Cambridge Studies in Oral and Literate Culture

THE INCORRUPTIBLE FLESH

Cambridge Studies in Oral and Literate Culture

Edited by PETER BURKE and RUTH FINNEGAN

This series is designed to address the question of the significance of literacy in human societies; it will assess its importance for political, economic, social, and cultural development, and will examine how what we take to be the common functions of writing are carried out in oral cultures.

The series will be interdisciplinary, but with particular emphasis on social anthropology and social history, and will encourage cross-fertilization between these disciplines; it will also be of interest to readers in allied fields, such as sociology, folklore, and literature. Although it will include some monographs, the focus of the series will be on theoretical and comparative aspects rather than detailed description, and the books will be presented in a form accessible to nonspecialist readers interested in the general subject of literacy and orality.

Books in the series

THE INCORRUPTIBLE FLESH

Bodily mutation and mortification in religion and folklore

PIERO CAMPORESI
University of Bologna

Translated by Tania Croft-Murray
Latin texts translated by Helen Elsom

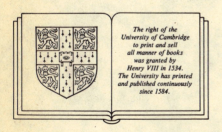

The right of the
University of Cambridge
to print and sell
all manner of books
was granted by
Henry VIII in 1534.
The University has printed
and published continuously
since 1584.

CAMBRIDGE UNIVERSITY PRESS

CAMBRIDGE

NEW YORK   NEW ROCHELLE   MELBOURNE   SYDNEY

Published by the Press Syndicate of the University of Cambridge
The Pitt Building, Trumpington Street, Cambridge CB2 1RP
32 East 57th Street, New York, NY 10022, USA
10 Stamford Road, Oakleigh, Melbourne 3166, Australia

Originally published in Italian as *La carne impassible* by il
Saggiatore, Milan 1983 and © il Saggiatore, 1983

First published in English by Cambridge University Press
1988 as *The Incorruptible flesh: bodily mutation and
mortification in religion and folklore*

English translation © Cambridge University Press 1988

Printed in Great Britain at the University Press, Cambridge

British Library cataloguing in publication data

Camporesi, Piero.
The incorruptible flesh: bodily mutation and mortification in
religion and folklore. –
(Cambridge studies in oral and literate culture; 17).
1. Funeral rites and ceremonies.
2. Mutation of the dead.
I. Title. II. La Carne impassible. English.
393   GT3150

Library of Congress cataloguing in publication data

Camporesi, Piero.
The incorruptible flesh.
(Cambridge studies in oral and literate culture; 17).
Includes index.
1. Body, Human – Religious aspects. 2. Body,
Human – Mythology. I. Title. II. Series.
BL604.B64C3613   1988   291.2′2   87-26808

ISBN 0 521 32003 8

CONTENTS

FOREWORD BY PETER BURKE

Although it may be something of an exaggeration to speak of a 'Bologna school' of historians, a number of important and innovative studies have been produced in that milieu in the last few years. The books of Carlo Ginzburg, from *The Night Battles* (originally published in 1966) to *The Cheese and the Worms* (1976) are now celebrated the world over. Also important, if less well known, are the essays of Carlo Poni on the economic and social history of Bologna and its region, the researches of Adriano Prosperi on the Counter-Reformation, and – rather more difficult to label or classify – the shelf of studies published by Piero Camporesi.

Camporesi teaches Italian literature at the University of Bologna, but what he writes might be better described as a kind of socio-cultural history, which takes literary texts as its point of departure but widens out into a reconstruction of popular mentalities. He first attracted the attention of historians with his *Book of Vagabonds* (1973), an anthology of texts dealing with the language and indeed the world of beggars and thieves in early modern Italy. One of these writers on vagabonds was Giulio Cesare Croce, a popular poet who lived in seventeenth-century Bologna. Camporesi considered Croce's work at some length in *The Mask of Bertoldo* (1976). Like other popular poets, Croce often composed his poems for Carnival and about Carnival. In order to put this poetry in context, Camporesi therefore discussed Carnival and, more generally, parody and the carnivalesque.[1]

The literature of Carnival is preoccupied with food, so it was hardly surprising to find Camporesi, like a good Bolognese, making food the centre of attention in three books: *The Land of Hunger* (1978), *Bread of Dreams* (1980), and *Food Folklore and Society* (1980).[2] The first of these studies had two complementary themes, times of feasting and times of famine. On one side the description of images of abundance associated with Carnival and the Land of Cockaigne; on the other the absence of food and the quest for food (taking us back to the territory of the vagabond). *Bread of Dreams*, on the other hand, is more concerned with the everyday hunger of ordinary people and the means they took to satisfy it; chestnut bread, bean bread, herbs and hallucinations. In this

[1] *Il libro dei vagabondi* (Turin, 1973); *La maschera di Bertoldo* (Turin, 1976).
[2] *Il paese della fame* (Bologna, 1978); *Il pane selvaggio* (Bologna 1980), English translation forthcoming); *Alimentazione Folclore Società* (Parma, 1980).

collection (Camporesi's books are generally collections of essays), the author goes so far as to suggest that many people in early modern Italy lived in a state of almost permanent hallucination, drugged by their hunger or by eating bread adulterated with narcotics such as darnel. Finally, *Food Folklore and Society* moves into the nineteenth and twentieth centuries and concentrates on the traditional peasant cuisine. This cuisine, he notes, lacked both variety and abundance, consisting (outside harvest-time and festivals) of one course served twice a day. In Italian peasant society, even salt and eggs were luxuries. In bourgeois society, of course, the situation was very different. Nineteenth-century Italy was two nations, two cultures, or as Camporesi puts it, 'two different alimentary languages'. The grammar of the language of bourgeois food was *La scienza in cucina* (1891) by the bachelor banker Pelegrini Artusi. Is it significant that the Italian Mrs Beeton was a man?[3]

From the history of food the natural next step was the history of the body, the subject of Camporesi's latest studies. *The Incorruptible Flesh* has been followed by *The Juice of Life* (1984), which deals with the symbolism of blood, and *The Workshops of the Senses* (1985), a collection of essays on medieval and early modern attitudes to the cosmos and its microcosm the human body.[4]

Like the narcotic bread eaten by his peasants, Camporesi's essays are mind-blowing. They are intensely exciting to read but almost impossible to summarise because they do not offer arguments so much as images – phantasmagoric processions of giants, pigs, vagabonds in rags, and so on. They resemble mosaics, built up by the patient juxtaposition of texts, in order to reconstruct and evoke the experience of ordinary people. The author's interests span Europe from the twelfth century to the nineteenth, but the texts he cites most frequently come from Emilia and the Romagna in the sixteenth and seventeenth centuries.

Camporesi does not limit himself to the description of popular culture. His aim is to decipher it. To do this he relies on the close reading of texts, together with the stimulus of theory. From the theoretical point of view, he is an eclectic. He probably owes most to the great Russian critic Mikhail Bakhtin, whose work on the carnivalesque, neglected in its own time (the 1930s and 1940s) is only now making an impact on social and cultural historians.[5]

---

[3] Artusi's text was reprinted in 1970 with an introduction by Camporesi.
[4] *La carne impassibile* (Milan, 1983); *Il sugo della vita* (1984); *Le officine dei sensi*, Milan 1985. His most recent book, *La casa dell'eternità* (Milan, 1987), deals in part with the symbolism of the Eucharist, at once food and body.
[5] See especially M. Bakhtin, *Rabelais and his World* (English trans., Cambridge, Mass., 1968). On him, D. LaCapra, 'Bakhtin, Marx and the Carnivalesque' in his *Rethinking Intellectual History* (Ithaca and London, 1983), ch. 5.

Structuralism is another important ingredient in Camporesi's concep-
tual soup, in both its Russian and French varieties (represented by
Vladimir Propp and Claude Lévi-Strauss). Something of Antonio
Gramsci and Gaston Bachelard has also gone into the pot. This heady
mixture is powdered with references to Fernand Braudel, Emmanuel Le
Roy Ladurie, and other socio-cultural historians. However, the interpretations remain more or less within the folklore tradition. Giants are
symbols of fertility, round cakes served at funerals represent resurrection, the kitchen is a sacred space, cooking is a ritual, and the chimney a
tunnel communicating with the supernatural world (it is not difficult to
predict how Camporesi would interpret the English folklore of Father
Christmas).

Plain empiricist historians may find this mixture a little difficult to
swallow. Hermeneutics, like its sister iconography, must be intuitive in
the last resort, but one wishes that Camporesi would show a little more
awareness of the possibility of alternative interpretations of his data. All
the same, no one interested in popular culture or in symbolism can afford
to neglect either the wealth of material or the richness of interpretation
which Camporesi offers us in his remarkable shelf of books.

TRANSLATOR'S NOTE

Where necessary, to aid understanding of the original text, I have added explanatory material. This is indicated by the use of italicized square brackets. In the case of quotations, I have taken already-existing English translations or versions, as close as possible in time to the Italian original, with the two-fold purpose of illustrating English contemporary interest in the topics under discussion in this book and of conveying the flavour of the Italian quotations themselves.

T. C.-M.

PART I

1

THE 'PRODIGIOUS MANNA'

It was said that from the dead bodies of God's virgins and the buried flesh of his saints there gushed forth a healing sap, a wondrous balm. A 'most gentle odour', a 'marvelous odour' were unmistakable signs of the thaumaturgical presence of a saintly corpse, that aromatic liberator from 'all manner of sickness'. The dead might become a source of health, givers of life, indeed. When St Nicholas of Bari 'was buried in a tomb of marble, a fountain of oil sprang out from the head unto his feet; and unto this day oil issueth out of his body, which is much available to the health of sicknesses of many men'.[1] Upon capturing the city of Miren, the iconoclastic Turks opened the 'tomb of St Nicholas' and found his bones to be 'swimming in oil'.[2] Medieval fascination with the behaviour of saintly bodies under post mortem sets the scene for a morbid and nightmarish drama of which their bones, flesh and blood are the tormented protagonists, engaged in a long and restless *iter* which persisted, in some cases, across the ages. One catches glimpses of nocturnal life in convents, of macabre and spine-chilling operations more akin to butchery, of rudimentary dissections carried out with knives and razors by hands which, while devout, shook with inexperience.

Having decided that the body of Sister Chiara of Montefalco, known as 'of the Cross', who had died in an 'odour of sanctity' and had been declared blessed by all, should be opened and embalmed, the Augustinian nuns – whose abbess she had been – deemed that 'it was not proper for that virgin flesh to be touched by any man whatsoever', and that 'her saintly body' which had been a 'living temple to the Holy Ghost', should not be contaminated by the hands of a barber-surgeon. Therefore, one hot and still Saturday night in August 1308, while the convent slept, four of their number, tucking up their sleeves, embarked on a series of (for us) astonishing operations.

> They went into the oratory and with the utmost respect undressed the saintly body. Sister Francesca, inexperienced though she was, opened it as best she could with a razor. They

1 Jacopo da Varagine, *Leggenda aurea*. English translation taken from *The Golden Legend* printed by Caxton, 1483; ed. F. S. Ellis, London, 1900, vol. 2, p. 117.
2 Ibid. p. 117.

then began to remove the intestines. She noticed that the gall-bladder was white and when she touched it she felt inside it three hard objects like stones, which were round in shape and together formed a triangle .... As they continued removing the intestines, they reached the heart and all saw that it was inordinately large, larger than an infant's head .... The nuns decided that it was right and proper to put the heart to one side: this they did, and placing all the other intestines in an earthenware jar, they buried them within the oratory itself where the saint had died, to one side of the altar where to this day they are thought to lie. Taking up the heart again, Sister Francesca said 'behold this heart, in which the Lord has worked so many wonders'. Placing it in a wooden bowl, they locked it up in a chest. This done, they dressed the body again and set it to rights.[3]

After being told the results of the autopsy carried out by their four dissecting colleagues, the thought of this heart of extraordinary dimensions caused the nuns to lie awake at night. It began to be suspected that the matter 'was not without mystery'. Some of the nuns then recalled that Sister Chiara had been much given to contemplating Christ's Passion, and that during her final illness

she had more than once repeated these words: 'I bear the crucified Christ within my heart.' All the nuns were agreed that in this heart there lay Christ's cross. 'I am the more inclined to believe this', added Sister Marina, 'since I remember our holy Mother Abbess saying to me seven years ago that Christ had appeared to her in the guise of a Pilgrim bearing a cross on his shoulder, and told her that He wanted to plant the cross in her heart'; the nuns finally decided that her heart should be opened for the purposes of embalming, whether a mystery were found or no.[4]

And so one Sunday night, with this in mind, Sisters Lucia, Margarita, Caterina and Francesca betook themselves to a room where the heart lay locked away in its box; and taking it up they all four knelt. Sister Francesca opened it, uttering with great humility the following words: 'Lord, I believe that in this heart there lies your holy Cross, although I believe my sins to be so many that they make me unworthy to find it.' Thus saying, she took the heart in one hand and in the other a razor and, not

[3] B. Piergilii, *Vita della B. Chiara detta della Croce da Montefalco dell'ordine di S. Agostino*, Foligno, 1663[2], pp. 193–4.

[4] Ibid. p. 196.

knowing where to make her incision because the heart, consistent with the general condition of the body, was all covered in fat, she finally decided to start the incision at the top where the heart is broader, took it to the lower extremity, and thus opened the heart easily with one cut.

The excess of blood was such that they did not at first see what was contained therein; they knew well enough that the heart is concave and divided into two parts, being a whole only in its circumference; then Sister Francesca felt with her finger that in the middle of one section there ran a nerve; and when she drew it out, they saw to their amazement that it was a cross, formed of flesh, which had been ensconced in a cavity of the same shape as the cross. Upon seeing this, Sister Margarita began shouting, 'A miracle, a miracle' . . .

It occurred to Sister Giovanna, after observing this phenomenon, that the heart might harbour other mysteries: so she told Sister Francesca to continue her inspection with greater attention . . . And in so doing, she encountered another small nerve standing up in the heart, like the Cross; and studying it carefully, they realized that it represented the Whip, or Scourge, with which Christ was beaten at the Pillar.

The nuns were so astonished at the extraordinary nature of these mysteries, that they could do no less than praise the Lord, who worked such miracles.[5]

The news spread like wildfire outside the bounds of the convent and an 'heretic of the sect of the Little Brothers' [Minorite Friars], feigning devout orthodoxy, and at the instigation of the Devil, hastened to the Bishop at Spoleto, Berengario Donadei, in order to denounce this 'credulousness born of gossip and the fantasies of women' and the probably bogus nature of the operation performed by 'meddlesome hands'. Having thanked the heretic, Berengario set off for Montefalco to 'bury the news which he already considered scandalous and foolhardy and severely to punish those nuns'.

Before a chosen gathering of theologians, judges, doctors and churchmen of every kind and persuasion, Berengario caused the heart to be brought to him. He took it and 'with a gesture of scorn and disdain he opened it'.

Whereupon he observed both Cross and Scourge with great circumspection, as he did the whole heart. And behold an even greater miracle: both he and the others foregathered discovered,

Ibid. pp. 196–7.

when they touched the heart and examined it carefully, that there were other mysteries of the Passion, to wit the Pillar, the Crown of Thorns, the three Nails, the Spear and the Pole with the Sponge, all so truly represented that Berengario on touching the point of the Spear and the three Nails was pricked by them as though they had really been of iron. At this point everyone was awe-struck and filled with amazement . . .[6]

The same fate awaited the gall bladder which, when disinterred and taken from the jar together with the other intestines, and separated from the liver and dissected by Sister Francesca again with the same razor, yielded three globules or balls, linked together to form a triangle. These were washed in wine by Sister Tommasa, dissected and examined by the theologians, who decreed that 'the three globules were without doubt a symbol of the ineffable mystery of the Holy Trinity'. It was found that the heart and its mysteries remained miraculously intact

since these were never kept in any preservative; indeed, for a period of some years at a time, the chaplain or some other priest exhibited them, and taking the heart he would open it, remove the Crucifix and the Scourge from its cavity; after showing these to the congregation, he would replace them . . .[7]

The blood which 'was collected from the heart of this saintly woman . . . is still today to be seen in a phial and it is red in colour just like a ruby'. At times this blood would boil, portentously and 'terribly', especially in periods of mourning or catastrophe, war or epidemic.

The remainder of the body was placed in a coffin and lowered into a deep grave inside the church of Montefalco. It became necessary, nonetheless, to satisfy the 'devout importunings' of the populace which 'clamoured repeatedly to be allowed to see Chiara's saintly remains', and the chaplain of Montefalco ordered 'that the body be disinterred and kept in a place where it might be seen by all'.

As in the case of the intestines hidden away in a jar which, when exhumed were found 'to have no unwholesome odour',

it being the fifth day since the death of this saintly woman: her body, despite its being plentifully covered in flesh and fat, and although it had not yet been embalmed, the day being hot too – for it was the twenty-first of August – not only remained intact and unblemished in every way but with a countenance fresh, nay, almost resplendent, she exhaled a gentle odour, a heavenly fragrance.

[6]   Ibid. p. 200.
[7]   Ibid. p. 217.

The nuns had requested of the apothecary, Tomaso di Barto-
lone, the necessary ointments in order to embalm the body. It
was God's will that the apothecary should bring the said ointments ten days after the death of the holy woman. He delivered
them into the nuns's hands and showed them what to do.
Accordingly, the nuns undressed the body and following the
apothecary's instructions, removed the brain and embalmed the
body in its entirety. They then wrapped it in the fine cloth which
they sewed up, allowing face, hands and feet to show – just as
they may be seen today.[8]

Every year on the eve of the feast of St John the Baptist, the remains
were taken from the coffin and placed upon the altar. The night prior to
the solstice (*sacrum*) of antiquity, 'they undress the body, cleanse it with
a powder and dress it again', to show it the following day to the multitude
of the faithful. The uninhibited familiarity with which the nuns of
Montefalco opened corpses, removed intestines, heart, liver, gall, dissected the organs, bored into skulls, extracted brains, embalmed bodies,
powdered mummies, opened and shut coffins, repeatedly manipulated
age-old cadavers, may be disconcerting nowadays, but the nuns of
Montefalco were only one among a number of communities indulging in
such activities. In Ferrara, the body of the most noble and blessed
Beatrice II of Este 'was often exhumed and found to be undecayed',[9]
wrote her anonymous seventeenth-century biographer who, barring
certain additions, virtually reproduces the biography compiled by the
Archpriest of Cento, the plagiarist, Girolamo Baruffaldi. It is true that
the cadaver of one who had been blessed represented a useful source of
exploitation in all sorts of ways, although this only provides us with half
an explanation for the unreservedness with which the physical side of
death was treated – something incomprehensible to us.

There exuded from the grave of the saintly Beatrice d'Este 'a supernatural fragrance so sweetly aromatic and unlike any earthly odours, that
it filled any who drew near to that holy repository with joy, solace and
enchantment'.[10] This extraordinary perfume had a tendency to grow
stronger, according to the chronicles of old, 'at times when Holy Mass
was celebrated, almost in token of her pleasure at the entreaties
addressed to her'.

8   Ibid. p. 216.
9   *Vita della Beata Beatrice seconda d'Este. Fondatrice dell'Insigne Monastero de
       S. Antonio in Ferrara della Regola di S. Benedetto*, Ferrara, 1777, p. 91. This
       biography of the Este saint (mentioned also in *Orlando Furioso*) compiled by
       Girolamo Baruffaldi, was printed in Venice in 1723.
10   Ibid. p. 92.

> In descriptions of the past [the goodly lady was born during the
> first half of the thirteenth century] it was especially noted how
> the sick who drew near to her sepulchre to pray for a return to
> health were overwhelmed by this remarkable fragrance which,
> far from being ephemeral, was of a lasting nature, to such an
> extent that a nun who was visiting the tomb in order to renew her
> votive offering marvelled so greatly and for so long at the
> fragrance, that she fell to her knees and recited the whole Office
> never once losing her perception of the sweet scent, which grew
> from moment to moment.[11]

Through the medium of the 'saintly cadaver, which, the tomb being
opened to reveal the 'miracle of the aroma', 'was seen to be intact,
beautiful and resplendent as though still alive', those heavenly odours
permeated the earth, sweetened the air, inebriated and stunned the
senses. A fragile, precarious and ephemeral transmission system was
formed, with the holy cadaver at its centre, from which there flowed an
aromatic radiation. The 'odour of sanctity' was no mere metaphor but a
matter of deep importance: it was a tangible presence fed by collective
hallucinations. The aromas of paradise, transmitted through the bodies
of the blessed were regarded as real by an emotional, impressionable and
easily excitable sensibility always ready – in a manner totally alien to us
today – to capture the essence of the supernatural, the emanations of the
uranian, the taste of the ineffable. This hallucinated sensitivity was a
direct product of the high degree of religiosity which permeated people's
everyday lives, people who were used to illogical and irrational forms of
perception and knowledge, which were nonetheless soothing and comforting in themselves, and at once stimulating. This experiencing of the
sacred (or magic – which is almost the same thing) by absorption all one's
waking hours, day after day, at table, at work, in the street, in bed,
brought with it a form of fideistic knowledge, based on contacts and
conversations with impossible and ultrasensitive worlds; it was stranger
to the subtle yet tormenting, illuminating yet destabilising notion of
Reason. The most subtle logic and honeyed arguments were brought to
bear to justify a world whose order was based on the irrationality of faith,
on the paradoxical myths of oriental fables or the tightrope acrobatics of
fanciful theologians. The Montefalco nuns who opened Sister Chiara's
heart and thought they found there the Mysteries (the instruments in
miniature) of the Passion, the Vicar-General and theologians who
confirmed their discovery and set the seal of authority on the miraculous
event: every one of them participated in a fantastic drama produced by
collective hallucination and set upon a dark and gory stage. The three

[11]   Ibid. pp. 92–3

'globules' discovered in the gall-bladder – 'a proven symbol of the ineffable mystery of the Holy Trinity' according to the theological doctrines of the time – were found when placed upon a pair of scales to be of equal weight and quality. But far greater was the

> astonishment when, after deeper examination, it was found that not only were they equal in weight, but that if one were placed in one tray and the other two in the other tray, the two weighed as much as the single one; and upon weighing two together and then all three, the two weighed as much as the three; and the one weighed the same as all three together: a tangible proof of the profound mystery of the Holy Trinity, whom St Augustine described as follows: 'One Person is as great as the three at once, and two are in no way greater than one; and in Themselves They are infinite things in each singly, and also all things in each singly, and single things in all, and all things in all, and the one is all things.' ... And so with the stones, as verified by other reliable books and by many proven tests; one weighs as much as two and two as much as three. In our present day, this test was carried out in the presence of more than thirty people and was found to be thus – and may God who allows me write on such matters be witness thereof – but I believe that when someone seeks to discover something which is of curiosity, God would not make him worthy of discovering it *for he who hides his knowledge only reveals his own smallness of mind*.[12]

To the eighteenth-century biographer of this Augustinian nun, a layman from Bevagna called Battista Piergilii, the 'rational experiments' of Galileo take place in a remote, improbable and demoniacal setting pertaining more to the sphere of pseudoscientific 'curiosity' inspired by the Evil One; they are inimical to the magical order upon which the revealed world rests. Many continued to think like this obscure village intellectual for a long time after him. They were probably wrong. But they found in the impossible, improbable and visionary, a heavenly consolation such as modern science with all its 'objective' equipment has failed to provide.

After being transferred to its new sepulchre, the disinterment of the body of the noble Benedictine abbess of the Eremite monastery of St Anthony of Ferrara became a ritual and every year, on the anniversary of her death, on 18 August:

> They brought that saintly body from its sepulchre and laid it on the marble slab near to the altar so that they could array it in

[12] B. Piergilii, *Vita della B. Chiara*, pp. 206–7.

clothes and carefully wash it, anointing it with cotton soaked with wine and water, and the flesh was found to be still soft, as though living, and firm . . . .

For this fluid and the impregnated cotton rags with which the holy body had been washed and wiped, another use was found: they were distributed among the sick of the town and hospitals, because their beneficial qualities, which derived from Beatrice herself, were such as to cure all manner of disease.

The disinterment and the practice of washing the body continued for many years . . .[13]

The practice was abandoned at the beginning of the sixteenth century, however:

The nuns had already decided to abandon the practice of washing the holy remains, whether with water or any other fluid, their supply of the ointment being finally exhausted, when there began to flow from the marble slab of her altar a copious stream of the purest water . . .[14]

This 'wondrous nectar' with supernaturally therapeutic powers could be used to correct nature's excesses, by controlling the processes of preservation and stabilization of wine. If, as sometimes occurred, during its long sojourn in the dark recesses of a cellar, the wine lost, through some unforeseeable cosmic and meteorological disturbance, its normal relationship with the sun, which while remote and invisible, nonetheless governed the lengthy process of ripening, gradual fermentation and ageing; if the wine turned sour in its barrels, if it seethed and bubbled, the supernatural liquid originating from the cadaver had power to restore peace and order to the turbulent barrel. It might indeed be that the wine in turning was trying to subvert its preordained rôle as mere neutral begetter of riotous drunkenness in men; instead, it 'had gone mad' itself and become drunk on its own account.

In the month of July of 1501 on the eve of the feast of St James the Apostle, so great was the heat of the season and so ardent the fiery vapours that descended from heaven, that even the wines in their subterranean casks boiled as though they had been placed before a fire, and the corks began to shoot out impetuously from their bung holes as though from a cannon. The nuns in charge ran to the scene and found that all the casks were affected by the boiling. Great was their dismay, and they prayed to the holy Beatrice that she might help them preserve some of their wine to

[13]   *Vita della Beata Beatrice*, p. 95.
[14]   Ibid. p. 105.

bring to table; they deemed it prudent to place a few drops of saintly nectar or the water with which her body had been washed in each of the barrels. Later when the hour of supper arrived the nun appointed to fetch wine confidently descended to the cellar expecting to find things changed; and indeed, she found all the wines sound and incorrupt, and wholesome and good in flavour, as though they had never suffered any evil effect whatsoever.[15]

The wine thus 'laced' with sap from the incorrupt bones and flesh of Beatrice who 'placed among the ranks of the saintly / shall be honoured with incense and votive offerings' (*Orlando furioso*, XIII, 64), and the decay of the dancing and rebellious enzymes of fermentation thus having been overcome (the enzymes and fermentation tended to be identified with hobgoblins and the spirits which presided over the phenomena of leavening, ripening, curdling and putrefaction), cosmic order was restored to the once turbulent cellar. This episode, if true, fits in perfectly with the Egyptian thaumaturgic-cum-pharmacological logic of the old world, according to which the human body and its derivatives possessed a great variety of medicinal and curative properties. *Homo homini salus*: human beings were a source of precious medicaments for their fellows, both dead and living, by providing excrements and other by-products of the body, and 'we can see how by its various parts and functions the human body can benefit human health'. So wrote a canon of the Reformed Lateran Order in the seventeenth century, Ottavio Scarlatini, archpriest of Castel San Pietro and member of the 'Gelati' academy of Bologna: 'since it is inevitable that the body dies, whether anointed and embalmed artificially or naturally, it may yet provide medicaments vital to human health'.[16]

Only a few generations divide us from 1685, the year in which these observations were made, yet these words seem to come from a very different age and imbue us moreover with a sense of discomfort and unease by evoking ghosts we thought buried in the anthropophagic pharmacology of a past which saw in a seasoned, embalmed – or otherwise manipulated – human being a first-rate remedy for the conservation of human health. Modern sensibility, however, bridles at the idea that the body of another man, our neighbour, might be used to safeguard our health. The relationship between man and his body, and that between a man and the bodies of others, has undergone a radical change in a very short period of time. The bacteriological revolution of

15   Ibid. pp. 134–5.
16   O. Scarlatini, *L'huomo e sue parti figurato, e simbolico, anatomico, rationale, morale, mistico, politico e legale, raccolto e spiegato...*, Bologna, 1684, part II, p. 180.

the eighteenth century and pharmaceutical chemistry have dealt a mortal blow to the image of the therapeutic flesh and of human excrement as agents of physical well-being and health. Indeed, as late as the sixteenth century, Ulisse Aldrovandi, the great father of the human and natural sciences, was confidently writing: 'I believe that there is no part of the human body, no residue which comes forth from it, out of which the doctor cannot derive enormous advantage on behalf of the sick.' At the same time as the illustrious doctor and pharmacologist was writing these words in his *Antidotarium bononiense*, Gerolamo Mercuriali of Forlì was echoing them in his lectures at Padua University, transcripts of which were made and posthumously published by Paolo Aicardi in his treatise: *De morbis cutaneis et omnibus corporis humani escrementis (1601) [Of skin diseases and all excrements of the human body]*.

Children's hair was a cure against gout and a 'podagric balsam' was concocted from an oil extracted from the cranium and from other bones of one who had been 'made to die a violent death'. The ashes of human bones when imbibed 'in broth or wine or another liquor' might 'most usefully and profitably' cure 'any ailment whatsoever its cause might be'. An 'extract from the human cranium' was recommended as an invaluable cure against epilepsy and as an

> ointment known to be 'sympathetic' or indeed 'preventive' . . . was given even by the great Paracelsus as a gift to his Imperial Majesty, Maximilian Caesar; it is so efficacious that with suitable application it even heals wounds when they are a thousand miles away, by merely anointing an item of clothing of the patient's or the arrow with which he was struck, or a cloth impregnated with the patient's blood.

Teeth, also (as long as they were children's teeth)

> had beneficial properties, principally in the treatment of uterine ailments, if tied to the right arm and the latter be then extended so that the teeth hang down and touch the ground . . . . Besides there are other human bones: these Haubert . . . reduces to ashes and mixes with conserves, so that they are valuable in curing headaches and attacks of gout . . . . Nor should the virtues of the umbilical cord be underestimated, for if a portion of the umbilical cord of a new-born child be taken and worn in a silver ring, it discourages every kind of cholic passion.[17]

The mummy or 'desiccated human body', is different from the true *mumia*,

[17]   Ibid. pp. 180–1.

a Persian word describing a certain balm, present in those sepulchres where cadavers had been kept for many a year, embalmed and treated with spices. This *mumia* takes its name from other *cerops*, perhaps because, according to Renodeus, it has the consistency of wax, and was only found in the tombs of Egyptian kings and heroes. The Egyptians had some conception, albeit imperfect, of the resurrection of the body: they wished to delay the body's decay for as long as possible and so embalmed it with myrrh, cinnamon, aloes, cedar gum and other rich and valuable spices; and thus, when after many years these sepulchres were depredated and levelled out, it was possible to collect a fluid that ran out like thick and aromatic honey.[18]

If this thick liquid was greatly sought after by doctors, we can hardly be surprised at the avid demand for the 'prodigious manna' flowing from Nicholas of Bari or the body 'fluid' of the blessed Beatrice d'Este, and the popularity of many other products of a similar nature. Upon this point, there was a perfect consensus between secular and religious medicine. The search for the best *mumia* like the search for the best quality 'manna' answered the same yearning for good health, the same desire for protection from disease.

This was not a unique case – as the hagiographer of that pious member of the Este family reminds us – but 'in many other stories of saints, written by reliable biographers, we have read of various marvels most similar to ours concerning body sap'.

So do we read in the life of the blessed Beatrice d'Este, formerly known as 'di Gemola' [sister to Azzo Novello, and a nun at the convent of St John the Baptist on Mount Gemola in the region of Padua. The other Beatrice was Azzo's daughter] written by Monsignor Tommasini . . . . So do we read also in the biography of St Nicholas of Bari, to whom Father Buonafedi Lucchese devoted a whole treatise printed in Ferrara in 1729 on the subject of the miraculous manna which flowed from his sepulchre; and so was it too with the blessed Pietro Gondisalvo of the Dominican order, and with St Lawrence – the priest and Spanish martyr in Novara in Lombardy, and in the story of St Winefred of England according to Baronius' description, and with St Catherine of Alexandria as Adricomio recounts, and so was it written of the Archbishop St William of Evora, and of St John the Evangelist and of St Andrew, as St Gregory of Tours relates, and finally as it is told of St Julia – virgin martyr of Corsica . . .[19]

[18]   Ibid. p. 182.
[19]   *Vita della Beata Beatrice*, p. 117.

Precious as a relic was the authentic *mumia*, and eagerly sought after. To this balm

> were attributed great and unique powers by physicians, and consequently they would apply it to patients with many different ailments and afflictions; later, with increased boldness, they even sought the balm in the tombs of other magnates and princes, and when these were emptied they even tapped the tombs of ordinary men and those of the lower stations, still finding balm, but of inferior quality, which was nonetheless, though to a lesser extent, useful in the treatment of certain conditions. However, it must be noted that the balm from a man's corpse that has been dried in the oceans of sand such as those of Arabia whence it is sent for use as medicine and for display, is not real and authentic: which causes the learned Aldrovandi to comment: 'therefore, I conclude from my observations that the true *mumia* survives very rarely in our ministrations; and although some people today compound a balsam in order to preserve the human body from decay, this balsam is nevertheless very different in recipe from that of the ancients'.[20]

In Aldrovandi's day, it was virtually impossible to find the true *mumia* in Bologna pharmacies. The ointment obtained from the real *mumia* was not only useful in a wide range of therapeutic treatments but also in the embalming of corpses.

As to the latter application, it is not clear what technique was employed in preparing the body of the blessed Chiara of Montefalco: if she was anointed in the ancient or the modern manner, if she received the treatment reserved for the rich or that accorded to the poor, which involved less cost and time. The 'manner of anointing the bodies of the poor', relates Ottavio Scarlatini, in referring to ancient times, was distinguishable from more expensive methods in the following manner: 'the body was not opened, but the intestines were removed by means of a rod of cedar wood, as for an enema, and the body sprinkled with salt all over for seventy days'.[21] Salting and smoking were the methods favoured by his contemporaries in the sixteenth and seventeenth centuries:

> The method normally used for embalming bodies nowadays [we must remember that the theologian from Bologna writes his work in the penultimate decade of the twelfth century], is described by the Neapolitan Giovanni Battista Porta; namely, in the first place the skull [that is the cranium] of the cadaver should

[20]   O. Scarlatini, *L'huomo e sue parti figurato . . .*, p. 182.
[21]   Ibid. p. 183.

be sundered, its brain drawn out and the eyes thrown away, the spinal cord and intestines removed. The body should then be hung for four hours by its feet and then washed with distilled vinegar and spirit. When it is dried out, it should then be sprinkled with quick lime, alum and salt, and hung for two days over a smoke of myrtle wood, bay, rosemary, cypress and other aromatic plants. The body should finally be anointed with a mixture made from quick lime, alum of burnt stone, salt, aloes, myrrh, spikenard oil, ashes of green rosemary, verdigris, cypress, tartar, crocus, seed of bitter apples, antimony powder, musk and amber; for three successive days the body should be rubbed with this compound in an open place . . .[22]

Let us now return to the preparation of the *mumia* 'which as has been seen, it is difficult to achieve perfectly and truly'. The 'very experienced' Osvald Crollius prepares it in the following manner: 'take the corpse of a red-haired man of twenty-four years of age, and after it has been hung, sprinkle it with a powder made of myrrh and aloes, after which it must be rubbed with vinegar, thus drying part of the body suspended in the air, and from this will be obtained a brilliant red tincture'.[23]

These strips of human flesh hung up to dry like washing might strike us as barbaric and evil. But what really shocks us is the impassivity and total lack of compassion, not to mention piety, betrayed in these lines composed by a man of the Church, archpriest of a small town not far from Bologna. Moreover, the words for cook's recipe and chemists's prescription (the latter originating in the dispensary, apothecary's shop or the spicery) are not even distinct from each other linguistically: *ricetta* being the word in both cases. Both make mention of blood, flesh, oil, fat, condiment, cooking, salt, vinegar, rosemary . . . . A reading of Della Porta's recipe for embalming bodies ('dressing' them *[in the culinary sense]*) may awake in us a feeling of discomfiture because of its analogy with drawing and quartering, salting and smoking, seasoning, cooking, not only animal but also human flesh. A pharmaceutical laboratory, a kitchen, a slaughter-house, a mortuary – all have a certain chilliness in common. The culinary treatment of human flesh has something threatening and sinister about it: 'take some liver . . . and cut it in strips', 'cut the liver in little pieces' . . . (the nuns of Montefalco had done a similar sort of thing to the liver of their abbess), 'chop the liver well . . .', 'take the head of a calf, boil it and remove the bones, then cut it up in pieces and cook

22   Ibid. p. 182. For the 'cadaverum conditura' (seasoning of corpses – Tr.) cf. Joannes Veslingius's note in part II of Prospero Alpino's *Rerum Aegyptiarum*, that is to *De plantis Aegyptii*, Lugduni Batavorum, 1735, p. 60.

23   O. Scarlatini, part II, p. 183.

it', 'mince the liver thoroughly', 'take some lamb's offal, cut it in pieces and pass it in flour', 'take a bullock's or a calf's tongue, boil till half cooked, peel it and make a number of holes in it with the point of a knife'. 'Pluck', 'empty', 'cleave', 'chop', 'gut', 'clean and bone', 'clean and gut', 'scrape and gut', 'peel and gut': these are not orders issued by an executioner to his assistants but mere practical injunctions in cookery, of a cookery that has now fallen into desuetude, and these mortuary-like instructions sound increasingly remote to our ears. The present generation which has 'abolished' death, as though it were something indecorous and dirty, is also at pains to abolish the slaughter-house kitchen, the blood-stained kitchen where animals were slit open, skins were scraped and what was left was minced. But now cellophane isolates this impure matter, ennobles it and redeems it. Blood must not be seen, the edible substance must not in any way remind us of death, suffering, the visceral. Those women who plucked, hacked and gutted chickens, drew veins, who slit rabbits' throats and skinned them alive, who strangled geese by breaking their vertebrae with a broomstick, who ate the feet, neck, liver, gizzard and entrails of farmyard animals, who sucked rabbits' eyes and the parson's nose, are a memory of the past to us.

Cooking reflected a sense of death, the relationship man has with his own body's fate. The ephemeral colours everything in our present day and 'eternity' has become a forbidden, unmentionable word. The sole exception is perhaps the Jewish tradition with its taboos, its abominations, its protracted and ritual butcheries during which the animal has to be bled to the last drop; and circumcision as a reminder of a healthy and correct rapport with both body and blood.

Amongst all the effluvia of the human body – saliva, 'excreta of the ears', sweat, urine, faeces (studied in detail by Mercuriali for variations and type), milk, sperm – human blood certainly enjoyed undisputed supremacy. 'Blood is the best of sauces, the food and pasture of life';[24] this was believed (and put to practical use) above all in its role as the prince of foods, of vital sustenance: a juice, a precious element of the body, a sauce brewed in kitchens.

> Human blood has countless uses, possessing as it does the main animal and vital qualities .... Human blood can effectively alleviate epilepsy, if an incision being made between the patient's shoulder blades, three drops of blood are taken forcefully, mixed with the contents of a crow's egg and ingested by the patient at the end of his paroxysm. It may also be used to treat

[24]   L. Lennio, *Della complessione del corpo humano libri due*, Venezia, 1564, c. 70r.

another and equally dangerous sickness which keeps the patient almost permanently at death's door: in this case the big toe is cut and the patient's face sprayed and sprinkled with the blood thereof. Weckerius [Jacobus Weckerius of Basle, author of *Antidotarium generale* (Venice 1602) and of *Antidotarium speciale* and *De distillatione*] merely by moistening the lips of the subject, professes that he can banish all ailments and physical complaints; other physicians intent upon eradicating so ruthless a tyrant of human life, openly give those affected by the malady human blood to drink. Fallopius instructs that this blood should be distilled as many as seven times, so as to eliminate any humidity from water, and that this should be done by proper means; the substance resulting can be used in the treatment of nervous disorders. Evonimus combines it with eggs and meat to extract a fifth substance which is called quintessence by chemists; the latter, at the instigation of Albertus Magnus, produced a water from this substance by means of glass apparatus. This water is noted for its efficacy in curing all manner of illnesses, both internal and external; Crollius placed this 'water' in the opthalmic category of medicaments; other experts compound from it a poultice which is greatly beneficial in the treatment of hernias. However, Galenus prefers pig's blood, and in today's laboratories, pharmacists and physicians make a plaster for application in the case of hernia out of a goat's skin which yet contains a proportion of human blood. Moreover, pharmaceutical laboratories do produce an oil from human blood. But Gordonius, and other authorities, maintain that this blood should be extracted from a red-headed man in his twenty-fifth year of life, who has been sublimated with great care, and for this reason the blood may be called 'living oil', effective (according to Gordonius) in expelling many illnesses, indeed in maintaining a human being in a good state of health .... Weckerius mentions, too, the extraction of a salt from human blood, which is useful in alleviating all kinds of physical pain. Modern chemists are producing an *elixir vitae* which has shown itself to be most beneficial and profitable in treating obstinate fevers and a weak constitution. It is also used in the treatment of haemorrhages, and when the haemorrhage is considerable, a certain quantity is taken and allowed to dry over embers; the powder thus produced is then blown up the nostrils of the sufferer.[25]

25   O. Scarlatini, *L'huomo e sue parti figurato* ... part II, p. 181.

That this noble liquid should have had an eminent position in the preservation of health and that its power should be reflected in a very broad area of symbolic attributes, is a well-known fact.

In Jewish funerary rituals, a bird's blood mixed with dust was included in the rites as a sign of purification, 'because they were convinced by the precepts of the prophets that blood is effective for the removal of a stain which has been incurred, and for the purification of the spirit. 'But', continued Pierio Valeriano, 'They do not understand that this sign refers to the precious blood of Christ, which sprinkled will wash away the stain of all our sins, if we wish to do penance.'[26] The association soul/blood was particularly strongly felt in the Jewish religion. 'You must not eat fat, or blood', warned Leviticus. 'Blood is not to be consumed', interpreted the humanist, 'because the life in any particular piece of flesh is thought to be in the blood.'

> The phrase: *the life of any individual is in the blood*, should not be understood to mean that blood is the substance of life, according to Hesychius, but rather that life and flesh are connected by means of the blood. For this reason, some call the blood the *carrier of life*: for when it is lost and the flesh begins to grow cold, the life is separated from the flesh and flies away. For this reason, the Egyptians used the picture of a hawk to signify blood. Of course, many have actually thought that the blood is life, or, as Empedocles claimed, that life was in the blood. Hence we read in the poets phrases like: *He spewed forth his purple life*, or *He poured out his life with his blood*, and others of the same kind.[27]

Among the many abominations, Leviticus forbade not only blood but also fat: 'all fat pertains to the Lord' (3:16). The fat of the sacrificed animals ascended to the Almighty, who delighted in the aromas which wafted up to Him from the offerings made Him by mankind. On the other hand the consumption of fats in modern Europe was very high, both in cooking and in other areas. As in the case of *mumia [mummy]*, or the 'oil extract of human blood', the oil from a person's cranium, or 'extract of brain marrow or human backbone', human fat was likewise used in official pharmacology (much as it was in necromancy and witchcraft). Let us not forget that salt from human blood was used in the preparation of *lapis rubeus*, a red stone of 'wondrous efficacy and

---

[26]   G. P. Valeriano Bolzano, *Hieroglyphica, seu de sacris Aegyptiorum aliarumque gentium literis commentarii*, Lugduni, 1602, p. 214.

[27]   Ibid. p. 213.

virtue'.[28] The obsession with grease, in which the pre-industrial mentality was immersed, led to sinister and gruesome therapies:

> ... but it is certainly true that human fat is effective as a pain-killer and anodyne against any hardening of the nerves and gumma formed in the body: and I recall having known a certain individual who, reduced to senility, suffered from these very maladies and being knowledgeable on these matters, had himself taken to a particular wood where there hung the remains of criminals who had been executed. Having allowed the grease of these to fall upon the afflicted part of his body, he was very soon cured.[29]

We have no serious reason for disbelieving the episode related by Scarlatini. We could, with some reason, suppose that human fat was so keenly sought after also for purposes which were not purely therapeutic.

It would indeed be difficult to pass off the practice of total and scientific paring of flesh from the bones of human bodies as merely gratuitous and bestial, in an age where on occasion the main square became a 'butcher's yard' (as described by a late-fifteenth-century writer of Forlì, Leone Cobelli). Wishing to avenge the death of Girolamo Riario, the executioner Babono di Castelbolognese and Nicolò Macto of the Alban hills performed the most lurid executions in true professional style, although the 'dastardly mercenaries' were their equals in ferocity:

> some used bill-hooks, some sabres and some swords to hack the body in small pieces like meat at the butcher's and threw the pieces about the square. Oh, reader, you will find it hard to believe the square was called the 'bloody lake', but it was no lie. I can confirm this for I saw it with my own eyes: there was so much blood, so much entrails, so many bits of flesh, entrails and intestines ...[30]

Equally grim was the fate that awaited the head of the rival family, Andrea Orsi (nicknamed 'the Bear') who was captured in a monastery of the Dominican Order: they began by 'spitting in his face, throwing filth in his face (the excrement of insult and hatred, customary in bloodthirsty charivaris) and in his mouth, they flogged him, put a halter round his neck and dragged him around the citadel'. He was then made to watch

28   A. de Sgobbis da Montagna, *Nuovo, et universal theatro farmaceutico*, Venezia, 1667, p. 89.
29   O. Scarlatini, *L'huomo e sue parti figurato*, part I, p. 177.
30   L. Cobelli, *Cronache forlivesi dalla fondazione della città sino all'anno 1498*, ed. G. Carducci & E. Frati, preface & notes F. Guarini, Bologna, 1874, p. 337.

the 'annihilation', the total demolition of his palace, after which he was dragged three times round the square by a horse. And lastly:

> they pierced his body with so many holes like a sieve, drew and quartered him, opened him and removed the fat and the intestine and strew them about the square; they then removed the entrails, one of those cur-like soldiers took the heart cut it off and threw the entrails in the middle of the square; then he put that bloody heart into his mouth and bit it as a cur would.[31]

To be sure, this spectacle must have been somewhat shocking, even for a town which had reduced Martin IV's eight thousand Bretons to a 'bloody heap'. But the demolition, the near disintegration of the human structure was a common spectacle. A chronicler of the generation succeeding Cobelli's, Andrea Bernardi, known as 'Il Novacula' (a barber and therefore an expert on blood, social intermediary and privy to the town's secrets), tells of another victim.

> who was wounded in the back by a dart, after which large chunks of flesh were hacked from his thighs and arms with a dagger . . . then his prick was likewise cut off, his guts opened and entrails taken out and all of this person's fingers scattered around the square like the points of a mace. And so much fat did they take from him, upon my word, from both the front and the back of his thighs that it was two inches thick down to the knee; and likewise with the breast and arms; and thus was nearly every part of him removed, so that no flesh was left upon him back or front. The bones of his torso having been thus laid bare, for several days did youths of the town drag them around . . .[32]

There was so much purposefulness in this act of destruction, which made the 'bones of his trunk', his flayed skeleton, a boys' plaything, that it must surely lie beyond the bounds of mindless slaughter or pure ferocity. It certainly makes one's hair stand on end to read, not merely of hands, but also of teeth and mouths being used as instruments of laceration. A taste for blood there certainly was, coupled with carnivorous frenzy; but there was something beyond that:

> Immediately, they cut off his prick and placed it in his mouth; and they removed his entrails and intestine. And lucky was the man who might grind the entrails between his teeth and rub them with his fingers. They cut him up in small pieces to remove his fat

[31]   Ibid. p. 337.
[32]   A. Bernardi (Novacula), *Cronache forlivesi, dal 1476 al 1517*, ed. G. Mazzatinti, Bologna, 1895, vol. I, part I, p. 264.

because he was young, being probably twenty-eight years of age, tall and slim in build.[33]

The fact that he was young made the fat particularly attractive not so much from the gastronomic point of view (the raw flesh, the intestine torn by hands and teeth, whilst only arguably a gastronomic experience, are certainly expressions of popular cannibalism), as for their therapeutic possibilities, because – as we have already seen – human fat must

> like other fats and fatty tissues, be processed and compounded before it can be put to practical use, and then be kept in the laboratories of pharmacologist-doctors, for it is beneficial to all nervous ailments ..., and in using it those who suffer acute pleurisy and podagra are freed thereof and their health is much improved.[34]

But the adipose parts of men may have been used to achieve other, more covetous aims, for there existed a belief (we do not know how widely held) that 'if a candle made of human sebum or fat is placed near a presumed treasure-trove, its crackling will indicate the position of the trove, and its extinction that the trove has been reached'. This piece of information, reported by Johannes Jacob Wecker in his *De secretis*, was received sceptically by Ottaviano Scarlatini who, however, expressed the notion shared by others that 'this could occur from a certain sympathy, since fattiness has its source in blood and from this emanate the instruments of the spirit, which in its turn is motivated in this life by a lust for gold and silver'.[35]

Given these assumptions, it was almost natural to suppose that because of

> an unbridled yearning after certain things ... some individuals are lead to perform most rascally deeds; on which matter, the erudite Aldrovrandi and most scholarly Martino, not limiting themselves to the uses of human fattiness, also describe how witches and other wicked people who have sworn allegiance to Satan and who practice their atrocities by night, drain milk and bleed infants, and take away the little juice and fat that they have upon them.[36]

The presence of occult properties in human fat explains why, in a society permeated by magical culture, fat was extensively used and why everyone participated in a certain measure in some form of sabbatical

33   Ibid. vol. I, part I, p. 263.
34   O. Scarlatini, *L'huomo e sue parti figurato*, p. 181.
35   Ibid. p. 177.
36   Ibid. p. 177.

activity, with an end either to assuaging their physical ills or gaining easy wealth. Amulets, spells, magical formulae for instant wealth abound in the books and manuscripts of the time. A young inhabitant of Modena and his girl friend were found in 1601 in the fields of Albareto di Modena 'in the midst of diabolical characters with candles, nails and other instruments'. This was, it seemed, because 'they wanted to cause a storm to gather over the villa at Albareto and perhaps by some spell become rich'. Moreover, the literature of folklore exudes a passion for gold – the Devil's gold hair, capricious old witches handing out secrets, rootless and vagabond soldiers with magical crowbars who force entry into impenetrable strong-boxes, dragons and monsters who guard underground treasures – all part of a vast continent of magical/necromatic mythology which testifies to a pulsating collective imagination thirsty for comforts, riches, luxury and beauty: all things out of reach of the man-in-the-street, the aged, the ugly, the disinherited, the sick and the great majority of the commonalty and working class. The sabbatical dream forms part of the search for joys forbidden to the poor, from which the humble were debarred, out of bounds to the old. Broadly speaking, the witches' sabbath amounts not to a search for a new and revolutionary god, so much as to the overturning of a social state or the superseding of a *classe d'âge*, to the escape from the ghetto of a humdrum daily existence, to the relinquishment of the usual meagre vegetarian diet of beetroots, chestnuts, cabbages, beans, onions and broad beans, foods which in themselves tend to induce 'turbulent dreams'. A tendency to flight, to nocturnal journeys, to dream-like visions, all belonged to the hard business of living. An ointment formed from the fat of a child or a youth was perhaps not just a metaphor illustrating the rivalry between youth and age. Ultimately, the wisespread practice of anointing was perhaps not so far removed from the many paths of expression that mass escapism took (even if only in fantasy) into forbidden and impossible areas. Intoxication grew with age and the elderly became prey to states of dementedness and stupor, to raving hallucination, unknown to the young. Whole communities, whether rural or from mountain regions, entire valleys fell into long-drawn nocturnal, wintry and senile lethargies and hibernated with ointments and potions:

> ... following this prescription, it seems that amazing visions were seen. There is discussion in another place of things which appear to exist but do not exist. The mixture is made, they say, from the fat of children, the juices of parsley, wolfsbane, cinquefoil and nightshade, and from soot. People seem to be asleep while they are seeing these visions; it seems, however, that they hope to see theatres, gardens, feasts, fine furniture and

clothes, gilded youths, kings and magistrates; in short, all the things in which they take pleasure and which they even believe themselves to be enjoying. But they also see demons, crows, prisons, isolation, torture . . . . In this way also shamans believe that they are carried to distant countries and undergo various experiences there, in every case according to the disposition of the individual, with the help of the ointment. I append here another ointment which is of similar effect in producing a deep and long-lasting sleep:[37]

Seeds of lily, henbane, hemlock, red and black poppy, lettuce and purslane, fifty-three parts; berries of deadly night-shade, one part.[38]

Unguents and ointments compounded from narcotic, toxic and hallucinogenic herbs produced an effect of temporary madness: 'the intelligence is either removed altogether or confused: the result is that anyone who uses these ointments seems to be crazy in his speech, his hearing and his answering of questions, or else he falls into a very deep sleep for many days on end'.[39] In the midst of his delirium, the subject would dream theatres, gardens, sumptuous displays, fine clothes, lovely maidens, real people and people in authority: a *transfert* into the realm of the forbidden, of pleasure, beauty, youth and power. But at the same time, the consciousness, whilst yet dreaming, remains awake in a gallery of sinister symbols (devils, crows, tortures, dungeons) to their ineluctible solitude. The reticent and maniacal old washerwoman, engrossed in suicidal rumination upon a barren mountain-top of the Apennines, surrounded by a frozen and enamelled world of ice, the lonely and mediumistic old woman created by Silvio d'Arzo in *Casa d'altri [Another's home]* belongs to this suffering world of ageing hypochondriacs, eaten away by frustration, despair and the worms of loneliness.

These were 'wicked and infamous' people whose only desire was to sleep and dream. Ulisse Aldrovandi, who as a leading physician had all the pharmacies of Bologna and the surrounding area under his control, was also an expert pharmacologist and a compiler and reformer of the *Antidotario* of Bologna. He was familiar with the unguents of 'witchcraft' based on human fats, which can be 'made to boil in a bronze pot together with smallage, wolfsbane, poplar leaves, lime, bat's blood, nightshade, opiate, mandragora, darnel, broad beans, henbane, poppy, opium and other similar things which induce the deepest sleep. Wecker-

---

[37] G. B. Spaccini, *Cronaca modenese (1588–1636)*, vol. II, Modena, 1919, p. 176.
[38] Johann Jakob Wecker, *De secretis libri XVII*, Basileae, 1588, p. 178
[39] Ibid. p. 718.

ius also reports that when these substances are in the body, they cause strange and remarkable visions'.[40]

[40]   O. Scarlatini, *L'huomo e sue parti figurato*, part II, p. 177.

2

THE 'IMPASSIBLE' SAINT

To mediaeval and renaissance minds paradise was a mirror image of the real and historic worlds, an image in which the human condition was totally recast and the quality of life reached absolute perfection. Paradise was the world turned upside down: illness was banished, hunger forgotten, the flesh's corruptibility abolished, sweet scents were daily inhaled rather than the stench of putrefaction. It was a dream of permanent embalming, of 'impassibility' /'incapacity to suffer either pain or detriment', OED/ – according to the expression – of the blessed, of the incorruptibility of the flesh, of itself mortal and perishable. The embalming of corpses reflected this search for permanence and renewal through rebirth. It was an ancient dream that the human world vainly sought to propitiate by simulating the appearance of longevity in the cadavers of the famous, 'treating' them according to certain funerary recipes. 'It was the practice ... of the ancient to prepare some of these cadavers with balsam, myrrh and saffron, as well as other sorts of seed and aromatic herbs, as it is the custom to do with the dead bodies of our princes.'[1]

The impassible could take on a fragrant and aromatic reality: it was only necessary to trust completely in death, in 'goodly' death, in the death of the just, went the sales patter of preachers. 'Give us a heavy body and we shall restore its lightness, a feeble body and we will restore its impassivity, a malformed body and we shall restore its beauty, a gross body and we shall restore its subtlety so that it will be like the spirit.'[2]

Paradise, in this dialectic of reversal, is portrayed as a laboratory of physical restoration, an exemplary clinic where the boldest plastic surgery achieves a one hundred per cent success rate. The 'qualities of these exalted bodies' resurrected in all saintliness from their tombs, the 'bodies of the virtuous' recomposed and returned to eternal bliss, were their amazing perfection, their total 'impassibility, incorruptibility, non-transience', their immunity to the withering and drying up processes of old age:

[1]   F. Imperato, *Historia naturale*, Venezia, 1672, p. 365.
[2]   Padre F. Zuccarone, S.J., *Prediche quaresimali*, Venezia, 1671, p. 325. 'Le doti de' corpi glorificati. Predica ... della Resurrezione nel giorno di Pasqua.'

Impassibility is a gift which according to St Thomas does not merely have the negative advantage of not inflicting pain upon a sick or dying man but has the positive and delightful quality of enabling every sense to cull an overwhelming abundance of pleasure from its corresponding excitant. As far as the negative aspect goes, we see the body totally embalmed and wrapped in a coat impervious to the arrows of the serried ranks of diseases that, like executioners of divine justice, penetrate the chambers of monarchs not subject to temporal justice, find their way between the pearl-embroidered curtains of high born princes, seek out the finest ladies in their labyrinth of secret rooms, and heedless of all entreaties and the aphorisms of pundits, pin them to their couches with podagra and migrain and imprison them in their houses with leprosy. But those who die in sanctity have no need of fortresses like that of Louis XI in order to preserve their lives, as though death could be afraid of bodyguards. Nor do they think of preparing foods with a pure magnet inside after the fashion of the King of Zeilan who judged that since he had lead a hard-working life and had demonstrated steel-like character-istics, he would retain these beyond the grave with the aid of magnets. Nor would they . . . keep a unicorn constantly by them as princes do, for protection against every kind of poison. The blessed are more adept at handling vipers than are the Psilli, less burnt than those of the Hellespont when carrying live coals, lighter than Abide of Galicia when he strode across the water, safer than the young St Medard when playing with lions. Hurl stones at them and they will not be harmed; would you wish them to be less fortunate than Fortunatus? Shoot pointed arrows at them and their skin will remain unbroken. . . . Unleash the bolts of a cross-bow at them and unscathed they will kiss them. . . . Where are time and death now, that you should even compare these saintly lives with the short span of our mortal existence? . . . . How poorly you make your reckoning: 'He who will be accepted as Blessed has no end.' The nine hundred or so years lived by the Patriarchs is nought when compared with the length of their lives. The life of the blessed is only measured against the golden locks of Aged Eternity. 'He who is accepted as Blessed has no end.' This is the negative side of impassibility.

We now come to such positive merits as the harmonious warmth of the blood, the delicate economy of unchangeable humours which predisposes our senses to a heightened enjoy-ment of beautiful objects, without however affecting the physical organs; a total enjoyment of every kind of pleasure,

without agitation; a continuous feast of the senses, without
satiety; an incessant delighting, without surfeit. For the eyes
what a variety of scenes, for the nostrils what distillations of
springtime, for the touch what flattering softness, for the palate
what flavours of unforgettable exquisiteness![3]

In this Jesuitical sermon on resurrection dating from the second half of
the seventeenth century, full of 'magalottian' sensitivity to the inebriating odour of 'distillations' and sensuous sublimation of desire, entrapped
and assimilated by the body, are reintroduced the fundamental notions
of pleasure, of health, of physical contentment, of the humours in
calibrated equilibrium with each other and of 'blood at an harmonious
temperature': a sense of perfect (physiological) well-being, a paradise
where healthy organs work efficiently, indeed, perfectly. In the land of
the blessed the spirit appears to have become volatized. The five senses
will at last enjoy their moment of triumph, of absolute fulfilment:

> Whilst the eye feasts upon gardens, loveliness and fine views . . .
> the ear is entertained with sweet sounds, songs and symphonies
> of unsurpassed harmoniousness; the nostrils with amber, civet,
> scents and thyme, all undiluted; the palate with juices, nectar,
> ambrosia and all that is most delicious in one sip; the flesh with
> joys, delights, tender embraces, rest and peace, all that can be
> enjoyed in its quintessential form.[4]

God himself is transformed into a cross between a cow and a mother,
abounding in honeyed milk, exuding ineffable sweetness from his
breasts. 'Ah, what abundance!' exclaims a Capuchin preacher, closer by
birth and upbringing to country folk, 'he who is blessed will suckle the
nipples of divine goodness, he will imbibe sweetness, almost as a chalice
immersed in a sea, which floods . . . '.[5]

In an age when it was reported, even on the evidence of trusted men of
science, that there existed widowers from whose teats there issued milk
which nourished orphans, God himself appears in the guise of a bosomed
and loving wet-nurse.

The empyrean heaven of the eighteenth century lived in a perpetual
state of kinaesthesia and continual triumph of movement, of physical
dynamism. In heaven 'the gift of agility [has] wonderfully grown',
together with 'the insubstantiality and transparency of the blessed, who

[3]   Ibid. pp. 325–6.
[4]   Padre Pacifico da Venezia, *Prediche quaresimali* . . . In attestato d'umilissimo e
         divotissimo ossequio alla Santissima Vergine, Padova, 1722, p. 87.
[5]   Ibid. p. 89.

are so insubstantial that, the body being dressed in the livery of the spirit, it can barely be distinguished from the soul'.[6]

Heaven appears like a crystal-domed sports hall where these saintly and scented bodies, gleaming like the sun and clear like glass, remote from the 'kingdoms of the world' which 'stink, almost like a tomb',[7] free of 'the worm infested carrion' of the 'rotten, leaden, tormented body',[8] dart about with supersonic speed between the heavenly spheres. Appearing on the scene and talking in the first person, the personification of 'Saintly Agility' explains to his audience the dazzling opportunities he provides:

> 'Compared with me the fastest winds are lame, the airiest light wears leaden boots. How often have your raised your eyebrows in astonishment at your irrefutable calculations which show that each star situated in the Equinox devours 42 million miles in an hour, which is as though a postilion mounted on a good horse encircled the earth two thousand times in an hour? How often have you been beside yourselves with astonishment at discovering that the sun runs one million, one hundred and forty thousand miles in an hour? And you have noticed, moreover, that when compared with the planets, lightning is the epitome of celestial laziness and eagles mere aërial tortoises. And I, in anointing these blessed bodies with quintessential balms, in endowing these glorious bodies with invisible feathers, enable them to go and to come, to circle and walk repeatedly from Earth to Heaven, from the high *Zenith* to the diametrically opposed *Nadir* in less time than you need to bat an eyelid.' So speaks, dear Sirs, the 'Agility of Blessed Bodies', and he says but little: so you may understand how St Bernard's saying to the effect that all the blessed own the whole of Heaven and each one is a master of it, is proven. 'All have it [Heaven] and each person has the whole' . . . to cross a world it takes only an act of will for the blessed: 'wherever the spirit will, thither will it with its body go'.[9]

The lightning agility and slenderness of these saintly bodies must have captured the imagination of the swollen, corpulent people of the day, bloated with putrid phlegm and flatulence, tortured by gout, of the upper classes accustomed to hypercalorific diets and lack of exercise. But Jesuitical astuteness quietly slips into a paradisiacal rhetoric which is still

6   Padre F. Zuccarone, *Prediche quaresimali*, pp. 327, 329.
7   Ibid. p. 330.
8   Ibid. p. 329.
9   Ibid. p. 328.

largely 'mediaeval', and fits in with the gaudily attired fantasy world of the delician paradise, full of myth and dream. New, however, in that era of mathematics, was the taste for arithmetical hyperbole, for accurate astronomical computation, for precisely measured distances, for the sounding of uranian abysses and for cosmic exploration. New, too, was the mathematical frenzy with which Father Clavius ('our Clavio, the new Archimedes of Bamberg') had infected the order of St Ignatius.

In this age of form in motion, of curving, interrupted lines, of darting and unpredictable trajectories; during those long decades dominated by restless and neurotic baroque invention, by gushing waters, gyrating dances, trilling voices, where metamorphosis and change are symbolically personified in the figures of Proteus and Circe, where 'reluctant' dandies like Glisomiro experiment with fantastic carriages (see Girolamo Brusoni's novels), and Alessandro Capra invents new configurations with jets of water and moving machines, the blessed state cannot react to this intoxication but by indulging in untrammelled and lightning agility, in lightness itself and in vertiginous *motus ad perpetuum*. And so the world pours itself out into the heavens, bringing with it the neurotic frenzy of postilions, messengers, libertines, astronomers, adventurers, vagrants and travelling actors.

The heavenly vault, hitherto site of blissful contemplation and stillness, was now transformed into an acrobatic gymnasium, a whirling track of precipitous journeys. Stillness (synonymous with sapient beatitude) was rejected in favour of new forms of beatitude based on movement, on change, on mobility. The classic notion of beatitude which in the sixteenth century was still identified with the cessation of movement, with the alternation of day and night, of the seasons, of light and darkness, faced a deep crisis. The old world, the 'gyrating theatre' should have been reborn on the eighth day, in a 'new form' refashioned by 'the eternal Maker' according to a new scheme from which all movement would be excluded. This 'frail mass, the Universe' rebuilt in

> ... more admirable a form,
> Will not change with the changing of the years,
> Nor fear renewed destruction or decay.
> But this inconstant temple of the sky
> Will stand still with the sun, as will the
> Tortuous course of other wand'ring stars.
> Thus will the Blessed find constant shelter
> In an eternal and a tranquil peace,
> Untouched by tempest or by violent turbulence,
> A pure light invisible in a still day
> That will not end in hated night.

Neither will it run from morn till dusk,
Nor will the shadows chase away the day,
Nor will it vary with the season's whims;
But a recompense awaits these noble spirits:
A prize of rest and glory all in one,
A supreme honour in supreme quiescence.
    Torquato Tasso, *Il mondo creato*, VII, 366–82[10]

'Rest', 'stillness', 'quiet peace', and an absence of all activity and movement; stability not mutability are the sweet rewards of the blessed. With the discarding of a 'weak and sickly nature', of the 'weary and wakeful/World' and of 'toil and motion', they cannot but look forward to ultimate immobility and repose, to an 'immutable resting place', to a final embalming. Tasso's world is diametrically opposed to that of the subsequent generations of the seventeenth century and of a large portion of the eighteenth.

Hand in hand with this inebriated passion for movement went the attraction of musical effects of a suavity bordering on languor, of harmonious feeling for the 'sighs and swooning languor' of baroque music absent from the austere tones of Gregorian chant.

The soft strains of music in the paradisiacal garden induce a state of abandon and oblivion, analogous to aromas which induce forgetfulness, balms and incenses which intoxicate, to temporary lapses from consciousness, all of which lull the walker to harmonious forgetfulness: the scent of music, the music of scent, a neat and subtle mixing and remixing of the senses, a sublimation of all the channels through which the vigilant and sensitive body absorbs voices, messages, and the presence of secret things and essences. Music is absorbed and diluted in the veins as an elixir, a potion that intoxicates, overwhelms, enchants and transports into unknown spaces and dimensions.

> He who has the courage to explain the delightful harmony that will fall upon saintly ears, must explain to me the tale of the fortunate Paphnutius who, while meditating once upon the prophetic tract (Psalm 90:4: 'For a thousand years in thy sight are but as yesterday when it is past'), was detained in a wood by the song of a small songster, an Angel it was, for three hundred years, which barely seemed like the passing of an hour. Who can believe such an extraordinary tale? Fortunate wanderer, why did the delay not pall? How was it that you did not tire of being on the same spot, that you did not perish in the sun's rays, were not overwhelmed by rain or prostrated by wind and storm? Three

10   T. Tasso, *Il mondo creato*. English translation by J. Tusiani *The Creation of the World*, Binghamton NY, 1982, 7th day, pp. 196–7, vv. 365–81.

hundred times over did the ancient trees over your head lose
and put on again their yearly foliage, and each time was your joy
renewed. Three hundred times did the barren earth of winter
beneath your feet yield up the tender shoots of spring, and yet
your little goldfinch made a perpetual May of the year's cycle.
The days and nights passed and the little bird's song transformed
them into perpetual day. Many thousand times did tempests
rage and thunder, but for you his music was never discordant.
The years and the centuries fled by, but your transport and
delight remained unchanged. Who will count the many reigns
that the song lasted? How often the world's generations came
and went while you never tired of that charming melody or were
satiated. How often did the phoenix change its feathers while
your feathered songster never changed a feather nor changed his
voice.... And so, my little musical angel, I turn to you and ask
with what consort of viols, with what passionate skill contained
in your chromatic warbling, with what sweetness in your flats
and languor in your sharps, with what tuneful magic did you
enchant the soul's ear?.... Perhaps a whole orchestra of lutes
plays within your throat. Perhaps you ordered, with angelic
wisdom, your high, clarion voice to follow the soul to a joyful
heaven of serenity. And again cascading in harmonious scales,
then to throw the soul into a dark state of sweet melancholy....
I fancy that sometimes on hearing those sublime notes he
[Paphnutius] would experience the very heights of divine nature;
or if the voice sank as though into an abyss he discovered in it the
profundity of divine counsel. Now at one moment it was as
though he saw the divine consort gently languishing of love,
while hearing the fainting sighs of that voice: 'I faint from love';
at another moment the succession of long and majestic notes
might evoke the divine monarch himself, seated upon a diamond
throne and speaking in thundering tones: 'I am God'.... Or
with the remoteness of a receding voice, dying away, it led him
by the hand into the distant regions of Eternity. But either I am
as innocent as if I were born yesterday or I am unable to
understand how one single angel is capable of filling three
centuries with a variety of different sonatas, a multiplicity of
songs and open countless doors to new melodies with so meagre
a range of keys? What matter, if I fail to understand how a little
bird, a singing fleck in the sky, so to speak, an invisible drop in
the Ocean of beatitude, can enable a man to forget the weight of
his body, the weariness of his limbs, his aged and hoary head,
not only its white locks but also the snows, the hunger suffered,

the ravages of time, the voraciousness of the centuries, so that after three hundred years of music, shaking himself, he commented: 'I set off this morning an hour ago, so by now it must almost be the third hour'.... Oh Christian hearts, who keeps you in so deep a lethargy, who caused you so sadly to sicken and who deprived you of understanding so that, desirous of pleasure, alas, only of a sordid and ephemeral kind, you are apt to question and even to judge the ineffable joys of the blessed?[11]

The weight of the flesh and the lightness of the blessed: the spellbinding and at once amnesic effects of heavenly music, the loss of sense of time, the elimination of the 'pangs of hunger', of corporeality in all its forms through the astonishment and wonderment caused by the music of the angels; melody as a drug and a surrogate of reality, as a prelude to ineffable happiness, re-establishes the circuit which leads to a seemingly 'bewitched' (in a positive sense) paradise, a free and infinitely voluptuous space where sensuality undergoes the ultimate sublimation, where the frontiers between body and soul become intangible, and the flesh mingles with the spirit to produce a new mixture: the impassibility of the blessed body.

This image of paradise lasted, until well after the Marinistic declamations of Father Francesco Zuccarone, with surprising tenacity in the collective imagination of the gentry well into the heart of the eighteenth century. If, in order to evangelize the rich and urban populations, it was necessary to woo them with promises of future pleasures which, even if they were of an intense and sublimated kind, did nonetheless count as pleasures and gratification, what vision of heaven prevailed among the unlettered and country folk? This is not the place to answer this question; one thing is certain, however: that in sermons of the time, the soul was referred to with caution and even casually, as if to avoid spoiling this dynamic, sensuous and full-blooded view of life with the spectre of spirituality and insubstantiality. Paradise beckons with promises of unsurpassed physical delights, not of spiritual joys. It is a far cry from Dante's paradise, which is indeed absent altogether and of which no mention is made at all. Visions of the Land of Plenty (Cockaigne), 'Indian' mythology, oriental dreams are the 'scene' in the package put forward by preachers who were versed in the mental attitudes and psychological make-up of their audience.

> You would like to immerse yourselves in sensuous delight and in sensuous delights immerse yourselves you will [so wrote the Jesuit, Cesare Bottalini in his *Quaresimale* of 1738], but it is too

[11]   Padre Zuccarone, *Prediche*, pp. 326–7.

soon. You must wait a little longer to cull the fruit of the divine
promise: 'You must observe patience, and your promises will be
fulfilled', which is as much as to say: a human body possessing
impassibility is more lasting than any jasper, agility is speedier
than any dawn, transparency is more penetrating than any
flame, light is more luminous than any sun. It is a body that can
boast of all the joys of every age, the candour of childhood, the
charm of youth, the strength of manhood, the decorum of old
age. It is a body that will enjoy, as it never has before, all that it
craves after: unimaginable beauties for the eye, melodies for the
ear, flavours that make the mouth water, perfumes for the
nostrils, delights for the insatiable tactile sense: a body, in fact,
(need we say more?) similar to the glorious Body of Jesus
Christ.[12]

That 'the corporeal parts' of God should have been deemed manifold
and that it should have been thought possible by the ecclesiastical
community to see and to 'read' God in corporeal terms is not a fact at
which we should wonder. It is enough to peruse the *Trattato de
l'emulazione, che il demonio ha fatta a Dio, ne l'adorazione, ne' sacrifici,
et ne l'altre cose appartenenti alla divinità. Con la dichiarazione di molti
nomi essenziali di Dio, et de le parti corporali, che si danno a Dio ne le
scritture* (Venice, 1563) *[Treatise on how the devil sought to emulate God,
in adoration, sacrifices and in other things pertaining to Divinity. With a
list of many names essential to God and to his corporeal parts, that are
given him in the scriptures]* by Giovanni Andrea Gilio. If the ambiguity of
a divine image which is simultaneously sacred and profane, corporeal
and spiritual, may strike 'purists' of the sacred as a piece of grotesque
nonsense (although Gilio's treatise points to an infiltration by Christ's/
God's human corporeality even into the higher levels of ecclesiastical
culture), among common people (and here we need only remember the
standing of the Virgin both then and now in the female sector of society)
the corporeal attributes of Christ reflected the nature-bound and mater-
ialistic sensibility of popular culture which, immersed since time immemorial in a double stream of currents both sacred and profane, had never
been able to interpret spiritual matters except in material terms. The love
of life was too strongly rooted for a purely ethereal Beyond to be
contemplated, a Beyond of insubstantial shadows indulging in acrobatic
games, or of non-existent and intangible saints, who were not 'impassible'. The abstractions of theologians were incomprehensible to those
who, while accepting mystery, the miraculous and impossible, were
accustomed to visualize these on a human scale and to measure them

12   Padre C. Bottalini, S.J., *Quaresimale*, Venezia, 1738, p. 193.

with a worldly measure. A man-sized concept of divinity which may disconcert those who are accustomed to see only mass and number, and fearing (or desiring?) their extermination, view with horror the rebirth of non-serialized man.

A beatified Land of Cockaigne is the furthest horizon, the remotest Thule towards which pre-industrial man might venture in his meditations on death: a different – though not too different – land where, if not peace, at least 'luxe et volupté' reign; a 'pays de rêve' where the senses rather than being mortified are sublimated. This land of acrobatic lightness constituted a great attraction for the army of gouty individuals who displaced themselves only with great difficulty and pain, and were for the most part susceptible to attacks of 'migrain', of cephalitis induced by metabolic malfunctioning such as would make a modern dietician's hair stand on end: hyperglycaemia, hyperproteosis and hyperlipidaemia. It is impossible to overlook the great disparity between strict theological rationalization of the irrational and the collective consciousness of the imagination, the beliefs of folklore which, by reason of their ineradicable syncretism and ambiguous scepticism, pursued contradictory dreams. Life's logic proved stronger than any theological theorem, and preachers, like good brokers who are aware of the temperament of their client, set about bridging the gap between the improbable and the impossible.

'Corporeal delights' (*bona corporis*) was always a central theme in this type of sermon: if it was hard to accept the sacrifice and flaying of the body on God's remote and inaccessible altar, then at least as a single, unique and unrepeatable good, the body was considered a treasure to guard by every means possible. Compared with the careful preservation of the body, any moments of exaltation, whether private or collective in nature, were typically a minority activity. The fear of hell (of a long darkness, and always within the bowels of the earth), was more widespread by far than the belief in a celestial paradise, located in some improbable and unimaginable zone. By and large, people found it hard to believe that a human body could be in the image of God. It seemed impossible for anyone who was saved to cry: 'these eyes of mine are like Christ's, these hands like his hands, these feet like his feet, my body is like his body'.[13] Many did not find it credible that a human body 'could overflow with sweetness, like a beehive in Ibla, brimming with honey'. In order to become celestial honey, many venerable men of God had undergone unspeakable tortures. 'And are you then amazed to hear that the saints used to mortify their flesh by fasting,' exclaimed the preacher at his Lenten sermon, 'they tore it with flagellation, destroyed it with punishments?'

[13]   Ibid. p. 192.

For, however much you cherish it, it always suffers a thousand pains; if only because time erodes it, as the Apostle Paul says, and death destroys it: *Seminatur in corruptione [*it is engendered in corruption*]*. But there, above the stars it will enjoy the most perfect age of all, and be immortal and free from all troubles. *Surget in incorruptione [*it rises in purity*]*. Here, no matter how much you idolize it, it is always like a sickly and clumsy clod of earth that needs a bridge at every valley it tries to cross: *Seminatur in infirmitate [*it is engendered in sickness*]*; but there above the stars it will be endowed with such transparency that, even were the walls of this church of pure diamond, it would penetrate them with an agility surpassing that needed to pass through a door: *Surget in virtute [*it ascends in strength*]*.

Here, no matter how much you try to keep it agile, by dancing at balls, riding proud steeds and throwing javelins, it is always lazy, reluctant and intractable: *Seminatur corpus animale [*it is engendered animal*]*; but there beyond the stars it will always be alert for action at a prompting of the will; so that at the batting of an eyelid it can leap from one hemisphere to another, and not tire: *Surget corpus spirituale [*the body rises spiritually*]*.

However much you cleanse it, its natural condition will always be dull and blind, a web of shadows, a tissue of darkness: *Seminatur in ignobilitate [*it is engendered ignoble*]*; but up there beyond the stars you will find it so luminous that were it to extend one single finger from Heaven, it would illumine the whole world as the Sun does when it rises over the Indian Sea: *Surget in gloria [*it rises in glory*]*.

But if God has prepared your body for such perfections, what joys will he bestow upon it after? According to St Lawrence Justinian, visions for the eyes, of a beauty never before witnessed [St Joseph of Copertino, in a paroxysm of ecstasy, saw among other things a 'great hall full of beauteous things']; singing for the ears, whose charm surpassed anything they hitherto had heard; flavours for the sense of taste exquisite as never before, textures for the touch of such pure delight as it had never known before; all the senses were regaled as they had never before imagined possible: *Caro spiritualis effecta per omnes sensus suos multimodis exuberabit deliciis [*the spiritual flesh will abound in all manner of delights through all its senses*]*.[14]

The spiritual flesh, that theological paradox and oxymoron, could in today's climate be transformed into a heavenly orgasm.

[14]   Ibid. pp. 191–2.

3

THE DUST OF DEATH

Popular religiosity appears to have no limits when it comes to accepting the weirdest, most grotesque and most spectacular traits in the 'man of God'. What people expected of the person who lived in a privileged relationship with the divine can be surmised from numerous beliefs: a faith in the impossible, in the ability to realize the unrealizable, in the possibility of overthrowing the established order, to impose a contradictory logic, one which is turned on its head and paradoxical, to attempt 'eccentric deeds' and to 'get oneself a reputation as a madman' (Segneri). The saint is the man who overturns physical laws, who reveals the unexpected, who prophesies a change of state, who inhabits another dimension full of remarkable, unheard-of and spectacular phenomena. He is a magician-cum-prophet who has succeeded in mastering the occult world, in reading the future, in penetrating the most jealously guarded secrets of the present, in sounding 'occult thoughts, secret temptations and the tormentings of the soul'. Even his body obeys physiological rules founded on the impossible and formulated in miraculous terms. After the death of the holy Joseph of Copertino, according to custom:

> death having been legally certified by public authority, the body was then opened and embalmed with sweet-smelling herbs and spices. The surgeon found in the process not only that the pericardium was dry but also that the ventricles were devoid of blood, indeed the heart itself was dry and desiccated, not through the natural burning of a fever, but through the supernatural flame of Divine Love; a phenomenon which the surgeon had encountered previously during his experience and therefore attributed in this case.[1]

[1] *Vita di S. Giuseppe di Copertino sacerdote professo dell'Ordine de' Minori Conventuali di S. Francesco*, Firenze, 1768, pp. 165–6. For an analysis of the complex question of 'sanctity', seen also from a modern interpretative angle, such as that of ethnopsychiatry, cf. J.-M. Sallmann, 'Image et fonction du saint dans la région de Naples à la fin du XVIIe et au début du XVIIIe siècle', in *Mélanges de l'Ecole française de Rome*, tome 91, 1979, 2, pp. 827–74; *idem*. 'Il santo e le rappresentazioni della santità. Problemi di metodo', in *Quaderni storici*, 1979, 41, pp. 584–602; *idem*, 'Il santo patrono cittadino nel 1600 nel Regno di Napoli e in Sicilia', in *Per la storia sociale e religiosa del Mezzogiorno d'Italia*, ed. G. Galasso & C. Russo, Napoli, II, pp. 189–211.

The fever of divine love had dried out the heart, the surgeon believed – perhaps the same phlebotomist who during his last illness opened one of his veins:

> thus seated [wrote the surgeon in his report attached to the deeds of beatification], with his leg resting upon my knee while I was carrying out the operation, I observed that he was completely alienated from his senses, his arms wide apart, face and eyes were likewise open and cast heavenward, and his mouth was also open although he gave not the slightest sign of breathing; I also observed that he was raised almost a whole palm above the chair. I tried to lower the leg I was holding but failed. Furthermore, I noticed that a fly had alighted in the middle of the pupil of his eye and however much I tried to chase it away it always came back, so I finally left it there.[2]

The pupil of the eye and its fixed insensitivity, the molesting fly that walks upon it, are two recurrent themes in the ecstatic state of this disconcerting saint from the south of Italy, mistrusted by a Holy Office which suspected that beneath his habit there hid a consummate imposter, a past-master in the art of simulated sanctity, a subtle magician. In death as in life he was a worker of 'resounding miracles' which, occurring as they did within silently claustral surroundings and segregating walls, provide the observer with a useful spyglass whereby he may penetrate the mentality of these monasteries, a mentality partly decipherable through monastic nosology. He will catch glimpses of atrocious clinical cases, of mental disorders, of unimaginable instances of physical disintegration. One example among many is that of Sister Teresa Margaret of 'San Giuseppe', a member of the Discalced Carmelite order at St Nicholas of Lecce.

> This noble sister [writes the hagiographer of St Joseph of Copertino] suffered for the duration of eight years roughly, from so great and so racking a series of diseases, that even on the first occasion – a fierce attack of epilepsy on 8 May 1727 – it was feared for her life. This attack passed, the following month of December, she succumbed to raging attacks of cephalea, which gradually reached such painful intensity as to make her not only delirious but, what is worse, caused her to beat her head against the wall; and unable, due to her overwhelming distress, to stay in bed, she would lie on the ground and, tying sharp and jagged pieces of stone about her head, she would hit it against the floor and the blood would flow from her wounded forehead, as if she

2   Ibid. p. 159

were seeking to calm the ruthlessness of her internal suffering by the infliction of external pain.

All remedies tried were of no avail, so much so that the doctors almost despairing after a thousand attempts, decided to made a small incision in her cranium to discover the cause of so unremitting a pain. Indeed, on the hard meninx they found a tubercular growth of about the size of a chickpea, which they dispelled with medicaments. But the cephalea did not disappear as a result and, as though dissatisfied that it was unable to cause enough suffering on its own, it called in other ailments: painful abdominal spasms that racked her, agonizing pains in the chest which prevented her breathing, epileptic fits and a cough so fierce that whenever she swallowed she was obliged to throw up again what she had eaten; and she was often seen to spit blood, due to swelling and subsequent breaking of blood vessels in the chest. So beleaguered was her poor body that the nervous system in her spine was greatly affected and she was unable to stay on her feet or to walk and she was reduced to dragging herself about on all fours like an animal whenever she wanted to get from one side of her cell to another. She eventually became cachectical, developing mouth and throat ulcers, together with other tumours of a scirrhous kind in the stomach. She was constantly affected by fevers, her legs and feet swelled up prodigiously; she was in one word, reduced to a mass of ailments, unable to find respite or rest, to breath easily, to eat without vomiting, all the nerves and muscles of her body were tormented by unbearable pain and a thousand other terrible symptoms.[3]

When later she fell into a deep lethargy and lay dying of an acute inflammatory fever, a paper image of St Joseph of Copertino was laid upon her body: after two days 'she at once rose from her bed and sat herself in a chair', 'the acute fever was gone, so too had the pains, spasms, cephalea and every gnawing symptom . . .'.

This mind-boggling clinical picture of the epileptic Carmelite sister, whose cranium was bored into, who beat her head against flagstones in an attempt to find relief from unbearable encephalitis, whose meningitis was 'dispelled' by the physicians' corrosive medicines, who was forced to crawl about the floor like an animal because of the lesions in her medulla, with her tumours of the lower abdomen, her whooping cough and coughing up of blood, all throw but a dim light on the secret torments in so many monasteries, whose few escape valves from a cruel and

[3]   Ibid. pp. 292–4.

delirious existence took the form of battles with demons on the one hand and visionary aerobatics on the other.

In this world of possessed souls, where convulsions were more common than the common cold, where hysteria and cephalea were the inevitable companions of melancholy nights, and of days that were ennervating, monotonous and repetitive to the extent of provoking manias, where closed rooms emphasized the claustrophobic oppressiveness, men and women lived tortured lives amidst flagellations, penances, wakes, fasts, humiliations and mortifications.

Already at the age of seven, the flying and jumping Joseph of Copertino, born in the land of the tarantella *par excellence*, where the 'tarantula' supposedly compelled its victims to dance and jump about, was familiar with the havoc caused by the worst sicknesses:

> assailed internally in a fleshy part of his body by an abscess, which had grown in size and developed finally into a horrible gangrene, which in turn gave rise to other ulcers in the head, he was obliged to submit – unavailingly – to a treatment by iron and fire. For four years that young body was plagued with the sickness but at the end of the fourth year, the Divine hand that heals took pity on the stricken boy and restored him to health when a hermit, to whom his devoted mother had brought him, applied a small quantity of oil from the lamp of the Virgin of Galatone.[4]

He arrived at the hermit's cell 'gangrenous and on horseback', but he was able 'to do the return journey of nine miles in health and on foot, without any other help than that of a stick'.[5]

'Freed now from so severe a sickness, he offered up thanks to God and then determined to devote the life he had newly gained to His service.' And, though still convalescent, so as to mortify the body and keep it subjected to the mind, he began a régime of the 'sternest penance'.

> He therefore assumed a hairshirt of the coarsest prickles which he wore against his bare flesh, he fed only on bread and fruits; if perchance he ate cooked vegetables or herbs, these he sprinkled with powder made of bitterest wormwood. He fasted frequently and often spent two or three days without touching food . . .[6]

Inured and toughened by so strict a régime, it is hardly surprising that this master of 'astonishing and admirable things' should, without any precautions, set about performing some acts of basic surgery on himself:

[4]   Ibid. pp. 3–4.
[5]   Ibid. p. 4.
[6]   Ibid. p. 4.

Wherever God surprised him with an ecstasy, there would he kneel: and as a consequence of the prolonged contact between his knees and the ground which was sometimes stony and uncomfortable, he developed a painful tumour in one of his knees. However, ignoring the pain of the operation, he cut himself with a knife and left the remainder of the cure to God, who immediately healed him.[7]

Turned down by the Minorites as an untutored boor, a man of 'little or no learning', he entered the Capuchin convent of Martina as a lay brother, but his odd behaviour caused them to suspect he was 'slow of mind, or infirm of body', and he was dismissed from the order. He resumed his previous existence as a roaming and saintly beggar, as 'a clumsy tramp', a crazy angel, until an uncle of his managed to place him with the Oblate convent at Grottella as a tertiary, where his sole duty 'was to look after the convent's mule'.

Lean-faced and bare-footed, he now added a 'rough iron chain tightly girded about his thighs'. He subsequently took orders within the Minorite fraternity and

> . . . for seven years ate no bread and for ten drank no wine.
> Whether he ate herbs, or dried fruits, or cooked beans, these were always sprinkled with a bitter powder. Someone who once tried some of the powder thinking it pepper, nicknamed it – like David – *death's powder*. On Fridays his only food was a particular herb which was so bitter and disgusting that if only touched with the tip of the tongue it caused nauseous feelings for several days. During Lent, called *the blessed* by the Franciscan Order, he only tasted food once a week. On fast days observed by the Order his only sustenance was the usual bitter herbs or fruits or broad beans on Sundays and Thursdays, whilst on the other five days he would survive solely on the Eucharist. It was noticed moreover that before Holy Mass he was so weak and languid that he seemed moribund but after Mass, he would be so bright and active and his face so happy and full of colour, that it proved indeed that his best source of nourishment was the Bread of the Angels.
> Meat was out of the question: so much so that on one occasion when the Superior of his Order had instructed him to eat some, he obeyed with his usual promptness, but his overcharged stomach immediately rebelled and rejected the meat. So it was with fish, too. He ate some once to obey the inhabitants of Lecce

[7]   Ibid. p. 7.

who had arrived with a gift of fine fish; but at the end of the meal he lightly excused himself from the others at table and, returning to his cell, he was heard, unbeknown to himself, to vomit what his weak stomach could not withstand. He then grasped an iron chain and brutally beating himself with it fifty times, uttered the words of his Seraphic Father: 'Now, brother Ass, you are well again.'

Not only was he parsimonious in his eating habits but he also limited his hours of sleep, these being a meagre two or three hours a night ... [8]

Those given to ecstasies and visions had to observe a 'bare minimum'[9] diet. St Francesca Romana used to subsist on a

small amount of bread, or what was enough to ensure survival, and as an accompaniment sometimes beans or lupins; occasionally she would allow her obedient and mortified body a drink, or a feast of cabbage or borage; but so as to avoid enjoying these too much, she made sure that the vegetables and herbs were cooked without oil or other condiments, deeming a little salt to be sufficient condiment.[10]

He who aspires to be free of 'worldly labyrinths' must opt for a perverted cuisine, an anti-cuisine which scorns the body and upsets the culinary norms. Even dietary practice must be turned on its head, must obey the call to disillusionment and avoidance of every kind of indulgence of the appetite.

Suppress your taste for food [suggests John the Baptist to Francesca Romana during one of her visions] by introducing something that makes it distasteful, by for instance eating cold what others eat hot, by not eating any delicacies but only common foods, by not seeking variety; you should always subtract something from your food; you should never satisfy your hunger ... [11]

The Capuchin monk from Faenza, Carlo Girolamo Severoli (1641–1712) never 'took salt', nor ate meat or fish and to 'abstinence from these foods', wrote his biographer, 'he added so rigorous a fast that it is best described as continuous; not being accustomed to eat in the evening,

8   Ibid. pp. 22–3.
9   Padre Don Bernardo Maria Amico di Milano, Monaco Olivetano dell' Ordine di San Benedetto, *Vita di Santa Francesca Romana Fondatrice delle Oblate Olivetane di Torre de' Specchi*, Venezia, 1710, p. 257.
10   Ibid. p. 257.
11   Ibid. p. 181.

excepting on certain of the main feast-days, his sole nourishment consisted of a salad of raw herbs dressed only with vinegar.[12]

At midday his 'customary meal'

> consisted always of the same ordinary soup: if ever it ran the risk of tasting at all good, he would pretend it was too hot and would add a fair amount of water. Indeed, to mortify his sense of taste . . . he would sprinkle the bread soaked in the soup with ashes which he carried hidden about his person for this purpose. Thus at Bertinoro, having reached the age of 69, he ordered Friar Umile da Bagnara that every Monday, Wednesday and Friday, he should pick the worst kind of bread, soak it in cold water and place it under his napkin, which he would then sprinkle with ashes, and this was his customary food. Though Guardian and 'Definitore' at the Bolognese convent, he never dined in the refectory but remained instead in the choir, whereupon after an hour or two he would go to his cell and taking a piece of discarded bread and a cup of murky water left over from the washing up, he would add to it a few drops of wine and would take his nourishment in this form. This might yet appear little, had he not taken even more remarkable steps to mortify his appetite, which he seemed to wish to extinguish completely. According to Friar Domenicantonio da Ravenna, he actually witnessed Father Carlo Girolamo, while he was Vicar at Cesena, placing his bread to soak in stagnant and verminous water, whereupon he would eat it and drink some of the water after it; and God knows how often he did this secretly, since he was very keen that acts of mortification should not be witnessed . . . [13]

Not only did he observe the compulsory fast days of the Church, but on those which were left to the pious discretion of the faithful, the *novenes*, God's servant from Faenza (of noble extraction, unlike Joseph of Copertino)

> would fast on bread and water, kneeling on the bare ground as he ate, after a long penance performed in the public refectory. Thus not a week went by without his performing one or other of these extraordinary penances from which he never attempted to excuse himself, no matter how weary he might be from an exacting journey or the weakness of old age, even though he

---

[12]   *Vita del Servo di Dio Padre F. Carlo Girolamo Severoli di Faenza Dell'Ordine di S. Francesco dei FF. Minori Cappuccini della Provincia di Bologna.* Compilata da Romoaldo Maria Magnani sacerdote faentino, Faenza, 1733, p. 34.

[13]   Ibid. pp. 32–3.

practically always observed harsh abstinence by eating stale bread dipped in rank water from washed crockery in the cellar, to which he added ashes as previously described. Moreover, he was accustomed to take all the foods offered him at the refectory table together with his fellow monks, not so much to hide his abstinence as to be doubly worthy in God's eyes by depriving himself of these foods. He would treat himself with harshness by letting his appetite for food be whetted and then refusing to eat it by way of mortification. . . .

If he had become rather frail and sensitive in his old age through his unrelenting penance and self-inflicted hardship, eating soaked and ash-besprinkled bread, how difficult it must be to imagine the extent of the fasts and penances practiced by him when he was younger and stronger, whether in places of retreat or in the strict Province of Umbria for twelve unremitting years.[14]

This self-inflicted hardship, this destructive anger turned on one's own body, this hatred for one's own physical being, considered foul and corrupt, may startle the modern reader by its harshness (living as he does in a totally different dimension, one in which he is used to hearing of the body as a treasure to be tenderly cherished, caressed and sheltered, as a casket laden with wonders and speaking a language of its own), but it had its own logic and a sublime coherence. It has taken only a few generations for our relationship with our bodies to change so radically and for the punitive and destructive attitudes, which were the glory of saints in an age not so long past, to seem incomprehensible to us now.

No one, in these days of mass beauty culture and sublimated corporeality, would be prepared voluntarily to transform his or her body into a gruesome dummy of dead and larval matter.

The devout penitents burned, on the other hand, with a desire to annihilate and deform their physical selves in the most repugnant manner possible.

Such was the manner and number of his self-inflictions and abstinences that his appearance was completely transformed: his countenance was pallid and his bones were barely covered by his bloodless skin so had he wasted away; a few meagre hairs sprouted from his chin and his frame was bent and transfigured, so that he had become bare like a skeleton, a living image of penitence. He suffered as a consequence most grievously of languidness, fainting, swooning and a death-like pallor, so

[14]   Ibid. pp. 35–6.

extreme that on journeys he was sometimes obliged to stop and he would sink to the ground to recover some little strength in his flagging limbs; or to relieve the pains of a hernia and other ills, for which he refused to seek any remedy.[15]

The image of this Capuchin monk on his travels could be easily mistaken for that of a wretched and forelorn tramp, a beggar riddled with ailments, all skin-and-bones:

> ... you might meet him on the road, wearing some threadbare garment with patches, and bearing a rough stick under his left arm, a wooden cross from his neck and a paltry basket between his hands; and any who knew him not might well have imagined him to be one of those sad tramps who beg a crust of bread. Naturally, he had difficulty remaining on his legs on journeys because of the poor constitution of his body, with one shoulder higher than the other so that he lost all the agility required to avoid muddy puddles or obstacles. But what hindered his steps even more was the feebleness of his emaciated limbs which, owing in large measure to meagre sustenance, possessed so little strength that even when standing, it would have been possible to knock him down with a single light touch of the hand. It would often happen (likewise because of his short-sightedness) that travelling on muddy roads in winter he would sink into some murky pool or fall headlong in some ditch ... [16]

The 'straight and narrow path' that lead to (eternal) life was as follows:

> castigate and mortify the body, pray for whole nights while keeping vigil, eat a little bread, drink water in moderation, receive cheerfully the salutory and purgative draught of humiliations, insults, derision and sneers, disappointment, frustrated desires, without complaint; suffer persecution, repression and scorn ... [17]

The 'filth of the world' as exorcised by the destruction of the self, by voluntary annihilation of the 'foul and bestial' flesh, by acceptance of putrefaction on earth so as better to breathe heavenly aromas. The anachoretical extremism of Thebaid and Sinai was re-lived also in

---

15   Ibid. p. 36.
16   Ibid. p. 37.
17   Johannes Climacus, *Sermoni di S. Giovanni Climaco, Abbate nel Monte Sinai.* Ne' quali discorrendose per la scala di trenta gradi, simili a gl'anni della pienezza dell'età di Giesù Cristo, secondo la carne, s'insegna il modo di salire brevemente alla perfettione della vita monastica, religiosa e santa, Venezia, 1570, p. 19.

socialized versions of the punitive experience in certain 'religions' of the Christian west, at least into the eighteenth century.

'Let us kill this flesh', 'let us kill it just as it has killed us with the mortal blow of sin', cried John Climacus, as he climbed the Holy Mountain or – to quote the title of his work – the *Santa Scala*, the holy ladder to monastic perfection:[18]

> And thus did those saintly sinners behave; whose knees, through repeated and assiduous genuflexions, were dry, hard and full of callouses. Their eyes were dull, concave and sunken deeply into their heads, and all their lashes had fallen out; their cheeks were wizened, burned and full of sores from the hot and fervent tears that had coursed down them. Their faces were thin, dry and pale, not unlike the faces of the dead. Their chests likewise had sores and contusions from self-inflicted bleeding and they suffered great pain from the beatings they had given themselves. From their mouths there came forth blood rather than saliva, because of their beaten and broken torsos. . . . Their clothes were all ragged, full of filth, flea and lice-ridden. . . . They prayed to the universal Bishop, exhorting him under oath not to let them be worthy of human burial, but that he should cause them to be thrown like beasts into some river or in some field so that they should be devoured by wild animals. . . . These men full of wretchedness, and growing day by day more bent and more dismal, exhaled and gave forth an intolerable smell from their decayed and blistered bodies. Having no thought or care for their bodies, they would forget to eat their bread, while their tears and sighs would mingle with what they drank. They ate their bread rolled in ashes. They were dried out like hay, so their skin stuck to their skeletons. . . . You might see them sometimes with their tongues hanging out like dogs so burnt were they. Some would torment themselves by standing in the burning rays of the sun. Others, on the other hand, would make themselves suffer bitter cold. Some, so as not to dry up and die of thirst, might occasionally drink a drop of water and thus had some relief. But others when they ate a little bread, would throw away the rest declaring themselves unworthy of normal fare as if they had performed the deed of some irrational beast.[19]

[18]   Ibid. p. 98.
[19]   Ibid. pp. 99–100, 95–6.

4

SUPERHUMAN AND HEAVENLY LIFE

In the Middle Ages, a hermit's cave of a monk's cell was a kind of distillery for an elaborate cobweb of visions, ecstasies, illuminations, of imaginary games with the ineffable and impossible. It was a Middle Ages that never seemed to end: during the age of the Counter-Reformation, new and wonderful acrobatics were invented by conjuror-saints as they progressed from astonishing 'raptures' (in the Franciscan tradition) to levitations, then to fly along the corridors and around the chambers of their convents. One of these 'enlightened' saints, who enjoyed an intimate rapport with the supernatural world, was confined by his superiors to hermitages or remote convents, or was at the very least expected to live a segregated life in his cell, but once the aerobatic Baroque Age was in full swing, his popularity soared, together with his breath-taking defiance of gravity or 'flights' that swept him off the ground, and abducted him heavenward with sudden and irresistible violence:

> ... the ecstasy that occurred in the morning of Pentecost was prodigious beyond all measure. As he was celebrating Mass, upon intoning the *Veni Sancte Spiritu*, he was so brimming with grace and spiritual completeness that he was swept away from the altar and sped, more impetuously than swiftly, like lightning around the whole chapel breaking into so weird and resonant a cry that the convent [of Fossombrone] trembled from it; where-upon the monks ran tumultuously out of their cells and cried 'an earthquake, an earthquake', filling the whole convent with sudden terror.[1]

This fortress-cum-heritage at Fossombrone 'was', according to one biographer, 'a continual paradise of ecstasies and raptures in God'. The acrobatic excesses of this semi-illiterate Minorite friar, innocent as only the piously simple can be, a fool or *salòs* who, sleeping 'always in the same habit, half-sitting and half-lying on three boards, his head on a small cloth-covered pillow and his body upon a worn bear-skin',[2] emanated inexplicable heavenly aromas, multiplied in number most alarmingly in this convent of the Marche.

[1]   *Vita di S. Giuseppe di Copertino...*, p. 135.
[2]   Ibid. p. 146.

No sooner had he caught sight of a devotional picture than he would utter a cry and be wafted up into the air in ecstasy. Whenever he heard reference to the Christ's passion or praise of his Virgin Mother, he would fall into a gentle swoon. On one occasion in an orchard, a Capuchin monk happened to remind him of the Virgin's greatness, and he straightway threw himself into the other man's arms, hurling them both to the ground, whence Giuseppe cried out aloud praising God's plenitude whilst the Capuchin exclaimed in terror. Their companions, hearing the sudden uproar, ran to the scene calling to each other: 'They've both gone into an ecstasy', but they then realised that the one in ecstasy was Giuseppe, who remained prostrate, immobile and insensible upon the ground for a full hour and a half, the Capuchin having taken to his legs in utmost terror. There had been similar occurrences before in the library and later in the dormitory. On perceiving a Crucifix nearby, he would collapse spread-eagled upon the ground like a dead man, his eyes and mouth filling with flies.[3]

This 'total communion with God', the 'holy rapture', the 'arcane fainting fits', the 'ecstasies' (which he preferred to call a 'numbing of the senses') were often heralded by impromptu 'dances'.

While still a young man and attached to the Grottella convent at Copertino,

> At his invitation, a goodly band of shepherds came one Christmas eve to play in the church at La Grottella. He came joyously forth to meet them and no sooner had they started to play their bagpipes and whistles than he began to dance in the middle of the nave as David had done before the ark. After this he sighed and with a great cry, flew up like a bird above the main altar a height of over five canes [c. 2–2.60 m] and embraced the tabernacle with his arms. The prodigiousness of this spectacle filled the pious shepherds with holy terror.[4]

Not only was he often 'apt to fly up in the air' but also 'had the unwonted and unprecedented capacity of carrying others to God upon the wings of his rapture'. One day, 'he drew nigh to the caretaker and grasping him about the thighs in a strong embrace, he cried "Lovely Mary, lovely Mary!" so loud that, surprised by a sudden ecstasy, he was transported upward taking the caretaker with him.'[5] This 'idiot',

---

3　　Ibid. pp. 133–4.
4　　Ibid. pp. 25–6.
5　　Ibid. p. 89.

'simpleton'[6] who 'could hardly read', who spoke in symbols, when not expressing himself (always in dialect) in the aphorisms of popular proverbs, had nonetheless been 'ravished by God' and received the 'gift of wisdom'. This saintly elf of unpredictable habits

> was present at the robing ceremony of some novices of the convent of Santa Chiara, when he heard from the corner of the church where he was praying, the musicians intone the *Veni Sponsa Christi*, whereupon he uttered his customary shriek and ran towards a father reformer, a native of Secli who was also attending this function and the nuns' confessions, and seizing him by the hand, swept him joyfully off his feet and launched into a frenetic dance around the interior of the church, performing a continuous gyration . . . until both of them rose in the air carried by Giuseppe . . .[7]

Born in the land of the *tarantella*, where penitence was a way of life, this faithful speaker of the 'natural and rough dialect of his native village, which he spoke till his dying day', had only to hear the *villanella* sung – as happened to him one day in the house of the vicar of Nardò in the province of Salento – for him to fall into an ecstasy and levitate. 'He gave his customary howl and rose above the edge of the table',[8] relates his biographer. Who knows what unconscious associations the Salentian peasant girl evoked with her song or what conditioned response had been triggered by that rustic and folkloric message in this rough diamond, this rugged and 'simple-minded' vagabond. An acrobat of the faith, a 'placid' visionary, a fakir,

> he was seen to go towards the altar at the Convent of Grottella at Copertino, wearing a cope, and to bounce from the last step of the pulpit; he then flew through the air and landed near the sepulchre of Jesus Christ on Maundy Thursday; he again flew above the altar of St Francis on this saint's feast day and rose above the ground on that of the Virgin of Carmel; he also flew over the altar of the Holy Virgin on hearing the *Sancta Maria* intoned. Likewise, he was seen to levitate in his cell while holding a flaming torch in his hand without harm to himself; he also flew up once from his seat in the refectory with a sea urchin in his hands; in the countryside he was seen to fly over an olive tree and another time over a tall cross, carried by him to that spot with miraculous energy . . .[9]

6   Ibid. p. 91.
7   Ibid. p. 90.
8   Ibid. p. 40.
9   Ibid. pp. 27–8

He was a nomad, who 'at times was laughed at like a beggar, at others apprehended like a tramp, or ignored like a mendicant',[10] and because of his 'penances his body was reduced almost to a skeleton and he could only walk with great difficulty'.[11] He was kept isolated in his cell so that his flights, warblings and shouts would not disturb the holy services, and kept at bay from the crowds of faithful by his superiors. He was ill-regarded by the Inquisition, who suspected him of pretended devoutness.

> Visited on one occasion by Cardinal Bichi Vescovo and interrogated on I know not what doctrinal point, his answer was to rise swiftly from his chair and kneel upon the floor with his arms flung out and eyes wide open in an ecstasy so profound that a fly walked upon his pupil for some time without his closing his eyelid, so alienated was he from his senses. His raptures were frequent ...[12]

What this curious 'man of God' actually saw during his ecstasies is an only partially revealed mystery:

> He told Cardinal Laurìa, who had put the question to him in the third person, saying: 'what do mystics see in their ecstasies?', answering also in the third person: 'They find themselves in a great gallery of beautiful things, and in a resplendent mirror hanging therein they see with one glance the wandering essence of all these things, that is, of the arcane mysteries which God is pleased to reveal to them in that superb vision.'[13]

The Archbishop of Avignon, Monsignor Libelli, recounts how he once paid him a visit at the convent in Città di Castello:

> closeted with him in his cell, I asked him if he was happy. He answered me that he was happy everywhere because he knew he would find God everywhere. We then turned our conversation to spiritual matters and there arose the issue of man's ingratitude. He answered that he marvelled that every man was not overwhelmed at the sight of the Crucifix and he enumerated Christ's sufferings: his agony, his flagellation, his thorns, the nails, and while he thus spake, I thought I perceived a certain puckering of his lips as though he had tasted strong vinegar. Upon the instant, I saw him fall violently upon his knees from a

10   Ibid. p. 38.
11   Ibid. p. 39.
12   Ibid. p. 153.
13   Ibid. p. 27.

> chest upon which he had been seated, doing this with so much
> noise that I thought he must hurt himself. I know not how, but
> there he stayed his eyes wide open, so that only the whites of his
> eyes showed, the pupil being under the upper eye-lid, and his
> arms spread out in the shape of a cross, just as St Francis is
> portrayed receiving the stigmata. I likewise knelt down and gave
> thanks to the Lord and after carefully considering his attitude, I
> tried with difficulty to move his arm; once I had done this it hung
> limp from the shoulder and I was able to swing it back and forth
> as though it were a trailing plant in the wind. A good quarter of
> an hour had elapsed before he recovered himself, and addressed
> me in Neapolitan dialect: 'I crave pardon; how pleasant a dream'
> and sat himself again upon his chest.

The archbishop adds that he reprimanded him, exhorting him to abstain
from these disconcerting ways in the future. The prelate then turned the
conversation only to what God might show him during these trances. He
replied

> that 'At times one saw God's things all jumbled up together
> without distinguishing shapes, at other times He would reveal
> some particular mystery, according to the wishes of his Divine
> Will.' At this point he asked not to be further questioned, and
> knew not how to discourse.[14]

The 'great gallery of beautiful things' and the dazzling mirror seem to
give us glimpses of a sumptuous edifice, something like a fairy land (both
of charms and of deceit) or a procession of visual treasures. The
'wandering essence of all these things' mingles ambiguously with the
'arcane mysteries', passing from awed amazement at such extraordinary
phenomena to an intuitive acceptance of the ineffable.

Even St Francesca Romana (1384–1440) of the Oblate order was one
day 'transported in spirit to a vast place full of remarkable treasures, all
springing forth from the wounds of the Saviour, who sat upon a majestic
throne'.[15] During another ecstasy, as she passed from one light to
another, she entered another 'splendid hall':

---

14   Ibid. pp. 116–18.
15   Padre Don Bernardo Maria Amico di Milano, *Vita di Santa Francesca
      Romana...*, p. 153. The life, visions and struggles of the Roman saint dictated
      to her confessor, Giovanni Mattiotti, vicar of Santa Maria in Trastevere were
      brought together in a Vatican codex dated 1469: *Narratione delle sue visioni e
      delle sue battaglie. Libro de' più nobili tractati della nostra beata Francesca da
      Roma dicta altramente delli Pontiani*. Published for the first time by Mariano
      Armellini in 1882 (*Vita di S.F.R. descritta nell'idioma volgare di Roma del XV
      sec. ...*), parts appeared in two treatises by M. Pelaez on hell and purgatory,

Here she saw seated upon a noble throne the Virgin Mary, with her head adorned with three crowns, bearing the Infant Christ in her arms. Francesca, heedless of all else, fixed her eyes upon the divine Infant; and, gazing upon his, she so burns with love as nearly to die of agony, so desirous is she to enfold him in her arms. He, however, dallying with St Ponziana, repeatedly hides behind the effulgent light and then reappears to her, as though causing the light to melt. The saint is so dismayed by the hide-and-seek of the divine boy that the Queen of Heaven reveals the game to her ...[16]

An angelic sabbath, a pious *ludus*, 'holy game' played in a hall irridescent with light, the 'Queen of Heaven' in the guise of play-group leader, a divine baby who appears and disappears in a great halo of light, eluding the embraces of the saint, while she, mother of three children, dreams in her repeated ecstasies, of touching, embracing and hugging the divine child to her bosom: 'her only treasure flourished for a good while in her embraces and then vanishes from her arms', and touched to the quick, her motherly feelings are so outraged, that when she is carried away 'in ecstasy' (in 1413) to hell by the Archangel Raphael, she sees abortion punished by the severest chastisements. Those women who 'by means of a beverage or some other method try not to conceive or to induce abortion, and those who were mother and have murdered their own babies' are drowned 'in vats of boiling human blood' and then thrown in an 'icy pool', their flesh being torn with 'iron hooks', quartered by demonic butchers, their hearts opened and their entrails thrown into a 'boiler full of bubbling pitch', but not before they have been roasted 'inside the belly of a great bronze serpent of fire, where they howl in agony'.[17] This hell seen through female eyes, together with its abundance of horrific equipment such as to conjure up hallucinatory visions of a subterranean torture chamber, has however a particular implication in the sense of acting as a highly socialized instrument of punishment. In it, sins are catalogued, classified and punished according to a professional taxonomy. This is a hell which resembles a guild, where fraud and perversion of trade, where the 'demonic in art' (in the guild sense) are pitilessly punished. Shopkeepers, merchants, innkeepers and butchers, who either by 'hidden deceit have adulterated their goods' or have

tricked their customers in a number of different ways, mountebanks, gamblers, fortune-tellers alongside judges, lawyers,

'Visioni di S.F.R.', in 1891 in *Archivio di Società Romana di storia patria*, XIV (1891), pp. 364–409.

16   Ibid. pp. 153–4.
17   Ibid. p. 49.

attorneys, notaries, who by their pens have done more damage than a thunderbolt . . . those who upon hearing the jangle of gold and silver prolonged their cases . . . sit upon thrones of fire in hell, are made to wear a cap of flaming metal on their heads, while their feet are placed under a torture table. They are then removed hence and placed in urns of boiling gold and silver, after which demons hoist them out with hooks and throw them to be torn limb from limb by lions.[18]

Doctors who

read proscribed books, who provoked death in the sick through ignorance or malice, or prolonged the sickness in their own interests . . . and because they disobeyed the orders of the Church forbidding them from visiting the dangerously ill who refused to confess, in the hopes that by visiting them they would induce them to confess . . . surgeons who exacerbated the condition of a wounded man and delayed the healing of his wounds for monetary gain. Pharmacists who did not follow prescriptions in making up medicaments, who sold one medicament for another or placed poor quality ingredients in them.[19]

are 'hung up by their feet and scraped with iron combs . . . have their eyes gouged out and their hearts torn out, these being given to dogs as food, whilst they themselves are placed in cesspits'.[20]

This infernal 'den', whose life-span lasted from the fifteenth to the eighteenth century, (the hell of Francesca Romana, liberally interpolated, that is, with that of her Counter-Reformation biographer, Bernardo Maria Amico, of the Olivetan monastery at San Benedetto – where medical assistance was denied to the sick who did not confess within three days) was much closer to a penal court or a slaughter-house infested with putrefaction and 'filth' than to Dante's infernal smithy. It was seen as a lurid and rotting uterus (the nose had a large rôle to play in the perception of misdeeds and their punishment) where 'huge glasses of filthy matter and evil-smelling, boiling wine'[21] are gulped down, where basilisks stare 'with poisonous glances', serpents 'send forth toxic bile'[22], where the great dragon's head occupies 'the higher regions, and spits out a perpetual stream of stinking and smutty flames'.[23] The worst sensation

[18]   Ibid. pp. 47–8.
[19]   Ibid. p. 47.
[20]   Ibid. p. 47.
[21]   Ibid. p. 43.
[22]   Ibid. p. 42.
[23]   Ibid. p. 42.

felt by St Francesca in this abyss is the 'great heat and stench'.[24] In this 'theatre of atrocities',[25] perjurers, blasphemers, magicians and fortune-tellers all have their tongues torn out and transfixed for having been 'poisonous instruments',[26] whilst worms play the part of torturers, much as their victims have with other mortals. Those who had confessed poorly or insincerely had their thighs torn open and 'in the throbbing wound demons would inject boiling oil, so that it immediately rotted and produced a great quantity of worms which in turn tormented the wound'.[27] Those who 'did not keep their vow of chastity and had illicit intercourse with women or those women who had been unfaithful in wedlock, widows who had succumbed to the sensuous desires, and those who hid the truth in confession because they were ashamed' among other tortures, also underwent one called the 'virgin of Nuremberg', during the course of which they were 'held down by iron plates with nails sticking out of them', they were fed on 'stinking and worm-infested fare'.[28] Other sinners (wine-merchants and butchers) the former for 'watering their wine', the latter for 'giving short measure',[29] having previously waded along a street of 'boiling wine polluted with burning refuse', are struck hard in the face with pieces of 'rotten meat'.[30] Married women, because of their 'sinful vanity or wicked desires and lascivious fantasies about those who did not belong them', after being slit 'down the middle from head to foot . . . had worms placed in the cut by devils'.[31]

In this re-feudalized post-Tridentine hell, 'dancing and wakes'[32] were ruthlessly punished – in accordance with the ordinances of the diocesan synods and the edicts of authority. As to 'virgins who either because they had been slandered by wicked tongues or because of lack of opportunity, had not lost their maidenhood in the eyes of the world, but had no qualms about losing it in the eyes of heaven by secret immoral actions or indulging in impure thoughts and desires', 'they are beaten by flaming chains while lying on fiery boards, and made publicly to confess their misdeeds'.[33] A 'house of wailing and sighing'[34] was this, where thoughts, intentions, deeds were imagined not committed. It was a hell of its own

[24]   Ibid. p. 42.
[25]   Ibid. p. 40.
[26]   Ibid. p. 44.
[27]   Ibid. p. 44.
[28]   Ibid. p. 45.
[29]   Ibid. p. 46.
[30]   Ibid. p. 46.
[31]   Ibid. p. 46.
[32]   Ibid. p. 44.
[33]   Ibid. p. 46.
[34]   Ibid. p. 40.

making, which specialized in penetrating the darkest corners of the subconscious: the worst hell of all.

In this inverted picture of the world, even God and the Devil, good and bad, the sacred and the sacrilegious, are perceived in olfactory terms: 'if by some mischance it befalls a man or a woman to mention or be seen committing some dishonourable and sinful deed, so great is the stench that this person is forced to breathe from this sepulchre alive with ordure, that he is obliged to stop his nose'.[35]

By contrast, after the episode of the 'eucharistic manna', an ecstatic Francesca continues on her way,

> her soul filled with a sphere of light, and there she encounters a man who is all resplendent and yet more beautiful than the sun, his name being Tabernacle, because in place of his heart there is a large tabernacle: and into this the saint enters, bowing with humble confidence. There her ear is charmed with a celestial melody and her spirit restored with the waftings of a gentle fragrance. Within this tabernacle there lies a pool of sweet-smelling water, shimmering like gold on a bed of most precious jewels ... and several times she tries to grasp one of those precious stones, but unavailingly, whereupon she decides to plunge her head in and manages to drink but one drop; she is immediately sated by the exquisiteness thereof, and such is the state of her inebriation from divine love, that she deems her heart would burst if the vision were to continue longer.[36]

Even these struggles with the Devil, who had identified her highly developed sense of smell, are seen in terms of 'fetor'. The stench of hell pursues her wherever she goes:

> Suddenly the room is filled with so foul a smell that there is no way of describing it except that it must surely emanate from hell. And then, like some grotesque porter, the Devil appears carrying upon his shoulder a worm-infested corpse, or rather a demon heralded by a stench. He lays it on the ground and with an impertinent gesture he bodily draws our Francesca – that heavenly flower – pale and swooning, into the very midst of that foul odour. Suddenly, he throws her on that heap of putre-scence; but by dint of twisting and turning, and divine intercess-ion, the Devil and the corpse vanish whence they came from, leaving the room full of an intolerable fetor and the face and body of the nauseated saint all befouled. Francesca takes off her

35   Ibid. p. 36.
36   Ibid. pp. 148–9.

habit hoping to dispel the dreadful stench by removing all that had taken on the smell by contact. She then throws them in another chamber, that in its turn becomes almost a cemetery in consequence, and she is amazed that the whole house does not perish of suffocation from such a stench . . .[37]

'Tall, well-complexioned, large-boned and physically alert', such was the description of Giuseppe di Copertino, 'resilient, vigorous and able to withstand great pain . . . with a beard that waxed long and thick . . . his eyes sparkled and were like his hair, black, and gracefully turned heavenward through his habitual ecstasies'.[38] This image of a healthy, vigorous man, with his feet firmly on the ground contrasts oddly with the gaze turned to heaven, the ecstasies, the dizzy flights. The impression that Giuseppe di Copertino made on the Italians of the south was profound: publicly declared 'Apostle of the Kingdom', 'so great were the hoards of people that flocked to see him, that in order to flee from their acclaim, he was obliged to travel across country, by night or in the heat of the day, or when the skies showered lightning, hail or copious rain'.[39] The fanaticism of the multitudes alarmed the upper échélons of the Church, culminating in an anxious letter to the Holy Office in Naples which ran thus:

> in those provinces (so said the charge), a man of thirty-three years in age, draws to himself whole populaces like another Messiah, by performing miracles wherever he goes, which are believed by the gullible multitude, which is unable to distinguish between pretended truth and real truth.[40]

He was said to be endowed with extraordinary powers and he enjoyed the gift of 'continuous prophecy, continuous reading into the innermost secrets of others, and even of discovering charms and spells from a distance merely by his sense of smell'.[41] Possessed of so prodigious an olfactory sense, rather like an extraordinary bloodhound, he was able to scent evil and witchcraft. Witches were no match for his nose.

A healer of 'all manner of illness',[42] a multiplier of food and wine, a king of rain ('storms and whirlwinds obeyed him . . . the clouds obeyed him'), a restorer of health by touch and the sign of the Cross, or with holy oil, he followed in the footsteps of St Catherine of Siena, and 'in order to conquer the sense of revulsion which is natural to the senses', he went so

---

37 Ibid. p. 36.
38 *Vita di S. Giuseppe di Copertino. . .* , p. 164.
39 Ibid. pp. 38–9.
40 Ibid. pp. 46.
41 Ibid. p. 28,
42 Ibid. p. 28.

far as to 'eat leaves filled with rottenness'[43] produced by his patients' sores; so attuned was he to Christ's Passion, that he seemed to take leave of his senses and 'talk as though on familiar terms and face to face with God like another Moses on the Mount',[44] while exuding a 'celestial fragrance'; it was his custom to 'restrain the passions of the flesh' with deadly rigour and vehement fury: 'Twice a week he beat himself so ferociously that thirty years later the walls of his cell still bore not merely marks, but veritable encrustations, of blood upon them.'[45]

His obsession with the passion and flagellation, this existential model of *imitatio Christi*, drove him (as it did many fellow holy men) to a bloodthirsty butchering of self.

> Not satisfied even with this, he would ask others to flog him so that he was sensible only of pain. If ever he was assailed by impure thoughts or vain fancies, or some distraction, he would flog himself to the very bone. His favourite instruments of self-torture were ropes tipped with crooked needles, followed by steel rowels with sharp points which tore his flesh so that the blood streamed down and he would fall into the deepest of swoons.[46]

Torture and ecstasy, blood and intoxication, pleasure and cruelty, combine to form in a perfect cycle of sexual perversion, the ultimate in tortuous and obstinate neurosis.

> The exaggerated rigour of his penance, which gave rise to fears for his sight, was restrained by the prudence of the Father Superior who reduced it to a small scourge of brass wires applied once a month; this being a source of cruellest torture since, while causing severe bruising, it did not actually lacerate the flesh; he had therefore to submit to a surgeon's intervention to open the lesions and squeeze the bruising. His many wounds had only his rasping hairshirt to dress them; and the fearful chain that he wore about his loins made the wounds stick to his hairshirt and the hairshirt to the chain, so that his soaking and wounded body resembled more a corpse than a living human being.
>
> He went even further in inflicting harm on himself. He superimposed upon the knotty chain, an iron plate, which pressed and drove the links of the chain even further in so that they almost broke his bones. But this pitiless and ingenious

43   Ibid. p. 233.
44   Ibid. p. 152.
45   Ibid. p. 20.
46   Ibid. pp. 20–1.

martyrdom was soon halted, since he was met one day by Don Girolamo di Domenico – a lay priest who was fond of the convent at Grottella – who saw Giuseppe return to his cell dragging himself along as though on the point of expiring; he immediately brought this to the attention of the Father Superior, exhorting him to make an investigation of his person. Together they visited him and having, under the rules of obedience, made him take off his habit and also his cassock, which was none other than his usual bristly and evil-smelling hairshirt, they saw to their horror not flesh but wounds, chains and an iron plate, which when removed also under orders, revealed a man who, in his underpants, was all one sore, and alive only in the sense that a scant breath of life still remained in him.[47]

'Bloodthirsty penances' were also spectacular instruments of conversion, when theatrically performed after sermons. The saintly Jesuit, Francesco di Girolamo (1642–1716) was accustomed to throw himself between the flagellants and 'joined the others in scourging himself so harshly and with such holy vehemence that it finished always in a great loss of blood'.[48]

This 'missionary of the people', and indefatigable preacher who, in true Jesuit style, 'would usually finish his sermons with a description either of some horrendous punishment ... or of some extraordinary example of divine pity', would then pass to the culminating act of

contrition and bloody penance, which he performed on bended knees, wet with tears, at the base of a Holy Crucifix, while the congregation likewise wept bitterly and begged pity and forgiveness. In proof of this, I allude to certain circumstances, occurring in Orta in the diocese of Aversa, where the Franciscan Father was engaged in his Mission: the congregation having left the church after the sermon, there was found scattered about the church a large quantity of hair, which men and women had torn from their heads as a demonstration of their contrition.[49]

The manipulatory techniques of these rural missions excited the countryfolk and provoked mass hysteria and bouts of devastating, self-inflicted torture. With the help of a fraternity/guild of craftsmen, the 'oratory of the missions', organized by Francesco di Girolamo to follow

---

47   Ibid. pp. 21–2.
48   Padre Longaro degli Oddi, *Vita del B. Francesco di Girolamo sacerdote professo della Compagnia di Gesù*, scritta dal padre Longaro degli Oddi della Medesima Compagnia, Roma, 1806, p. 240. The first edition was printed in Rome in 1761. A reprint was made in Rome in 1839 by the Tipografia Salviucci.
49   Ibid. p. 29.

him wherever he went, maintaining order, tracking down sinners and bringing them to him, seems to have succeeded in mobilizing enormous crowds. The intermediate cadres, the lay apostolate, were a useful vehicle for his 'evangelizing' activities.

The inhabitants of villages, subjected from morn till dusk to an unremitting bombardment of collective confessions, of communal communions (usual on the third Sunday of the month), of masses, of sermons (at the end of these, Francesco di Girolamo 'would every time effect upon himself a ruthless penance on his bare shoulders'),[50] of prayer, of spiritual exercises, of novenes, of choreographic first communions with children 'all well indoctrinated and dressed in the manner of angels in pictures, their heads adorned with flowers',[51] they would abandon themselves to remarkable excesses and fanaticisms.

> The largest number of penitential processions were reserved for the last day; and they were such that only a heart of stone would not have wept, watching the many ways in which the already contrite congregation gave vent to their devotion, tearing at themselves in a thousand ways in proof of their internal repentance. Self-flagellation to draw blood, carrying heavy crosses on their shoulders, wearing sharp-thorned crowns on their heads, could be said to be the very least. There was more than one Mission where [the penitent] would progress along the road dragging his tongue along the surface until it bled; not to mention those who had themselves dragged by a rope and would bump about like any ass, and other holy oddities.[52]

In 1713 in Barletta

> a thirty-year-old man, on hearing another preacher inveigh against the monstrous wickedness of sin, was so horrified at himself and at the sinful life he had lead, that he ascended the platform where the preacher stood and baring his shoulders, back and arms, he flogged himself so mercilessly that he even spat blood from the mouth and nostrils, and the appeals of the man of God were insufficient to stay his hand.[53]

Such was the obsession with blood (which had its genetic source in the 'Divine Bood' of the Redeemer who 'in his infinite mercy . . . had for this purpose opened his Divine Bosom . . . ready to take him to his heart',[54]

---

50   Ibid. p. 106.
51   Ibid. p. 107.
52   Ibid. p. 108.
53   Ibid. p. 119.
54   Ibid. pp. 28–9.

and the most noteworthy and dramatic cultural model in the Passion) that descriptions of Francesco di Girolamo's sermons have it that whilst terrifying his audience in the first half and regaling them with melting expressions of human compassion in the second, he did not merely cause 'the blood to freeze in the veins of those sinful breasts' by 'the excited vehemence of his words', but:

> frequently in the very act of preaching, he was seen to spit forth blood from his mouth ... and on one particular occasion did he dwell so long fulminating against the iniquities of a woman who obstinately refused to reform, that he succumbed to a fit of swooning and abandoned by his senses, he fell into a dead faint and was of necessity carried thence to a place where he might be revived.[55]

Such sensitivity was no rarity in a century given to convulsions, swoonings, hysterical passions, ambiguous pathological states, 'strange illnesses', frequent occurrences, particularly in nunneries. Francesco di Girolamo, by touching Sister Maria Colombo Cerbini, of the Neapolitan convent of Santa Maria della Splendore, with the relics of Saint Cirus and making her drink 'pollen from his flowers dissolved in water', cured her of 'severe articular pains, accompanied frequently by fainting fits and convulsions so violent as to throw her often out of bed onto the ground'. A parallel, though diametrically opposed, syndrome was displayed in the convent by a sixteen-year-old Sister Maddalena Sterlicco. She 'suffered such strange ailments in bed sometimes, that they caused her to bounce out of bed so that she almost touched the ceiling of her cell, to the fright and horror of all who witnessed this'.[56]

The blood of the saintly, after death, could effect miracles. The 'cadaver' of Francesco di Girolamo caused 'something to happen of great astonishment to all':

> His nurse, wishing to keep some remembrance for himself of this holy man, before clothing him in his priestly raiment, took his scissors and secretly cut a corn that the saint had upon the sole of his foot. But, however much he desired to hide his pious theft, it manifested itself of its own accord, as blood flowed forth so copiously from the cut that, as well as soaking several linen cloths, it was possible to collect three to four ounces of it in a jar, and it remained liquid and red in colour for more than three months and subsequently was found to lead to the performance of many miracles ...[57]

55 Ibid. p. 28.
56 Ibid. pp. 207, 208.
57 Ibid. p. 223.

On the last day of the funeral

> the populace, always indiscreet whilst yet devout, having thrown
> to the ground all barriers that stood in their way, ran towards the
> body, anxious to have some small part of the holy man to keep as
> a cherished relic, principally some blood, which still trickled
> upon the funeral bier for many hours from the aforementioned
> cut.[58]

The blood of the virtuous, of those who had died in an odour of
sanctity, of the most venerated of God's servants, was the most sought-
after and miracle-producing of relics. This was the very blood, the very
symbol of physical vitality which, with grim fury and maniacal intent,
they forced out of their living bodies, in their headlong frenzy to destroy
that filthy and impure vessel of vice. Francesco di Girolamo 'pleasant in
manner . . . always cheerful and with a sweet and discreet smile upon his
lips',

> wore permanently next to the skin a jerkin of chain-mail,
> embroidered with sharp steel points .... In calculating the
> number of times in a day that he subjected himself to his many
> merciless penances, whether publicly or in private, by night or
> by day, once with iron chains, another time with scourges tipped
> with nails, tearing at his innocent body (some of these punish-
> ments lasted a full half hour), it can be said with certainty that at
> least three times a day he inflicted so harsh a torture on himself
> as to draw blood every time. Nor were these the only instru-
> ments he used to torture his body. Many others of his own
> invention were discovered in his room after his death, causing
> repugnance at the mere sight of them.[59]

This grotesque machinery designed for self-torture, this armoury fit for
a fakir, created out of an 'avidity for pain', and resulting in 'blood baths'
(Paolo Segneri), are proof of the extraordinary persistence of the taste
for torture, for sanguinary mayhem (our man of God died in 1716); his
continuous fascination with the Passion lead him to enact the rôle of
Christ when celebrating Mass and Holy Week services. On Maundy
Thursday he would visit all the Sepulchres 'bare-foot, crowned with
thorns, bearing a heavy cross upon his shoulder'.

If monasteries contained the sinister weapons of torture, ingenious
instruments of punishment, seminaries (like the Jesuit monastery at
Naples) were training-grounds for penance and suffering, centres of

58   Ibid. p. 224.
59   Ibid. pp. 179–80.

conditioning and self-abnegation. A visitor would have had trouble distinguishing between a seminary and a prison.

> And it was in truth an object of much amazement, on the sign being given for the period of meditation to begin, to see so many hot-headed and vivacious young men walk into the hall with downcast eyes, some crowned with thorns, others with ashes upon their heads, others with their arms crossed and tied to a piece of wood, and other similar attitudes of contrition. A stranger entering upon this scene was so overcome with astonishment, that he was moved to comment that the seminary seemed to him like the famous prison of St Climacus . . . . Harsh flagellation which drew blood was a daily occurrence for many.[60]

Father Paolo Segneri (1624–94), the 'inventor' of the rural missions, used to perform his penitential exercises with an instrument of his own devising which he named an 'excoriater',

> . . . a round cork encased in a tin box, stuck with a good fifty pins or needles, inserted in it and somewhat protruding: with this he would strike his bared chest during the final processions of penitence and used it further to overcome the obduracy of those who adamantly refused to make peace with their enemies.

The blessed Luigi Gonzaga – a keen creator of 'devices for punishment' – when an adolescent used to gird 'his bare thighs with sharp riding spurs', as we read in the *Panegirico* Father Segneri wrote of him.

The spectacle of a penitent innocent flagellating himself in public held such morbid fascination that it would sometimes precipitate conversions which were nothing if not clamorous.

> Captain Giuseppe Fumo, the so-called 'Standard Bearer', a corsair of the high seas, a man of evil ways and a famous robber, of whom it was said notoriously that, on finding himself in the hands of the Turks, he had repudiated his faith in Jesus Christ: this man upon encountering the blessed Francesco, while the latter was preaching, and desirous of acquaintance with a man of whom such great things were said in Naples, attended a sermon. And in that very place, Divine Mercy lay in wait for this wild beast. Hardened sinner though he was, the words of the man of God did not fail to make some impression in his heart. But when, the sermon once finished, he saw the other grasp an iron chain and beat himself to the bone most horrendously . . . he could no longer contain himself at the sight, and mounting the

Ibid. p. 68.

platform himself, he took the chain from the hands of the blessed Girolamo and saying 'let me strike myself for I am he who has repudiated Jesus Christ', without more ado bared his shoulders and beat himself for some while with such asperity that blood flowed all over his body, and he would had done worse had he not been restrained by the holy Francesco himself.[61]

This was one of the revered Francesco di Girolamo's most notable achievements. He operated in Naples for forty or so years as an urban missionary, inveighing mostly against 'the idle and lazy mass [who] seeks largely to be entertained on feast days, by listening to charlatans and mountebanks, and enjoying other intrigues and forms of revelry', whilst not omitting to attack in his sermons to the various quarters of cities that 'filthy vessel' that is an 'infamous woman'.

A strategist of Divine Majesty, he worked with consummate ability waging implacable and holy guerrilla warfare against urban abuses: against the 'base profession' of quackery, and all 'people already hardened to vice'.[62] Consequently, the 'first upon whom he declared a vehement and implacable war were actors and mountebanks who, by bringing women to the stage, shameless and brazen young women, and by the obscenity of their plays, encouraged wicked behaviour, particularly in inexperienced youth'.[63]

The offensive launched by the Church authorities and by intellectual Jesuits like Ottonelli, the author of *Christiana moderatione nel theatro [Christian moderation in the theatre]*, was reinforced by teams of Christian 'vigilantes' and by missionaries aided by members of the monastic fraternities. Francesco di Girolamo, who in the course of these crusades underwent physical attacks at the hands of irate adversaries, acted with scientifically thought out tactics and premeditated strategies.

> At the appointed hour, having hoisted up the Holy Crucifix, they all came forth in procession with the Servant of God in the rear together with some of our young monks whose task it would also be to preach, and as they intoned fervent prayers and praised God, they brought the Cross to the chosen place; whereupon, the young preachers having had their places allotted at the head of each street, [di Girolamo] kept for himself the spot which was busiest and most in need of attention; and from this place; whereupon, the young preachers having had their places allotted at the head of each street, [di Girolamo] kept for himself the spot which was busiest and most in need of attention; and from this

[61]   Ibid. pp. 81–2.
[62]   Ibid. p. 46.
[63]   Ibid. p. 45.

place or from some higher eminence such as a table, or even on the very actors' stage, who on his appearance, losing the audience's attention, were obliged to withdraw, he would embark on his sermon.[64]

The 'holy activities' of this urban missionary culminated (according to his biographer) in the conquest of the enemy stronghold. The 'missionary theatre' of the rural missions provided a distraction even within the city walls. The history of conflict between these ecclesiastical gangs and the popular theatre highlights, albeit in another guise, the age-old pre-Christian *conflictus* between the culture of the divine and that of the actor. A state of conflict which in being absorbed by the ecclesiastical structures of the Middle Ages, is reaffirmed by the Counter-Reformation in a climate of intransigence, of severe tension and imposed Christianity, in accordance with the Jesuit plan for a 'society of discipline' and of integral Christian living.

[64]   Ibid. p. 23. For the importance of Padre Segneri's rôle in missionary organization, cf. V. Marucci, 'L'autografo di un'opera ignota: le missioni rurali di Paolo Segneri', in *Filologia e critica*, IV (1979), I, pp. 73–92. The passage on Padre Segneri's 'smagliarino' [instrument of flagellation] (taken from the biography by G. Massei, 1701) is to be found in V. Marucci's study, p. 77. For the relationships of comedy to tragedy and sacred to secular in pre-industrial culture and theatre, see P. Camporesi, 'Cultura popolare e culture d'élite fra Medioevo ed età moderna', in *Storia d'Italia*. Annali 4. *Intellettuali e potere*, Torino, 1981, pp. 81–157.

PART II

5

DECAY AND REBIRTH

The remarkable fasts and virtuoso-like excesses to which venerable servants of God of the Counter-Reformation resorted in their hunger for heaven, eliminating calories, treading the narrow path between survival and *exitus*, indulging in extraordinary balancing games upon a tightrope that somehow stretched far into the improbable, represent the ascetic world's answer to the passion for gastronomic display typical of the late Renaissance and Baroque periods: for pasty, glazed, waxy and funereal dishes reminiscent of anatomical structures; whilst at the same time engrossed (like the restless skeletons on Baroque tombs) in a search for a dance of the elements, of a movement of matter, of a tension of form and shape. The main courses were masterpieces of ephemerality in which culinary architects exhibited ingenious dexterity, alternating heraldic motifs (emblematic displays, embodiments of heroic feats, aristocratic coats-of-arms), and sculpted enactments of kidnappings, battles, hunts, sieges, threatened ships in tumultuous seas.

Just as the plot of the Baroque novel unravels itself in a tenebrous game of disguises, of ambiguous masking, which mingles, confuses, camouflages identity and sex (take for example the whirligig of disguises and continual loss of identity of the protagonists of *Calloandro fedele [The faithful Calloandro]*), so do the masters of the Baroque cuisine (consummate actors hiding behind masks and make-up) play at disguising substances, masking tastes and quality in their hunt for culinary ecstasy, for palatal deceptions in which fish is camouflaged to taste like meat, fried foods like roasts, boiled foods like smoked, products of fantasy and imagination, which turned the dinner table into a gallery of artificial and frothy creations, a theatre of deception and illusion in which the palate lost its way in a maze of contradictory encounters, in a puzzle of unexpected conceits, dictated by a culinary poetics of surprise, of unpredictability, of wonderment which prepares it for a journey in Marino's 'land of dreams' which 'has an undefinable touch of futility/that appears and disappears in the eyes of others', where 'monstrous ghosts wander/elusive dreams of the sun, enemies of the day/forgers of illusion, fathers of deceit'.

The aristocratic banquet was nonetheless an exception in a country of declining fortunes, in which compulsive ritual fasting, nights spent in prescribed fasting and abstinence at table became daily more tedious to the point of obsessive scrupulousness. It is no surprise that the precept of abstinence from meats, fats, eggs and milk products, governed by a meticulously comprehensive set of rules, which gave rise to a frenzy of hair-splitting and dialectic bordering on the absurd, became the social norm in the seventeenth and eighteenth centuries, when ecclesiastical power invaded the domain of civil power: an age in which theologians and confessors became the arbiters and governors of the mechanics of social coexistence.

The shadow of the holy fell upon the Cinquecento, as it never had before in Italy, in the kitchen. A thick web of taboo enveloped the dining table. The kitchen clock was set to match that of the sacristy. The week's dietary pattern was 'evangelized' with an intransigence and purposefulness hitherto unknown. Moral theology became mixed with dietetics by prescribing styles and rhythms, dictating production, trade, economics; it discouraged certain goods and encouraged others, it conditioned production by establishing a different balance between demand and supply and creating an alternation (at certain liturgical times of the year and week) between consumption and the conservation of foodstuffs. The sacred spread its sphere of influence to the economy. During the game of condition-making, regulations and controls made their appearance, together with a 'precept-bound' approach to food, and a diversified gastronomic sensibility. The *regimen sanitatis* incurred the somewhat burdensome privilege of pre-requisite to the *regimen salvationis*. Diets and religious timetables came together in an ever tighter bond: a low-fat diet became a sort of viaticum for the soul's health. Cooking by precept sharpened culinary skills and heightened the sensitivity of the taste-buds so that they might discover new areas of choice and unsullied delicacies, of snowy fields of pure food, as bloodless as they were beatifying. There were unheard-of displays of talent for the benefit of the alimentary canal; all the unexpressed potential of a sterile and spineless, though chaste, voluptuousness, is squeezed from the vegetable and aqueous worlds. Red meat takes a back seat, ousted by white meats. New liturgical soups and devotional recipes were invented; there is a rise in the production and consumption of ritual and patronal sweets, in which the promises and augurs of religions of the ancient world interlock syncretistically with the contemporary worship of saints and the *nominatio* of the heavenly protectors. The forbidden and the permitted meet in a game of alternating patterns for work-days and feast-days, which reflects the rotation of sacred and secular throughout the calendar year. It is immediately obvious, in particular during the seventeenth and eighteenth centuries, how nutrition is at the heart of a complex intersection, expressed in rituals whose rhythms reflect the sacred and eschatological. The overlapping of the religious and nutritional worlds, and the parallel connections between health in time and health/eternal salvation draw ever closer to each other.

In a theocratically run society, in which control, supervision and liturgical rules are at the core of everyday lay existence, and in which the conventual model predominates, Lenten discipline is fundamental to ecclesiastical political culture. Lenten discipline sets in motion a whole series of doubts, cases, exceptions, and gives rise to a sophistical concern with minutiae, verging on the lunatic and paradoxical, and to almost ridiculous demonstrations of subtlety.

Arrayed upon the battlefield are theologians such as Cardinal De Lugo and Bellarmino, Leonardo Lessio and Saint Alfonso de'Liguori, not to mention pontiffs, law-givers, bishops, polemists and Jesuits. The *Disciplina antica e moderna della Romana Chiesa intorno al sagro quaresimale digiuno [Ancient and modern disciplines of the Church of Rome for the period of Lenten Fasting]* (1742) by the Dominican theologian Daniello Concina, a strict chastiser of all dietary laxity and opportunism, constitutes a peak of achievement in the intricate art of secular 'discipline' and in the fight against dietary infringements.

The casuistry which explores the delicate relations of wedlock, the 'burdens of marriage', the duties of the conjugal state, sheds light on private and little-known territory, and goes to the length of arguing for dispensation from the obligation to fast for 'married women who are less able to fulfil their matrimonial function'.[1] The casuists cast penetrating and voyeuristic glances upon the relationship linking sex and the table, the kitchen and the bedroom, sensing the close bond between these two spheres, even if they do not quite alight on the 'modern' theory of the mutual contaminations between mouth and vagina, throat and genitalia, orality and anality.

The thesis which held that women could abstain from Lenten fasting for fear that 'by fasting they might become emaciated and unattractive to their husbands'[2] had not a few adherents.

It would be mistaken to believe, however, that this dispensation came out of a respect for the holy status of matrimony, as solemnly reaffirmed by the post-Tridentine Church. Whether a *sacramentum magnum* or no, the 'married state' was not regarded much above concubinage: another case pleaded dispensation for a certain person who complained of the 'lassitude caused by the long journey undertaken to visit a concubine'.[3] The particular attention reserved for sexual matters, and the understand-

---

1   D. Concina, *La Quaresima appellante dal Foro contenzioso di alcuni recenti casisti al tribunale del 'buon senso' e della 'buona fede' del Popolo Cristiano,* Venezia, 1744, p. xiii.

2   Ibid. p. xiii.

3   Ibid. p. xiv.

ing of the problems pertaining thereunto, may be a source of surprise. There are also those who favoured the idea of release from the require- ment to fast for those who suffered 'weakness and impotence born of intemperate fornication'.

Perhaps it is superfluous to remember all the long debates on the topic of chocolate (the *theobroma* – a potion of the gods) as to whether or not it constituted a violation of holy fasting. Of great interest (and also a point of dispute) was the thesis that 'it can indeed happen that travellers wishing to fast are denied lodging by the innkeeper if they do not dine'. Or, indeed, the contrary situation in which 'for fear of losing custom', innkeepers are allowed to prepare fare for travellers in periods of fasting.[4]

The subjects of dispensation (the cases number of fifty) go to show that the flood of printed material on the problem of regulating fasting reflects the importance in day-to-day existence of all possible shades of meaning and the applications of fasting.

In the disciplinary-minded society of the Counter-Reformation, even secular existence bases itself ultimately on religious sensibility. The 'physical canons of health' and the 'apostolic canon' are not a far cry from '*sobrii estote et vigilate [be sober and watchful]*, whereby the Church is using the word 'fasting' refers to any form of abstinence undertaken by a man in conquering his desires'.[5]

In his *Dialoghi dell'Infinito*, Ludovico Agostini (Pesaro, 1535–1612) draws attention to the doctrine that 'a physical remedy may also be a spiritual remedy' and, in attributing exceptional powers to 'physical abstinence', he evolves the theory of a

> rule of temperate and long life on earth and a happy and blessed existence in eternity, avoiding all manner of illness: since by removing from the body all excess and diversity in food, it is protected from an over-abundance and variety of humours, and by denying it atrophying sleep and soft beds, the intellect retains its sharpness and the body the strength and vigour of all its limbs; as in the case of the aged Paul of Thebes, Anthony the Hermit, Hilarion, Ammonius, Honofrius, Macarius, Agathon, Serapion, together with the whole school of the hermits of Soria, Egypt and Thebaid who, for the most part, lived to be over eighty without any marked defects in the soundness of their health . . .[6]

---

4   Ibid. p. xiv.
5   L. Agostini, 'La repubblica immaginaria', in *Utopisti e riformatori sociali del Cinquecento*, ed. C. Curcio, Bologna, 1941, p. 178.
6   Ibid. pp. 177–8.

A generation or two after that of Alvise Cornaro, in which *Discorsi* (1558) the high Renaissance 'life of sobriety' is triumphantly predicated, as the respectful and conscious awareness of one's own metabolic destiny, the total realization of self in terms of *joie de vivre*, creativity and energy, brought about by a diet of 'natural medicine' and 'rational order', thebaic/hermetic observance, monastic practice, anchoretic living in place of 'social discourse', 'abstinence' in lieu of mere temperance, moderation and 'continence', are all indicative of the new cultural approach taken by the Post-Tridentine model.

If Alvise Cornaro was fortunate enough to look forward quietly to 'being in possession of an earthly paradise beyond the age of eighty',[7] Ludovico Agostini, only a few decades later, believed in a heavenly paradise, to be won only *post mortem* through fasting and abstinence of the eremitical kind.

In the gloom of urban utopia, in the dull imaginary space inhabited by aristocratic Pesaro, the real city of the Counter-Reformation wiped out any indication of a happy utopia. In this case, the imaginary coincided almost exactly with the real. The suggestion that 'at such a time when man will come to his senses, and abstain from excess in pleasure and excess in nourishment', the order should be promulgated 'that from the greater part of the city should be heard the voices of monks celebrating death',[8] points to a move from the conventual model to the lay model, the projection of a religious superstructure for the whole of urban society.

The shadow of 'regular' penance returns to cast its gloom upon meal times and dwell upon the link between food and disease, between lunch among the living and the death knell. The ear must have been attuned to and conditioned by the funereal tolling of bells which always accompanied the most delicate moments of life's daily course. In the evening 'may all the bells of the city ring together nine times mournfully and distinctly in memory of the souls of the dead, severe punishment being meted out to those who do not immediately kneel down and pray'.[9] The 'melancholy nights' of those condemned to death – this being the depressing and harrowing title which the Jesuit, Giacinto Manara (1598–1662), gives to his manual for a 'good death' – become even darker through an injection of additional sorrows for all concerned. The clanging of 'sacred bronze' impinges disturbingly on the private world, and the network of city belfries of the Post-Tridentine era becomes a

---

[7]   A. Cornaro, *Discorsi intorno alla vita sobria*, ed. P. Pancrazi, Firenze, 1942, p. 97. English translation by W. Jones, A.B., *Sure Methods of attaining a Long and Healthful Life...*, Edinburgh, Donaldson, 1768.

[8]   L. Agostini, 'La repubblica immaginaria', p. 176.

[9]   Ibid. p. 176.

contrivance for suggestive psychological conditioning, a mechanism for inflexible control.

Pleasure in food is dolefully transformed, if not indeed destroyed, by the inexorable pealing of 'bells':

> The Avemaria for the dead, which it is customary to ring in nearly all Catholic cities after luncheon and after dinner, is no mean reminder, without assistance from other voices, and fills with distaste whosoever has just tasted the necessary sustenance from his continued mortal survival.[10]

The bipolarity of taste/disgust epitomizes that of liking for/dislike of life, and the bitter and neurotic bulimia of the Post-Tridentine age.

Controlled nourishment and 'controlled worship by Christians' reflect the aspect of one and the same problem: the relationship between gastronomy and holy living takes on extraordinary significance in the issue of 'penance' in the moral and civil life of a theocratic society, which had undertaken the arduous task of looking after the soul's health in every possible way and of guaranteeing a modicum of pleasant living in the next world for everyone, at whatever cost on earth: in a manner of speaking, general and obligatory salvation awaited everyone.

The alternation of emptiness and fullness sets the pattern for secular living conditioned by the life of the soul, and by 'men reformed' (*Riforma dell'huomo*), as suggested by the title of a posthumously published work by Fra Simone di San Paolo, a Discalced Carmelite, hailing from Volterra and who died in Milan in 1622, a Provincial of that Order. Little known to us today, this man of God, who had been a physician before he came to the convent, came to call Galenus a 'demon', because it

> appears that he tries to give health and keep us in health, but in reality he is a most dangerous demon. May he who falls into the hands of this demon beware, because I believe that, neither for the common good of all religion, nor for the particular welfare of the monks, there be a crueller tyrant than this man.[11]

The fear of 'losing one's health' was held to be 'pernicious in the extreme'. This sort of fear, suggested by the Devil, should be severely 'mortified'. *Prudentia carnis inimica est Deo* ['To be prudent about the flesh is inimical to God'] warned the Apostle. Consistent with this premise and with the obsessive desire for mortification, the biographer of Fra Simone recalls a 'truly outstanding deed' performed by the master while still a novice:

[10]   Ibid. p. 176.
[11]   Frate Simone di S. Paolo, *Riforma dell'huomo. Opera spirituale*, Venezia, 1694, p. 258.

> While all were engaged in the daily recreation, it happened that
> the Father Superior was called to the door . . . and the latter told
> the novices that in his absence they should each of them engage
> in some virtuous act. Padre Fra Simone chanced to be beside a
> consumptive brother, who coughed up some catarrh from his
> stomach, and pretending to kiss it, the father ingested it from the
> ground.[12]

This intrepid member of the Carmelite Order who

> during his secular existence in Rome had, because of his actute
> mind, been esteemed one of the most famous physicians of that
> city, once a monk became so sworn an enemy of medicine,
> because it favours the flesh, that Galeno – whom he had
> previously so esteemed and revered as a master – he sub-
> sequently named the 'devil Galenus', and this with such earnest-
> ness that he used to teach it as a spiritual axiom to his novices,
> and wrote it into his books.[13]

This case may appear surprising today, but the demonization of
medicine had a very real rôle in the cult which denigrated the human
body. The logic of salvation encountered a forest of varying symbols,
created a thick network of reversals, upset worldly values. A bitter,
humiliated life, a life mortified by suffering and privation, was the only
one that lead to heaven: tribulations became the passport to the blessed
life, which could only be gained by scaling *Il Monte Santo della Tribu-
latione* [*The Holy Mount of Tribulation*] – the title of a work dated 1602
and written by Fra Giacomo Affinati d'Acuto. 'Mortification both
internal and external of the self' was the right key to open the gates of the
Kingdom of Heaven. Absolutely true to the stereotype of the good
Christian who cannot agree with the image of man turned on his head,
Fra Simone di San Paolo

> inspired all who saw him with wonder and amazement, due to
> the many penances and infirmities, particularly gallstones, from
> which he suffered, when he not only faithfully pursued a normal
> existence as was his wont to do with great tenacity, but he also
> took so little care of himself, that for the most part though in
> great pain, he would take no remedy, but indeed would, on
> purpose and to spite the medicine he knew, often partake – and
> this joyfully – of foods which would exacerbate his malady; but
> what is more remarkable is the secrecy and cheerfulness with

[12] Ibid. c. 2v. of the anonymous *Breve relatione della vita dell'Autore*, preceding
Riforma dell'huomo.
[13] Ibid. c. 2v.

which he would do this, that even those only merely acquainted
with his manner of living could not but notice, try though he
might throughout his life to disguise this, for he was but all skin
and bones.[14]

This erstwhile doctor who, now a Carmelite monk, in spite of his
knowledge, acted against science, and subjected himself to diets which
were intentionally mistaken and deleterious to the health, in order to
demonstrate, by predisposing his body to anticipated destruction, how,
man being a 'plant which is upside-down' with his head in the earth and
his feet in the air, it was necessary to replant him the right way up with his
head in the sky and his feet in the ground.

During the same period, and in the same cultural ambience of Rome
which was to witness within a few years the sublime eccentricities of San
Filippo Neri, Fra Giacomo Affinati d'Acuto, whilst compiling *Il mondo
al roverscio e sossopra [The world inside out and upside-down]* (Venice,
Zaltieri, 1602), harped on the image of Christian man, whom he
regarded as the mirrored reversal of a tree:

> the academics of antiquity called man *antropos*, that is, inverted
> tree. . . . This fine plant that is the human being is planted the
> reverse way from other plants, in that these have their heads in
> the soil, being the roots through which they subtly steal their
> nourishment from the earth, while the branches are turned
> skyward: but man has his head towards the sky and his branches
> are downward upon the ground; consequently, he is the contrary
> of the earth's plants and is upside down. The head is a man's
> roots, and therefore he has upon it a great number of hairs which
> are like small roots turned heavenward; his arms and his hands,
> his fingers, his thighs and legs are like trunks and branches, the
> skin is in place of bark, the apertures for excrement are in place
> of the openings from which exude aqueous and viscous
> humours, rubber and so forth. The nails on his hands and feet
> are instead of green fronds. This microcosm was created in a
> shape contrary to that of all the animals, with an upright body
> and his head turned towards the sky: in reference to the rectitude
> of our soul, which should always be concentrated and rooted in
> heaven . . . [15]

[14]   Ibid. c. 2r. & v.
[15]   G. Affinati d'Acuto, *Il mondo al roverscio e sossopra*. Diviso in quattro
dialoghi, ove si tratta di tutte le cose create, Venezia, 1602, pp. 232–4. Cf. M.-L.
Launay, ' "Le monde renversé sens dessus-dessous" de Fra Giacomo Affinati
d'Acuto', in *L'image du monde renversé et ses représentations littéraires et
para-littéraires de la fin du XVIe siècle au milieu de XVIIe* Paris, 1979,
pp. 141–52.

This divine plan having basically failed, it is not hard to notice that the 'microcosm has his head where his feet should be, and his feet where his head should be, in such a way that he treads the sky with his feet and has his head planted in the earth like a leek'.[16]

Vice and sin are the agents of this anthropic reversal. Like the Dantean simoniacs 'buried with their head down' (the term, which belongs to the vocabulary of the torture chamber, originated in the agricultural techniques of vegetable propagation) many are those who have their heads downwards and their bottoms upwards.

> Those who, on the contrary, fix their every thought, desire and care upon the earth and on earthly affections as if the world were their ultimate goal, they are undoubtedly upside down and their heads are planted in the earth while their feet tread the sky and they trample celestial things with the soles of their feet, as they hold them in no esteem. . . . Nor does the miser have his head planted in the sky, but rather in the earth where he has placed his treasure. . . . The lustful man does not have his head in the sky but in a muddy, putrid and verminous bog full of carnal filth. . . . The envious man does not have his head turned towards the sky, but rather towards his neighbour's goods and this gnaws into his soul. *Putredo ossium invidia.* The glutton is a bent plant with its branches pointing to the ground and its head in the cook-pot, its feet in a stove and its heart on a spit, its hands being on the dinner table.[17]

In righting this wayward and upturned man so that his head and soul faced heaven again, as a 'reformed man' he might yet refuse the *regimen sanitatis*. Similarly 'lay' medicine was discarded in favour of therapeutic cures of a supernatural kind. Invisible healers dispensed with the unreliable and uncertain science of the physicans. Trust in the 'Heaven's doctor' superseded confidence in 'carnal medicine'. The holy Mother of God consoled and cared for the sick and dying with ineffable grace. As the old Minorite friar of Soffiano, Fra Liberato da Loro, a man of 'great devoutness and full of grace', lay dying, the Comfortress, the Virgin Mary, appeared to him in the company of 'three holy Virgins, who bore three caskets of an electuary overpowering both in smell and sweetness'.

> Whereupon the glorious Virgin took one of the caskets and opened it and the whole house was filled with the scent thereof; and taking a spoonful of the electuary, she administered it to the sick man, who no sooner had he tasted it than he felt such

16   Ibid. p. 232.
17   Ibid. pp. 235–6.

comfort and sweetness, that it was as though his soul could not stay in his body; and he began to exclaim: 'Enough, Oh gentle Mother and blessed Virgin, who is the saviour of human creatures; enough, Oh blessed Doctor; enough, for I cannot bear so much sweetness.' But the compassionate and good-natured Mother, by repeatedly administering this electuary to the sick man and making him take it, completely emptied the casket. Then, having finished the first, the blessed Virgin took the second casket and prepared to give him a spoonful of it, at which the latter gently remonstrated saying: 'Oh, most blessed Mother of God, since my soul is almost completely liquefied by the aroma and sweetness of the first electuary, how will I be able to bear the second? I beseech you, blessed above all the Saints and above all the Angels, not to compel me to take any more.' And Our Lady answered: 'Taste, my son, taste some of this second casket also.' And giving him some, she said: 'By now, my son you have a sufficiency. Be of good cheer, my son, for I will soon come and lead you to my Son's realm, which you have always sought and desired.' So saying, she took leave of him, and he found great relief and comfort in the goodness of that nourishment, which enabled him to live, sated and strong, for some days without earthly sustenance. Some days later, while talking merrily with the friars, with great happiness and joy he passed from this wretched world to the blessed life.[18]

The aroma, gentleness, sweetness of electuaries, of celestial confections administered by the 'blessed doctor' – all these removed the need for 'corporeal' nourishment, prolonging one's last days indefinitely and transforming the ritual of passing to another life into a serene, nay almost jolly, triumphal march amidst rejoicing and delight. The dying man imbibes an aromatic comfort so inebriating and narcotic in its effects that his soul liquefies from the 'aroma and sweetness' of the medicament. An aromatic and fragrant death will be the least reward that God's humble servant may expect for himself for a devout existence, though he may never have tasted the delights of the world. His rugged flesh, made gaunt by fasting and racked by penances, will not know the horror of the sudden decay that pitilessly attacks the body which has been pampered, petted and caressed all its life. The *exemplum*, recounted by St Peter Damian, of the elegant wife (from Constantinople) of the Venetian Doge whose 'body totally succumbed to putrefaction, having formerly over-

[18]   St Francis, *I fioretti di San Francesco*, introduction C. Segre, preface and notes L. Morini, Milano, 1979, pp. 198–9. Translation taken from *The Little Flowers of St Francis* by Dom Roger Huddleston, London, 1953, pp. 104–5.

indulged in delicacies', consists of a short disquisition on the flesh, on the essence of the body (putrefaction with the outward appearance of beauty) which unfolds itself against a background of disgust for cadaveric stench and the horror of corruption.

> A certain Venetian Doge had married a lady of Constantinople, whose way of life was very refined and exquisite, and who cossetted herself with pleasures which were not only excessive but, if I may use the expression, perversely contrived, with the result that she even scorned to wash herself in the common water-supply. Her servants were kept so busy collecting dew from all quarters, from which after great labours, they made her bath. Nor would she touch food with her hands: her meals were cut up by her eunuchs into small crumbs, which she lifted to her mouth with little two-pronged golden forks and nibbled daintily. Through her room there wafted so many kinds of incense and perfume that it would be disgusting for me to relate them, and the reader might perhaps not believe it in any case. But her arrogance was hateful to Almighty God, as the punishment which befell her in judgement clearly shows. For the sword of divine justice was brandished over her, and her whole body began to rot so that every part decayed and filled her whole appartment with an unbearable stench as a result; there was no one who could endure such an assault on the nostrils: not her couturier, nor her houseboy, nor scarcely for a while her maid (with the help of some kind of perfume) who remained with her to look after her. But even the maid quickly succumbed, and retired forthwith in retreat. So the woman was ravaged by this disease for a long time and pitifully tortured by it, and then, to the joy of her friends, she gave up the ghost. Let the flesh itself reveal its own nature: let the living flesh bear witness to the spectacle the dead provide.[19]

Corruptio optimi pessima [equivalent of 'Lillies that fester smell far worse than weeds']. The punishment of flabbiness and soft living (which the monk of Ravenna smells as a vile stench merely in telling his tale) falls inexorably from the sky, inundating the scented chamber with a nauseating stink of rotting meat, of corrupt and decaying tissues. It was almost the reverse of the situation of the saints who, on the point of being raped by lustful men, were enveloped by divine intervention in a fetid and protective leprosy. For the men of God, at the beginning of this by now declining millennium, *caro* [flesh] and *putredo* [decay] were essen-

[19]   St Peter Damian, *Institutio monialis,* in *Opera omnia,* Bassano, 1783, vol. III, col. 780–1.

tially the same thing, and life but camouflaged death. Putrefaction was not a *post mortem* process but one which ran concurrently with life, was inherent to life, inside life itself, for life was but corruption and stench, disguised and beautified. Indeed, as an inescapable counterbalance, the flesh decays in a manner more atrocious, the more it has been fed on sophisticated and refined foods:

> ... because the flesh, which is now nourished on exquisite meals, will in a little while of necessity be swarming with worms: the same flesh which is now pleasantly fattened on delightful foods will then be food for worms; and it will give forth a viler stench as it decays according to the delicacy of the pleasures which it procured for its nourishment.... For what it will be then is shown clearly now. It could be said that human flesh, which now seems to be alive, does not in fact bring forth decay in itself after death, but only then declares itself openly to be the rottenness which it has always been.[20]

Decomposition occurs not after death but before it, because that which is called life is nothing but stench and dung, as we are startlingly informed in the church of the Salvatore in Rome, by one of the deceased: 'I have been shameful sperm, I have lived as the home of murky Dung; in this place I live as food for worms.' This is reminiscent of St Bernard, who, in his *Meditationes*, peremptorily wrote: 'Man is nothing but stinking sperm, a sack of excrement and food for worms.'

'When a man dies', said Syracides, 'his heirs are snakes, animals and worms.' A serpent could in fact, according to Pliny, be born from the decaying human spine or spinal medullum. So it was said centuries later of Carlo Martello whose tomb was found to be full of serpents. Up to about two centuries ago, it was commonly thought that 'serpents are born of the medullum of a human corpse'.

Whether serpent, earthworm or cockroach,

> After the human being the worm, after the worm, decay and
>   revulsion,
> Thus every human being is turned into what is not human.

The obsessive belief (manifest in many cultures) that the interior of the human body was little more than a latrine, swarming with worms and lice ready to feast on the intestine, is almost timeless. It is effectively confirmed by mediaeval Christianity which bases itself on the assumption that procreation happens *ex putri*. In the periods of Rome's greatness, these fears are buried under the remains of exotic, peripheral and

[20]   Ibid. col. 779–80.

immigrant populations. People's fears were exorcised by dumping them on those who inhabited the edges of the known world, who were lesser in some sense: whether troglodites or pygmies. The centre (*Roma caput mundi*) could not tolerate the thought that the object of horror might not take root like nasty infection in the ghettos of the more distant suburbs of the world. Moreover, even nowadays, the *bidonvilles* of the outskirts are felt to be infected zones, where all kinds of monstrosities are possible, and where a different man is born, an aberrant from the prototype who inhabits the centre of things.

The terror of *animacula* (Sulla, it was said, died with his intestines devoured by fleas, of pediculosis) gave rise to legends about sad, wretched people with short, dismal lives like the *Acridophagi* communities which inhabited the desert adjacent to Ethiopia (another inexhaustible source of monsters) 'men of lower stature than other men, leane, and very black'.[21] These short-lived people, whose sole nourishment consisted of salted locusts, ended their days riddled through by horrible winged lice, that destroyed them, causing unspeakable pain.

> Their death is strange: for when they draw near to their old age, there breed in their bodies certain winged lice, of divers shape, stinking, and ougly to behold, which in a little time eat their belly, after that their breast, and at last their whole body. The disease beginneth with an itching, which the patient feeleth intermingled with griefe and pleasure, and scratching himself untill he have made an open passage for the lice, and for the matter that floweth forth; the sickness groweth so grievous and vehement, that with greedie nailes and lowd cries he teareth all his bodie, out of which the vermin come forth in such abundance (as out of a pierst hogshead) that it is impossible to cleanse the poor bodie of them: but the same, by reason of their blood so corrupted with the aire, and with the feeding, being no other thing but rottenness and vermin, doth in that sort miserably die and perish.[22]

From worms life and from worms death. But fear of little creatures, of parasites and 'entomati' (as they used to say) was real enough and not limited to areas covered by African desert. In the *Nuovo et universal theatro farmaceutico [New and universal pharmaceutical theatre]* (1667) by Antonio de Sgobbis, are listed at least ten ointments (for the rich and

---

[21] Ph. Camerarius, *Operae horarum subcisivarum sive meditationes historicae auctiores quam antea editae*, Centuria prima, Francofurti, 1658 [1644] vol. I, p. 83. English translation by I. Molle, *The Living Librarie*, London, 1621.

[22] Ibid. pp. 83–4.

for the poor) against scabies (so far however not thought to be caused by parasites).

As with the Biblical plagues, the peoples of Europe were tormented by grasshoppers, frogs, mosquitoes or gnats, hornets, wasps, the common fly, lice, crab-lice, bedbugs, earthworms, caterpillars and worms of all kinds. They all drew blood, caused sores or ulcers: the scourges of olden times. Pliny and Solinus recount how in their day:

> the Eleans, so as to guarantee themselves against the pestilence which often beset them due to an invasion of flies, solemnly instituted a yearly sacrifice to some idol of theirs called Mingrone, that is, the killer of flies; so that on the very day of sacrifice to this bogus diety, all the flies in Elis should die together. The Eleans had perhaps learned about Mingrone from the inhabitants of Accaron, one of the chief provinces of the Philistines: since, as we know in the Scriptures, the Accaronites worshipped Beelzebub, the first almost among their gods: Beelzebub, as I say, in our common parlance, as the learned St Jerome observes, is the god of flies, or is held to be the god of flies.[23]

In the seventeenth century the Jesuit missions – so wrote the hagiographers – brought spiritual solace not only to 'poor peasants', to 'wretched yokels', but also in certain dramatic situations, to the 'countryside itself [which] greatly felt the benefit, since that land was still infested by death-dealing caterpillars, which when blessed from the terrace of the house by the man of God [Francesco di Girolamo], all vanished instantly and never were seen again at that time nor for many years to come'.

> At the time of this same mission, an endless army of caterpillars had invaded the whole countryside and the land [Andria]: a scourge to vie with the famous plagues of Egypt, bringing with it death and famine wherever it chose to alight. The news having reached the man of God, he fell upon his knees and implored Divine Compassion on behalf of the wretched multitude that would be left without any means of sustenance. God made no delay and consoled his Servant, so that the caterpillars now satisfied their hunger with weeds, respecting the good crops, for which by nature they are very greedy.[24]

It was worms above all that were to harass Western peoples for millenia. While endemic, in certain years they became so virulent as to constitute epidemics. The notion of putrefaction was itself associated

[23]   Q. Rossi, S.J., *Lezioni sacre*, Parma, 1781, vol. II, pp. 245–6.
[24]   Longaro degli Oddi, *Vita del B. Francesco di Girolamo*, p. 118.

with the smell they produced. When their reign of terror came to an end, so too did the terror of putrefaction, of unpredictable and uncontrolled childbirth. Giovan Battista Codronchi, a physician from Imola of no mean repute and author among other works of *De christiana ac tuta medendi ratione* (Ferrara, 1591), wrote a treatise at the beginning of the seventeenth century on the diseases which raged in Imola and the surrounding area in 1602: *De morbis qui Imolae, et alibi communiter hoc anno MDCII vagati sunt. Commentariolum in quo potissimum de lumbricis tractatur.*[25] The clinical picture is horrifying, depicting a formidable battle fought by men, children, women, young and old against death-dealing earthworms (*ferae*) intent upon strangling (*iugulare*) their human prey, gnawing their veins and pestering them ferociously. This scourge acquired particular virulence and malignancy in 1602. Associated with a form of pleurisy, it 'grassavit' or redoubled its attack (this verb being more associated with the idea of wholesale plunder) on the inhabitants of Imola, more particularly on the poor ('praesertium pauperes et ignobiles homines') who by the end of the winter and the beginning of spring had almost exclusively eaten fat foods and foods which are 'cold' by nature: vegetables, greens, corn-meals from various grains, fish, all of which involved slow digestion and produced – so it was thought – 'melancholic' excrements and putrefaction. And thus

> it happens that a substantial quantity of denser and less refined juices accumulates in the stomach; once this has decayed along with sooty excrement which has been retained under the influence of a great fiery heat, a great number of worms come forth from it. Although worms are not born directly from decayed matter ... they nevertheless come forth from the substance which is produced in matter by the process of decay.... For there is a lifegiving heat which not only predisposes matter to take on form, but also gives form to and brings into being the creatures themselves; this is especially the case since the part of the body in question is highly conducive to the generation of worms.[26]

Giovan Battista Codronchi, whose theory of *ex putri* generation is not so remote from the Aristotelian *De generatione animalium*, actually thought there were places, regions, nay indeed whole countries infested by earthworms and others which were completely immune. Romagna, in particular Imola, was crawling with them: 'horum animalum satis

25 Imprint: Bologna, 1603. In 1607 there appeared Fernando Salando's *Trattato sopra li vermi, cause, differenze, pronostico e curatione*, dedicated to the Duchess of Mantua (Verona).
26 Ibid. p. 21.

feracem esse' ('was very productive of these creatures'). Women especially were susceptible, being idle, greedy, sedentary and inclined to an excess of mucous humour.

> Women, in particular, I assert, are prone to suffer from this kind
> of disease, since many unrefined humours are to be found in
> them as a result of imperfect digestion; and these humours give
> rise to worms. Moreover, they stay indoors much of the time and
> are idle, and this is the origin of great quantities of phlegm,
> which are also increased by too decadent and varied a diet, of
> which women are fond above all.[27]

According to this intellectual who straddles the sixteenth and seventeenth centuries, women were fuller of vermin than men, an opinion shared by official science; for it was held they had a weaker digestion, were fuller of bad juices and phlegmatic humour, born of their irresistible fondness for variety and richness in food.

Like the toad 'is said to be born of the putrefaction and corrosion of mud, of themselves and of rotting blood', so a *maître á penser* of late sixteenth-century science, a contemporary of Codronchi, Giovan Battista Della Porta, maintained that

> neither is it hard to generate Toades of womens putrefied
> flowers; for women do breed this kind of cattel, together with
> their children ... And so, he saith [Paracelsus], you may make
> them of womens flowers; and so, he saith, you may generate a
> Basilisk, that all shall die which look upon him.[28]

However, Della Porta deemed this 'very untrue', while at the same time sharing the widely-held view that 'serpents are easily engendered of mans flesh, especially of his marrow'.[29] If Avicenna had conjectured that man and beasts could be born from the putrefaction of dead bodies with the aid of celestial influence, the Neapolitan 'magician' had no hesitation about stating that 'daily experience teacheth us that many living creatures comes from the putrified matter of the earth'.[30] Putrefaction was possessed indeed of a 'marvellous potency to produce animals', like mice, an additional scourge and source of fear, because, since they had 'a supernatural birth', their death could not 'occur in a normal fashion,

27   Ibid. p. 22.
28   G. B. Della Porta, *Della magia naturale*, libri XX, 'translated from the original
       Latin by the author himself and extended under the name of Gio. De Rosa
       V.I.P'. Napoli, A. Bulifon, 1677. English translation by Young & Speed, *Natural
       Magick* in 20 books, London, 1658, p. 28.
29   Ibid. p. 29.
30   Ibid. p. 27.

because in a few days not one was to be seen'. The fable of the Pied Piper reflects the anxieties and fears of a collective imagination which creates vast and unstoppable hoards of mice.

> *Pliny* could not find how it should be; for neither could they be found dead in the fields, neither alive within the earth in the winter time. *Diodorus* and *Aelianus* write, That these field-mice had driven many people of Italy out of their own Countrey: they destroyed Cosas, a City of Hetruria: many came to Troas, and then drove the inhabitants. *Theophrastus* and *Varro* write, That mice also made the inhabitants of the Island Gyarus to forsake their Country; and the like is reported of Heraclea in Pontus ...[31]

'Frogs,' writes Della Porta, 'are prodigiously conceived of rotten dust and rain.'[32] Bees were engendered (remembering Virgil) from the putrefaction of an ox, wasps from that of a horse or, better, from its 'rotting marrow', hornets from a horse dead and buried, cockroaches from the carcass of a donkey and 'unserviceable bees' – drones – from the rotting carcass of a mule.

So was it with many fish who, unequipped either for coitus or for the production of eggs, were born of rotting matter. Likewise with eels who, being devoid of gender, were supposedly conceived of rain, and other creatures of the lime of marshes and decaying mud. Shellfish were born of 'putrefied lime fcam'.

To be avoided at all costs as food, warned Tommaso Campanella, were 'fish without scales', 'because they are born of rotting scum, and have little life since they have not enough heat in them to enable them to expel excrement or to form scales'.[33] It was necessary to be particularly careful about diet, because 'according to how foods and beverages are combined and constituted, they lengthen or shorten the span of life'. The physician

> recognizes these things from their heat, taste and smell, and crass or slow consistency, and where he sees all manner of evil flow together, he cannot doubt but it is poison; when the colour is black but the rest is good, it gives rise only to melancholy; where the colour and smell are fetid and sad, disease and putrefaction of the blood occurs and heaviness of spirit; where the taste is itself an enemy of the tongue and the consistency is

31   Ibid. p. 28.
32   Ibid. p. 28.
33   T. Campanella, *Del senso delle cose e della magia*. Unedited Italian text with variants from the codices and two Latin editions, ed. A. Bruers, Bari, 1925, p. 246.

dense rather than slow, as with hellebore and hemlock, and if it retains the humour greatly, it is certain poison; but if these things do not occur all at one time, they nonethess make poor nourishment and gradually dispose the body for death and infect the mind. My argument, therefore, is that all things that smell evil, are evil, and all carcasses and fodder born in dung and manure, which are induced and not natural, whether trees or grain, grasses or any animals that feed from decaying matter or vegetation and fruits with little life, will shorten our lives. . . . Consequently, this nourishment will gradually and insensibly bring about a change in the person nourished. . . . And thus must rotting water and wine be eschewed for they turn rapidly to vinegar, but more especially those that easily become an oily and stinking liquor. . . .

Moses, a divine and natural magician, in his exceeding wisdom forbids all meat taken from carcasses, from any animals which do not ruminate, because they swallow gross foods, in haste and without digesting them, and in consequence they are full of viscous, gross and malignant vapours and of raw meat, which has not been cooked by natural heat; and he also forbids the meat of animals which do not have cloven hooves, such as the horse, the ass and the camel, for being too stout and with little life, and that of swine, for in Palestine this engenders leprosy, and that of predators because they fill us with harmful juices and bad habits. . . . On the other hand, I say that meats which are too dry are corrosive, such as that of crows, eagles and old animals, because they produce a salty humour, they dry the temper and induce hectic fever, and those that are old, being nearer to death bring death nearer, whereas those with longer life communicate this to us.[34]

Long life and short life were sucked, absorbed, eaten from animal flesh and liquids. Long-lived animals, elixir of human blood, honey which 'putretudini resistit'. 'Among the main remedies to stave off old age, some authorites include the meat of deer, because they are long-lived, human blood prepared by alchemy. . . .'.[35] Diet seemed as complicated as a puzzle, like a forest thick with traps and sources of energy, with substances congruent with the body and revivifying juices; or, indeed, like a dark reservoir of liquids and substances that poison, intoxicate, dry up and parch: impure, evil, muddy and rotting substances that saturate

[34]   Ibid. pp. 245–7.
[35]   B. Codronchi, *Commentarius de anni climactericis, ac ratione vitandi eorum pericula, vitamque producendi*. . . , Bologna, 1620, p. 126.

the blood with toxic elements, which lack life and abound in death, kilos and kilos of death. In a hard and hostile reality, rife with animal poison (spiders, wasps, scorpions, vipers, rabid dogs, insidious worms, leeches), where the air was often charged with the odour of 'marches and carcasses', polluted by 'poisonous gasses', in which meat rotted quickly surrounded by myriads of flies and worms, where the corruption of inert matter reigned supreme and implacable, it was of the utmost importance, in the fight to survive and to prolong one's time on earth, to identify and recognize 'all such things [that] lengthen life, which are inimical to poison and which resemble ourselves and contain as much as possible of the first mixing of seed and pure blood (not menstrual) such as we were born of'.[36]

Among the extraordinary things that Neapolitan legend attributed to the magician Virgil:

> apart from the slaughter-house where meat would not rot, Neckam recounts how Virgil, with a golden leech, freed Naples from a cloud of leeches that infested its waters, over which he built an aerial bridge which enabled him to be transported wherever he wished, and which surrounded his wonderful garden with an impenetrable wall of immobile air.[37]

Ridding the water of leeches, wrapping a garden in immobile air, macerating flesh without perpetual fear of immediate decay: three 'miracles' corresponding to three potent wishes, to three unfulfilled dreams; water free of filthy slimy creatures, Eden with a controlled environment, the 'impassibility' of the flesh like that of the blessed in heaven.

In a highly toxic world where poisonous plants lay in wait at every corner even within a city's walls (Antonio Musa Brasavola in his *Examen omnium simplicium medicamentorum* ... 1539, describes how some citizens of Ferrara were killed when taking hemlock and other straightforward poisons by mistake), to combat poisoning it was first necessary 'to comfort the spirit with aromas'.[38]

> First aid [advised Campanella] should first be administered to the spirit by way of pleasing and nutritious perfumes, then to the ventricle [the stomach] and intestine with restoratives such as cinnamon, mace and any spices whatsoever as may overcome the deleterious odour that insinuates itself within the body, and

36   T. Campanella, *Del senso delle cose e della magia*, p. 250.
37   D. Comparetti, *Virgilio nel Medio Evo*, new ed. by G. Pasquali, Firenze, 1941, p. 66.
38   T. Campanella, *Del senso delle cose e della magia*, p. 249.

from without [the body] cupping-glasses [shall be applied] that
will draw the vapours and blood, and lavages with a potent
wine.[39]

The 'fetid exhalation that infected the mind', at a time when it was
thought contagion spread aerially, was the most feared enemy of health.
Bodily decay sprang up everywhere and behind every street corner there
lurked the danger of poisonous, nay lethal, pollution. The desire for
aromatic 'restoratives' was particularly marked in urban centres which
most often lacked drainage, or whose streets served variously as a
pasture-ground for pigs, or a dumping ground for liquid sewage. Town-
dwellers lived perpetually immersed in atrocious stench, which in the
summer grew to be intolerable. Alessandro Tassoni likened Modena to a
'city half buried in a bog, where whomsoever chanceth to pass that way is
sure to become befouled from head to foot'. His quarter 'ran with mud
and shit in mid-summer'. 'Upon corner stones/and by gateways
everywhere/untidy and scattered mounds of old manure'. Valladolid
reminded him of a filthy latrine:

> Odourous turds and heaps of chamber-pots
> upset and scattered about and lurid torrents
> of urine and rank and foul-smelling broth,
> that you cannot walk without boots;
> the liquid dung of animals,
> dead . . . fish whose stench assails from afar.

In 1694 (or, according to another source, 1718), the Duchess of Orleans
wrote:

> The smell of mud is terrible. Paris is a frightful place; the smell of
> the streets is so revolting as to be unbearable; the great heat rots
> large quantities of meat and fish, and to all of this is added the
> mass of people who . . . emit an odour so repellent in the street
> that it cannot be borne.[40]

Even making allowance for the fastidiousness of the *grande dame*'s
nasal apparatus and its sensitivity when faced with the acrid smells of the
urban-yet-not-parasitical world (certain streets where dyers and tanners
worked put us in mind in Bernardino Ramazzini's writings of the bowels
of hell), one thing was sure and that is that the preservation of food was
closely connected with the preservation of health. In a society crawling
with animals and parasites, where mud and sewage, rotting meat and

[39]   Ibid. p. 249.
[40]   Quoted from N. Elias, *Über den Prozess der Zivilisation*, vol. I . . ., Frankfurt,
         1969.

decomposing corpses (of offenders who had been hung and quartered), increased the level of reeking exhalations, there was a high probability of seeing worms, caterpillars and flies appear from everywhere: from putre-fying carcasses, from mud, from wood, from barns, from butchers' shops and graveyards: a melting-pot of birth, death and verminous prolifer-ation. Surrounded by a Nature, both living and lively, sentient and sensuous, in which the organic and the inorganic merged, the loves of men and those of animals found correspondence in plants, like immobile animals. Among the palm trees and carob trees of the hot countries

> male and female lean towards each other, kiss, and the female is impregnated, and without the male she makes no fruits, indeed she seems to pine, wretched and mournful. In Nicastro, I won-dered even more at cedars I saw that were shaped some like the male member and others like the female organ, with such precision as those in men and women. Moreover, there are plants in Scandinavia whose fruits become flying animals and worms are born in all plants . . . [41]

A Nature like this, which was a swarming cosmos full of myriads of ephemeral metamorphoses, gave rise to dreams of extraordinary creatures, even of birds which were born of the rotting fruits of trees.

> *Munster* saith, there be certain Trees which bring forth a fruit covered over with leaves; which if it fall into the water under it, at the right season, it lives, and becomes a quick bird, which is called *Avis arborea.* . . . *Gesner* saith, that in the Islands Hebrides, the same birds are generated of putrified wood. If you cast wood into the Sea, first after a while there will certain worms breed in it, which by little and little become like ducks in the head, feet, wings and feathers; and at length grow to be as big as Geese: and when they are come to their full growth, they flie about the Air, as other birds do. As soon as the wood begins first to be putrified, there appears a great many wormes, . . . *Ficinus* reporteth, and he had it out of *Albertus*, That there is a certain bird, much like a Black bird, which is generated of the putrefac-tion of Sage: which receives her life and quickning from the general life of the whole world. [42]

If the fruits of trees gave birth to birds and waterlogged wood to worms which turned likewise into birds, how much more probable was it that the tombs of churchyards in urban areas might spew forth 'a multitude of worms'. In Forlì in 1427:

[41]   T. Campanella, *Del senso delle cose e della magia*, p. 215.
[42]   G. B. Della Porta, *Della magia naturale*, p. 46; p. 31 in *Natural Magick*.

it being the month of June, it happened that in the churchyards, more in the large ones than in the small, there appeared an enormous multitude of worms, their heads shaped almost like [those of] grain parasites and wingless like grasshoppers, but not with long legs, and seeming as though of gold and silver, so did they shimmer; around their necks they wore what looked like a monk's cowl. And they were so numerous that the nettles and mallow did not suffice and they left not a leaf on the stems of plants in these places. And these creatures abounded remarkably for eight or ten days, and crawled along the ground like as worms are wont. And it became necessary, because of the devastation they made of these places, that fires should be made in the cemeteries; and so they [the worms] were burnt and soon dispersed.[43]

Even the corpse is an organism in some sense still alive and capable of feeling: seed turned to foam, blood coagulating in the uterus which by increasing in volume becomes flesh, melts into pus ('homo de humore liquido', says St Bernard) and dissolves the fine 'machinery of the body' into horror and stench, ferments flesh inside the tomb like wine in the butt; for even inside the lifeless body there is 'hidden feeling and warmth which never forgets to move, being by nature active'. The process of putrefaction therefore

grows and liquefies and reduces the human frame and makes it smell, for the smell is none other than a gross and hotly immoderate exhalation that overwhelms our spirit and while distasteful to us, is not so to other creatures with a grosser and hotter spirit than ours, and therefore what to one is a stench to another is perfume. Heat being thus generated and the fine thread of life being unable to detach itself from the viscous, the spirit gives birth to worms . . .[44]

In Campanella's world, where 'death of simple things is a transformation into something else',[45] a loss of 'human consciousness and of the living spirit, but not of the obtuse, material and everyday',[46] death signifies a change of state and decomposition, a mutation of form into a sensuous mobility of matter. Worms are but a projection of man, of his inside shape, and the fine, shiny caterpillars may have something human about them and appear anthropomorphic.

[43]   Giovanni di M. Pedrino Depintore, *Cronica del suo tempo*, Roma, 1929, vol. I, p. 160.

[44]   T. Campanella, *Del senso delle cose e della magia*, p. 254.

[45]   Ibid. p. 253.

[46]   Ibid. p. 255.

Thus in June 1498 in Florence:

> On the meadow of the *Servi* and of the *Tiratoio* certain caterpill-
> ars appeared, which devoured everything, so that the sloe-
> bushes became white and peeled; and within the space of four
> days these caterpillars turned the colour of gold. The boys
> caught them, saying: *These are Fra Girolamo's caterpillars*
> [Savonarola]; and some looked like gold and some like silver.
> They were as follows: they had a human face, with eyes and
> nose, seeming to have a crown on their head, and round their
> face a diadem (a halo) as used to be made, whilst between the
> crown and the head was a little cross, their bodies were golden,
> and they had a small and slender black tail (*sic*) with which they
> ate these sloe-bushes. It seemed miraculous that they were never
> seen again, and as if it must signify something[47]

An ambivalent monster, a 'wicked worm' (*Inferno* XXXIV, 108) like
the Prince of Darkness, the rebel and fallen angel, or 'worms/born to
make the angelic butterfly', the earthworm and the caterpillar are man's
other face or, better, his image. 'What are all men', wondered St
Augustine, 'born of flesh, if not worms?' (in John 1.12). Fear of worms is
in the last analysis fear of oneself. These creatures, like mankind, were
born of decay; man from fetid sperm, from stale blood, fed in the womb
by the same putrid blood that also produced snakes; worms of rotting
blood and decomposing flesh. The difference was only superficial.

---

[47] L. Landucci, *Diario Fiorentino dal 1450 al 1516*, continued anonymously until
1542, published in the codices of the Comunale of Siena and by the Marucelliana
with annotations by Iedoco del Badia, Firenze, 1883, pp. 179–80. English
translation by A. de Rosen Jarvis *A Florentine Diary from 1450 to 1516*, London,
1927, p. 144.

6

ENTOMATA

By association, the verb 'to swarm' gives rise to a sense of discomfort and anxiety.

> Since the main animal categories are defined by their typical movement, 'swarming', which is not a mode of propulsion proper to any particular element, cuts across the basic classification. Swarming things are neither fish, flesh nor fowl. Eels and worms inhabit water, though not as fish; reptiles go on dry land, though not as quadrupeds; some insects fly, though not as birds. There is no order in them. Recall what the Prophecy of Habakkuk says about this form of life: 'For thou makest men like the fish of the sea, like crawling things that have no ruler' (I,V:14). The prototype and model of the swarming things is the worm. As fish belong in the sea so worms belong in the realm of the grave, with death and chaos.[1]

This funeral prototype of the world of corruption, of deviation from 'regular' and 'normal' forms of life like many other *imperfecta animalcula*, was powerful enough to elicit sombre fears since, according to the ancient theory of spontaneous generation, of birth *ex putri*, it could burst forth everywhere suddenly.

In commenting on the Dantian episode of the slothful, Benvenuto de' Rambaldi da Imola (Battista Codronchi's fellow countryman) glosses the lines:

> [...] were stung exceedingly
> By gadflies and by hornets that were there.
> [*Inferno*, III, 65–6; tr. Longfellow, 1867]

illustrating them by means of images of people afflicted by the most repellent ailments, from whose bodies are born foul creatures:

> Dante's image is most appropriate, in that these wretches, because of the monstrous nature of their lives, suffer from the scab, leprosy and other most shameful kinds of disease, and they lie sick with them in a wretched condition, in the infirmaries and

---

[1]   M. Douglas, *Purity and Danger. An Analysis of Concepts of Pollution and Taboo*, Harmondsworth, 1970, p. 56.

often on the streets and in ditches; and no one attends to them except the flies and wasps; for these creatures are born from decay and excess, and it is therefore meet that they should be tormented by these wretches. 'By noisome grubs was he assailed': for they often reach such an appalling state that their festering limbs bring forth worms; hence flies also breed worms in the heads and limbs of sufferers.[2]

It was believed that lepers and those suffering from scabies generated worms in their semi-decomposed bodies. One catches glimpses of hospitals, lazzarettos, of mere shadows of human beings, abandoned in ditches and highway tramps forsaken and rejected by all but a host of flies and wasps that followed them. A dismal picture of 'shameful' sickness (a sick person was in certain cases according to mediaeval ethos, a sinner, one who was guilty and whom God was punishing), and of unfathomable human loneliness. The distasteful portrayal of these 'historic' diseases acquires even more sombre and repellent colours in a distressing account of the condition and appearance of elephantiasis (in ancient medicine the 'elephant man' was confused with the leper) given by Areteus of Cappadocia 'with tragic eloquence and remarkable medical precision',[3] and which includes 'astonishing and incredible' cases in which individuals suffering from

> elephantiasis had, through fear of contagion spreading from them and because of the horrible appearance of the disease, been taken away from their next of kin into the mountains and to solitary places there to be abandoned, as testified by Aurelian to be the normal practice, but were subsequently found and cured.[4]

Monstra, the wicked aberrations of nature (*vitia naturae*), were consumed ostensibly by an inextinguishable lust akin to *satyriasis*, with their enflamed cheeks, like those of insatiable fauns, 'from the insatiable and shameless desire of copulation'.[5]

This slow, inexorable disease came to be called 'elephantine' not only because of the deep furrows it drove into the skin of its victim, but also

---

2 *Comentum super Dantis Aldigherii Comoediam*, ed. Lacaita, Firenze, 1887, vol. I, p. 121.

3 A. Cocchi, *Del vitto pitagorico*, in *Opere*, vol. I: *Discorsi e lettere di A.C.*, Milano, 1824, p. 235.

4 Ibid. p. 237.

5 Aretaeus Cappadocii, *De causis et signis acutorum, et diuturnorum morborum libri quatuor. De curatione acutorum, et diuturnorum morborum libri quatuor.* Editionem curavit H. Boerhaave, Lugduni Batavorum, 1735, p. 69. English translation taken from: *Aretaeus, consisting of Eight Books, on the Causes, Symptoms and Cure of Acute and Chronic Diseases*, translated from the original Greek by John Moffat, London, 1785, p. 96.

because of the lengthy duration and the interminable process of decay, whose 'longevitas' put people in mind of elephants. 'This affection is likewise called *leo*, from the similitude of the corrugations in the extremity of the forehead ... besides the name Herculean has been attributed to it, because there is nothing greater or more powerful in its effects.'[6] This nightmare continued to plague the patient over the years 'until the patient is torn limb from limb':

> tumours arise one after another, but not adjoining, of a thick consistence and rough to the touch, the interstices likewise are cleft . . . . The hairs on every part of the body die away especially those on the hands, thighs, and legs, they appear but rare on the *os pubis* and chin, the hair of the head likewise falls off ... the prominence of the lips is thick, and the inferior part is livid, the nose is swelled, the teeth are not white but of a black appearance, the ears are red with a mixture of black, obstructed, and have somewhat the appearance of those of an elephant, so that their magnitude is apparently greater than usual, there are ulcers at the basis of the ears attended with an ichorous fluxion and pruriency. The whole body is ploughed with rough wrinkles, and the clefts are deep like the black furrows of leather, on which account the name *elephas* has been affixed to the disease. It is attended with fissures of the heel and heart of the foot, which reach as far as the middle of the toes, and should the evil still increase more and more, the tumours of the cheeks, chin, fingers, and knees are ulcerated, and the ulcers are not only attended with a bad smell but become incurable, for one rises upon the back of another and continual succession takes place. The different members are lifeless and dead before the patient, the nose, fingers, feet, with the genitals and hands fall off, nor does the evil produce death, or a change from this miserable state of life and excruciating torture, until the patient is torn limb from limb. The disease is of long duration, and in this bears a resemblance to the life of the elephant.[7]

From time immemorial there had circulated horrible stories, lurid like hell, tales of evil metamorphoses, worthy of Dante's blackest imaginings.

> There is a report that one of those exposed in a desert, on seeing a serpent creep out of the earth, devoured it alive being compelled from hunger, or pain of the disease, in order to

6   Ibid. p. 69.
7   Ibid. pp. 69–71.

exchange evil for evil, and that he did not die until the members of his body putrified and fell off.[8]

A decanting of poisons, a toxic exchange, almost a belated genetic transformation as if the elephant wanted to become a viper. It seems as if the virus of metamorphosis that affected Dante's thieves made itself felt in this 'incredible' tale. These tales, though seeming to hark from Asia, Africa or the tropics, were also indeed European.

Leprosy aside, prolonged skin diseases (but also those of shorter duration such as that suffered by St Anthony, which made short shrift of its prey, afflicting him with the most horrible gangrenes and burning into his flesh so that his limbs were reduced to little more than ashes), represented a real scourge, whether induced by internal causes or the product of parasitical attacks. Over a very long period, and still only very slowly after the discoveries of early parasitology (first of all Francesco Redi, then Giovanni Alfonso Borelli, Diacinto Cestoni, Giovancosimo Bonomo, Antonio Vallisnieri, Lazzaro Spallanzani) generation after generation tried to neutralize these tormenting afflictions by abundant use of mercury-based medicaments. For a long time European blood was largely luetic/mercurial. The supra-cutaneous tissue, in a sufferer, was richly and elaborately incised with a variety of cutaneous diseases, from the mildest such as vitiligo or ephelis, to the more virulent herpes, impetigo, St Anthony's fire (erysipelas), leprosy/elephantiasis, thyriasis, 'famous among eminent people, rulers and sages, who have been left painfully to perish by so dire a malady'. A variant of this was scabies or the itch, a social evil of unimaginable proportions today. The 'virulent itch', the 'pertinacious and painful itch' might last for many years and by coursing though the whole body, would by its 'aggravating irritation' make like a perfect hell.[9]

> On 10 September 1748 in Pisa, Sister Annafrancesca, born of Sire Pietro Magani of Pistoia, and a nun in the Ceppo convent of that city, came to our baths when aged thirty-eight. Sanguine of temperament, robust of constitution and somewhat plump of figure, on reaching the age of twenty-two or twenty-three there had begun to issue from her legs a salty cutaneous discharge, which then spread gradually, defying all remedies and cures attempted, so that after a few years the whole of her body was afflicted by what became an obstinate and malignant ichorous scabies. This fierce and relentless scabies caused our nun a great deal of suffering, and such were the excruciating heat and intolerable irritation that tormented her day and night, that she

[8] Ibid. p. 71.
[9] A. Cocchi, *Trattato dei bagni di Pisa* in *Opere*, vol. II, Milano, 1824, p. 169.

was forced to spend a large part of the time in her bed during these last years. The number of medicaments, both internal and external, prescribed by physicians to free her from this horrible and tormenting illness was countless; yet they were all fruitless, for the malady continued with the same force.[10]

This occurred when the nun was twenty-three, and fifteen years later not only had the scabies not disappeared or diminished in force, but it had reach unbearable proportions. This is just one among an infinititude of similar cases, whose number whilst inestimable must be very high.

It was only after Francesco Redi and, to an increasing extent, during the eighteenth century that people began to realise that it was not dirt and an excess of sanguinity, or the putrefaction of evil 'foul and stagnant'[11] humours that spontaneously engendered 'vile and minute animals':

> It is not a defect in the internal humoural system that causes scabies directly, but a type of living species called *pedicelli*, or rather *pellicelli*, as our old folk chose to call it in the vernacular language. The insinuation of these minute creatures under the human skin, with the consequent irritation caused by their movements and the sores produced by them as they take their nourishment, the inflamation caused by a man's own nails, their propensity to multiply fast, provide altogether a very good reason for the symptoms of this sickness.[12]

The 'multiplication', the 'multitude' of these 'minute anthropophagic animals' – when their provenance appeared mysterious and unverifiable, yet not regarded as 'foreign bodies' which had insinuated themselves into the human body, but as 'altered parts of the human body itself' or as a foul corruption of organic substance and of 'turgid and corrupt' humours, as putrid excrescences of moral vices turned into mobile, living and aggressive excrements, there to punish the vile and sinful body – had created a nightmare seen as asiatic.[13] A dark obsession, a disease of the 'Arab' genre akin to those maladies which seem to grow worse in the darkness of the psyche than in the blaze of Oriental sunshine.[14]

Redi's 'little beasts', his 'little animals' and 'insects', which should be observed and described calmly and without trepidation as

> ... so many other kinds of insect like flies, wasps, bees, scorpions, singing crickets, mole crickets which we Tuscans call *zuccaiole [zucca* means 'pumpkin' and therefore with a head like

10   Ibid. pp. 175–6.
11   Ibid. p. 167.
12   Ibid. p. 170.
13   Ibid. p. 168.
14   Ibid. p. 168n.

one,] naked slugs, silk-worms, all kinds of caterpillars, sea
scolopendra, leeches and blood-suckers, and very many other
species of similar little animals ... [15]

each with their appointed rôle in an ordered nature, properly born of
their own eggs and not of putrefaction or corrupt humours; whilst but a
few generations earlier (for physicians like Battista Codronchi or the
scientific/philosophic 'theorists', like Fortunius Licetus, who favoured
the 'spontaneous birth of living creatures') they had played a very
different part as man's diabolical and invincible adversary, as carriers of
obscure infections, as a mass of ghastly putrefaction, carrying with them
symptoms which spelt undefinable and incomprehensible danger. Born
then of death, putrescence and coital blood rather than life-giving seed, a
product of death rather than of life, they were felt in that earlier period to
be doleful messengers of corruption and decay.[16]

Infecta animalia, 'not having blood (and they are worms)', abnormal
and incomplete (*imperfecta*) creatures, cruel tormentors and murderers
of mankind, born tumultuously, chaotically and almost instantaneously,
these toxic individuals were spewed forth in myriads by some evil and
hostile agent, presaging imminent catastrophe, epidemics, bad harvests,
famine, corrupt and insalubrious aerial conditions.[17]

These creatures were 'turbulent' (Cocchi) *anthropophaga entomata*
for the most part, suckers of human blood and capable despite their
microscopic size of perforating the skin. Endowed with a mouth, teeth or
something like them – an internal proboscis, a sting or rostrum with
which implacably to gnaw and perforate. Consequently these creatures

> inflict bites and stings which are remarkable and sometimes
> fatal, namely, some kinds of fly, fleas, gnats, bugs, lice, wasps,
> 'tines', moths and leeches .... Some flies have a sharp beak,
> which they use to penetrate human skin and draw out the blood;
> the flea likewise scrapes through the hides of animals and sucks
> out blood through the opening, and also draws more blood to the
> surface with the result that the area around the bite is reddened.
> Lice, which Aristotle ... calls animals, but which most people
> call pests, have a bite which is so dangerous that from time to

[15] F. Redi, *Osservazioni intorno agli animali viventi che si trovano negli animali viventi*, in *Opere di F.R.*, Venezia, 1722, vol. I, p. 91.

[16] Cf. his *De spontaneo viventium ortu libri quatuor. In quibus de generatione animantium, quae vulgo ex putri exoriri dicuntur, accurate aliorum opiniones omnes primum examinantur...*, Vicenza, 1618.

[17] B. Codronchi, *De morbis, qui Imolae et alibi communiter hoc anno MDCII vagati sunt. Commentariolum, in quo potissimum de lumbricis tractatur*, Bologna, 1603, p. 40.

time it causes blood to burst out from the rectal vein or through the nostrils . . . . The leech, also known as the bloodsucker, bites and then by opening up the surface of the vein makes the blood flow out and causes a triangular wound. The 'dog-fly' makes a perforation and draws out blood, attacking in particular the ears of dogs; lice puncture the skin of human beings, while the gnat breaks through the hides of animals and draws out their blood, the bug bites humans; I have thought it best to pass over in silence the wounds inflicted by many other creatures of this kind.[18]

Vampire-like haematophilic insects, tissue-borers, blood-suckers, bloodless creatures of death. Those 'worms' that did not directly attack people, assailed them instead in a roundabout way: for instance, aphids that destroyed their corn, moths that ate into the wool and linen, woodworms that riddled their wood, snails, moles, crickets, mice, caterpillars, grasshoppers that infested their orchards and fields; blood-suckers and salamanders that nested in their water, cockroaches that visited them at night, like ominous shadows of demoniacal pollution.

The roach is another species of bug; the book of natural history says that it shuns the light and goes about in the darkness. The demons which appear to people at night in dreams to corrupt and deceive them with fantastic visions are represented in the form of this worm.[19]

As a means to combat the ants which devastated their larders, they resorted to incantations and charms (traces of which can still be found in country songs). Magicians and exorcists tried to stem the ubiquitous tide of invaders:

I exorcise you, pestilent worms, mice, birds, locusts and other creatures, cursing you: wherever you are, may you be accursed, shrinking and shrivelling into yourselves from day to day, until none of your remains are found anywhere that are not service-able for the use and well-being of men.[20]

These 'worms' together with the whole of their genus and all the other excommunicated and damned creatures, associated with death and chaos, could become therapeutic agents and instruments of consolation and physical cure, or liberators from illness. Toasted and pulverized earthworms or ones which had been squashed to extract their oil (with

18   Ibid. p. 39.
19   Thomas Cantimpratensis, *Miraculorum et exemplorum memorabilium sui temporis libri duo*, Duaci, 1597, p. 451.
20   H. Mengus (Girolamo Menghi) *Eversio daemonum e corporibus oppressis*, Bononiae, 1588, p. 539.

pestle and mortar and later in alembics), and so, too, mouse blood, millipedes (against epilepsy), shrimps' eyes, scorpions, provided a basis for a medicine reminiscent of witchcraft, the only one feasible in a mental and medicinal world which used the very ingredients exorcized by the sorcerer who, while invoking their extinction and annihilation, nonetheless recognized in their 'reliquiae' a source of health, '. . . necessary to health and useful to mankind'.

Given the ambivalence towards magic of societies of the past, the sacred overlapped with the sacrilegious, filth with purity and healthiness, satanism with angelic attributes.

It was a dangerous and fearful world, a world hostile to man, to his life, his work, his achievements, the animals useful to him; it was a world which swarmed with insidious and maleficent creatures vomited forth by death and felt through biblical tradition to be man's antagonists, imbued with a strong quota of the demoniacal. It was a frequent vehicle for malignant spirits to infiltrate the body disguised as insects and take permanent 'possession' so as to bewitch and corrupt it. The 'world of the approximate' goes hand in hand with the world of spontaneous generation (and is therefore uncontrollable, unverifiable and immeasurable in an objective sense): to be shapeless is to be approximate, to be putrescent is to be approximate.

This was a swarming and 'nilotic' (where the notion of illness is associated with the worm/parasite) world, over which the Egyptian magician had to some extent the power to reproduce and counterfeit, changing rods into snakes, water into blood, quagmires and filth into frogs (the means to combat mosquitoes proved ineffective); and yet over this power, Moses and Aaron with their rods (prototypes of the magic wands of mediaeval sorcerers) reign supreme – with help from the Omnipotent. Frogs, mosquitoes, flies, grasshoppers, stench, ulcers, hailstones, impenetrable darkness, blood . . . the plagues of Egypt seemed nightmares that reared their heads from the depths of farming and grain-producing societies, which the agrarian magic of Classical times had tried to neutralize through spells, purgations, exorcisms, fumigations, recipes and 'black magic': fat of a bear, heart of an owl, henbane blood, spleen of owl, concoctions of black hellebores, deer's antlers, goats' hooves, foul-smelling smoke to keep these *monstra noxia* at bay. And the menstrual blood of a near-naked woman: '. . . they make a menstruating woman with no fastening in her clothes, her hair loose, her feet bare, walk around as a protection against canker-worm and other garden pests'.[21]

These are the very same monsters against which the Christian exorcists then inveigh with holy diatribe, camouflaged by devils, or driven by

[21] Palladius Rutilius Taurus Aemilianus, *De re rustica*, in *Scriptorum rei rusticae veterum latinorum tomus tertius*, ed. Io. Gottlob Schneider, Lipsiae, 1795, p. 47.

demons. Abominations sprung out of the darkness, corruption, evil (like malignant spirits) tormentors of bodies, souls, fields, and all of them 'diabolic filth'.

To this category belonged the *dracunculus Persarum*, carrier of the disease called, predictably, *dracontiasi* by Greek physicians, and a gnawing nasty little monster, of which Agatharchises, author on so-called 'asiatic' matters, in a passage quoted by Plutarch, says:

> some of the sick by the Red Sea were to have certain little snakes that came forth from their skins and gnawed at their legs and arms and when touched turned and went in again and in turning caused intolerable inflammation.[22]

Three decades from the end of the seventeenth century, the city of Pesaro in the Marches on the eastern side of Italy, where the *mirabilia* of old Italy had not yet been magnified out of existence by the advent of the microscope, became the site of a remarkable occurrence, of an 'Indian' or 'Arab' nature. A Capuchin monk, after 'thirteen months of urinating blood ... emitted through his urine a creature similar to a small viper'. The chief medical officer of the Duchy of Urbino, Alessandro Cocci, 'the Aesculapius of our times', succeeded in extracting from the monk's insides

> a small serpent [a *dracunculus* would have been the term used by a scholar of asiatic matters] with a head like a viper's, ashen in colour, measuring the width approximately of a little finger and a span in length, indeed two ounces more; a thing quite incredible but true.[23]

On the morning of 4 April 1677, Brother Stefano da Camerino, a Capuchin friar who for many years had been suffering from kidney stones (in February of that year he had retired to Pesaro to be treated by Alessandro Cocci), after many days in atrocious pain and of discharging blood in his urine, had a decisive attack of shooting pain:

[22]   A. Cocchi, *Trattato dei bagni di Pisa*, p. 168n.
[23]   *Relatione del caso successo in Pesaro sotto il dì 4 aprile 1677. In persona d'un Padre Capucino, che doppo 13 mesi d'urina di sangue curato ultimamente dall'Eccellentiss. Sig. Protomedico Alessandro Cocci trasmise per urina un'animale simile ad una viperetta*, Pesaro, s.a., p. 35. This 'report' appears in Carlo Lancilotti's work (pp. 37–117) *Chimico disvelato, che chiaramente dimostra il modo di conoscere le falsità, che far si possono in molti medicamenti spargirici, e l'elettione loro...*, Modena, 1677. The same case, together with Athanasius Kircher's remarkable explanation, was analysed by Antonio Vallisnieri, stern discreditor of 'old wives' tales' and 'whimsical tales', in *Considerazioni ed esperienze intorno alla generazione de' vermi ordinarj del corpo umano*, Padova, 1710, pp. 20 ff.

he was assailed, he said, by extreme pains which lasted two to three hours and then he felt some elongated object tear itself away from his right kidney and travel towards the pubic parts rather like a stretched cord, which would gave him no respite whether standing, or sitting, or in bed, or in any other place, but groaning, restless and urinating blood copiously twice . . . . When then he had the urge to urinate a third time, he felt the object he called a cord detach itself from his kidney – causing him such extreme anguish that he lept up and cried out aloud. Subsequently, the pain abated when wishing to urinate, but he could only produce a few drops of blood, and feeling a great pressure and irritation, he beheld a long narrow object about three inches in length discharge itself in the urinary meatus, which object he grasped firmly and vigorously attempted to draw out and remove. In this he failed, finding himself with a truncated piece in his hands, his urinary meatus blocked and himself a prey to the torments of death. These then abated after an hour as the long object, spanning two Roman inches, was ejected in another discharge of blood. This left him exhausted and drained of blood, as it can be imagined, but free of pain, load or incumbrance in the kidney and free of suffering. Indeed, he soon began to acquire a good colour, recover his strength and spirits, causing observers to wonder and rejoice to see him released from so much anguish and torment.[24]

The author (a medical man) of this passage saw, 'to his great astonishment' and after careful cleansing of the object, 'a small animal with a head like that of a small viper'. For two days this 'unprecented monstrosity' was exhibited to the public gaze; and then in the presence of the Vicar General, the Archdeacon and various representatives of the nobility, and with the assistance of the expert surgeon and anatomist, Carlo Antonio Grana, he proceeded to dissect and make a thorough examination of the creature. On examination of its internal organs, using a *microscopio pulicario* (the scourge of fleas weighed so much in people's minds that it even gave its name to the instrument, probably a bi-convex lens, with which fleas were examined), it was established with something approaching certainty that the rejected intruder was not of the verminous kind. Those present, most of all the physician and the surgeon, were in agreement in identifying it as belonging to the 'serpentine species', the head and intestine being different from those in worms.

It is most probable that Francesco Redi, or others of his school, would have been of a different opinion. The 'spell-free' observers of the Grand

24   Ibid. pp. 43–4.

Duchy of Tuscany would not, like the doctor from Pesaro, have spoken of 'a new prodigy of nature'. Nature, a fecund and capricious progenitor of monsters and *mirabilia*, was changing its old image beneath their impassive gaze and controlled experiments. The magical/conventual culture of the Marches (like that of nearly all of Italy in the second half of the seventeenth century), even when it was conducting 'sensible experiments' remains prisoner – at the unconscious level – to the old logic of monsters and marvels. The antiquated paradigm of spontaneous breeding in a state of slow change was a fertile source of chimeras and monsters of nature besides being (supposedly) a stimulant of the 'intellect'. The observer's vision, no matter how it was assisted by the new precision instruments (the microscope, in this case), remained nevertheless conditioned by the old mental frame of reference, by the logic of putrescence child-bearing, by the spontaneous fermentation of organic matter and of birth *ex putri*. All in all, it was 'prejudice' that swayed, and the coherent substance of dreams that guided observation, diverting it towards distant zones populated with abominable and loathsome creatures, beyond the bounds of any norms and genetic laws. With the exception of certain isolated outposts, the overwhelming majority (among whom many educated people and 'literati') remained the subjects of that realm, with its ill-defined boundaries, which moved and expanded, shifted and was self-propelled, like certain maps we make in our dreams or an imaginary land: a realm that by long tradition had come to be known by the name of its ruler, Father John. To him did potentates of the Middle Ages direct their messages, plenipotentiaries, epistles and bulls. And from him there circulated apocryphal answers about mediaeval Europe. This incredible correspondence, which was half true and half imaginary, was kept up by kings and popes with a pinch of the non-existent, the sovereign of nothing, of dreams. It was a logic of unreality mixed with *raison d'état*, of delirium programmed in chancelleries. Much of this long Middle Ages survived into the last decades of the seventeenth century. Scientific evolutions became mental revolutions only very slowly. Even the most hardened culture looks to the past with half its mind and follows well-beaten paths and ancient sheep-tracks. Even in the most advanced and intellectual of capitals, like Pisa and Florence, led by the cultivated and enquiring minds of the last of the Medici, old and new lived side by side, sometimes in one and the same person. The botanically minded Grand Duke Paolo Boccone, a great correspondent with other learned Italians, a passionate traveller and indefatigable observer, dedicates the thirteenth part of his *Osservazioni naturali* (1684) to the 'miraculous feeding' that an Umbrian infant received from 'his father's breasts in the absence of his mother': 'from the milk-bearing breasts of a man who, upon the death of his wife, suckled his child'.[25] There co-existed, in the mind of this cultivated gentleman of Palermo, 'botanist to his Excellency the Grand Duke of Tuscany', and in certain respects a forward-looking experimenter and meticulous observer of reality, whose name, moreover, Linnaeus bestowed upon a genus of the papaveraceae family (*Bocconia*), two contrasting systems: that of the approximate and hearsay, of the fabulous and impossible, and that of scrupulous investigation and rigorous assessment of fact. Deep pockets of resistance to new scientific methodology, had entrenched themselves like some sombre legacy of the passing millenia in the cultural make-up of this learned and well-travelled intellectual, who lived in constant contact not only with the finest minds of the Pisan school but also with the 'cavalieri', 'literati' and philosophers of Europe and Italy, among whom there numbered Marcello Malpighi, the father of vegetable citology. This stubborn body of ideas from the past could lead to wild observations, of which I cite one (among the many), concerning the 'extraordinary and miraculous discharges of certain plants and animals':

> The prawns were transported to Vienna alive and in baskets on carts, since in Austria, Moravia and other German provinces, they abound greatly and are three times the size of those fished in Italy. If it so happen, however, that a pig pass beneath one such cart, they immediately die, all of them [the prawns]. Consequently, the peasants are obliged to take certain precautions to safeguard the waggon on its journey; and before resting themselves and their horses at a tavern, they remove the wheels of the waggon so that it will lie upon the ground and so will the passage of pigs beneath it be prevented. The potency of effluvia from pigs appears to be damaging to the constitution of prawns.[26]

A trick of the imagination, a tumble into the well of dreamed treasures, of mythology, a fairy-tale maybe, but hardly a scientific 'observation'.

It is not entirely for fortuitous reasons that this member of the 'Accademia Caesarea Leopoldina Naturae Curiosorum', changing his

[25]   P. Boccone, *Osservazioni naturali ove si contengono materie medico-fisiche, e di botanica, produzioni naturali, fosfori diversi, fuochi sotterranei d'Italia, e altre curiosità. Disposte in trattati familiari da P.B., e dirette a varii cavalieri, e letterati del nostro secolo, secondo lo stile delle Accademie fisico-mattematiche d'Europa*, Bologna, 1684, pp. 194 ff.

[26]   P. Boccone, *Museo di fisica e di esperienze variato e decorato di osservazioni naturali, note medicinali, e ragionamenti de' moderni*, Venezia, 1697, pp. 147–8. Osservazione vigesima sesta [26th observation]. 'Intorno gli effluvi stravaganti e prodigiosi di alcune piante e di alcuni animali'.

name from Paolo to Silvio, returned in later life to Sicily and retired to become a monk in a Cistercian monastery.

That he should have undergone an existential crisis was but a natural development of a religiously fervent mind, prompting him also to dedicate his *Osservazioni naturali* to the Almighty Father himself as 'Inspirer of science'. But it is also a symbolic journey, a relapse, or a retracing of his steps towards that magical and conventual world whose fascination he was unable ever to shake off. His action, typical of a thinker of the Baroque period, has something in common with that of the eccentric secretary to the Academy of the Cimento, Lorenzo Magalotti, who abandoned academy and court, forgot Pisa, Florence and Europe and proceeded to shut himself up in a cloister of the Philippines, which in its turn he also forsook after a few months.

Here it is quite irrelevant, indeed senseless, to talk of encyclopaedic dilettantism. The conflict, or at least, the co-existence of old and new was (and is) a problem that faces every thinker, even one who has 'pushed back the frontiers of knowledge'. For its part, the science of the human body lagged behind the revolutionary sciences of astronomy and physics. The skies changed, the macrocosm revealed a hitherto unknown order, the age-old cosmologies were overturned, but man as defined by Galenus persisted in his unchanging quaternary form, his equilibrium perpetually threatened, always on the point of succumbing to malfunctioning humours, corrupted blood, or the poisonous decay inherent in food. The past signals to us its countless dangers: widespread toxicity, putrid water and air, vital foodstuffs in decay; from a world sunk in a nightmare of corruptibility and constantly overshadowed by putrefaction; from a muddy, excretory and dungy world full of pungent smells, acrid odours and inescapable stench. The antidotaries, pharmacology and prescriptions of the past are valuable and so-far untapped sources of information for anyone wishing to explore more deeply into the make-up of man of the *ancien régime*. Moreover, the history of pharmacological science is a useful key to a better understanding of man's relationship with his anxieties, fears, hopes, physical malfunctions and mental dystonia. We need hardly add that medicine in the past, concerned as it was predominantly with matters of diet, governed the state of one's health through a therapeutic taxonomy of foodstuffs, classified according to their effect on bodily constitution and on temperament which, in their turn, reflected upon the typology of the humours. The *hortus sanitatis* [orchard of good health], the garden of salutory, nutritious, restorative and stimulant herbs, supplied both apothecary and housewife. It served a double function: alimentary as an extension of the kitchen, and therapeutic as the laboratory of man's health, of his physiological well-being, of his dreams and obsessive fantasies. It was a kitchen full of drugs reminiscent of the electuaries or 'confections' of the apothecary's repertory, prepared in ovens, in cauldrons, on hearths and in domestic slaughter-houses, just as in the back-rooms of an apothecary's shop. Ritual soups, sacrificial deserts, medicinal and intoxicating bread, pap and runny potage providing relief both internally and externally, to be taken both internally and externally; jams, gelatines, compots, 'condiments', tit-bits, pâtés; alimentary poultices and therapeutic cataplasms were part of the same double matrix, where eating meant not only continuing survival, fuelling life's fire, maintaining nature's warmth and replenishing vital juices, but also knowing oneself from within; it was a tonic, a cure, a weaving of dreams and fantasies, an evoking of journey and mirages. Culinary art and pharmacology belonged to the same sphere and were practiced in the same premises. The *spezzeria domestica* [home spicery] of the Bolognese physican, Azzoguidi (this being the title of his book written on the threshold of the nineteenth century) had its roots in home cooking. Management of the human condition lay somewhere between the laboratory bench and the mortar.

This dual function: the provision of nourishment and therapy (the latter being the province of the 'medicinal' apothecary), is readily observable in pharmacological texts. In order to appreciate how long this duality lasted and how the image of Hippocrates's man or Galenus's man persisted until the time (it may be said) of the Industrial Revolution, it is only necessary to examine the antidotaries.

The *Antidotarium bononiense* of 1771 ('a very newly compiled codex of matters relating to medicine', the previous work dating from 1750), among other galenic medicaments, has one named the 'Requies magna' ['great repose'] in a preparation created by Niccolò da Salerno, Arnaldo di Villanova's 'diacatholicon', Mesue's 'cardiac confection', Avicenna's pills, Niccolò da Salerno's 'pills I do not wish to be without', his 'long-life pills', his 'pilulae melanogogae', and his 'hysteria pills', together with sow thistle, turnip jam, sorb-apple jam, violet jam, rose jam, poultices made of bread crusts, the sweetest and most refined sugars and rose-waters.

Writing at the beginning of the same century, Giambattista Morgagni describes in his *Consulti medici* how viper's fat, powdered human cranium, woman's milk, earthworm oil, viper flesh, mouse blood were regularly prescribed, together with bread and parsley, in 'a decoction made with chicken broth', dandelion, fumitory, hop and lemon-balm. Millipede powder (considered an excellent diuretic) took its place alongside aniseed and saffron bread 'most beneficial to the lungs', endive soup with poultry meat, tower pigeons, skylarks, 'sweetened mercury', orgeats and spelt soup, as a prescription for scabies. 'Cheerful in mind and sound in body', 'gay and genial in conversation: lemon-balm and alkermes decoction', 'enema made from sweet almonds ...: tranquil, happy and contented mind'. Bread boiled in water and citron peel:

> Immediately before the broth I would take a small handful of coral and shrimps' eyes [an hors d'oeuvre which could well be a delicacy of the *nouvelle cuisine* served, say, with five grams of chervil] prepared and bound together with borage-leaf jam, dried rose syrup, or quince juice. And if it is judged inadvisable to suspend treatment whilst awaiting the arrival of spring, other forms of treatment can be devised using small quantities of either lentisk, citric sandalwood, quince wood or root of red rose, and adding to these borrage, violet flowers and the juice of sweet apples, an infusion then being made from this by adding to it the above-mentioned *bouquet garni*, or similar ingredients which should however contain extract of hypercium flower in which there is no alcohol.
>
> But whatever the season, well-regulated living-habits are always necessary and the best of all cures [so he advised in 1736 in a presumed case of aneurism]. The foods eaten should be veal, poultry and the occasional frog, though not from a swamp, and shrimp tails, rice soups, often with cow's milk, cooked sweet apples ....[27]

This founder of modern pathological anatomy, author of a path-breaking study in medical science: *De sedibus et causis morborum per anatomen indagatis* (1761), this ruthlessly precise and scientific investigator of the human cadaver, when assuming the guise of therapist, returned to his chamber of wonders with its herbal concoctions and black magic. Oak mistletoe, oil and powder of earthworm, bound with sage leaf conserve, 'tit-bit of yellow amber and human cranium', horn of a deer, 'tit-bit of powdered shrimps' eyes and mother-of-pearl bound together with seasoned rose jam', 'viper meat bound ... in mouthfuls', 'jaw of a pike'.

When it came to 'blood of a mouse', recommended by other leading physicians of the eighteenth century, he did have his doubts, but not so far as to reject it altogether:

> ... the blood of a mouse is apparently effective in preventing the progress of scrofula swelling for, without anointing the affected part, it is cured simply by laying on the neck a cotton cloth impregnated with this blood; while I find it hard to believe, nonetheless, no remedy however simple and ingenuous should

[27]   G. B. Morgagni, *Consulti medici*, ed. from unpublished minutes by E. Benassi, Bologna, 1935, p. 203.

be rejected out of hand when highly recommended by Great Men.[28]

In matters relating to 'the factory of mankind' (*opificium Dei*), popular lore and academic culture agreed, remarkably, on several points. Revolutions in attitude towards human physiology tended to encounter more obstacles and were more fraught than revolutions of a celestial kind. In 1832, powder of millipede was still the prescribed remedy against dropsy; and in 1833, it was still considered effective as a diuretic. The eighteenth century had seen the publication of *Dissertatio de millepedibus* (1711) by Elvert and *De millepedibus* (1771) by Richter. The French Revolution and the whirlwind of the Napoleonic era caused traumatic upheavals, sweeping away kingdoms and heads. But in Venice of the post Napoleonic age, apothecaries were still mixing Andromachus's so-called theriac, a special drug, dating back at least a millenium and a half, in which the viper had a fundamental therapeutic rôle.

[28]   Ibid. p. 228.

7

HYPERCATHARSIS

It seems that the corpses of Roman soldiers were easily distinguishable on the battle field from those of Persian soldiers for the reason that, unlike their oriental counterparts, the bodies of the Roman dead decayed so rapidly as to be unrecognizable after four days. According to the antiquarian expertise of Filippo Camerario (who develops Ammiano Marcellinus's 'first-hand experience'), the corpses of Roman soldiers decayed fast, whereas those of Persian soldiers appeared to desiccate and become seasoned like wood:

> For those of ours ... after they are killed, doe presently melt away, so that the fourth day a man cannot know a dead Roman by the features of his face. But the bodies of the Persians wax drie like a woodden stake, so that a man cannot perceive them to melt, or marre with corrupt matter; because while they live, they eate little, and withall their native country is extremely hot ... they had made their bodies drie, that they never spet, nor blew their nose and were marvellous active and nimble. Therefore, as *Xenophon* writeth, They did eate commonly watercresses, because, saith *Suidas*, this herbe staieth spettle and urine, a thing that our Phisitions utterly deny. However, it be, the Persians abstaine much from spetting, pissing and blowing their nose.[1]

The *questio* surrounding the properties of the nasturtium, on its inhibiting and desiccating 'virtues' ('it heats ... and refines and burns, draws, resolves and cuts deep, and when eaten [it was also used in baking] sharpens the mind'), sheds light on the image of death in western man, an image which has its roots in the late Classical period. It is remarkable how the picture passed down to us of the fourth century by Ammian Marcellinus[2] effectively fixes the mediaeval stereotype created by theology and ascetic culture in its most intransigent form. The rapidly putrefying cadavers of these warriors, their fast melting flesh reappear in the gloomy anthropology of death of the Middle Ages with its vision – as in a tragic obital radiography – of living man as already dead, orthanatologically alive, a putrescent and fetid yet mobile corpse, defunct *ab ovo*.

[1] Ph. Camerarius, *Operae Horarum subcisivarum...*, vol. I. pp. 86–6.
[2] Ammiano Marcellino, *Le storie*, ed. A. Selem, Torino, 1976, p. 383, [XIX, 9, 9].

So western man is watery and excremental, muddy and 'pituitous', not dry, purged and desiccated like the people of an arid climate, whose diet is sparse and who are as tough by nature embalmed in preparation for death. The prototype of the hermit belongs in the latter category: dried out by the torrid and scorching sands of African and oriental deserts, he requires only a few scanty crumbs of bread and herbs for his survival, attains awe-inspiring longevity whilst reducing himself to a fragile skeleton and acquires in some measure the wooden, mummified attributes of his Asiatic model. The metaphor of the tree of life finds an echo in the body of this ancient, rugged, yet vital and buoyant old ascete, hardened by vigils and dehydrating sapless diets, from which cooked foods were banned (even oil was often forbidden), and which rationed both water and sleep ruthlessly. These dietary regulations, which played with life and death, lead to a constant flow of visions and temptations, where carnal desire naturally loomed large and obsessively, whether of the gastronomic or the sexual kind. Given the states of physical exhaustion into which our subjects were plunged, they were constantly assailed by temptations and visions, a prey to endless cyclic and epic battles with the personifications of pleasure. As everyone knows, even Jesus Christ at a very vulnerable moment of his life was tempted by Satan who, taking advantage of his weakness from fasting, tried to 'make him fall into evil ways'.[3]

There was a kind of beauty, a sacred and inhuman beauty – which exuded 'an odour of life', as St Paul would have said – about the adherents of the *mensa sacra atque sobria [sacred and sober diet]*: 'Moses with gleaming aspect, Elijah controlling his body at will as though it were the spirit.'[4] It is probable that Christ followed a *regimen bonitatis*, too.

> Moreover, he made their bodies most fair in appearance by abstinence from earthy foods and an abundant consumption of those which are bright, and he made them tractable by instilling throughout their bodies the sensible and mobile spirit of the intellect; thus in a friendly manner he fortified his followers against vice and evil spirits, watched over them, made them pure as is appropriate for the temple of God, and reconciled their minds and spirits to God; indeed, there is nothing more conducive to health and a moderate disposition. For no food in nature should rather consumed than that by which nature itself is best fortified. For some say that Christ limited his consumption of

---

[3]   P. Franceschino Visdomini da Ferrara, *Discorsi morali sopra gli Evangeli correnti...*, Venezia, 1566, c. 31r.

[4]   Thomae Philologi Ravennas, *De vita hominis ultra CXX annos protrahenda*, Venetiis, anno sactissimi Iubilei 1550, s.n.t. I, c. 47v.

food, so that it did not overburden the digestion. Moreover, many, by sparing consumption of food, have enjoyed health and physical activeness even after a fast of forty days . . .[5]

The human body, 'almost an uncontaminated temple to God', if cleansed, purified and squeezed dry of the humours which represented the easiest channel of access for tempting and possessive devils, was in privileged communication with the divine ('the mind and soul are married to God'), was easily able to span a century or more. But the theories of Thomas of Ravenna, otherwise known as the 'Philologist' (1493?–1577), to whom Alvise Cornaro's *Vita sobria* owes not a little, were exaggeratedly optimistic. The *De vita hominis ultra CXX annos protrahenda* [*How to prolong human life beyond 120 years*], a handbook that this physician regularly dedicated upon the death of a pope to his successor so that he should be made aware of the correct technique to ensure maximum longevity, failed in its objective. None of the popes to whom it was addressed ever reached the age of a biblical patriarch. If Paul IV (the longest-lived of the three dedicatees) had a good haul, Julius III and Pius IV did not even make it to seventy.

A paste of mud and water, pituitary and mesenteric pulp in which verminous filaments hide and endlessly reproduce – the favourite pasture ground of earthworms of all kinds (in women particularly, gourds with swollen wombs full of liquid impurities), fermented sperm, hardened foam, frothing fleshy matter, opprobrium of the 'world of filth' (Iacopone):

> This flesh . . . is no better than filthy Rags [and] that thou art reduced so low as to be esteemed Nothing. The flesh . . . is in it self no better than froth and bubble, cloathed with a gay, but frail and decayed beauty; and time will shortly come, when all its boasted charms shall sink into a rotten Carcass, and be only food for worms . . . Consider a little those constant evacuations, the discharges of thy mouth, and nose, and other passages, without which the body cannot subsist; and ask they self how much this differs from a Common Shore . . . . For indeed this gaudy creature is no better than a bundle of Corruption, and food for Insects: First, Blood, then Man afterwards Worms and no Man.[6]

After St Bernard, the attack redoubled under Innocent III who remorselessly completed the debasing and hyper-realistic portrait of excremental man, the emanator of 'filth', excrement, urine, spittle,

---

5   · Ibid. c. 47v.

6   St Bernard Abbot of Clairvaux, *Meditationes piissimae ad humanae conditionis cognitionem* in *Operum tomus quintus. Aliena, dubia, notha, et supposititia,*

faeces, lice, worms and stench: a puny man 'formed . . . of foul sperm . . . food for worms which never cease to gnaw and consume: a mass of putrefaction, ever fetid and horribly dirty'.[7] Iacopone, for his part, writes on this cadaveric theme in sombre and desolate litanies:

> Behold a tree, Oh man!
> how delicately it bears its fruit,
> how scented and how
> tasty in the eating . . .
> Oh man, think of your burden:
> of the many lice and nits
> and the pitiless fleas
> that give you no peace.   (*Laude*, 76)

In a world pervaded by the 'deadly stench', in which 'stinking prurience' feeds the 'rotting lair' of 'carnal love', man seems to carry within him a miniature hell, one full of needling, relentless parasites, lice and fleas, which give him no respite, that deprive him of peace and repose. An infernal life, before falling into a revolting pit, in the 'putrid' chasm of hell which, particularly before Dante, was perceived as a nauseous abyss, where there accumulated a 'great stench', like an over-sized tomb where the body became 'very fetid and putrescent' and the flesh 'is consumed by worms'.

Old flesh, a carcass fading with the years, constituted – in this pitiless light – a horrible image of unmitigated filth:

> of surly and abrasive character,
> ugly and smelly
> with half closed eyes
> reddened and runny,
> upturned eyelids
> which seem bloody,
> a perpetually runny nose
> like water under a millwheel;
> his teeth, like a boar's fangs,
> are bared, the gums red
> as though always bloody;
> with a horrible expression
> and wretched countenance:
> and because of the great fetor
> that he exhales from his mouth,

Lugduni, 1679, pp. 140–1. English translation by George Stanhope, *Devout meditations; with regard to the state of human nature*, London, 1701, p. 365.

[7] Cardinal Lotharius (Innocent III), *De miseria humanae conditionis*, ed. M. Maccarrone, Lucani, 1955, p. 8.

the extreme stench
befouls the earth;
the thick cough
(irksome to witness)
with its smelly spittle
troubles the mind;
dry scabies
that seems one with the skin
like a dog with the mange;
he waves his hands like a windmill;
and now you'll see him playing
for he's scratching
the old man with lumbago
like a bent violin bow.   (*Laude* 57)

A grotesque monster dripping with mucous and phlegm, contaminating the earth with his evil, pituous and scabious smells, ceaselessly scratching himself, an unholy mass of catarrh.

It was inevitable that, in this dark and oppressive atmosphere of denigration of the human flesh, the earthworm should end by acquiring the role of an exterminating angel, of a ruthless avenger of human corruption and depravity, and be as invulnerable and everlasting as one of the terrible celestial punishers unleashed by the Almighty on earth to correct and annihilate: *vermis immortalis* (Innocent III). The earthworm reaches its macabre and triumphal apotheosis in ecclesiastical culture, when raised to the level of a sacred and inescapable instrument of divine justice, of an official 'executioner' in the system of and reward and retribution planned by the judiciary of the other world.

But the ever fragrant and often incorruptible bodies of the 'men of God', of the blessed, who were a 'special' kind of dead, would escape the atrocious demolition that awaited all common mortal flesh. The flesh of God's revered servant, hardened and virtually mineralized by tough vigils and pared to the bones by pitiless dieting, would smell after death as 'sweet as a perfumed apple' (Iacopone). The harsh discipline of the desert, the asceticism of the cloister were a prerequisite of the purification of the flesh. Mortification was a premise for preservation, *post exitum*. After five years, San Romualdo's corpse was found intact in its tomb: 'exhumed in this fashion from the tomb, the body was recovered almost entire and sound'.[8] An almost constant rule among these 'men of God', according to the legendary hagiographer, was the perfect preservation of their remains. Moreover, weird and wonderful things could

[8]   St Peter Damian, *De vita sancti Romualdi*, in *Opera omnia*, Venezia, 1783, vol. II, col. 483.

happen if one lay on top of a holy tomb. A disconcerting instance of this (undoubtedly an occult manifestation of divine grace) was the loss of hair that befell a certain Gislardo, a cowherd from the Haute Dauphiné near Vienne.

> One evening, having lead his oxen to pasture at nightfall and left them to graze before the sacred tomb, he chose a corner of it, lay down and fell asleep. When he awoke after a peaceful slumber, he arose to find all his hair and beard had fallen off, in the place where he had slept. He had been hirsute, for sure, according to the avowals of those who had known him previously, and had sported a flowing beard.
>
> On another occasion, a division of soldiers had gathered together at the monastery to pray. While the others refreshed themselves that night with sleep, one of them who had been charged with looking after the horses, having let them loose in the already mentioned field so that they should graze, followed them closely but as soon as he lay down and slept, he lost all his hair from his head. And when he arose his head immediately looked bald and shining like one who bears a splendid and sparkling helmet upon his head. His friends, as soon as they saw what had befallen him, were amazed and said to him: 'To be sure, you must have fallen asleep on the tomb of a saint.' And he, bathed in tears, to his shame and anguish, was forced to bear these signs for evermore.[9]

Though strangely manifested, this is an example of a taboo to protect the holy cubiculum.

When the theology of the worm began to wane, medical literature stepped in to support the cause of these instruments of death that bored their way into the delicate and defenceless human frame, with blind and uncontrollable fury. In the seventeenth century and to some extent in the following century, these creatures continued to be seen in the threatening and ambiguous, erroneous and ambivalent light of 'possessor'. White, and born of 'putrid, pituitous matter', or red derived from 'putrid blood', 'the putrescence being transmitted to the veins, and through these to the heart, they cause cardiaglia and swooning', 'they inflict dreadful and ghastly apoplexy on anyone who is possessed by them'.[10]

Mainstream medical literature, from Hippocrates to Alessandro Tralliano and from Galenus to Gerolamo Mercuriali, who devotes the entire second book of his *De morbis puerorum* to worms, had never ceased to

9   *Cronaca di Novalesa*, ed. G. C. Alessio, Torino, 1982, pp. 123–5.
10   A. Salando, *Trattato sopra li vermi, cause, differenze, pronostico e curatione*, Verona, 1607, p. 3 *passim*.

be concerned with them. On the other hand, popular imagination, closely reflected in the books of 'secrets' (a widely-read form of literature which provides an important source for the reconstructing of the mental outlook of bygone days), held them responsible also for convulsive attacks affecting children. In one of the most popular of these books, the *Secreti* of the self-styled 'Reverend Donno', Alessio Piemontese, he proposes a remedy intended to cure infants who are moonstruck, that is when they tremble and fall into a faint, an illness which occurs in children often because a two headed worm insinuates itself near to the heart and this causes them to tremble and often to die . . . . And many infants that have died from this sickness because the right remedies were lacking, have been opened and found with a worm attached to their heart.[11]

But the phantom of the *vermiculus rodens* turned up everywhere, in the books of wise man, as well as in grandma's fairy tales and nurse's stories. It was a visionary dogma which encompassed the most surprising beliefs: for instance, that worms might be the cause of dumbness. These projections of humanity's worse sides, these slimy incarnations of the worst physical and moral excrements of *homo sapiens* are subjected to a slow process of anthropomorphization which transforms them in the seventeenth century into destabilizing agents of physiological and psychological balance. 'The vital processes are affected not a little. For the sick are irritable and unstable.'[12] These voracious predators attack the morsels of food in the stomach, devouring them and thus depriving the body infested with them of its nourishment; 'A ravenous hunger also occurs from time to time, for no other reason than that these creatures are occasionally so voracious that they snatch food directly from the stomach and then, as Galen says, the body becomes horribly emaciated.'[13] In Aldrovandi, and even more so in Codronchi, his contemporary, the signs of infestation are increasingly alarming:

[11]   D. Alessio Piemontese, *Secreti* del Reverendo D. A. P. divisi in quattro parti. Nuovamente ristampati e da molti errori corretti. Con un'ottima regola per la conservazione della vita umana, secondo molti eccellenti uomini per tutti li dodeci mesi dell'anno. Ed una tavola copiosissima per ritrovare i rimedj con ogni facilità, Venezia [1780], p. 22. The first edition of this most excellent book, of European renown, is dated 1550. Cf. N. Zemon Davis, *Le culture del popolo. Sapere, rituali e resistenze nella Francia del Cinquecento* [corresponds to *Society and Culture in Early Modern France*, London, 1975] Italian trans. Torino, 1980, pp. 340, 359. The French transl. of the *Secreti* is dated 1559. Cf. J. Ferguson, *Bibliographical Notes on Histories of Inventions and Books of Secrets*, London, 1981.

[12]   U. Aldrovandi, *De animalibus insectis libri septem, cum singulorum iconibus ad vivum expressis. . .* , Bononiae, 1602, p. 667.

[13]   Ibid. p. 667.

... the eyes glaze over all of a sudden, the cheeks grow pale, at night they run with cold sweat, their mouths drool excessively, by day they suffer from an enormous thirst, their tongue and lips are dry, they suffer from terrible halitosis, their general appearance is sickly, they suffer from nausea and frequent vomiting, they reject food, their teeth chatter, at night especially they bite their tongues ...[14]

The worms that inhabit men are seen in the dubious and murky role of malevolent scourgers of the flesh, goaded by a collective conscience so that they become a permanent affliction, which could always creep up and attack the heart. In Alessio Piemontese, as already observed, the affliction of being 'moon-struck' and the motor crisis in the young lunatic, for which the worm was held responsible, has many traits in common with the shattered limbic system of those who suffered convulsions and felt their 'hearts being devoured' (Florian Canale). In both cases the heart is the organ on which the maleficent agent has evil intentions:

> ... worms [explains Battista Codronchi] from time to time cause great and dangerous fevers from the vile and putrescent fumes which arise from them and reach the heart by means of the veins and arteries. If the worms grow very many in number and make a significant assault on the vital nature of the organism, the pulse becomes weak, unclear, irregular and from time to time absent altogether; sufferers are overcome by mental disorders of greater or lesser degree because of the viciousness and evil nature of the worms. Occasionally there arises from the same cause a palpitation and trembling of the heart; around the stomach and bowels there occur gripes, stabbing and incredible gnawing pains and heartburns. They attack the stomach in such a way that, either because of their essential nature or because of the vile and malodorous vapours they give off, the appetite is completely lost .... Because the stomach has a close relationship with the brain, worms, either because of their strange movements or through their bites and perforations, or through the putrescent and evil vapours which rise to the brain, cause dizziness, epileptic fits, convulsions, mental wanderings and lethargies, and they also cause a swelling of the belly so that sufferers seem to be afflicted with dropsy ...[15]

[14]   Ibid.
[15]   B. Codronchi, *De morbis qui Imolae, et alibi communiter hoc anno MDCII vagati sunt*. Commentariolum in quo potissimum de lumbricis tractatur ... auctore Baptista Codronchio, medico imolensi, Bononiae, 1603, p. 21.

The clinical picture is impressive: fading heartbeat, loss of appetite, relentless fevers, lacerating pains and insect bites, bloated stomachs as in dropsy; and more: deliriums, lethargies, convulsions, dizziness, epilepsy. An overwhelming and devastating attack which mounts up from the stomach irrisistibly and invades the brain.

Paolo Egineta (quoted by Codronchi) claimed that 'many perished eaten by worms and suffering convulsions'. Other medical men maintained that they had seen them issue forth from the groin. Nicola Fiorentino recalls the case of one patient who had been saved because 'many worms had erupted from the navel'. Trincavelius recounts how a five-year-old child 'in whom worms had gnawed through the belly and come out of the navel'. Marcello Donato relates that at Trent at the time of the Council, 'there was a certain woman who, in addition to the fact that one month her menstrual bleeding came out of her navel, regularly also brought forth living worms'.[16]

This woman who ejects menstrual blood and earthworms from her navel seems the very image of putrid and contaminated, yet living, flesh, generating 'animalia infecta' from decaying, unclean menstrual matter.

Many people managed to survive by vomiting them, with the aid of emetics: such a case is recorded by Amato Lusitano, in which a woman who had a lipomatic attack and 'with much vomiting expelled a fair mass of worms and cured herself of the gnawings and lacerations of the stomach which had often caused her to fall into seizures and faints'. The same physician describes the case of another young woman who was dying, but who after taking a vomitory draught, threw up 'hairy-backed worms' and was saved. Antonio Benivieni recalls for his part the case of a carpenter who having suffered continuously from heart pains, regained his health no sooner had he 'thrown up a worm, four inches in length, replete, with a small, red and rotund head'.

The convulsions brought on by these worms could be so impossible to contain that Vittorio Trincavelli described how he saw some boys: '*qui a verminibus adeo male affecti . . . retrorsum adeo convellerentur, ut pene calcaneis caput contingerent* [they contorted themselves so desperately that they even reached the napes of their necks with their heels].

A similar case was also observed by Codronchi, Imola's chief medical inspector, that of Arrigo Fontana's fourteen-year-old son who died five days after an attack: 'because of the savage nature of the worms, he was tormented by great convulsive spasms, along with mighty screaming fits and twistings and turnings'.[17] There were still, however, some 'evil women' who 'judged that this had happened through witches' spells': a victim of witches, it was said, because it was difficult to distinguish

16   Ibid. p. 29. The preceding quotations also come from this work.
17   Ibid. pp. 30–1.

between a poisonous spell and poisoning by worm. If the effects were the same, the causes (it was held, not without a thread of logic) could not be very dissimilar.

If the affected person did not die, the worms had of necessity to jump out of his body and in so doing would take all sorts of different routes. On a certain occasion in 1587, Codronchi saw them come forth, one from the mouth and two 'from the backside', in this case, of an attorney's wife, named Rosa. That same year, Sister Francesca, a Capuchin nun, delirious with pain, expelled a great number of these from her stomach. Black earthworms five foot in length and and all hairy would appear from the anus. But they might also make their way out through the ears and nostrils. Antonio Benivieni recounts how a friend 'suffering from intense headaches, dimmed eyesight, a wandering mind, dulled voice and flagging spirit', at the end of his days 'expelled worms a palm in length from his right nostril'. On the other hand, a peasant woman (according to the indefatigable Codronchi) who suffered 'incredible palpitations and fluctuations of the stomach' which was distended and swollen as though she were pregnant, rid herself of a great number of worms. It is said of a barber that: 'he had a belly which swelled up spontaneously, and brought forth from it, as well as a lot of putrid liquid matter (such as often appears as a result of worms) a long string of worms like cucumbers, all hanging together'.

These images of man as a latrine, a dung-heap (*sterquilinium*, St Bernard was fond of saying), 'a bag of excrement, food for worms' (*idem*), 'a mass of putrefaction' (Innocent III) fit perfectly in a theological world which had to exist side by side with revolting pathological states and with a medical system that saw mankind through his excreta, using this even as medication. In a world infested with worms, verminous man who spat forth evil-smelling creatures from every orifice and pore could hardly have enjoyed a less noble picture of himself than that painted by these men and women who dreamed of purity and perfection, of shining angels softly born aloft, of uncontaminated heavens and incorruptible places.

Wild beasts (*ferae*) was the word Hippocrates applied to worms, the Latins used 'saeva animantia' and Suidas κακὰ θηρια. With a distinct penchant for children, young people and women, the cruel and murderous worm did not however overlook the elderly. In Imola in the ill-starred year of 1602, the eight-year-old Sebastiano Mariani died a few hours after ejecting two worms from his mouth. Alberico Pasini had a young maid who died after ejecting 'either from above or from below' fifty or more worms of not inconsiderable size in the space of seven days. Oliviero Mazzolani, a carpenter in his sixty-fifth year, passed from this world after lying in bed for many days and then expelled 'many thin worms'. An old woman called Pirunda, after likewise expelling a large number of worms 'passed from this life'. Tommaso Arduini's wife, who was seriously afflicted, 'having excreted a worm of wondrous length . . . exchanged death for life'. A blacksmith by the name of Cesare Canevari, 'one day was troubled by a worm and becoming hydropic, his belly swelled, he excreted a long worm and went from this life'. Rinaldo de Albana, a young peasant also died of a swollen stomach. With bloated belly, feeble, irregular and faltering pulse, Antonio, Lodovico di Trarivio's son, who was convalescing from pleurisy was forced to take again to his bed after a day or two, and 'after excreting a live and slippery worm with spotted skin, gave up the ghost'.

Earthworms were presumed to be the prime cause of fatal lethargies: they were seen as death-dealing hoards invading the vital centres of the body in a series of relentless marches. In his *Sepulchretum* (a sombre gallery of pathological cases brought to light 'by the examination of anatomies', a *pynacotheca imaginum* of bodies quartered and disembowelled by a surgical lancet), Theophilus Bonnet, the great collector of 'extravagant' anatomies, reconstructs synthetically the clinical story of an eleven-year-old girl who had fallen into a gloomy and rapid lethargy from which she had no hope of recovery:

> A lethargy was fatal to a girl of eleven years within the space of five hours. When her skull was opened, her brain was found free from inflammation and its ventricles were intact. But in her bowels there were found a dozen long slender worms in a mass, and the bowel was found to be inflamed with remarkable redness, in spite of the application of enemas, a cautery to the coronal suture, and cupping glasses.[18]

They were ubiquitous: not even the brain escaped their rapaciousness. Violent migraines that induced delerium and madness were attributed to them.

> In the case of migraines, whose pain is very violent, worms are present only rarely, although Hollerius says that this occurs . . . . The Poles call this affliction *Stowny roback* and the Germans *Hauptwurm*; it was once common in Germany and Hungary, and its sufferers all fell into a frenzy or manic fit; after their death their brains were dissected and worms were found . . . . Cornelius Gemma, discussing the lethal haemotrite in the appendix to his book, *Cosmocrit*, relates that a woman in a town near the

[18]   Theophile Bonnet, *Sepulchretum sive anatomia practica ex cadaveribus morbo denatis proponens historias et observationes omnium humani corporis affectuum, ipsorumque causas reconditas revelans*, Lugduni, 1700, vol. I, p. 167.

Mosel was overcome by a very violent and protracted headache; after her death her brain was dissected, and there was found in it a great mass of decay and worms.[19]

Jean Fernel relates how a canon of the Anthonian Order, tormented by cholic pain, after taking a special draught: 'deposited a worm, like a lizard in shape, but fatter, hairy and standing on four feet'. Having expelled this bloated and hirsute verminous monster shaped like a lizard, the good canon gave up the ghost.

Such disquieting clinical sagas (described by Fernel who was highly regarded by Jérome Cardan, considered by Fallopius to be the greatest doctor and philosopher of his time, hailed by Guy Patin as a 'saint, alongside Galenus') were more frequent than might be imagined. Strange and amazing they plunge us in a nightmarish world (it is hard to say whether visionary or real) in which the human body apparently harboured phalanxes of nasty sadistic animals.

The episode narrated by Benvenuto Cellini is well-known and, in the presence of so many witnesses, we have no reason to doubt it. While convalescing, he had Cardinal Cornaro transport him to the villa on Monte Cavallo. On arrival, he relates:

> I started to vomit, and with this vomit my stomach expelled a hairy worm, a quarter of an arm in length: its hairs were long and the worm hideous, with patches all over of differing colours, green black and red . . .[20]

It would now seem that the stomach has been changing over the centuries and is no longer that dark sack of wonders from which there might spring forth, in vomit, the most extraordinary objects: little polychrome monsters, undefinable and gelatinous things and, in the case of any who had a spell cast upon them, whole loads of bric-à-brac.

This remarkable vision of the human stomach as an eccentric laboratory of unstoppable fertility, spewing strange and disturbing objects, is illustrated by the case witnessed by Leonardo Fioravanti in October 1558 at an inn not far from Spoleto. The innkeeper's wife who, for twenty-five days 'had been unable to rest either by day or by night and had terrible attacks whenever she ate', after being examined by the travelling doctor, took two grams of 'diaromatic', one of this genial Bolognese charlatan's miraculous remedies. (He was a contemporary of Benvenuto Cellini and Berengario da Carpi.) Two hours after swallowing it:

19   *Insectorum sive minimorum animalium theatrum.* Olim ab Edoardo Wottono, Conrado Gesnero, Thomaque Pennio inchoatum, tandem, Tho. Moufeti Londinatis opera sumptibusque maxime concinnatum, auctum, perfectum. Et ad vivum expressi iconibus supra quingentis illustratum, Londini, 1634, p. 283.

20   B. Cellini, *La vita*, ed. G. Davico Bonino, Torino, 1973, p. 188.

> she began to vomit, as will indeed occur after taking a diaroma-
> tic, and spent the whole night vomiting the rubbish that lay in
> her belly. And amongst the other things that she brought up,
> there was an object like a uterine tumour , but round and hairy in
> form, and alive, which filled me with wonder, because I had
> never seen the like before. I washed it and placed it in a box in
> cotton wadding so that I might show people this portentous
> object; but no sooner had we arrived in Pesaro, the fine city of
> the Duke of Urbino, than upon inspection I found that it had
> dissolved and that so small a quantity remained that it had no
> shape; nonetheless, when the woman had vomited it, it was large
> and wondrous, as I have said . . .[21]

Like starfish at the bottom of the sea, so did unidentified objects surface
from the depths of men's stomachs, living thromboses, obscure furry
creatures which torn from their environment, melted after a few days
leaving nothing but a jelly-like blob.

This rounded object torn from the stomach by the emetic force which
sucked it in, can be placed side by side with numerous other exhibits
expelled from the intestine, in a museum of the imagination or, indeed,
in a chamber of nature's wonders and miracles; or, if preferred, in a
exhibition of satanic art, of diabolic ephemera.

However incredible it may seem, collections of this kind, of objects
thrown up by the possessed during exorcism, did actually exist in the
past, thus belying the opinion which held that 'objects' thrown up by the
possessed were no more than artefacts out of the Devil's box of tricks, an
example of the great juggler up to his pranks, indulging a whim, enjoying
a joke or a confidence trick. Those who believed in this theory held that:

> in order to deceive men the better, Satan causes these things to
> appear [needles, hair, nails, stones . . .] in this manner, so that
> they should seem miraculous, these objects being seen and
> considered natural; yet it being impossible by reason of their
> form and essence that they should have entered the body
> naturally, they are in truth far from being real and natural; they
> may so seem because they come out and are emitted by the body
> or in vomit or from beneath and appear chiefly among the liquid
> matter expelled by the body; but if you were to keep them for a
> matter of six or eight days, you might see them turn to liquid and
> become nothings . . .[22]

21   L. Fioravanti, *Il tesoro della vita humana* Venezia, 1570, cc. 80v–81r.
22   G. Menghi, *Compendio dell'arte essorcistica, et possibilità delle mirabili, et*
stupende operationi delli demoni, et de i malefici. Con li rimedij opportuni alle
infirmità meleficiali, Bologna, 1582, p. 160.

The round, hairy 'thing', which Fioravanti had caused to be vomited with the aid of his powerful emetics (even he was basically performing the exorcist's function by cleansing the pit of the stomach of its sickness) would seem to fit well into the catalogue of fantastic forms designed by demons, which then melted away in a few days.

However, one problem remains. According to a great exponent of the technique of exorcism, the objects ejected by the possessed were solid, real and not transient or ephemeral: they were destined to last. The pre-eminent sixteenth-century expert in the 'art of exorcism', Girolamo Menghi (a Minorite friar), rejected the theory about spells cast by a conjuror/devil, 'a creator of [illusory] trifles', a fabricator of evanescent baubles, and called instead upon a variety of different experiences, quoting, for instance, the 'astonishing events' which had taken place at a Franciscan sanctuary:

> In the Marches of Ancona, in a certain place called by the name of Monte Brandone, there stands a church built in honour of the Virgin, and here God works many miracles in honour of his mother and here do many who are possessed come from distant places to be freed of their malady; here does the mantle of the blessed Jacob of the order of St Francis, no sooner laid upon the shoulders of the possessed person, because of its holy properties, cause him to be immediately delivered of the evil; and if he is bewitched, then he throws up all manner of maleficent objects, which the friars gather and hang on the walls of the church, where (I understand from persons worthy of trust) they still hang and can be readily seen by all, which means that if they were fictitious . . . they would not last and be seen for so long a space of time.[23]

We have it from reliable sources, however, that these 'maleficent objects' have disappeared into nothingness and that the friars have no memory of them today . . . But Girolamo Menghi assures us that in Bologna (and here we return to the home-ground of the exorcist/doctor Fioravanti) in the home of a rector of St Antonio's church 'a man well-versed in averting devils, a fearless expert in exorcising and expelling them', not only saw 'many remarkable things vomited by the possessed' but was also able to pick them up with his very hands:

> these [things] I have touched several times with my own hands, and among them have seen two very large chestnuts, in one of which there was embedded the rare silver *paolo* [coin minted under Paul III], and it was hard to see how it had come to be

23   Ibid. p. 161.

placed inside, the shell not even being broken to the size of the coin. The other was full of mallet or pommel needles that transfixed the chestnut from one side to the other with such artistry that they seemed to have been born there; and many other things worthy of wonder, which were preserved for a long time, and such things I have seen with many other exorcists.[24]

Among the pernicious objects and 'wondrous things' thrown up by the treacherous stomach or otherwise disposed of by the body, it appears that in past centuries the body contained within its internal organs a kind of *Wunderkammer*, a reservoir which could pour out the weirdest things: outsized worms, small, hairy and oddly-coloured monsters reminiscent of lizards, breathing lumps, chestnuts into which some mysterious hand had inserted nails, needles and 'marvellously adorned' locks of hair (Girolamo Menghi).

From the pit of the stomach there might surface fakir-like objects, an abnormal quantity of swallowed items, culinary bric-à-brac. In a book which came out in the last decade of the sixteenth century, the Florentine doctor Antonio Benivieni records the case of a patient who seemed 'to have a new and remarkable kind of illness': a woman in her sixties who appeared to want to tear out some mysterious and raging pain in the lower stomach.

> She broke out in a terrible scream, and her whole belly began to swell to such an extent that you would believe that she was seven months pregnant; once her voice was exhausted, she flung herself here and there all over the room, placing the soles of her feet against the back of her neck and then leaping back to a standing position: lying down like this and leaping up again, she repeated this action time and time again .... When she was asked what she was doing, she had absolutely no idea. But I, having investigated this kind of illness, believe that the disease is born upwards from the womb by reason of evil vapours which then reach and attack the heart and brain. So I was not a little surprised when the application of the appropriate medicine had absolutely no effect. But I judge that I should by no means abandon this arduous battle; meanwhile the woman had become more violent and would stare wild-eyed about her, until at length she began to vomit violently. In the course of this, she brought up long bent nails and bronze pins, together with hair and wax, all mixed into a ball. Finally she brought up a lump of food which was so large that no-one could have swallowed it whole. When

---

[24]   Ibid. p. 162

she had done the same thing several times before my very eyes, I judged that she was possessed of an evil spirit which deceived the eyes of onlookers while the woman was doing these things. She was therefore placed in the hands of spiritual doctors and has confirmed my diagnosis subsequently with clearer signs and evidence. For I have often myself heard her prophesying and, moreover, seen her engaged in the following . . .[25]

This frantic old woman with her rolling eyes and bloated tummy resembling a repugnant and impossible pregnancy, with her yells and convulsions, her vomiting of bent nails and torrent of undigested food, after passing from physician to priest is metamorphosed into an oracular prophetess. A grotesque caricature of maternity, a teratological symptom of painful and troubled old age, she casts an alarming light on delirium and witchcraft, again bestowing upon the stomach the rôle of multivalent store of ignoble and contaminated treasures. Fermenting sybils in the throws of convulsion, like bruised and suspect mushrooms, secreting poisonous clots, in a restless social environment 'swarming' with visionaries, prophets and pythons.

This turbulent scent, where soul merged with body, holy with profane, health with salvation, was part and parcel of everyday life, and in this doctor and exorcist ineluctably exchanged rôles. Antonio Benivieni's description causes us to make the following interesting observation: if this 'case' came to be classified as a new and extraordinary clinical event, it could be deduced that demoniacal obsessions were not yet, as far as the early sixteenth century was concerned, the commonplace affair that they were to become in the latter part of the century and the following one.

The techniques of evacuation and the art of the exorcist were so interlocked as to seem almost indistinguishable. 'Maleficent diseases', colossal indigestions, caused by 'objects' poisonous to the soul, were cured by emetics and purges. White hellebore or veratrum, and black hellebore (the most drastic and radical 'simples') reigned supreme: they were insidious, toxic and unsettling 'both disturbing to the body and liberating to the soul'. 'Extreme maladies require extreme remedies' seems to have been the Hippocratic precept. For those who maintained that therapeutic intervention was a *conflictus* between illness and health to be resolved by a hard battle using potent medicines ('the illness and therefore the medicament should be strong; for strength leads to victory'),[26] the *vomitoria* made of veratrum were preferable to purges

[25]   A. Benivieni, *De abditis nonnullis ac mirandis morborum et sanationum causis*, Firenze, 1507, Ch. VIII, c. bII.

[26]   P. Castelli, *Emetica. In qua agitur de vomitu et vomitoriis*, Romae, Ex typ. I. Mascardi, 1634, p. 1. Castelli, among other things, was the author of *Opobal-*

because 'the expulsion of vomit is powerful'. The careless, timorous or ignorant doctor, on the other hand, would usually prescribe remedies which, as Jérome Cardan also held, exacerbate the affliction irremediably because 'they go with gross and melancholic matter, take away what is insubstantial and leave behind what is thick, and render incurable what was previously a curable illness'.

Pietro Castelli, author of *Emetica* (1634) (a treatise, which is detailed and thorough to the point of obsession and which 'treats of vomiting and vomitories'), takes these lily-livered therapists to task ('who indulge and yield to an illness'), for ignoring either by incompetence or through fear, the necessity of attacking serious illness with powerful weapons. ('A powerful illness requires a powerful medicine.') In his opinion those who merely administer weak remedies, 'only use medicaments they call *benedicta*, which may mitigate the affliction, but never expel it completely if indeed it were great and violent', whence 'they use only those drugs which they themselves describe as *blessed*. These mollify the disease, it is true, but they do not drive it out completely if it happens to be great and powerful. Hence, these drugs ought rather to be called *cursed* by the sick, since they do not remove the disease.'[27] Pietro Castelli's treatise, in which 'the measures to be taken before vomiting, during vomiting and after vomiting' are subjected to a careful and thoughtful scrutiny, is a monument to the most drastic and terrifying of emetics: Areteus of Cappadocia's hellebore, which he called a 'sacred medicine', also known as 'melampod' (in its black form), 'for it is said', states Dioscorides, 'that the goatherd Melampus was the first to use it to purge and cure the daughters of Praetus, who had become insane'. This plant, the exorcist's plant, which was so singular that when picked it necessitated a special ritual for its protection ('when it is dug up, they stand and pray for help to Apollo or Aesculapius'), was also used by people in Classical times to purge their homes.

The ritual of liberation by purge using the hellebore began with a whole series of preliminary steps including lotions, baths to induce sweating, moistening of the body, poultices, enemas, fomentations and special diets.

During the expulsion fit it was necessary to keep an eye on matters to try to avoid the 'accidents', which happened not infrequently. 'Helleborism' could easily take a dramatic turn for the worse with the onset of cephalea, dizziness, impaired vision, hiccupping, convulsions, suffocation, loss of voice and strength. The toxic fit from alkaloids (veratrine) was inseparable in varying degrees from the 'heroic' drug that left the

---

samum. *Examinatum, defensum, iudicatum, absolutum et laudatum*, Messina, 1640; and also of a tract on the civet, *De hyaena odorifera*, Francofurti, 1668.
27   Ibid. p. 1.

intestinal linings in a state of severe inflammation, not to mention persistent thirst and blood-spitting. Moreover, in certain cases, even more
extreme forms of treatment were practiced, such as the *superpurgatio* (a
combination of induced vomiting and a purge) or *hypercatharsis*, during
which the patient was secured by means of 'chains or bonds': tied and
parcelled up. This was a therapy/torture, which bordered on sacrifice,
because just as the exorcists relied on supercatharsis so did the physicians
count on total liberation, *superpurgatio*: the expulsion of manifestations
of wickedness, whether in the form of pernicious objects, tapeworms,
ringworms, pinworms, black sooty or melancholic humours, or catarrhic
obstructions and overactive phlegm. There was certainly good reason to
pray for help not just to Apollo and Aesculapius but to the whole pantheon of gods, and to all the saints of the Catholic empyreum.

Presented with this mind-boggling picture one is prompted to ask how
far these harrowing cleansings leading to convulsions which were hard to
control or guide, how far these conditions of hallucinatory *transe*, of dizziness and loss of sight and speech, or nervous agitation whose intensity it
is difficult to fathom but was surely exhausting and shattering, and how
far these moments of visionary ecstacy and crisis, undermined the
psychological balance and mental order of those who subjected themselves to such techniques of purification. Beyond every mechanistic and
crudely deterministic account, it seems necessary to ask oneself what
impact such cures might have had not only on the development of the
whole range of human sensibilities, mentalities, dreams, or the collective
imagination of the superpurgated, but also on the establishment of cultural protocols and on the working conditions of the gnosological apparatus. It might be interesting to know if, how far and to what extent the
hellebore, an emetic/visionary drug, passed from being an inducer of
revulsive dizziness to acting as a stimulant 'object' of a modified or
altered culture. It would appear that, after an extended period of only
moderate use,[28] these vomitory and expulsive techniques reached their
peak in popularity in the second half of the sixteenth century, there to
remain unchallenged for over a century. The decades which knew the
highest rate of diabolism, the golden age of witch-hunts, the Tridentine
'reconquest', Catholic supremacy, the hegemony of theocracy, happened to coincide with the age of dizziness and superpurges, of ostanta-
tious and vehement cleansings of the sullied flesh, of obsession with individual catharsis and collective purification. Research for the furtherance
of purity (or of salvation in purity) inevitably lead to the medico-
ecclesiastical ideology of supercatharsis.

[28]   '... helleborus niger, preparatus per magisterium, paucis notum ... non est pro
          corporibus delicatis et nobilis complexionis' (A. di Villanova, *De conservanda
          iuventute et retardanda senectute*, in *Opera omnia*, Basileae, 1575, p. 815).

In the treatise of Pietro Castelli (the devout doctor who during his teaching post at the University of Messina had created a botanical garden, dedicated it to the Virgin Mary, and divided it into twelve sections corresponding in name and patronage to each of the Apostles), there seems to be evidence that it was written to promote and disseminate the use of a pharmaceutical technique which had been somewhat abandoned, perhaps as too risky and dangerous. His defence of 'heroic' medicaments, of strong and potent drugs, of radical and far-fetched remedies, tends – in the Hippocratic sense – to the heroization of medicine as a perfect reflection of the religious tensions of the Counter-Reformation, the agonistic fervour of saints and missionaries, the ecstasies and swoonings of female saints, the flights, raptures, screams and dizzy spells of male saints, friars, ascetics, hermits, soothsayers and visionaries. The ravaging effects of the hellebore, the hastening and slowing of the pulse, nervous system and brain, caused by veratrum, the fainting fits and therapeutic convulsions, the leaps into unreality, the loss of balance (to which should be added other kinds of permanent toxification caused by other herbs and self-punitory diets) may have had some imponderable relationships (though small and not verifiable) with the swoonings, catalepsy, warblings and flights of the armies of ecstatics, convulsionary visionaries, in that atmosphere charged with giddiness, raptures and loss of consciousness. The case of Giuseppe di Copertino is a symptom of a widespread neurosis, obscure in origin and complex in aetiology. Are we indulging in wild conjecture to suppose that 'helleborism', with the mutation in chromatic values and artificial blackouts, may have imperceptibly influenced the new sensitivity to colour or the theory and practice of *chiaroscuro*: the dramatic game of reverberations, of light and shade? Can psychic fluctuations be regarded as totally independent of visual fluctuations, of non-rectilinear lines, of forms in motion, of accentuated and dramatic contortionism, of the harmonizing of architectural and pictorial modes, of the excesses of a wild and unbalanced imagination, of a mental world devoid of remorse, a world full of frenzy; of the protean ballet of unfamiliar and jerky movements, of the game of mutation, of the climate of permanent metamorphosis and pathological sensuality? May we conjecture the existence of some point of contact between 'helleborism' and the 'baroque'? Perhaps the breathtaking excesses of baroque poetry and music, the 'deliriums from odiferous herbs' of the seventeenth century, of those who could 'change the square into the round', the transformed geometries, altered spaces, circles turned into squares, the new grammar of unreal and improbable forms, of mutated geometrical rules had all felt the acrid aura of emetic herbs, the 'great and awsome' (Leonardo Fioravanti) liberating giddiness of these toxic cures? We cannot escape the fact that the mental androgyny, disguises and masks of the seventeenth-century novel, to which ambiguous games of transformation and mistaken identity are fundamental (witness the taste for deforming mirrors, Circe and her peacock, *travestiti* ballets, the dance of opposites), even if they bear no immediate relation to the pharmacology of the period, seemed to originate in turbulent and disordered fantasies ('fantasy' *per se* was still regarded as a disturbance of the reason, quite close to diabolical 'ludificatio' or derision, different from 'imaginative' fantasy). Proteus is the emblem of mental metamorphosis. In the seventh Discourse of the *Criticón* of Baltasar Gracián, 'the Fountain of Deceptions', Critilo and Andrenio perceive arriving by an impossible road, a carriage:

> which was not usual on so bad a road; but being made so artificially, and with such nimble Joints; it passed through all the rubs, streights, and difficulties; the beasts that drew it were two flea-bitten Jades, like Serpents, and the Coach-man a Fox; *Critilo* asked if it were not a *Venetian* Chariot; to which the Coach-man replied in a manner far from the purpose, as if he understood not, what he demanded; within rode a Monster, or rather many, for so often changed he his colour, and shape, sometimes black, anon white, then young, anon old, sometimes Great, sometimes little, then a Man, a Woman, a Beast, that *Critilo* soon discovered him to be the famous Proteus.[29]

This many-faced monster, enclosed in a surrealist coach driven by a wolf and drawn by two snakes, gives us a startling image of the kind of raving madness and mental disorder induced by the pharmacological artifices of the age (seventeenth century), in which the apothecary's 'studio' acted as a testing ground for social fantasy. It is no coincidence that charlatans, anointers, *herbiers*, and barbers practiced the dual function of travelling actors and healers, experts in herbal secrets, potions, ointments and purges. Actor and purger in one – two sides of the same mask. All workers in the industry of dissimulation and of its opposite: simulation (even a youthful face could seem like the mask of a 'corpse disguised by artificial ageing'),[30] occult manipulators of those 'shadows that belong to the art of pretence', in a world dominated by cunning and false appearances, the undisputed domain of the *vulpeculae* or little foxes:

> ... there are foxes in our midst but we do not always recognise them; however, when we do recognise them, it is nonetheless

29 B. Gracián, *El Criticón*. English version taken from *The Critick*, written originally in the Spanish ... translated into English by Paul Rycant Esq., London, 1681, p. 108.

30 T. Accetto, *Della dissimulazione onesta*, ed. G. Bellonci, Firenze, 1943, p. 51.

inadvisable to use cunning against cunning, and in such cases a
wise person will feign stupidity since, by showing that he believes
the deceiver, the deceiver will himself be duped; and it is a sign
of great intelligence to make it seem that one has not seen when
one has seen all too well, so that we play a game as though our
eyes were shut, when indeed they are wide open.[31]

'Shut-eye' games with one's eyes wide open, the paradox and deceit of
the blind man who sees, mental *chiaroscuro*, two-toned truth, all emerge
in the limelight in those years of *superpurgatio*, in the bifocal ideology of
the pure and the sullied, the excremental and the spiritual. In an age
where social schizophrenia was rife, emetic science served as a prelude to
the sciences of divination and exorcism. In a world where everyone
dreamed a great deal, where taking leave of one's consciousness, where
flights, 'journeys' and excursions into lunatic behaviour, leaps and starts,
were the order of the day; where saints levitated (the 'dear to God are
raised aloft' Campanella wrote), where the female counterparts
ascended, flew and fell into ecstasies, where the 'men of God' were
mysteriously catapulted into the most unexpected of places at the most
unforeseen moments, or apparently fell down dead, glassy-eyed and
immobile, in a catalepsy, where there was no shortage of those who
'when touched feel nothing because the spirit is resting on high and
without it the exterior parts are deadened and when touched they break
like glass';[32] where the paths of flying witches crossed with those of
saints, *unguentis adiuvantibus* [helpful ointments], vertigo, ascent and
descent reigned supreme. Baroque man is *homo vertiginosus* par
excellence; he dreams about flying even when he is still and asleep.
Instabilitas, the obsession with movement, creates an empyrean into
which (as already seen) the blessed hurtle with untold speed. The usual
conception of beatitude associated with ideas of stability and non-
movement, suffered a total reversal and strayed into mental aberration.
The mediaeval monk sought beatitude in stillness not in motion. 'It is
impossible', writes St Bernard in his *Tractatus de vita solitaria*, 'for man
to remain faithful to his state of mind, unless his body reside in a given
place for some time first'.[33] 'A wandering body: a wandering and
unstable spirit.' The saintly hermits of the Counter-Reformation seemed
near allied to the deviant monks who practiced 'life-long vagrancy';
unstable and unhappy beings, 'in whom the very accursed wandering
sickness seemed to drive them on as though hounded by Vertunnus, a
kind of demon. The Vertunni were said by the ancients to be the demons

---

[31]   Ibid. pp. 85–6.
[32]   T. Campanella, *Del senso delle cose e della magia*, p. 198.
[33]   *Opera*, vol. V, p. 90.

whose scourge makes men dizzy when they are placed on a precipice .'[34] Harassed, bedevilled and goaded by Satan's bloated dreams: so would St Peter Damian have seen many of the inhabitants of the seventeenth century, as creations more of the Devil than of God. The world pullulated with 'possessed and bloated' (Campanella) vagrants and philosophers, unstable types and visionaries, all people who were oppressed with melancholy and bad humours, for 'those who are atrabilious enjoy much movement, and so do the Sybils and Bacchantes who appear to be inspired to this by God, whereas they are not, but it comes from their natural temperament'.[35] 'Ill-intentioned prophetesses', Sybils and 'Bacchantes' sprang up like mushrooms after the rain with the stars, the sinful humours and 'gross' foods as their accomplices.

> Ptolemy's comment on the prophecy of Jove, Venus and Mars concerning demonplessy [obsessive possession by the devil] brought on by the Moon and Mercury crossing Mars by day and Saturn by night, I have found to be true in some cases, for I have seen some remarkable things, but believe them to be only tendencies, for Jove and Venus in favouring Mercury, imbue us with nobleness of mind, make us lucid and fit to receive divine inspiration and angelic visions, as Origen said. Whilst Mars and Saturn when coinciding with Mercury and the Moon, which govern the senses and the reason, by natural influence ... will produce sourness of mind and great darkness of spirit, as for instance the minds of silly women and common folk who eat poor foods or derive bad vapours from menstrual blood or unpassed excrement, become dulled and all the readier to receive devils.[36]

It is in the light of this theory of witchcraft, seen as a mass phenomenon which took root mostly in the heart of peasant culture and among the lowlier and less protected sectors of society, where the influence and inclination of the stars crossed with the subculture of poverty fed by 'bad foods', its blood polluted by excremental sediment, that the practice of exorcism by vomiting, forced purgings, by expelling of 'murkiness' and 'sour spirits' acquires meaning and force.

> As a cure, Hippocrates [continues Tommaso Campanella] recommends – much to Plato's admiration – virgins to marry so as to purge the natural yearnings of youth, and old women to

[34] St Peter Damian, *Liber, qui appellatur Dominus vobiscum. Ad Leonem eremitam* in *Opera omnia*, Bassano, 1783, vol. III, p. 268.
[35] T. Campanella, *Del senso delle cose e della magia*, p. 200.
[36] Ibid. p. 201.

obtain purgation, and others fatty broths which clear the mind
and make it lucid, and sweet and rich wines. But without religion
there is no result . . . if the Devil has taken the uppermost. It is
true that many only suffer from natural melancholy, as did
Socrates, Callimachus, Scotus, Hercules and Mahomet, who
frequently fell into epileptic fits, and black smoke went up into
their heads even though they were sharp and intelligent when in
command of their reason; and others who are normally healthy
are affected, as I have seen in many old woman and others who
are bedeviled, like soothsayers . . . . Among my many observations, my sister Emilia was oppressed by the Devil at the age of
twelve years when the Sun, in the ascendant and in Aquarius,
moved into the opposite quadrant of Saturn in Leo and Mercury
was crossed with Mars; she then recovered under an excellent
configuration, took husband and lived an exemplary life till the
age of thirty-five, and two years later, favoured God and the
stars, she fell as though dead at the passage of Saturn, saw divine
visions and related astounding things of the previous century;
she became very knowledgeable on theology, though lacking in
formal learning. She could prophecy every event with accu-
racy . . .[37]

How many were there of these homely visionaries, prophetic
pythonesses, sententious prophetesses, raving old women, swooning
damsels, talking crickets, these convulsionaries haunted by *incubi*, who
'dropped down dead with epilepsy', how many the matrons desirous of
regeneration, and the old women seeking 'purgation'? How many the
'fountains of deceit', the 'amphitheatres of monstrosities', how many
have tumbled into the 'cavern of nothingness' (Baltasar Gracián).
Collective infatuations, 'epidemics of the imagination', 'filthy dreams'
born of 'obscene' and delirious 'fantasy', 'nocturnal flights through the
air', 'brutal releases of pent-up lust' by

melancholic women, endowed with vigourous imaginations and
ferocious animals spirits, or indeed old women consumed by all
manner of filthy and libidinous desires, which they abet with
generous quantities of liquor: no wonder, then, that when asleep
they are prey to such nefarious deliriums.[38]

The hellebore, a magic plant of pagan culture, an object of elaborate
apotropaic ceremonies at harvest time, considered a 'sacred medicine'
by Areteus, an electuary to be taken against madness, a liberating and

[37]   Ibid. pp. 201–3.
[38]   L. A. Muratori, *Della forza della fantasia umana*, Venezia, 1745.

purifying herb, held to be the sole barrier to the progressive invasion of elephantiasis (or leprosy), it is again regarded with favour by the 'holy medicine' of the Counter-Reformation and knew another hey-day under the doctors of the new Christian medicine, that had so keen an exponent in Battista Codronchi. His *De christiana ac tuta medendi ratione . . . Opus piis medicis praecipue, itemque aegrotis, et ministris, atque etiam sacer-dotibus ad confitendum admissis utilissimum* (1591) [*On a Christian and safe method of curing the sick . . . A work especially useful for devout doctors and also for the sick, those who attend them and likewise for priests summoned to confess them*], has very largely contributed to forming a picture of the functions of the 'pious' Christian physician, of the medicine of the confessor, and the exorcist.

In these very years, the 'melancholic' and 'frenetic' Tasso who came and went from the 'cavern of nothingness' with great assiduousness, anointed with oil of populeon, poppy juice, 'diacatholicon', infusions of 'hiera', 'euphorized',[39] and comforted by *pharmacopola* from the court, visited also by sprites and given to learned colloquies with the spirits of the air, or dazzlingly heavenly messengers, he sang a hymn of praise to this magical pharmacopeia with its psycotropic and hallucinogenic overtones.

A consumer of black hellebore (number one prescription against atrabilious complaints, an emetic with shattering effects, which inflamed

---

[39]   *Populeon* ointment took its name from the buds (eyes) of [black] poplars. According to Niccolò da Salerno's prescription, authoritatively backed and proven by Giovanni Marinelli, it was made of the following ingredients: poplar buds, pork fat or lard, leaves of a field poppy, namely the red poppy, mandragora, young blackberry leaves, white henbane leaves, morel, lettuce, violaria, namely the mother of the violet, leave of navel wort, Jupiter's beard – the major and minor kinds – bardana. It was recommended for its refreshing and sleep-inducing effects. The presence of mandragora, poppy, henbane, morel (*Solanum dulcamara* probably), containing actively narcotic elements and more or less poisonous according to dosage, clearly indicate the properties of this psychotrope. Let us not forget that deadly nightshade (*Atropa belladonna*), the so-called 'herb of witches', contains the same active elements: hyoscyamine and hyoscine contained in henbane and in thorn apple. Even mandragora contains an active alkaloid compound similar to atropine. 'Bitter-sweet' was also held to be narcotic, aphrodisiac and purgative.

    Without going into the dosages, the recipe for populeon ointment can be found in Antonio de Sgobbis's *Nuovo, et universal theatro farmaceutico*, Venezia, 1667, p. 512.

    According to the register of the ducal pharmacy, the consumption of drugs by Tasso was a daily and large scale occurrence. Among a forest of other medicaments, including populeon ointment, diacatholicon (a purge which was designed to expel bad humours), to *hiera* as an infusion (an electuary of aloes and spices melted in thyme), Torquato Tasso frequently resorted to black hellebore. Cf. A. Solerti, *Vita di Torquato Tasso*, Torino-Roma, 1895–9, vol. II, p. 39 ff.

the internal organs and irritated the central nervous system), of mandragora, solanum, henbane, poppy, this visionary who had had himself bled, purged, clysterized and anointed like a witch in preparation for her sabbath, this confidant and friend of exorcist monks (it is remarkable how 'necromantic' pharmacology and exorcism share the same vocabulary: the *antidotarium* of the apothecary became, in the hands of the exorcist Alessio Porri, *Antidotario contro li demoni*, 1601 *[An antidotary against demons]*), he 'flew' and 'travelled' through his melancholic nights. He was not the only intellectual to 'feel' and be in touch with invisible beings. A great intellectual and friar, Tommaso Campanella, who like Tasso (and much more painfully than him, experienced the hard and bitter trials of imprisonment) was wont to hear warning voices:

> I, who always have to suffer something, feel that I am between sleep and waking and a voice calls me: 'Campanella' clearly; from time to time I hear this and listen, but I know not who it may be, angel or demon; it must be the air which is troubled by my future passion or infected by him who plots it . . .[40]

The 'nocturnal anguish', 'endless melancholies', 'tricks and shadows', 'ghastly images and shadows' (Angelo Grillo) that haunted St Anne's nights, were cured by evacuative and vomitory practices taken from the medical/exorcistic theories of the time.

> For I say that a black and sombre humour mixed with blood engenders awesome spirits, and that if the blood be not purged, it creates werewolves, fears and dark thoughts, which results in delirium and a taste for stinking, filthy places, for graves and corpses, because the contaminated spirit yearns for these things and these things are often cursed because, as Origen wrote with great learning: melancholy is the seat of malignant spirits and the Devil, who, perceiving a human mind infected by these vapours and that the spirit is bound so that it cannot move he, who is himself impure and full of filth, relishing these sombre humours, enters and makes use of these to terrorize the mind and paralize it and he enjoys the siege he lays. But let no philosopher be amazed if the purgative rids the possessed of spleen, and of melancholy, cleanses his blood, from which is born the wicked idea that there are no demons but only a melancholic humour that causes such disturbances in the infected mind, for indeed, when the humour departs, so too does the Devil, depriving him of his sustenance . . .[41]

[40]   T. Campanella, *Del senso delle cose e della magia*, op. cit., p. 197.
[41]   Ibid. pp. 193–4.

8

THE 'CLOCK OF HEALTH'. BERTOLDO CHANGES DIET AND DIES

The 'clock of health' struck the hours with an irregular rhythm and a sombre chime. Yet those who recovered of their own accord and saw no shadow of a doctor stood a greater chance of 'prolonging their lives and remaining healthy without physician or medicine'.

Temperate and 'regulated living' together with a careful purging of the humours were the therapeutic techniques considered indispensable for anyone who would not or could not see a doctor. Men in authority, princes and monarchs could have everything save immortality. Of the 'two treasures most coveted and valued: health and life',[1] they almost always lacked the first. Some dark law of unhappiness and pain hung over their tormented lives. The sufferings and physical pain to which the great and the powerful were prey were unknown to their humbler subjects.

> They have absolute dominion, which brings supreme happiness to mortals; boundless power, abundant riches; the obedience and respect of their peoples; they are often born by nature with a strong constitution and excellent character, and yet in the flower of their youth they may be ravaged by gout, taken unawares by falling sickness, a prey to apoplexy, afflicted by gallstones, inclined to overweight, or riddled with festering ulcers; in a few words, more tormented by their many infirmities than they are consoled by their earthly goods: among these it is very rare to see one reach the first climacteric age of 56, or the second of 63, without spinal trouble or so great a burden of pain that it would have been better for them had they been dead rather than live through that unhappy age so ravaged by ills, destroyed by medicines, tyrannized by physicians, who lay seige to their diets, putting them through whole years of wretched servitude, denying them almost all that the appetite craves and permitting them only what it abhors, only to prolong their lives by two days. But what contributes above all to their misery is that their vain hope of good health makes them perforate and bore into their skin so that it becomes like a riddle; both the horrible blisters

---

[1] S. Mercuri, *De gli errori popolari d'Italia* libri sette, divisi in due parti, Verona, 1645, p. 429. The preceding phrases in quotations mark are from the same source (part 2, vol. 3).

appearing on their faces and these issues produce pus and are evil-smelling, so that these poor princes, formerly so handsome, become hateful and odious to themselves, their families and servants and even to their dogs.[2]

The 'issues' or '*rotturii*' were sores artificially induced by cauterizing the skin – an additional purge intended to cleanse the body of a 'sinful and poisonous humour', by extracting the 'virulent, corrosive and stinking matter' (Scipione Mercuri). This sore:

> continually purges the body of a part of its excrements, which is doubly effective, firstly because in expelling these, they are certain to harm him (the patient) no longer; secondly, because if he should be overcome by another illness, nature will cause this evil to be evacuated through the issues so that the illness is left without a leg to stand on as it were; and for the same reason (the issue) operates very well with unhealthy bodies by keeping the body always clean of the sinful humours that produce sickness, and in healthy bodies issues guard marvellously from many ills ... by extruding those humours continuously which with time might have lead to illness; it makes the body freer and lighter because it is unburdened of a large part of its excrement. . . . But it is not my purpose to recount the functions of cauteries [writes the doctor, Scipione Mercuri, an expert not only on 'popular errors' but author too of a manual which enjoyed a wide circulation: *La commare o la raccoglitrice*, on the problems of childbirth and breast feeding] because if I decided to do so, it would behove me to write a special book: I shall therefore merely limit myself to observing that in my home city of Rome, cauteries have been nicknamed 'doctor chasers' ...[3]

As a 'paediatrician', Scipione Mercuri was a convinced advocate of cauterizing and of 'scalding' administered 'to the back of the neck, beneath the nape' so as to protect or cure babies who succumbed to the 'evil sickness',[4] that is epileptic fits. The 'roasting' also of infants, whilst failing to catch on in Lombardy, was however widely practiced in Florence, where purificatory baptism and 'boilings' would occur on one and the same day and be enacted as part of the same liturgy.

> And therefore, the curative and protective remedy for falling sickness is to scald the infants immediately after baptism on the neck two inches below the nape, that is according to the doctors,

between the first and second vertebrae, which is indeed the second knuckle of the spinal chord if one counts from the head.

This custom is so popular with the Florentines, that I have seen women, immediately after having their babies baptized at St John's Church, go to the barber's to have fire applied so as to preserve them from epilepsy.[5]

Baptism by water, a ritual purification, was associated with a kind of baptism by fire for the purging of bad humours, of impure and stagnant waters. Evil and sickness were exorcised on the same day: priest and barber-surgeon with water and fire respectively (mutually hostile elements), purified the soul and the body of the little 'cherubs'. Caustic cauterizing was but a primitively mechanical enactment of the remote belief in the purifying and regenerating effect of fire. Water and fire were both felt to be fundamental vital elements, to which not only birth but also longevity and the quality of life were entrusted.

After opening the cautery artificially, there immediately arose the problem of its 'good management', that is keeping the wound under control, whilst allowing it to stay open so that it might weep. A variety of foreign bodies were used to endeavour to prevent the wound from healing: balls, peas, chickpeas and so forth. This gave rise, however, to evil-smelling sores, which were not only beset by all kinds of problems resulting from 'bad management' (not to mention the medical ones like gangrene) but which also constituted a social problem.

> I maintain that the bad management of issues is pernicious in three ways: the first to social living, the second to health and the third to that very benefit derived from the issues themselves. All social living and good upbringing requires that insofar as possible, one should not offend other people with personal foulness, dirt, or evil odour and stench. But when an issue is badly managed, it may cause much offence to other dwellers in the household, with the dirty rags and continual smells, and also in church, squares and public places to any who may draw near. For indeed, it is a kind of torment to have in the house a person with badly managed issues, to have always to wash dirty rags and smell that stench both in bed and at table, and it offends most particularly in the summer; whether in church, in a public square or in conversation with one who manages his issues badly, his interlocutor is always sickened to the heart by that evil smell . . . [6]

5   Ibid. p. 417.
6   Ibid. p. 337.

Chickpeas, ordinary peas, metal balls, balls made out of ivy wood, balls made of linen, were inserted in the wound to prevent its closing, but nearly all these led to complications of one kind or another and all, of course, caused pain and discomfort.

Chickpeas, for instance:

> swell notably and in growing larger they give continual pain, and when it is desired to remove them, the affliction grows greater and the issues become so irritated that an abundance of humour flows into the arms and legs and produces erysipelas, abscesses and fevers. In addition to which, in the summer, the rotting chickpeas or peas, mixing with the sweat and half cooked by the summer's heat, together with the stench of ivy, produce and stench so noisome and unbearable as to make even Polyphemus vomit. It is a grave error to place brass plates upon the issues instead of ivy: firstly because being a mineral it has little or no power to draw the excrements to itself; and then because as a solid body, while by its weight it contains the ball of chickpea on the one hand in the opening of the issue by pressing it against a bone or nerve and by-the-by causing considerable pain, on the other hand, in growing warm it adds another pungent odour to the smell of decay. The use of a gold or silver ball in place of a chickpea, is as vain as it is harmful: vain because it is done to show that one possesses enough gold and silver to be able to fill not only one's purse but also one's issues; harmful because it never remains in the mouth of the issue but sinking by its weight, it come to rest upon a bone or nerve and ends by causing endless torment, so making the issues a scourge even to Job.[7]

A new Job, odourous among such stench, with 'sweet-smelling waters and musk', protected by 'tender and aromatic substances', by turpentine, wounds dressed with fragrant plasters, with 'rose' ointment, washed in plantain water. Amber and musk were for the rich, 'those of the church and the poor may use roses and the roots of blue lily'.[8] So in this case poverty was entitled to 'aromatic' treatment, too. The social barriers were lifted also with the aid of smells and each class evoked its own. As never before in the old world where every guild, trade, profession was encased in a particular aromatic cocoon, the nose and olfactory system had become infallible instruments of social identification and professional diagnosis. The nose/chimney had become a sensitive and highly-tuned duct for the perception and recognition of reality, bringing together the private and public worlds: a sensory plumb-line, an aerial

7   Ibid. p. 339.
8   Ibid. p. 340.

receiving messages and olfactory information immediately decoded by the brain. Social memory also passed through the code and alphabet of smells: 'passions of bodily substances'.[9] A complex and varied alphabet that could be misinterpreted and interpreted in many ways. When used as a mask, the scent could disguise, beneath a cloud of odourous dissimulation, the most repulsive stench. It could also be used to distract, deceive, corrupt and create ephemeral and insubstantial images, a presence that hides an absence.

'Crippled by pain, murdered by drugs, tyrannized by physicians', 'pierced', their skin perforated 'in the manner of a sieve', honeycombed with 'festering ulcers', from a body exuding 'evil smells and pus from issues', producers and distributors of 'filth, dirt, fetor and stench', threatened constantly by irreversible and uncontrollable degeneration, 'crippled or slain' by cauterization, the powerful and the rich could not sleep in peace. Scipione Mercuri recounts to the chancellor of the *podestà* of Verona how 'the decision was taken to make an issue in his arm to help his head, as an opening, there immediately rushed out such an abundance of humours from the issue that it became impossible to manage the issue and the arm became gangrenous; there was no remedy sufficient to save him and he died perforce'.[10]

In an age when life was not only precarious, suspended as though from fine and insubstantial threads, but was also the cause of much bitterness and danger, those who enjoyed longevity were regarded with a mixture of wonder and respect, and would be interrogated in order to discover the 'secret' of long life. Their confessions seemed like precious testimonies of a wise and uncommon mode of existence from which a natural formula could be extracted for the creation of panaceas and elixirs. The more astute among doctors and charlatans travelled the world in search of such living witnesses of the technique of a prolonged existence. In his study on 'how a man may preserve his youthfulness and avoid senility and how this is done by reasoning', Leonardo Fioravanti, in combing the cities and countryside of Sicily, came across some monuments of dietary wisdom and circumspect care of the body. In Messina, just into the second half of the sixteenth century, he discovered an old man:

> who told me he was aged one hundred and four years; and I, who was hoping to converse with men of this age, simply to know what life they had lead and what regimen they had followed to live to so advanced an age, one day invited the aforesaid ancient to eat with me, to which to do me a favour, he aquiesced; and

9   U. Aldrovandi, *Moscologia*, Bologna, Biblioteca Universitaria, mss. Aldrovandi n. 84, p. 1.
10   S. Mercuri, *De gli errori popolari d'Italia*, p. 336.

being sat at table, the old man began to eat and ate most soberly that morning, he did not ask for more except for some things of his own choosing; and I asked him why he had not eaten some of those foods that had been placed before him and he replied: 'I may tell you that it is more than seventy years that I have always observed this regimen and that if I had done otherwise, this body of mine would be long ere dead and buried.' And when I asked him what had been his regimen, he answered: 'My regimen has been to rise early every morning and eat; I drink my first glass of wine of a morning and this the best I can obtain; and I have never eaten more than twice in the day, no matter if the day seemed a month in length; and in the evening I have always gone early to bed, nor ever have I gone later, as many madcaps do who ruin their lives for no purpose by staying up all night.' And then I asked him: 'Tell me, my good man, have you ever had recourse to any medicine?' He answered me: 'I never did take a medicine in all my life; but in truth, I take some soldanella in springtime, for we have this in abundance, and every time I take it, it makes me vomit thoroughly and leaves my stomach so clean that for a year I cannot fall ill. And still in the month of May, every morning I pick three sprigs of rue, three of sage, three of wormwood and three of rosemary and I soak them in a glass of good wine; this I leave overnight and then drink it on an empty stomach; this I repeat fifteen or twenty mornings; I still do this every year and now it seems a thousand years until next spring when I may take my remedy, with the help of which and that of God I am well all year.' And so said the old man to me, assuring me that he had done nothing else in all his life and that he had never suffered an evil day in all that time.[11]

The object of 'disciplined living' was in the first place to stay healthy and 'without afflictions' for an 'infinitude of years', and in the second 'to keep the stomach cleansed and offending humours desiccated'.

In Naples in 1552 he met another old man:

of eighty years of age, who was indomitable and lusty for his age, and when I spoke to him in order to know how he had kept him so well, he told me he had always been very disciplined in his living habits above all other things, but that he had nonetheless occasionally used certain medicinal remedies for the preservation of his life. On being asked what he used, he told me that

11   L. Fioravanti, *De' capricci medicinali*, 4 vols. Venezia, 1602, c. 53v.–54r. The 1565 Venetian edition is the first one. The second edition (Venice, Avanzo, 1568) is dedicated to the Duke of Ferrara, Alfonso d'Este. This noble family had dealings with charlatanry.

for a long time he had used white hellebore and taken it orally. The way he took it was the following: He took pieces of the root of white hellebore and placed these inside an apple or a pear and leaving them there the whole night, he would then cook the apple in hot ashes; once cooked he peeled it and removing all the twigs of the hellebore, he ate the cooked apple which he then vomited several times and thus was excellently purged.[12]

From this investigation, vomiting, which constituted first degree evacuation, and purging, again appear to be the chief measures used for ensuring a healthy and long life. Cleansed blood (even bleeding was an integral part in the methodology of purgation), especially when the stars and rotation of the seasons required it, provided it was free of noxious humours, strong and fine in colour, coupled with joyful serenity (laughter purifies the blood, regurgitates polluted humours and acts as an essential therapeutic) opened the way to long journeys in time. Spring, after the stagnation of winter, during which melancholy and phlegm quickened and 'fattened' the heart, was the season of ritual purification. Good wine, too, entered into this popular recipe book for the control of longevity. Blood of the earth and blood from the sun's rays filtering through vine-leaves were considered tonics and life-giving versions of human lymph, injections as it were of liquid sun, of 'humour and light', as Galileo was wont to say.

> I saw then another who lived in Naples, originally from Piacenza, about seventy years of age, a distiller, who told me that every morning, before going out he always drank a glass of Greek wine and ate a slice of bread and then he would eat as much as would absorb the wine, and several times after his meal he would drink a fine eau-de-vie and practised vomiting when he felt his stomach burdened; and in this way he had kept himself in health.[13]

Being itself a sensitive and finely tuned instrument, the body was able both to read and to regulate the clock of health, the hour of vitality, contained within it, realizing thus when certain operations were completed. Man listened to himself digest, came to understand that certain internal bodily processes took place regularly and behaved himself according to the messages received from that invisible processor of physiological data, the digestive apparatus: the black box and time-keeper of human cycles.

According to Fioravanti, it seems that besides wine, *eau-de-vie* was

12   Ibid. c. 54r.–54v.
13   Ibid. c. 54v.

commonly taken. The name itself is suggestive enough and, at the level of the collective unconscious at least, shows how the magical attributes of water were sufficiently influential to favour a kind of baptism in artificial, alchemic water: a distilled liquor encapsulating all the qualities characteristic of the liquid element.

Whilst it is impossible to establish an exact date, it seems that the use of acquavite greatly increased from the second half of the sixteenth century.

> Such madcaps and so foolhardy are the lower orders, being without forethought or consideration, that men feel the urge to drink acquavite in the morning with such avidity and desire that they might be drinking celestial nectar; but this fact is all the more ridiculous because common folk say that acquavite reduces phlegm in the stomach. Such a misapprehension is so widespread in Italy that I am quite astounded, and to such an extent that for fifty whole years, Italians have been distilling a thousand times more acquavite than ever known before; and this is because every city, village or castle consumes so much of its own that they appear not to drink anything else, and it strikes me that one day princes will impose a tax upon it. Perhaps this will stem the folly since the tax by increasing the price will make the liquor harder to obtain by the poor.[14]

Held to be most comforting to the stomach (once again the stomach becomes the focus of attention and popular myth) *eau-de-vie*, distilled in an alembic from wine, with an addition of aniseed and cinnamon, enjoyed, according to Scipione Mercurio, a sudden and tremendous boom in popularity in the second half of the sixteenth century. The 'desire' and 'avidity' with which people craved after this drink was perhaps a symptom of the growing longing of humanity who thought to find in this alchemical version of wine (the wine/water dialectic, the two sides of life, achieves a perfect balance in this artificial drink) an additional bonus of psychological comfort besides physical health. The stomach was always somewhat of a barometer, today just as much as in the past, not only of social climate but also of mental health, of an imperceptible pulse, of a dark well in which are concentrated the tensions and yearnings of generations. The social development of this organ, its changing image through time, the mythology which has grown around it, the popular myths and medical ideologies that it has inspired, form a misty path as yet explored by the intellectual eye.

Taken from the nosological point-of-view, one in which the melancholic humours predominate,

[14]   S. Mercuri, *De gli errori popolari d'Italia*, p. 329.

there is nothing so salutory for the elderly as the taking of purgatives: they can even purge the stomach of cholera and phlegm. And the reason is that when purged, an elderly man will be unburdened of an excess of evil humours. . . ; but besides this evacuation, it is also necessary to restore him to a sound diet and not to forbid him from consuming those foods that delight him, because *quod sapit nutrit*. This being the case, it seems that any food tasted which the stomach abhors, it will reject; whence is born the perfidy of many physicians: for the sick man, unable to taste them, will not partake of the unusual foods prescribed him by the physician, even though they nourish him, so this food gives him no sustenance, and he becomes enfeebled and wastes away. And for this reason do patients often pass away . . . [15]

It can be seen that the death of Bertoldo is presaged in the following quotation taken from his contemporary and fellow-countryman, Leonardo Fioravanti. Giulio Cesare Croce found in the pages of his fellow writer a medical justification and a scientific theory which explained why his hero died 'in acute pain / because he had not been able to eat turnips and beans', murdered by his doctors who:

> not knowing his constitution, gave him the treatment used for gentlemen and courtiers, but he, knowing his own nature, requested them to bring him a casserole of beans with onions and turnips, cooked on embers, because he knew that he would be cured by partaking of these foods; but the doctors chose not to comply with his request.[16]

The loss of vigour suffered by the village sage, his steady annihilation and the physiological decline which overtook him were above all the fault of ignorant doctors who, wise only after the event, 'understood he had died because they had not respected his wishes' *post exitum*. Croce found in Fioravanti's *capricci* the doctrinal authorization, scientific backing and inspiration for Bertoldo's murder: 'And whilst he was at court everything went very well; but being used to heavy foods and game, when he tasted these light and delicate foods, he fell fatally ill',[17] we read in the *Sottilissime astuzie di Bertoldo [Bertoldo and his crafty wiles]*. A few years earlier in *La sollecita et studiosa Academia de Golosi [The earnest and studious Academy of the Greedy]*, the omnivorous and widely-read

[15]   L. Fioravanti, *De' capricci medicinali*, c. 55r.–55v.
[16]   G. C. Croce, *Le sottilissime astuzie di Bertoldo. Le piacevoli e ridicolose simplicità di Bertoldino*, ed. P. Camporesi, Torino, 1978, p. 74.
[17]   Ibid. p. 74.

ballad writer, following in Fioravanti's wake, made the following sententious pronouncement:

> All those who devote their life to other people, should be aware, as experts are, of their patients' constitution, and apply the remedy which is most suited to their natural condition, because if they give a peasant some gentle medicine, he will undoubtedly 'kick the bucket', since his nature has been accustomed to heavy, rustic foods which respond only to heavy and coarse medicaments, which accord with their rustic origins.[18]

The error lay not only in the administration of a 'gentle medicine' to those who were used to 'heavy and rustic foods' and who should therefore be treated with 'heavy and coarse medicines', but it was above all in not taking into account their 'complexion', or their metabolism, the interrelationship of their humours, and the diet befitting their temperament. The 'changing of foods', the abandonment of foods consonant with the patient's profession and reflective of his social status had generally disastrous effects leading to alarming constitutional collapses. Bertoldo's father, in describing the build-up to one of his son's attacks, was certainly echoing the peripatetic doctor from Bologna in a writing of his in which he recalls a long-past clinical experience:

> It came to pass that in the year 1569, finding myself in the Kingdom of Sicily in the famous city of Messina, and practising my trade of medicine, I made many not unpraiseworthy discoveries. I went in the month of May to the abode of a most noble baron not far from Messina, and there resided from May to October, for that summer the villages were stricken with a great number of illnesses among the inhabitants, the disease being putrid fever, which killed a great multitude of people, for they lived not beyond the fourteenth day. And so it was that finding myself in that place I set about the treatment of a great number of these people, both men and women, and the medicament I prepared for them was the following. The first thing I did was to give them a bolus which made them vomit greatly. After this I gave them every morning for three to four days a syrup solution which moved their bowels strongly and followed this with a cupping-glass, whilst I anointed their bodies with oil of hypericum; having done this, I had them eat wild cabbage, salted tunny fish, salted sardines, salted cheese and drink wine. And in this order – for I never altered any treatment. Of the

[18]   G. C. Croce, *La sollecita et studiosa Academia de' Golosi...*, Bologna, 1602, c. a2r.

three thousand I treated, only three died, and these died from
old age. And in the district of Messina, between young and old,
there died more than eight hundred. But it was to my great
wonderment that they ate, whilst yet sick and purged, this
odious mixture of foods and in eight or ten days they were cured.
But now it is true that they eat nothing but these foods, so it can
hardly surprise us since these foods are their habitual nourishment. Moreover, if I attempted to give them delicate foods, they
could not take them and suffered great harm; from this occasion
I understood that to alter foods can cause great harm to the
patient and so true is this, that even in the healthy we may
observe how damaging it is to alter foods; this is to be seen
repeatedly. If it so harms the healthy, how much worse then for
the sick?[19]

The most noble baron and his peasants: this medical 'moral tale' of
country folk in Sicily falling ill and dying if they gave up their customary
diet in favour of 'delicate foods' is reminiscent of the case of the
Bolognese rustic who was deprived of his 'coarser foods'. The 'wild
cabbages' of country folk of Messina are but the southern version of the
'wild fruits' without which the cunning though impotent Bertoldo, fed
instead on 'gentlemen's food', ended in the grave, 'pushing up the
daisies', as Fioravanti would have said.

If the 'change of foods' was noxious and generally fatal for peasants,
for the nobility and the rich a 'variation in diet' was almost as insidious
and really a trap to 'satisfy untrammelled greed', in which the Devil 'sows
a thousand different diseases', a myriad of incurable evils'.[20] The 'unruly
and imprudent' appetite of the rich and noble, is the most obvious
example of their arrogant intemperance, their unnatural and distorted
living habits. Their lives were spent in an artificial world, where true
values were reversed and upside-down. No minute of their day was
orderly, disciplined or natural:

The nobility err in that they do everything outside its proper
time. For they never go to table at the right time and when they
do, they then forget the time to go to bed; and once they are in
bed they never seem to find the right time to get up and, indeed,
in winter when but a sleep of six to eight hours suffices, they find
when they get up that it is time for supper, and when it should be
time to have finished sleeping, they then go to bed; when they
should be up in the morning they are barely starting to digest,
and thus since they do everything outside its proper hour and

19   L. Fioravanti, *De' capricci medicinali*, c. 40r.–v.
20   S. Mercuri, *De gli errori popolari d'Italia*, p. 509.

time, they lose their health and enable physicians and apothecaries to triumph at their expense.[21]

If the lack of regular eating habits and of a varied diet killed the nobility, the abandonment of the peasantry of their customary eating patterns, their dietary 'simplicity', the 'flavourful and tasty sauces' of their cuisine sent them to their death. The eater of a diversity of foods found that:

> because these have mutually antagonistic qualities, they cause disturbances and overload the metabolism excessively ... and therefore produce blood of differing characteristics which, coursing through the stomach in a turmoil, offends its functions, instead of assisting it to make blood.[22]

From this 'turmoil' there emerges a blood which is 'half cooked and half raw, which is therefore a hotbed for a thousand ills and a sure recipe for a quick and certain death'.

> What I am saying here is well known to those who at one meal feast their appetite upon lamb stew, roasts, stews of a wide variety of animals, with all their varying flavours; upon the delights of pastries, cakes and ravioli; there are those who with a full stomach and satiated appetite take it, with renewed energy and heedless of satiety, to pastures new and attack a mountain of tarts and pasties accompanied by a host of cardoons, celery, sugars and so much other trash.
>
> Such individuals frequently fall ill, and die with much speed, and there is good reason for this, for by ingesting too great a variety among meats, fish, spices, herbs and sugars, the blood becomes more varied than Vertumnus. This even Polyphemus's stomach could not tame or digest and remaining so undigested, it can only lead to illness, all the more easily because the fieriness of the spices can quickly rot the liver and enflame it, the head and other important organs. But this defect is exacerbated by the consumption of yet more fish; this abuse is recognized and abhorred by the common people in a proverb which is very apt:
>
> He who eats meat and fish
> Death only does he wish.
>
> This is quite correct for fish is full of excrement, is cold and humid, and has little nutritional value; it rots like all that is born and lives in water, and likewise can corrupt other food present in

21   Ibid. p. 545.
22   Ibid. p. 510.

the stomach, so that if eaten in company with meat, the latter will be ill-digested and soon, like the fish itself, will decay and with the decay produced by the fish, lead to all the evils described above.[23]

But the ultimate calamity, a gastronomic symbol of evil, decay and death, befell the rich Italy of the later Renaissance, like a deadly bomb from Spain, in the shape of a noxious brew which induced speedy rotting of the blood and rapid deterioration of health. Even the name of this aberrant broth, which corrupted both simple tastes and the purity of the humours, is suggestive of its devastating propensities: *olla putrida* (putrid stew or rotting hotch-potch). It is the nefarious embodiment of putrefaction:

> But among the great variety of harmful and blameworthy foods, the worst is that which has penetrated Italy, for its sins, which has become the port of call of every passing fashion, and whilst offending all modesty and more gravely attacking good health, has been embraced and welcomed, nevertheless, at the most lavish banquets. This is of the pernicious Spanish variety, its name indeed bearing an indication of its iniquitousness. It is known in Spain by the name of 'putrid stew'; it is indeed quite capable of rotting on its own and putrefying other foods, not only inside the human stomach, but inside that of a colossus of bronze. This brew is composed of the following ingredients. Take a pot and boil in it all kinds of meat: beef, veal, bullock, fresh and salted pork; partridge, pheasant, quail, thrush, capon, chicken, poultry, pigeon, the muzzle and trotters of salted port, garlic heads, chickpeas, beans, cabbage, rice, onions, and a multitude of other rubbish. I myself twice tasted it and always condemned, damned and abominated it, as a food fit to kill a man, like the scythe of death.[24]

A sort of undischarged verminous alimentary bomb, in irreversible and unbiodegradable form, an infernal contrivance devised by the bizarre ingenuity of the *escorchadores* [the 'flayers'] of the West.

[23]   Ibid. pp. 510–11.
[24]   Ibid. p. 511. A less dramatic evaluation of this famous Spanish dish is given by Andreae Bacci, *De naturali vinorum historia, de vinis Italiae et de conviviis antiquorum libri septem*..., Roma, 1597, c. 165b.: 'Oglia Poderida in mensis hispanicis inclyta'.

PART III

9

FOOD FOR HEROES

An upturned *axis mundi*, a sad parody of the pure, healthy and luxuriously verdant tree, of vigorous and fecund vegetation overflowing with life-giving juices and sap; a feeble shadow of arboreal life, of aromatic and salutory herbs, Man, nature's discard, a living and walking incarnation of decay, like a contaminated and worm-infested blood clot, was the chosen pasture ground of the immortal earthworm which gnaws and devours ('esca vermis qui semper rodit et comedit immortalis'), a lurid 'thing', which rotted and became contaminated. A bag of excrement producing nothing but a foul stench, infected blood, purulent sperm, a ball of filth. 'Man is nothing but fetid sperm, a bag of dung and food for worms. After man comes the worm, and after the worm, stench and horror. And thus is every man's fate' (St Bernard).

In life, the human animal resembled a vessel brimming with a shameful 'stench', according to an olfactory description which was not that far removed from reality: flesh tortured by lice, mites, crab-lice, bedbugs, fleas..., scabies, herpes, gangrene, phlegmon, tumours, apostemes, fistulas, rhagades, sores, scabs, chilblains, pimples. A myriad of evil-smelling issues poured forth their contents from this worm-man. Pharmacological remedies reflect the image of this smelly monster dripping with moisture. Those who suffered from 'fistulas or gangrene' were prescribed: 'a man's dung burnt so as to make a powder and mingled with some poppy, likewise pulverized, that it may be placed upon the afflicted part.'[1]

A 'perfect ointment for ringworm' was prepared from:

> six ounces of pork fat; frogs ... forty in number. These should be boiled until they disintegrate; then the juice of wild mushrooms – of such as grow on walls – should be taken ... and boiled a little. Having mingled all the ingredients to make the ointment, this should be applied to the affected area twice a day ...[2]

Absinthe and bull's spleen 'to restore speech', oil in which worms have been cooked to calm 'ruffled nerves', rye or wheat bread in which, prior to baking, 'wall-wort juice' had been added, 'ox dung found in the

---

[1]   *Ricettario galante del principio del secolo XVI*, ed. O. Guerrini, Bologna, 1881, anast. reprint, Bologna, 1968, p. 125.
[2]   Ibid. p. 122–3.

countryside' distilled for gout, pigeon dung with a few feathers from a 'new' hen 'to give you beautiful hands', 'cream for the hands' based on 'fat from around the kidneys of a castrated billy-goat'.

Anyone who 'is spitting blood because of a broken vein in the chest' should, according to a remedy suggested by the Reverend Donno Alessio Piemontese (alias Gerolamo Ruscelli, d. 1566): 'Take mouse droppings, make them into a powder and place them in half a glass of plantain juice or *penneti* [a paste made from barley flour and sugar] and it should be drunk in the morning before breakfast and in the evening before retiring to bed; after only a few applications the patient is cured.'[3] There follows a 'first rate secret remedy, surpassing all others, for stones, be these in the liver, bladder, new or old, large or small', contained the indispensable 'base' of bovine dung:

> in the first, second, third or even last week of May when oxen are out grazing in the fields, their dung may be collected when neither too dry nor too fresh and distilled gently so that it does not catch fire, in a glass jar or one of glazed clay and a smelless and tasteless liquid will result which is perfectly suited to wash all garments and all marks on the face . . . [4]

These 'secrets' collected together by a contemporary of Pietro Aretino's, were very popular until the end of the eighteenth century. The editions ran into their tens in Italy, Lyons and Anvers, and before falling into oblivion they were matter for avid reading, part of a literature for the consumer, whose popularity was a sign of the strong association between 'secrets' and the hope of good health, between prescription and magic formula. It is almost as though the collective unconscious was attempting to exorcise evil by adopting a strategy of occultistic therapy immersed in a bath of necromantic pharmacology and natural magic. A Faustian dream lurked beneath this great desire to penetrate life's secrets and techniques and so keep death at bay. Fascinated readers saw a mirage of longevity, of sickness comfortingly banished:

> Method and secrets for the preservation of youth and postpone-ment of old age, for the continuing health and vigour of the individual as in the first flower of youth. All this is the picture and result of a long study and much experimentation made by a certain great man for very many years by order of a great lady. And during these experiments there is proof that a white-haired old man of seventy became as one of thirty-six or

3   D. Alessio Piemontese, *Secreti*, p. 48.
4   Ibid., p. 47.

thirty-eight years, where before he had been afflicted with a terrible constitution and all manner of illnesses.[5]

A highly clever polygraph and charlatan, this self-styled Piemontese (a 'trade' name that proved very marketable for his colleagues in the succeeding century) sells himself to his clients with supreme talent: he was born into a 'noble house by blood', 'was comfortably rich and possessing of a good fortune', he professed to have 'been a diligent student from childhood' and to being 'conversant with Latin, Greek, Hebrew, Chaldean, Arabic and other literatures'. But above all

> having immersed myself for my own pleasure in the study of philosophy and of nature's secrets, I travelled about the world for fifty-seven years in search of people versed in every subject; and most certainly I have acquired many fine secrets not only from men of learning and other great men, but also from humble women, artisans, peasants and a great variety of people. And I have been three times in the Levant, and have long searched in all the world; I can state for certain that I have never remained more than five months in any one land.
>
> This study of mine, this yearning for knowledge, both of the universal sciences and of particular secrets ... has always been sustained in me out of a real ambition and pretension that I might know what others do not, and I have always been very mean about sharing any of my secrets ...[6]

This Paracelsus and Faustus in one, this wayfaring and neurotic physician whose insatiable curiosity caused him to roam the world in search of knowledge and friendships, but with a touch too of the charlatan, was immortalized by Ariosto in his *Herbolato* as a herbalist, magician and alchemist, creator of potent and life-prolonging draughts.

*Renovabitur sicut aquila juventus mea. [*My youth was renewed like an eagle*]*. This was the dream of longevity, the 'grace' that the Lord in his goodness and mercy bestowed on Ezekiel, 'prolonging [his] life by very many years, and causing Moses to live one hundred and twenty years without ever losing a tooth or his strength being dimmed or impaired, or his ever suffering from a headache'.[7] In order to 'preserve and restore good health and youth' – so does Alessio Piemontese introduce the first recipe – 'I shall begin with the method for making a balm which miraculously preserves and restores natural warmth and fundamental

---

5   D. Alessio Piemontese, quoted from *La prima parte de' secreti del Reverendo Donno Alessio Piemontese, nuovamente dall'autor medesimo riveduti et ricorretti*, Pesaro, 1559, p. 1.

6   D. Alessio Piemontese, *Secreti*, p. [3], dedication 'A' lettori'.

7   Ibid. p. 7.

moisture, which are the two things upon which the body's health, strength and life depend':[8]

> This most precious and noble balm has no equal, for when a spoonful is taken one or twice in a week, it preserves health, relieves and cures the poor condition of the human body, it preserves, restores and heightens the natural heat and funda-mental moisture of the body, maintaining the person's vigour constantly, in head, body, mind, facial colour, and makes his breath sweet, fragrant, young and robust . . . [9]

The alchemistic and magical tone ('dissolve gold in a drinkable liquid so that it can be taken orally to conserve youth and health')[10] is indicative of a determined attempt to capture some small portion at least of a delician paradise, a fragment of an island populated with blessed, healthy, long-lived and incorruptible people. The journey towards a blissful land is lived in some deep region of the mind, hiding unimagina-ble treasures and miracles from consciousness. The march towards the impossible and the elusive was littered with recipes whose therapeutic recommendations issued from the same paradoxical and dream-like logic, as that which gave rise to fantastical geographies of journeys made to an earthly paradise or Indian *mirabilia*. Another demonstration of this astonishing evocation of symbolic magic is Donno Piemontese's recipe/ prescription with which 'as well as its many other qualities I cured a friar from St Onofrio whose left arm had for eleven years been wizened like a piece of wood, and nature sent no nourishment to it': the recipe for 'red dog oil':

> Take a dog whose coat is red, and who is not old, and do not feed him for three days. After this strangle him with a rope and leave him quarter of an hour thus dead. In the meanwhile have a pot in which water has been brought to the boil and place the dog, hair and all, whole or in pieces in the pot, taking care that every part of him with the coat is placed within. Make him boil until he becomes fragments, keeping the pot always covered. In the meantime, place up to eighty or a hundred scorpions in a copper pan and scald them till they become thoroughly angry, then put them in the pot with the dog and some oil, to which is added a plentiful bowlful of well-washed earthworms or red earthworms, together with a generous handful of hypericum . . . [11]

8   Ibid. p. 8.
9   Ibid. p. 12.
10   Ibid. p. 13.
11   Ibid. p. 31.

For haemorrhages, 'in order to staunch the blood of every vein cut', the following should be taken:

> soot from the oven, pulverized broadbeans beaten together with white of egg and goat's hair or cobwebs, and shake the ingredients together; failing this, take some flax, and place the powder on the wound as it staunches blood admirably, then place the flax together with the white of egg to which some plantain juice has been added.[12]

The ghastly drama of haemostasis, of gangrene resulting from these methods of staunching blood, forms a separate chapter in the story of human disintegration. These were desperate remedies that in the case of amputations, (carried out under dubious or indeed lethal anaesthetics) almost always ended in disaster. Bartolomeo Maggi (1477–1552), a Bolognese and physician to Julius III, applied a paste of clay and vinegar to stumps of limbs. And Cesare Magati (1599–1657), from Scandiano in the province of Emilia, who, starting life as a surgeon, later took holy orders and became a Capuchin friar, used in such cases ass's dung or horse dung cooked in vinegar and applied as a plaster. In the medication of sores, use was often made of hen's blood (and it appears the results were quite satisfactory in this case). A sow's belly, a pig's bladder and rabbit skin were widely used, too.

It was nevertheless the executioners who gave new momentum to the methodology for arresting the flow of blood, and faced with the problem of preventing their victim's death temporarily when they amputated his hand (usually it was tied to his neck by a chain) during the journey to the gallows, for execution by beheading or drawing and quartering. Some anonymous 'artist' of this form of massacre or demolition of the body – for the executioner was seen also as a 'master of justice' equipped with a team of assistants much as a 'surgeon' has at his disposal – is attributed with the idea (not in itself devoid of a kind of horrifying ingeniousness) of placing the bleeding stump in the bladder of an animal which was then tightly tied for the remainder of the time till the massacre had been duly enacted. It appears that haemostasis had by and large taken place by the time the bladder was removed. These were slaughterhouse techniques, suggested and corroborated by similar experiences witnessed by those who dealt with the dismemberment of animals, carcasses, and perhaps as seen during the course of anatomy lessons carried out on pigs in the absence of anything better. Butchers and pork butchers, on the one hand, and executioners on the other are, to a degree which is as yet inestimable, pioneer experimenters in avant-guard techniques combined with the experiences of the surgeons and barber-phlebotomists.

[12]   *Ricettario galante del principio del secolo XVI*, pp. 123–4.

Mechanics when applied to the problems of the human body, provided models, inspiration and suggestions. Sartorial and furriers' techniques came in handy when sewing together dismembered parts of the human body; particularly so when reassembling the intestine, 'some directly', as the surgeon, Giovanni Andrea dalla Croce, noted, 'following the practice of furriers in sewing together furs or as a sack is sewn together, so should a wounded intestine be sewn.'[13] Both the 'manner' in which this was done and the 'materials' for sewing (needles, pins, thread, silk, linen) transport us to the furrier's shop. The gravest danger (apart from the pain) was the wounds sewn in this manner 'easily reopened, rotted and festered'.

Certain techniques bordered on the surreal. Were it not for the fact that these are 'surgiens' who describe them, such methods might be taken for nightmares or the visions of an unhinged mind: but it appears that ants really were used to knit the soft parts of the body together, like the intestine:

> Some practitioners, according to Albucasis, joined together the edges of the wound with the heads of large ants, whose bodies were then severed from their heads once they had sealed the wound with their mandibles, the head alone thus remaining attached to the intestinal wound, and they believed that with the body thus separated, the heads thus applied would heal the wound . . .
>
> The use of ants is disliked by many, because they are not always to be found everywhere and after a short while they putrefy and fall off.[14]

If one is to believe the words of this technical authority, it would appear that this amazing expedient was attempted by a few people in Italy, too, and not just in the Arab world. There were even those who reduced animals to shreds in their attempt to make suitable thread for sewing intestines.

> Others would take the narrow intestine of some creature and would reduce it to something like a fine thread with which they sewed the human intestine . . . Not that the intestines of animals are recommended any longer, for from their innate humidity and natural heat, the fibres either slacken, putrefy or break, or at the very least cause the wound to fester.[15]

13   G. A. Dalla Croce, *Trattato primo*, 'Digressione prima. Nella quale di tratta la cura delle ferite del ventre inferiore e delle parti sue', in Giovanni di Vico Genovese, *La prattica universale di cirurgia...*, Venezia, 1622, p. 525.

14   Ibid. pp. 525–6.

15   Ibid. p. 526.

There was a constant threat that the sutured wounds might rot. And yet, in many cases, in the registers of old hospitals the note 'left cured' outnumbers the black crosses which symbolized the death of the patient, for the most part of peasant origin. The manuscript of the *Libro delle cure de maestri che si fanno giornalmente nel almo Hospedale di Santa Maria Nuova di Firenze (. . . cominciato questo dì 20 marzo 1631)* [*Book of masters' cures made daily at the Almo Hospital of Santa Maria Novella in Florence . . . begun this day of 20 March 1631*] abounds in admissions of peasants for bruises, peasants for concussion and peasants for dislocated parts of the body. 'Returns happily' can be read on the frontispiece next to the water-colour of a crutch.

The atmosphere was heavy with putrefying corpses, attended by all the nauseating fluid and purulent sap exuded by them, 'rot', cancerous ulcers, 'insidious goitre', benevolent scrofula, 'herpes esthiomena', 'disintegration', 'manure', the 'perfect corruption of the affected part and consequent removal of all pain . . . commonly known as St Anthony's disease',[16] 'gangrene' which 'brings about an excess of blood', the decay of flesh and bones 'when flesh is in contact with them, engendering a rotten and putrefying blood, which imbues them with a disagreeable and poisonous humour and induces stinking putrefaction'.[17]

The disease named after St Anthony, characterized by the lightening onset of a terrible gangrene and by the fatal necrosis which blackened the limbs, devoured as it were by the inexorable progress of a devastating fire; the so-called malady 'of the wolf', was a 'malignant plague which attacks the lower regions of the body, particularly the legs, and like a hungry wolf . . . rots and eats into the neighbouring parts';[18] common gangrene which caused the 'limbs to blacken, become limp and putrid, and producing a dreadful stench, becomes inert';[19] herpes induced 'delirium and corrosion', and 'bad and choleric pustules' of ant disease; the innumerable varieties of inflammatory tumour and abscess which 'matured and rotted' with melted wax and rose-vinegar, a 'mixture required with dirty wool which is impregnated with sweat and filth; take this and apply the lotion to the infection',[20] and in many cases the 'narcotic methods . . . are such that they mitigate the pain and benumb the limb, amongst these there being hyoscymine which has frequently been remarkably effective, as we ourselves and many others too have

---

[16]   G. Tagaultio, *La chirurgia*, tradotta in buona lingua volgare, Venezia, 1550, c. 47v.
[17]   Ibid. c. 47r.
[18]   Ibid. c. 93v.
[19]   Ibid. c. 48r.
[20]   Ibid. c. 38v.

had occasion to observe',[21] the 'narcotic and benumbing remedies' which 'are used with desperate diseases'.[22]

Rotting fluids, exuding putrefaction, 'grimy cotton wool' therapy with plenty of 'sweat and muck', surgical butchery, deadly purges by hellebore, dung-based health programmes using human faeces, both of adults and of children, steaming bird droppings, cow dung, goat dung, ox dung; urine, earwax, preputial smegma amalgamated with oils and fats obtained from distilling the lowest species of animals and insects are reflected in the attraction/repulsion dichotomy of 'cupio dissolvi' [I long to melt], in the recurrent obsession with *post mortem* decay. St Anselm's observation 'after the spirit has deceased, the body is full of horror and stench' (one of the many sombre litanies upon the theme of *ubi sunt*?) evokes the horror and disintegration of the mortuary, leads us to reflect on the human condition upon the Day of Judgement, and portrays decay as a melting erosion of the human frame, dwelling with repugnant sensuality upon the essential decay of the body. The theologian's pen becomes one with the anatomist's scalpel: cutting, dividing and demolishing the admirable symmetry of the living and vibrant microcosm:

> We should learn to contemplate in the following fashion ... In what disgusting and lamentable condition will my flesh be handed over after my death ... to be consumed by decay and worms. . . . Hiding, my eyes will be turned to face the inside of my head, eyes in whose empty and malicious wandering I often took delight: they will lie buried in terrible darkness which once absorbed gloatingly the hollow pleasures of the light. The ears will soon suffer an invasion of worms, ears which revel wickedly at present in the voices of slander and the rumours of the age. The teeth will be tightly and wretchedly clenched, which greed has gnawed away. The nostrils will decay, which now delight in various perfumes. The lips are crusty with a filthy scab, which used often to loosen in foolish laughter. The tongue will be bound up by a raging scum, which often proffered idle tales. The throat is constricted and the stomach stuffed full of worms, where both were stretched tight with differing foods. But why recall the individual details? The whole disposition of the body towards whose health, comfort and pleasure every concern of the mind strained itself, will dissolve in decay, worms and finally into basest dust. Where is the proudly held head? Where the boasting words, the adornment

[21]   Ibid. c. 39r.
[22]   Ibid. c. 409r.

of clothes, the multitude of varied pleasures? Vanished into nothingness like a dream ... [23]

Life, a rotting filth; and death, the embodiment of decay. All in all, no great difference can be said to exist between these two states. The *compositio corporis*, so hard to build and maintain intact and incorrupt on earth, finished underground melting away in a quagmire of grume. *Solvere* and *dissolvere*, release lived alongside decay, in a world where even the human smile looked like a foolish parody of dissolving mouth and lips, where the tongue, producer of words and tales, would disintegrate (as St Anselm smugly points out) in irreversible putrescence and punish that perfidious organ so hated by God: 'Grume binds the chaotic tongue, which so often uttered empty speeches'. The realm of putrefaction knows no bounds, neither spatially nor temporally.

In the paradise of the chosen, it was as though all the anguish, fears and pain, which held mankind in their thrall on earth, were projected in a reversed, negative form. The world of the blessed was the inverted reflection of the human predicament, of the stress which had dogged human existence for so many centuries, of hardship (for many), weariness (for most), terror and tears (for everyone). *Ibi*, up there:

> there, then, is no grief, no weeping, no pain, no fear. No sadness, no strife, no envy, no trouble, no temptation, no exchange of money or financial corruption, no fear of treachery, no political soliciting, no sycophancy, no slander, no sickness, no old age, no death, no poverty, no night, no darkness, no need for food or drink or sleep, no exhaustion. [24]

From this realm of 'perfect contentment', 'quintessential tranquility', 'supreme freedom from care', are all misery, drudgery, darkness and squalor banished: nor can 'deformity', 'poverty' 'toil [...] or age, night or darkness' dwell in this place 'which has overcome death and suffering'. The inhabitants are beautiful, rich, safe, healthy; they know no nightmares or gloomy nights; they are eternal and know not the curse of work. Heaven is dreamed as the reversed image of the world, the *speculum inversum*.

This yearning after a celestial home springs, of course, from dreams of escaping the miseries of home on earth, from expectations of being able to replace a hard and bitter terrestrial existence with a comfortable and secure one.

[23]   St Anselm, Archbishop of Canterbury, *Meditationes*, Roma, 1697, pp. 33–4. For Torquato Tasso even to indulge in laughter ('muoverci a riso') was a 'fraudulent activity ... because laughter is deceitful ('Il Gianluca overo de la maschere', in *Dialoghi*, op. cit., vol. II, Bk. II, pp. 679–80).

[24]   Ibid. pp. 245–6.

If we love this unstable and fragile life, which we maintain with a great struggle, since we can only with difficulty fulfil the body's needs for food, drink and sleep, how much more must we love eternal life: there we endure no struggle, where there is always pleasure, complete happiness, blessed freedom and bliss, where men will be like the angels of God. There will be no sadness there, no distress, no fear, no suffering, no death, but enduring health will always abide there.

No disease arises there, no discomfort of the flesh: there is no sickness there, no lack of anything at all: no hunger, no thirst, no cold, no scorching heat, no weakness from hunger ... but happiness and rejoicing reign everywhere. Men, together with the angels, will remain forever free from the ills of the flesh. There will boundless pleasure and everlasting joy reign; whoever is once taken into it will be kept there forever. There will rest from striving, peace from foes, perpetual enjoyment, everlasting freedom from care, sweetness and charm in beholding God, be the order of the day.[25]

In this perfect *locus amoenus*, this island of blessed creatures who have left behind them the curse and exertion of work, the torments of illness, hunger, thirst, the pangs of fasting, the 'pain of living', existential fear and insecurity, in this haven where *sanitas* (physical health) is eternal, even God was perceived sensually, as a gentle and delightful vision, as a honeyed blessing.

The body's disintegration and its putrefaction obeyed the universal law 'de corruptione et putrefactione omnium rerum', fundamental to alchemic thinking, which upheld the close dialectic of replacement and of the perennial osmosis between life and death: 'all matter is born', so believed Ramón Lull, 'receives a life and a spirit which naturally putrefy, as a mother giving birth to putrescence from her womb, through the interchanging elements'.[26]

The putridity of the womb, the warm vessel of the female uterus evoked images of dark, cosy incubators where essential metamorphises took place and where microcosms silently fermented in unison with the universal transformation of the elements. It was the archetypal dunghill, a feculent warmth:

From this you can learn that nothing can be given life, be born or be created without its own previous corruption, decay and mortification. It is then that the nature of matter is transmuted,

[25]   St Bernard, Abbot of Clairvaux, *Operum* tomus quintus., Aliena dubia, notha, et supposititia, Lugduni, 1679, p. 146, 2nd. col.

[26]   R. Lull, *Theorica* in *Theatrum Chemicum*, Argentorati, 1621, IV, p. 48.

like things which are easily broken and matter which is lacking the completeness of perfection. Therefore separate matter from its corruption and take the form separated from matter by the latter's corruption, in order that the form can become perfect by its transcendence.[27]

The analogy between the alchemic and vital processes is so close as to create a network of interdependent activities: test-tube research into life, a simulation of the creation of matter, the artificial engendering of bodies, all of which follow the logic of animal physiology.

Every operation, therefore, is based on decay [stressed Lorenzo Ventura], since if there were no decay, the universe would come to nothing.... Blackening follows decay, and these both take place in dampness. A moderate heat, moreover, is inducive of decay.... These three things, that is: dampness, decay and blackness, thus involve each other mutually.... There is no birth without previous corruption ...[28]

Putrefaction becomes thus a creative amalgam, the basis for a new and fermenting life: it is a kind of black copulation ('the signs of putrefaction are threefold: it is of course black, fetid and finely powdery'),[29] it fertilizes, swells and impregnates.

Images of nuptials and copulation mingle sinisterly with those of decay, even in far-away cosmic spaces:

This decay is the perfect and universal mixture of two bodies. Hence it is said in the book known as *Miserula*: since the sun is of one birth with the moon, it must drink and become drunk and drink still more deeply from the waters of the moon, go to bed with her lovingly and gradually join with her: because one nature rejoices in the other because both natures are alike. For then the sperm, that is the halo of the sun, penetrates the body of the moon and little by little mingles with it until they are intertwined in a complete mingling. By this means the moon becomes pregnant, and her pregnancy lasts fifteen days.[30]

Solar sperm, stellar fertility, celestial and fecund seed, all set in motion and generated the moon's putrefactory processes. It was thought that there rained down on earth like a heavenly sweat ('coeli sudor') or an undefinable saliva from the stars ('quaedam syderum saliva'), or a

27   Ibid. pp. 48–9.
28   L. Ventura, *De ratione conficiendi lapidis philosophici liber*, in *Theatrum chemicum*, Argentorati, 1613, II, p. 306.
29   Ibid. p. 307.
30   Ibid. p. 307.

secretion/excrement of the air ('purgantis se aëris succus'), a honey in the form of a gentle dew, the principal antidote to putrefaction, and thwarter of bodily decay, whether in life or death. It was said that Alexander defied time by besmearing himself with honey ('The corpse of Alexander, soaked in honey, remained whole and did not, as almost always happens, become defiled with decay').[31] As a product of heaven, honey contained a secret energy that regenerated life and embalmed the flesh, hindering the process of decay. When dissolved in wine, it was the sole food capable of delaying old age, 'many have attained a great age by means only of a drop of mead'. Pollio's anecdote about Romulus, who died more than a century old and lived off this celestial beverage, is well-known. He succinctly explained the secret of his physical and mental vitality to Augustus: 'Inside mead, outside oil'.[32] There it was in a nutshell: this was food for heroes *par excellence*. The past always returns, though in disguise and unrecognizable as such. The myths of longevity are restated with new formulae and the old syntheses in contemporary pharmacological dietetic terms.

The Riace bronzes, transmuted into an advertisement for a certain brand emblazoned upon twentieth-century walls, proclaim with energetic authority that:

> Two of life's secrets have at last reached us:
> *Pollitabs* 4: pollen nucleus freed from bark.
> Pure.
> Uncontaminated.
>
> E
> *Pollingel*: Royal jelly combined with pollen nucleus.
> Dry-frozen.
> Exclusive

FOOD FOR HEROES

We do not know if the heroic age was cognizant of pollens and dry-frozen royal jellies. On the other hand, we can recognize how this latest marketing venture on the part of the pharmaceutical industry has absorbed the mythology of potions and immaculate products uncorrupted by nature. 'Nature re-found', indeed, or a dream of 'purity' and 'the uncontaminated' emerge here from the mists of past mythology and hark back to lost havens and an Eden of physical beatitude. Astonishing, too, is the reappearance of alchemic esoterism and forgotten turns of phrase: 'Two of life's secrets have reached us'. From the recesses of mortuaries, royal jellies beckon us towards gardens full of honey and purity. The

---

[31]   L. Coelius Richerius, *Lectionum antiquarum* libri XXX, Lugduni, 1562, vol. III, Chap. XXVII, p. 550.

[32]   Ibid. p. 551.

journey towards death is sweetened by the offer of life and longevity, and this because the power of honey is ambiguous and ambivalent: divine and mortal, protracting and curtailing, delaying and propelling. If the people of antiquity saw in it an active and celestial power,

> this was seen to be the power of honey, imbued with a heavenly power and an unfailing natural potency, to conserve bodies miraculously from decay. . . . According to Pliny, the nature of honey is such that it prevents bodies from rotting, by means of a pleasant odour rather than an acrid one . . . [33]

On the other hand, according to a tradition reported by Rhodiginus, honey-based narcosis was thought useful to enable bodies which had been fortunate enough to be anointed to slip insensibly into the arms of death:

> Honey is said to be a symbol of death just as bile is a symbol of life: therefore libations of honey are poured to the earthly spirits, since death creeps in upon the soul through pleasure, but the soul is revived by bitterness: for bile is likewise offered to the gods, possibly because death is the end of the toils with which life abounds. [34]

Exuding balm and honey, redolent of incense and sweet aromas, such earthly paradises were mortal refuges where, being embalmed, life stood still, and in such blissful havens and 'fortunate' islands, life's bitterness was forgotten. The mythical power of honey to prolong life and the sickly taste of celestial dew are, in fact, a metaphor for the potent effects of embalming, or another version of the 'impassibility' of the saintly, whose skin was untouched by the ravages of time, the melancholy autumn of life, or the fading rays of sunset. The contraposition of *mel/fel* (honey/ gall), *dulce/amarulentum* (sweet/bitter), was quite fictitious really, just as that of sweet/salt. Indeed, salt was a remedy against putrefaction and decomposition, with similar results to those of honey.

> For salt tightens, dries and binds and it also preserves decaying corpses to such an extent that they last for centuries. The practices of the Egyptians, who used to bury corpses in salt, prove this . . . [35]

Egyptian science apparently discovered the natural clock present in the human heart, which marks the ascending and descending phases of life's course:

[33]   Ibid. p. 550.
[34]   Ibid. p. 551.
[35]   Ibid. Vol. I, p. 357.

... the Egyptians and Alexandrians experimented on the basis of the growth of the heart and showed that the natural span of human life is a century, as I will not hesitate to relate (says Johannes Langius). These people kept the bodies of those who had died without defilement covered in oil of cedar to preserve them from decay; in these subjects they observed that the human heart grew year by year until the fiftieth year, at the rate of two grains a year, and then for the same number of years shrank again by the same annual amount. Hence a human being cannot live beyond his hundredth year, that is, his twelve thousandth lunar cycle, because the heart will fail then.[36]

[36]   *Aurei Velleri, sive Sacrae philosophiae vatum selectae et unicae, mysteriorumque Dei, Naturae, et Artis admirabilium, liber primus* in *Theatrum chemicum.* Vol. v, 1622, p. 275.

10

'COCK'S BROTH'. THE COOK AND THE EXORCIST

The image of the 'anointed' body appears and reappears almost obsessively in the context of 'necromantic' medicine (witches 'anoint themselves and stun themselves with vapours from oil').[1] While thick, greasy broths, oils, syrups, sweet and sickly 'magisteries' lubricated the body's internal labyrinths, sugared 'clysters' softened its bowels, oil and butter moistened its surface. It was pampered with liniments, balm, ointments and creams; it was stroked, massaged and rubbed down by hand or with a sponge, poultices or cataplasms imbibed with wax or tinctures, plaster or preservatives; it was rubbed with scented or oil-impregnated cloths. It was sugared inside and greased on the outside. Women 'plastered not only their faces but also their backsides with ointments' wrote one seventeenth-century author. He used a fine sheath, a kind of greased and aromatic overskin as protection against the 'foul' disease (illness, curses, spells, frights . . .). In the event of penetration, he then resorted to evacuations to rid himself of the worst, and cleanse himself of dark and putrescent humours; he purified his blood with philtres and, where clysters, blood-lettings and issues had failed, he would induce artificial clearance of the body by means of 'vomitories' (liberation through cleansing). Vomiting advocated also by Hippocrates, was one of the chief techniques employed in the art of corporeal purification, in a society like that of the late Renaissance and Baroque ages, where the air could suddenly become evil and corrosive, bringing with it mysterious and widespread contagion, people might be easily stricken by a mere 'glance, kiss, flower, fruit or other form of food'. 'Curses', spells and witchcraft could even be transmitted by a mere glance or kiss, by smells or a fruit. Against these an amulet known as an 'Agnus Dei' was considered a 'salutory medicine' of 'remarkable efficacy', having also the power to ward off thunderbolts, not to mention the water and fire obtained from the 'purest . . . wax from a Pascal candle after the many ceremonies and benedictions of Holy Week'.[2]

'Christian' medical ideology (taken in the dogmatic sense of the Counter-Reformation), theology, exorcistic theory, quack medicine had built up between them an imposing consensus of opinion which was put

---

[1]   T. Campanella, *Del senso delle cose e della magia*, p. 281.

[2]   S. Mercuri, *De gli errori popolari d'Italia*, p. 419, Cf. V. Bonardo *Discorso intorno all'origine, antichità e virtù degli Agnusdei*, Roman, 1591.

into practice at all levels. Apothecaries in towns, travelling pork-butchers, nomadic herbalists, monastic apothecaries, phlebotomists, clyster-specializing barbers and embalming barbers, collegiate doctors of no fixed abode: all these people plied their trade within the same therapeutic framework. The only distinguishing factors between official (therefore legal) and unsupervised (illegal) medicine, which otherwise shared the same ubiquitous and homogeneous cultural inertia, were those of professional rank, income and dress.

Evacuatory oils and vomitories, taken internally and externally, were generally prescribed as good methods of purging the bad humours 'which harboured witchcraft'.

> Take an ash of silicon and flour from hay and therewith make a lye; once strained it may be applied to the whole of the patient's body from head to foot. The lye should again be well-strained for the cloth which has been used for straining will contain (as one author states) the instruments of witchcraft. Then must the sick man be again washed, the lye strained and the same procedure repeated until there are no more instruments of witchcraft in the cullender, for the patient will then be utterly freed; though the whole must have been preceded by the customary blessings and exorcisms.[3]

So the body had to undergo a treatment reminiscent of the laundering of dirty linen, with lye and lixivium. By subjecting the 'instruments of witchcraft' to a series of launderings and rinses, they were eventually sifted out and expelled.

An alternative procedure was to 'move' the stomach of the bewitched person, and the evacuatory purge then made a clean sweep of the humoural quagmire, the seat of fermentation for witchcraft:

> Take an inch or two of St John's wort, the oil thereof, and place this in a glass of malmsey, which the patient shall then drink at dawn, though under supervision, for he may vomit and move his stomach and so be rid of all sorceries; if not, then the amount of oil should be doubled.[4]

War was waged against evil spirits by means of 'confections' or 'vomitory syrups', or 'honey so made to cause vomiting', diluted with 'fatty broth of meat' together with wine, rose water, white hellebore and

---

[3]   F. Canale, *De secreti universali raccolti, et esperimentati trattati nove*. Ne' quali si hanno rimedii per tutta l'infermità de' corpi humani, come anco de' cavalli, bovi e cani. Con molti secreti appertinenti all'arte chemica, agricoltura, e caccie, come nell'indice alfabetico, Venezia, 1613, p. 180.

[4]   Ibid. p. 180.

cinnamon. But the preventive ritual was a great deal more complex: and a 'valuable defence against spells' which prescribed a far from easy series of operations:

> Take a sea onion, one grain of amethyst, two ounces of jet, one ounce of bezoar, one ounce of *morsus diabolis*, one ounce of coral, two ounces each of gold, myrrh and incense, a handful of rue, and one of St John's wort; one of half of these things shall be reduced to a powder to place in beds, that is in the mattresses upon which the patients lie, and the other half shall be placed in the corner of the bedroom, and in the doorway and about the sick man's neck.
>
> Moreover, the following bath shall be prepared daily. Take running water and make a gentle lye with ashes from an olive tree, in which there already boils a bunch of one sprig each of bay, sage and rosemary, a handful of bran and a pinch of ordinary salt. The patient should remain in this bath for an hour, even longer if possible, it being noted, however, that the aforementioned ingredients should have previously been blessed.
>
> After the bath, the body should be dried, anointed with butter and juice from the roots of wall-wort mixed over a fire in equal quantities and blessed.[5]

This holy butter is symbolic of a social ideology in which oil, anointings, unctions, fulfilled two purposes, hardly distinct one from another: those of holy lubrication and medical application. It served as a preservative, as did the baptismal herbal juices of exorcistic botany in the Counter-Reformation, themselves rebaptized and sanctioned with the names of angels or saints. The enchanted forest, the sacred wood, a shrine to the gods of vegetation, was converted and placed at the service of Goodness and watched over by the heavenly custodians. With help from herbs 'named according to the saints', an illness stood a chance of being cured more quickly, Bartolomeo Ambrosini, a pupil of Aldrovandi's, devised his *Panacea* to provide doctors, herbalists, surgeons and conventual hospitals with a new and more efficacious means of cure:

> not only trusting in our knowledge and in the virtues of these plants, but also relying on the watchfulness of the gods in times of sickness – for they have the sick primarily in their care – they will achieve a safer, swifter and more agreeable result.[6]

5   Ibid. pp. 180–1.
6   B. Ambrosini, *Panacea ex herbis quae a Sanctis denominatur concinnata. Opus curiosis gratum medicis vero et pharmacopoeis perutile*, Bononiae, 1630, c. [4].

In this new garden exuding supernatural kindness and virtue, the scent of some plants seemed like a foretaste of Heaven irrigated by divine grace. The routes of the rebaptized herb 'of the Holy Ghost', more commonly known as 'angelica', released an angelic voluptuousness:

> either because of its miraculous and enormous power against poisons and serious diseases, or because of the most pleasant odour which its root exhales, which seems to bring with it the grace of a divine perfume and angelic powers of great blessing.[7]

In this new blessed and dream-filled pleasure garden (in the century of new science, botany played a restraining rôle, stimulating the growth of a magical-religious folklore, protected by those very ecclesiastical institutions and that very political culture which strove, from another pulpit, to put an end to such folklore) Christian baptism by herb – alongside the programme of evangelization which had been specially entrusted to the 'missions' – introduces further confusion, if not chaos, into the already strained nomenclature of the vegetable pantheon. The name of St John represented at least four different 'simples', St Mary lent her name to the hand, mantle and rose of the Virgin Mary. Saints Cunegond, Gutheria, Barbara, Catherine, and Claire collaborated with their male counterparts, Saints Anthony, Albert, Benedict, James, George and Christopher and many other powerful patrons, to envelop mortal sufferers in a protective and aromatic veil.

'But since these types of illness are hard to cure without the previous application of vomitories', wrote Florian Canale, expert in demon-catching, a whole succession of 'emetics . . . of varying kinds, sometimes one, sometimes another, will be chosen, according to how the patient's constitution has been diagnosed . . .: some weak, some indifferent, some violent'[8] – from oxymel to ordinary oil mixed with barley water, radish juice or infusions made with dill, broom seeds and flowers or grains of antimony taken with rose sugar or in wine or in cinnamon and rose-water dragées.

'Wan, with rings under their eyes, there are those who suffer persistent headaches, others with a bone in their throat, others again with stomach aches: others are as if wrapped up in a mantle of thorns . . .[9]

> Some who are bewitched are ashen-faced, their eyes are as though shrunk, their limbs stiff and their humours desiccated. Other noteworthy sign is that they feel the mouth of the stomach and the heart constricted, as though they had a lump in their

7   Ibid. c. 3r.
8   F. Canale, *De secreti universali. . .*, p. 181.
9   Ibid. p. 179.

stomach. Others feel a kind of stitch in the heart like a pin prick; and others as though their hearts had been devoured. Some are so overwhelmed with pain in their necks or kidneys that it is as though dogs were tearing at their flesh, or they had a lump in their throat, or a tangle of thread that ascends and descends or, indeed, that their reproductive organs were bound. Others feel such discomfort in their stomachs that they throw up all they have eaten. There are those who have a chill wind racing through their body, and at times this is like a flame of fire.[10]

'Supernatural remedies' (the 'holy incantations' and 'powerful tones' of the exorcist/priest who 'challenges monsters to a formidable battle' so as to free the 'beautiful damsel possessed by the devil', 'fixed' by Tommaso Gaudiosi during an attack) were used alongside 'natural' remedies 'insofar as they remove the evil condition of the body'. There then followed the 'preparation' of the 'possessed' for exorcistic treatment, namely a long and extended peregrination among oils, baths, ointments, syrups, purges, clysters, vomitories and bleedings.

First the possessed should confess and take communion and be exorcised for seven continuous weeks . . . . In the meanwhile the following oil should be prepared. Take one pound and a half of carefully chosen clear turpentine . . ., one pound of yellow wax, which should be new and fatty . . . , three ounces of powdered dragon's blood . . ., six ounces of sifted vinestock ash . . ., a sufficient quantity of ground glass. Cut the wax into small pieces with a knife and melt it in an iron pot, then bind it together with the turpentine and the other ingredients over a low fire; this mixture then being shaped into small balls, placed in a glass retort and allowed to distill over a low fire until all the oil has been expelled . . . . The patient must drink this oil every morning for a month . . .[11]

Bewitched, spellbound and possessed, the patient had to undergo a whole ritualistic course of spiritual integration, a tormented and hallucinatory journey preparatory – provided no mishaps occurred during the demanding initiation period – to the expulsion of the evil spirits:

. . . certain [demons] are silent and others are not, and these issue from the mouth, as I have seen, in the form of an icy wind sometimes, or as a flame, and as they appear there is a swelling

10   F. Canale, *Del modo di conoscer et sanare i maleficiati, et dell'antichissimo et ottimo uso del Benedire: trattati due. A' quali sono aggionte varie congiurationi, et essorcismi contro la tempesta e cattivi tempi mossi da maligni spiriti*, Brescia, 1614, pp. 3–4.
11   F. Canale, *De secreti universali. . .* , p. 179.

of the throat; others come out from the ears in the same fashion, originating in the stomach or the heart; others issue from the lower regions in the shape of a ball, which spins until it is released; others appear in the form of frogs that wriggle their way out.[12]

In practice, in order to achieve complete purgation, the 'patient' was obliged to undergo a lengthy series of physical tortures during the course of which it not infrequently occurred that he was called prematurely to his Maker, as Florian Canale pointed out in a criticism of the 'abuses' practiced by certain clerics who

> undertaking the treatment of a possessed person, would purge him, without any advice from doctors, with highly potent medicaments which induce vomiting and do great violence to the stomach, such as antimony, white hellebore and other substances; this without regard to age, strength, constitution, the patient's disposition, or the time of year ... I wished to draw attention to this, in order to show how carefully exorcists should be in administering these powerful vomitories, remembering the risks incurred if they are applied without great caution, and I have seen some leave this life through the rashness of others ...[13]

The stages and halts in the journey towards liberation by exorcism were long, enervating, taking their toll to the extent of being almost irreparable. The treatment against demons made herculean demands on the patient's body: the purification of the corrupt body, the dialysis of the blood and of bewitched humours took the form of a taxing and gruelling ritual of initiation. The obligatory starting point was purgation, because:

> before applying other remedies, it is necessary to purge the whole body with lighter medicines so as to prepare it for more drastic treatment; and since purging of the body is better effected through vomiting or evacuation, it is best to resort to expulsion from the bowels, so that the body, which is full of excrement, may not cause the stomach to become overcharged, to the grave discomfort of the patient.[14]

The ceremony of *purgatio* was on the complex and delicate side, since it was a case of administering the right evacuant for the type of 'humour' predominant in the patient, and of establishing the compatibility of the

---

[12]   F. Canale, *Del modo di conoscer et sanare i maleficiati...*, p. 9.
[13]   Ibid. pp. 27, 33.
[14]   Ibid. pp. 25–6.

medicine with his 'complexion': whether choleric, phlegmatic or san-
guine. His temperament was judged more complex, however, if 'as well
as the humour induced by the sorcery, the patient was also of a
melancholy complexion'; and in this case substantial variants were
required.

On concluding this preliminary phase in the purificatory process, the
second phase was embarked upon, this consisting of 'preparatory medicaments':

> The offending humour being now reduced . . ., it is now a matter
> of preparing what remains of it, so as to extract it from the
> affected body through more potent medicines. For this purpose,
> the following syrups . . . should be used . . . for choleric complex-
> ions . . . for phlegmatic complexions . . . for melancholic com-
> plexions.[15]

And so the patient entered at this point on the syrup phase which, if it
was deemed necessary, was accompanied by a moderate dose of bleeding:

> While the patient takes syrups, a quantity of this blood may be
> removed in a variety of ways, according to his strength, the
> condition of his body and other considerations to be taken into
> account when performing this operation.[16]

Upon completion of this preliminary phase of sucrose and syrupy
waiting, there now followed the phase of 'more vigorous purgatives':

> The preparation having lasted for seven days or more, and the
> necessary bleeding being effected, it is at this point judged
> opportune to purge the whole body with the medicament most
> suited to the complexion, age, strength and nature of the
> patient, always bearing in mind that in the presence of a
> melancholic humour, particular care must be taken, as pre-
> viously stated.[17]

There then took place, after the due neutralization of humoural
excesses, a second cycle of purgations, to complement the first cycle, still
in accordance with the quaternary casuistry of the humours. But on
completion of the second phase, the patient was plunged into a sheer
purgatory, or cyclone, far more harrowing and dangerous than the
preceding operation:

[15]   Ibid. p. 28.
[16]   Ibid. p. 29.
[17]   Ibid. pp. 29–30.

The above-described evacuations having taken place, *it should not be thought* that the patient is fully purged, because there are some who are so full of excrement that not even a three or four-fold dose of medicament can purge them, but it is necessary to repeat the purgation of the stomach many times, and *finally* resort to the use of vomitories, for which the time has now come.[18]

It was upon reaching this phase of drastic vomitories involving also the use of poisonous emetics, that the greatest number of deaths occurred. Rough-handed and ignorant exorcists carried out extraordinary operations with the utmost casualness and apparent lack of concern, almost smothering their unfortunate patients sometimes, in a way that would arouse horror and pity in modern minds.

Milk from 'spurge' was judged by Florian Canale to be 'most dangerous if not used with great caution'. But even direr in its results, when compared with castor oil, or ricinus, was the white hellebore 'so frequently used by exorcists in the cure of bewitched patients'.

This medicament is very potent and its use is attended by great fear and danger because besides violent and immoderate vomiting, it causes fearful attacks and suffocation; and therefore it is necessary to know its use, or death will ensue where health was sought.[19]

Nonetheless, in spite of the 'fearful attacks', this vomitory was long favoured, to the extent that if its use were deemed unavoidable, the patient had to submit to 'preparation' for it:

If it is desired to use helleborism, it is advisable to prepare the patient's body to allow vomiting to take place with greater ease. Thus, for three days before, the area of the stomach should be anointed with sweet almond oil, fat from a hen, and marrow from a calf's shin. The patient should drink a relaxing broth made from mallow, althea, raisins, radishes, fumitory, with an addition of oxymel to counteract the viscose humours. This medicament should be taken after dinner, the patient having previously eaten heavy and greasy foods and drunk similarly greasy juices . . . . Vomiting having terminated, the stomach may be assuaged externally with oil of mint, wormwood and nutmeg, and within with aromatic rosewater or two slices of toasted bread soaked in malmsey.[20]

[18]   Ibid. pp. 31–2.
[19]   Ibid. p. 36.
[20]   Ibid. pp. 37–8.

Anyone thinking at this point that the patient's torture was at an end, at least from the 'medical' point of view, would be seriously mistaken. The protracted therapeutic journey was far from over: for other medicines, anointings, baths, fumigations and, last but not least, the formidable clyster, awaited the patient:

> ... it is time now to lay aside the vomitory medicaments and speak of some others that should be used after the body has been totally evacuated; some will be used internally and others externally: they take the form of powders, electuaries, preserves, waters, decoctions, jelly-broths, pills, juleps, and other confections; they can be summarized under four headings: baths, fumigations, anointings, amulets or similar items which are hung around the neck, or a limb, of the patient. Clysters are also used, varying in number according to the patient's internal need.[21]

Ointments were made from oil of hypericum or St John's wort (a good demon-chaser and highly aromatic), oil from bay leaves, rue, motherwort, marjoram; or from general purpose oil (against spells, the evil-eye, 'chills' and 'wounds'), or from pungent and bitter-smelling oils made from the flowers and leaves of St John's wort, rue, sage, whorehound, broom, the leaves and berries of bay, of verbena, root of white hellebore, angelica, *imperatoria ostruthium*, birthwort; or fresh juices squeezed from St John's wort, rue, *galega officinalis* (sweet cane), melted in malmsey and eau-de-vie, infused for three days, then cooked in a *bain-marie* and finally put through a press. To this 'extract' there might be added olive oil, holy water, nutmeg, cloves, cinnamon, cassia, spikenard, sweet flag. This new compound was allowed to marinade for twenty-four hours and, again using the *bain-marie*, it was cooked till it had absorbed all the liquid. The remaining oil was then strained, and further enriched with the following ingredients: incense, myrrh, storax, laudanum, aloes, red roses, saffron, scented amber, oriental musk, civet grains, Cyprus powder, live sulphur, *assa fetida*, gold leaf, wax from a pascal candle. Each item had to be blessed 'separately before it was compounded with the oil, and once compounded, it [had] again [to] be blessed'.[22]

If we add to this monstrous anti-diabolical apparatus, ritual fumigations based on sulphur, *assa fetida*, incense, hypericum, myrrh, laudanum burnt upon a fire that had previously been blessed, 'inhaled by patients through the nostrils';[23] if amulets were worn by the bewitched

21   Ibid. p. 39.
22   Ibid. p. 47.
23   Ibid. p. 43.

person around his neck (whether in the form of St John's wort, a piece of coral, a bell, a chunk of red bryony root, a fragment of palm, sprigs of verbena, motherwort, centaurea, southernwood, cyclamen, *teucrum Chamaedrys, salvia pratensis, salvia sclarea*, a wolf's heart), 'items which may be used about the home to impart scent or in other places to scare away all kinds of foul spirits and undo all kinds of sorcery';[24] of if we take into account the bunches of aromatic herbs placed 'in beds, about the house, above doors',[25] or in other places 'against every kind of witchcraft and sorcery', whether for preventive or curative reasons, the picture we receive is one of aromatic and nightmarish delirium, or of an olfactory bomb ready to explode when the contingency arose.

If every epoch has its own odour, the age of witchhunts (contemporary with the cuisine of the late Renaissance and Baroque periods, which favoured the use of vinegar together with sugar, madeira cake with pigeon meat – cooked together in milk and malmsey – were considered a delicious marriage of flavours; or pheasant stewed with pistacio milk and melon seeds, softened with cream, and lemon juice, which commanded widespread and unconditional approval) exhales an unmistakable aura of mutually incompatible essences which are here intermingled, blended, amalgamated to form a surprising and disconcerting mixture. *Assa fetida* used to be combined with incense, hellebore with myrrh, amber with sulphur, wolf's heart with marjoram. This was a cuisine in which the meal started with the dessert (sugared pine-kernels, raisins, marzipan, figs) as a deoppilate and aperitive, the prevailing taste being for sweet-and-sour, sugary, honeyed, treacly concoctions, imbuing the whole of the culinary cosmos with an aura of cinnamon, cloves, pepper, mace, and habituating the palate to the same volatile combinations as the organ of smell experiences in its own ultrasensitive realm. The alternation between taste and smell continued implacably and repeatedly with all the obsess-iveness and breathless monotony of a pendulum. The oxymoric taste of sweet-and-sour corresponded to the pairing of the sense of smell with what is smelt: the marriage of supposedly conflicting and dissonant odours and tastes, in an amalgam where attraction and repulsion formed a union in conflict. From such bold, irreverent and paradoxical juxta-positions of flavours there emerged a potentially life-giving, creative, and explosive synthesis between sacred and profane, pure and impure, hateful and enchanting, wild and tamed, field, and forest, orchard and wood, religious and sacrilegious, the buffoon and the sage, the fool and the prince. Weird and wonderful salads were devised from a wide range of disparate ingredients, as were 'farcies' (a multidimensional and internally contradictory category of recipe) which were the sensual

24   Ibid. p. 48.
25   Ibid. p. 47.

expression of the madness and incongruence that prevailed in ordinary day-to-day living. The symphony of discordant aromas and clashing flavours reverberated not only with the meaning but also with the secret and unobserved rhythm of paradoxical, dreamlike and enigmatic life-style and philosophical outlook. 'Life's a farce' is but a bare cognitive step from culinary 'farciment'; and from those stoves there wafts a hot, pinguid, succulent, humoural image of a comico-tragic society, living on two planes: laughing and crying, rejoicing and funereal, dismal and bright, violent and gentle, creative and destructive. The rhetoric of the kitchen provided a model for therapeutic theory (or vice versa?). Here was a culinary rule book which advocated the contradictory blending of heterogeneous and clashing elements in a beneficial *coincidentia oppositorum*. Pharmacology and cuisine, like two faces of humanity, one healthy and one sick, were closely intertwined, even if in its extreme form this two-headed monster appeared to leave a trail of victims in its wake through mere errors in dosage and proportion, or an overstepping of the boundaries set by an otherwise sound treatment. The kitchen, in which the activities of grinding, crushing, mixing, boiling, double-pot boiling, melting, spreading, greasing, kneading, leavening, fermenting, sifting, flattening, filtering occur, where herbs, meats, juices and dough are handled, is a cross between a sorcerer's or magician's lair and an alchemist's or apothecary's laboratory. The boundaries between 'ailment' and 'medicine' (both terms belonging to the vocabulary of the apothecaries of yore) are hazy and their rôles interchangeable. The same hand was expected to be adept at preparing decoctions and mustard, tisanes and preserves, cataplasms and candies, syrups and whipped cream, confetti and gelatines, *focaccia* and juleps; whilst their utensils, cauldrons and mortars are vessels common to the sciences both of cooking and of pharmacology.

The 'art of good condiment' (Bartholomeo Stefani) which received theoretic ennoblement by the great chefs of the seventeenth century is barely different from that of the apothecaries who prepared ointments, juleps, oils, creams and cataplasms, confections and syrups, broths and jellies. The confectioner's syringe is also used to extrude greasy ointments for clysters ('a glister of pure broth, sugar and butter' was advocated by the leading physician to the Grand Duke of Tuscany, Francesco Redi), and substances taken orally were also often taken anally: a perfect *coincidentia oppositorum*, totally lost by present-day man in his march towards the Quaternary age.

Jasmin preserve or violet jam exuded voluptuousness like the sacred and medicinal aromas brewed by exorcists for their oils or solidified by them to form ointments. The herbs that were intended to chase away one lot of devils (St John's wort and hypericum were 'against visions and phantoms', wrote Vincenzo Tanara in the mid-seventeenth century, 'therefore exorcists continually avail themselves of them'),[26] evoked in their turn other phantoms, conjured up other visions, and lead into other temptations.

Kitchens were pervaded by the smell of stewed, smoked, boiled meat; chopped, crushed, fried herbs; of omelets and sauces, of 'farcies', of decoctions, infusions, preserves, jams, gravies and poultices. Omelets, remedies, sauces, cataplasms and infusions were elaborated using the same herbs, the same hands, the same bodies. The kitchen and the apothecary's shop, the hearth and the alchemist's stove, a range of infinitely exchangeable items, the *bain-marie* of the alchemists was repeated in the techniques called similarly *bain-marie* of the kitchen, stewing in broth, slow roasting, slow boiling, fermentation by heat, the process called 'leavening' by the agents of fermentation and enzyme reaction, the controlled curdling and fermentation of milk, rosolio, julep, and 'confections' all come into being in the same environment.

> St Mary herb, also known as Greek mint, ... is suitable in omelets, and because of its bitter-sweet flavour it is a pleasing condiment on fast days and feast days and when chopped and mixed with eggs, the omelet is good. Moreover it imparts good flavour and odour to soups, when added with other herbs and salt. Women gladly partake of it and it eases their menstrual pains. If the roots be taken and divided it will multiply, and when made into a poultice and placed upon the male organ, it will aid the patient to pass water; heated with white wine and laid on the stomach it will strengthen it; when placed upon the ground this plant will frighten away devils, as too does smoke from it.[27]

Fires and fumigations, steam and herbacious smoke transformed kitchens into centres of homespun exorcism. Here, among vapour and steam, among ashes and embers, bellows and boilers, women watched over their daily task of miraculous transformation, over their pungent fumigations ('infusing the whole house with the scent of rosemary will banish all evil odours, poisons and particularly wasps and hornets').[28] This was where they mixed medicinal porridge, baby food, soups for adults, where they cleaned and scalded herbs whether for ordinary consumption or (as in the case of St Mary herb) for conversion into poultices with which to besmear the male member. An infusion of verbena – another of the exorcistic herbs ('with this plant they would purge houses, with this end they would pluck it in the presbytery'),

26   V. Tanara, *L'economia del cittadino in villa*, Venezia, 1687, p. 434.
27   Ibid. p. 237.
28   Ibid. p. 310.

It is used by women to bathe infants who have been afrighted, and also administered to adults to let blood ..., a crown of the herb is worn on the head to alleviate a headache, and it prevents loss of hair. The cooked roots when held in the mouth relieve toothache, it halts tooth loss and mouth ulcers; taken as a powder in a liquid form it cures the quartan ague.[29]

'Our women' used to take their own menstruum '... to alleviate the pain thereof, and frying it with eggs, they make an omelet which they eat'.[30] Motherwort.

called *arcimis* by country folk, it is a remarkable agent for inducing menstruation, it cures all afflictions of the womb and brings forth the foetal membrane; thus our midwives boil it together with aniseed and administer it to women before child-birth; to this end, not only do they flavour foods as with other herbs, but also fill ravioli with it together with parsley; the leaves thereof, applied as a poultice do cure the king's evil (scrofula). Some say that if a traveller carry its leaves about his person, he will not tire; but I'll warrant it is foolish to believe that hanging the leaves from the doors and windows of one's home will safeguard dwellers from witches.[31]

Motherwort is also effective in combating sterility which comes from excessive humidity. It should be pulverized with snakewood and nutmeg in equal proportions and administered to the patient in the morning in a powder and with wine as a decoction in the evening; or otherwise it may be compounded with apples in opiate form; or a bath may be prepared with motherwort and bay leaves, encouraging nature by such a decoction.[32]

Rue, also, which 'makes men chaste and women lustful' was prized for its apotropaic effects, as

... an enemy of every kind of poison ... it is said that when a person wishes to touch hemlock he should first rub himself with rue, so as to remain unaffected by the hemlock. It is held that a person who has covered himself with rue may approach a basilisk ... and if this creature rubs against him, it will be overwhelmed by the odour of the rue. It is most certain that the shadow or smell of rue will keep serpents away, so inimical is it

29   Ibid. p. 436.
30   Ibid. p. 425.
31   Ibid. pp. 425–6.
32   P. Bairo, *Secreti medicinali...*, cc. 194v.–195r.

to them. Indeed, they fear and flee from the scent of rue: so do toads and all other kinds of poisonous animals. Even the devil hates it, and with reason, for its flowers are topped with a cross.[33]

The cooking of these country matriarchs, as with that of all simple folks, was two-dimensional, nourishing, curative and protective. Gastronomy was crossed with home-made pharmacy, and in this cooking did common people seek for health, long life and appetite. It differed little in substance and taste (from the point of view of contrasting flavours) from the cuisine of the rich classes, except in the matter of quantity.

In fact, the cuisine of the rich also hid, under its for us incomprehensible plethora of ingredients, purées, elements, substances, a whole therapeutic programme or plan for cosmic recreation and revitalization, with the same ultimate purpose as that envisaged by the women who made necromantic concoctions using poisonous herbs. Like these women, the chef, besides being the great protector, the household magician, the creator of delicious fantasies appealing to sight and smell, the architect of ephemeral palaces in sugar and marzipan, was a sorcerer who brought together elements, distributed forces and quality, reintegrated and strengthened, restored and polished. Between the two cuisines there ran the same thread of distinction as that which ran between the great *theriaca* named after Andromachus and the small one destined for use by the poor, for rustic medicine, which was based on garlic or 'twenty leaves of rue, two old walnuts and three dried figs'.[34] Between the glamourous electuaries made from precious stones or pulverized gold and the salutory infusions made from herbs grown in peasants' vegetable plots, the difference was more a quantitative one than one of mental outlook. Dedicated as they were to the continuation of their species, the upper class ate salmés of bulls' testicles, or the rather more astringent soups made from 'the balls of a cock':

> ... washed, cleaned and boiled in a little capon broth, with the addition of six ounces of blanched, crushed pistachios, half a pound of top of the milk, four ounces of well crushed melon seeds, six fresh yolks of egg, the juice of two lemons, and the whole should be reduced into a broth; place the broth in porcelain cups which shall have been lined with Savoyard biscuits and serve with sugar and cinnamon.[35]

33   V. Tanara, *L'economia del cittadino in villa*, p. 254.
34   Ibid. p. 254.
35   B. Stefani, *L'arte di ben cucinare ed instruire i meno periti in questa lodevole professione*, Bologna, s.a., p. 166.

Revitalizing, energizing, regenerative, comforting, arrogant and warlike ingredients are to be found (these recipes came from a cook who appears to have been in the services of the Gonzaga household) even in the humble 'risole', capable of containing the wildest conglomeration of disparate ingredients:

> made of breast of turkey with parmesan cheese, fat ricotta, marzipan paste, candied cedar flower, ox marrow and a little lard beaten together with sweet-smelling herbs and fresh eggs. The whole shall be well mixed and a kite or lion may be formed thereof, or whatsoever may take the fancy. Upon this preparation shall be cast a sauce made of the yolk of fresh eggs, butter, sugar, a little grated apple and the whole dish shall then be sprinkled with powdered cinnamon.[36]

The processes of camouflaging, metamorphosis, herbal decomposition and ennoblement came into the cooking of vegetables also. Aniseed flowers which in peasant kitchens 'were used in meagre quantities because of their odour, and beaten into eggs to make omelets, or with ricotta and eggs to make omelets,'[37] became, at aristocratic tables a socio-culinary hyperbole.

> Take an elder flower, crush it well in a mortar and add three pounds of fat ricotta, eight ounces of parmesan cheese, four eggs, a quarter of cinnamon and six ounces of sugar. The whole shall be powdered and well compounded, after which water shall be sprinkled upon it and round fritters shall be formed thereof. The pan shall be well greased with butter . . ., the fritters shall be fried both top and bottom over the fire, and when half-cooked they shall be placed on plates, sprinkled with sugar and muscat raisins.[38]

The gastronomy which succeeded in uniting turkeys and snails, capers and marzipan, goose liver and sponge cake, which in its moments of architectural delirium produced pies shaped like eagles or 'castles full of minced veal sprinkled with icing sugar'; this cuisine of deceit and illusionism, of olfactory tricks and physiological contradiction, formed part of a pervading magical/alchemic craze, of a mysteriosophical naturalism full of the permutation and metamorphosis of the elements, intent upon discovering new frontiers on the road to the ultimate and impossible dream, to new broths, quintessences, unprecedented, astonishing and disconcerting feasts of the senses. Just as the 'great

[36]   Ibid. p. 168.
[37]   V. Tanara, *L'economia del cittadino in villa*, p. 311.
[38]   B. Stefani, *L'arte di ben cucinare. . .* , p. 174.

world' is a kaleidoscopic wilderness in which are born *ex putri*, sudden and uncontrollable myriads of 'minima animalia', waves of 'minutissima animalia', so in the cauldrons of baroque kitchens, fermenting in simmering broth (the only place where creation can take place) new monstrosities burst forth from the hum of organized putrescence. Audacious marriages of culinary alchemy, programmed with paradoxical logic while cultivating nonsense in the heart of dissonance, elevated the cook to the rôle of great orchestrator of unforeseen adventures for the palate, to that of inventor of novel variations in which the chimeras of the imagination had free expression in sauces and jellies, were imprisoned in preserves and in candied, sucrose, gelatinous dishes of heraldic semblance, were pondered over during nightly vigils. Funereal still lives, encased in icings of sorbet and sugar, crystallized in simulated ice and marbling (a caramel 'icing'), in a frustrated attempt to impose order, longevity and imperviousness on the ephemeral. 'Preparations' for an anatomy of the mouth which sought repugnant consolation in sweet-smelling mouthfuls of wax, balsam, amber, musk, honey, cinnamon, myrrh and incense. Culinary decoration smacked of the church and funeral biers, of wreaths and eternity:

> Bas-relief in gelatine scented with amber.
>
> Cold pie ... with larded pheasant.
>
> Tender chickens, finely larded with layers of fried pastry, crowned with cedar wreaths, adorned with split oranges, served with apricot flowers.
>
> Capons, salted and peppered and strewn with strips of icing, scented with musk and amber, and sprinkled with powdered sugar-cake.
>
> Mountain cock, roasted ... and upon it a flavouring made from pomegranate interleaved with sugar biscuits, upon a plate ornamented with myrtle leaves.

Relics of a funerary cuisine tasting of earth and death, saturated with drugs and emanating pungent aromas reminiscent of the services of the Roman Catholic liturgy, evocative of the exorcist's cuisine, in which 'remedies are given orally, subsequent to purging'.

The recipe for 'best broth' recommended by Florian Canale, who was a gastronomically minded exorcist, follows the same magical/therapeutic logic as that appertaining to the recipe for cock stuffed with enchanted herbs and transformed into an elixir:

> Take a cock, three years in age, and fill it with the below-mentioned items, boil in twenty pounds of water till only five pounds are left; then five pounds of malmsey, treacle and mithridate, an ounce each; anacardine honey, six ounces. The

cock shall be well minced and a goodly sauce be made with all the ingredients, which shall then be left for three days. it shall then be distilled in a *bain-marie*, taking care to place a little musk and amber tied in a muslin cloth in the neck of the lambeck. A quantity of four ounces shall be ingested every morning.[39]

The 'below-mentioned items', namely the ingredients and quantities thereof stipulated to fill the cock, are listed in Latin: hypericon tips, absynthe, motherwort, verbena, oregon, bryony roots, harts-wort, mustard seed, aniseed, cinnamon and nutmeg.

A popular symbol of fertility and male virility, of 'the resurrection of the flesh', insomuch as it is associated with the Easter liturgy, the cock, with its flesh and bones dismantled, minced, macerated, distilled, transformed by boiling and *bain-maries* into a revolting and smelly gruel, into an enigmatic elixir of life, in which honey melts in treacle, mithridate in malmsey; transmuted in a magical, regenerative and revitalizing liquid in which the sacrificed corpse of the sacred beast, offered up as a surety of physical resurrection and a new life from which all evil spells have been expunged, becomes the symbol/model for a chemical/gastronomic magic, or a theology of the kitchen where freedom from evil is interwoven with the recovery of health.

This exorcistic consommé, to which the flesh and blood of a cock mingle and act as restoratives for the weary body, belongs to a magical/cosmological system of therapy, itself an attempt to reinterpret in medical terms the mythology of creation, to reawaken primitive energies, to reinstate primordial elements and the physical momentum of creation, oblivious to the nutritional taboos recognized as existing (while half-heartedly condemned) by ecclesiastical punditry. Another concoction by a churchman, Don Timoteo Rosselli, was 'an oil called *elemental*, which by its action accomplishes incredible and desperate feats':

> Take the purest red blood of a human being in his twenty-fifth to thirtieth year, take the sperm of a fish called a whale and also the marrow-bone of a bull, of each five pounds, or of a male deer, and distill. The first water that flows will be white, the second yellow in colour and thick, the third will be very red and thick. But be careful that the fluid be well closed and sealed, lest that which is within breathe and exhale such a stench as would kill a man or at the very least do him great harm. For the last distillation will be an oil which shall be enclosed in a vessel well sealed as described above, so that none of the liquid be dispersed. This oil is called 'of the elements', that is of fire, air,

---

[39]   F. Canale, *Del modo di conoscer e sanare i maleficiati...*, p. 41.

water and earth and rises of its own agency when the moon waxes and likewise diminishes when the moon wanes.

The principal virtue of this oil may be called divine, when a person seems gripped by ecstasy and is unable to speak. He may take one drop of this oil to three of wine and his indisposition will vanish and he will recover his speech. Any man who drinks of this oil once a day, when overcome by lethargy, with a little wine, will be in excellent health all that day and feel his limbs full of energy and life. It prevents ageing in a man; indeed, he who uses this oil will most wonderfully extend his life . . .[40]

The charlatanry of the religious world hoped in these foul mixtures to find the secret of prolonging life: the copulation of fish sperm, human blood, bull's or deer's medullum, drawing on the welling stream of life's energy and sensuality, on the primordial fountain of the libido, to produce these miraculous brews so conducive to regeneration, though from an ethical standpoint, theology might have been expected rather to condemn these as symbols of moral depravity and fertile rottenness. An oil which had the power to restore life after life had apparently been interrupted or consciousness lost, after momentary and mysterious loss of strength or speech, seemed endowed with superhuman powers. The word often used to describe this state of suspended consciousness, of abandonment of physical control, is drawn from the terminology of saintly living practices: it encapsulates the supernatural phenomena of visionary crisis, visitations and celestial conversations.

The ecstasies of the holy fathers (a favourite subject of the art of the Counter-Reformation), characterized by loss of speech, the interruption of social communication, sublimation of the latter into mute and ecstatic conversation with the divine, form a spiritual backdrop for the enactment of physical rebirth and mental regeneration induced by an oil in which blood and sperm, decaying together (the ultimate symbol of impurity) in a 'deathly' stench, bring about a miracle of a contrary kind: that of restoring the blocked flow of vitality and suspended animation, by destroying the 'ecstasy' and state of sublimation.

[40]   T. Rosselli, *Della summa de i secreti universali. Sì per huomini et donne, di alto ingegno, come ancora per i medici, et ogni sorte di artefici industriosi, et a ogni persona virtuosa accommodate*, Venezia, 1619, cc. 14v.–15r.

11

'EVERLASTING PERFUMERS'

Pungent aromas and perfume were powerful, therapeutic, tonic and stimulating medicaments which revitalized a person's innermost being, and were particularly effective in combatting illness due to poisoning. In order to counteract the evil symptoms of poison, it was necessary 'to comfort the spirit with aromatic scents, and likewise with the heart and intestine'.[1] As for poisons which

> enter through the respiratory organs and rise to the brain or through the pores of the skin, the first antidote for the spirit is with pleasant and nourishing odours, which are then succeeded by palliatives for the ventricles and intestine such as cinnamon, mace and any kind of aromatic substance, to overcome the corrupt odour which insinuates itself within the body, and externally, cupping glasses to draw out vapour and blood, and bathing in good wine.[2]

Corruption and putrefaction insinuated themselves everywhere. If the 'Air is corrupted and putrefied' bread will moulder. If, on the other hand, the air was pure and bracing then the bread 'will remain without any change'.[3] And the 'malignity of the Cold'

> may be corrected, by artificially causing a good and sweet Breath, viz. by keeping in your Mouth Treacle, Mithridate, also the Confection called *Alcarmes* (a term of the *Arabian* Physicians, whereby they meant a Cordial made of certain little Scarlet Worms, of which also is Crimson made) rubbing the Teeth with this Antidote, which yet becomes better by the addition of Zedoary (a Root like Ginger growing in the East-Indies) and chewing therewith *Angelica*.[4]

[1] T. Campanella, *Del senso delle cose e della magia*, p. 249.
[2] Ibid. p. 249.
[3] C. Durante, *Il Tesoro della sanità...*, Venezia, 1596, p. 6. Translated out of the Italian into English by John Chamberlayne Gent., *A Treasure of Health* by Castor Durante Da Gualdo, Physician & Citizen of Rome. Wherein is shewn how to preserve Health, & prolong Life. Also the Nature of all sorts of Meats and Drinks, with the way to prevent all Hurt that attends the Use of either of them, London, 1686.
[4] Ibid. p. 6.

Among 'things [that] cleanse the Mouth ... [and] heal the putrefied Flesh' were elaborate 'dentifrices', made out of:

> Rosemary one Dram, of Myrrh, Mastick, Bole-armoniack, Dragons-Blood, Burnt-allom, *ana* half a Dram; of Cinnamon one Dram and a half, Rose Vinegar, Mastick-water, *ana* three Ounces, half a pound of Rain-water, of Honey three Ounces; boyle these together over a gentle fire, to the end that they may be well scummed; afterwards add thereto *Bezoar* (a kind of Precious Stone very Cordial, being an excellent Antedote to expel Poyson; by the *Arabick* Doctors it is called *Badzahar* i.e. *Alexipharmacon*, a remedy for poison) and as an Unguent keep it in a glass Bottle. Of this take a spoonful every Morning fasting, holding it in your Mouth ... [5]

Even one's house and home had its place in the realm of therapy, the choice of it being governed by its probable effect on the longevity of one's life: it could corrode it or conserve it.

> ... there is great heed to be taken in the choice of a House; see whether the Place and the ~~Air~~ be good or bad, wholesom or unwholsom to dwell in. The House therefore which you take, let it be seated in the highest place of the City; therein chuse your Apartment at least one pair of stairs high, and let it be very light, and so placed that it may always receive the Wind in the Summer, and the Sun in the Winter; and have Windows on all sides; that is, East, West, North, and South, if it may be, to the end, that no one Air may remain there long, which otherwise would putrefie and corrupt; and furthermore you ought to avoid not only lying in a Ground-Chamber, but also tarrying there long, for the highest are the most wholesom, where you breathe the thinnest and purest Air; then you receive this benefit, that dwelling in the highest and most open place of the House, preserves, and repairs the radical Moisture of the Body, and hinders Old Age; but to be in a dark, lower Room, or under the Ground, is very naught; for Life is maintained by the open Air and by Light, but in the shade a Man grows mouldy and corrupted.... 'Tis also commodious to have a Country House, whereto you may sometimes repair; for as the Country provides Food and Victuals for the City, and the City consumes it, so humane Life, by sometimes dwelling in the Country is prolonged, but by the Idleness of the City it is shortned. [6]

5   Ibid. p. 6.
6   Ibid. pp. 6–7.

It is hard to understand nowadays that one of the problems that beset the old world most and of which it was most acutely fearful, was the sense of material decay, the nightmare of universal putrefaction. Modern techniques for the preservation of meat and food in general (freezing, the effects of cold and heat, the exclusion of air to prevent the process of fermentation, hibernation and the miracles wrought by cloning) have eliminated from the canvass of our perceptions the stench of animal decay, the stink of corruption and the repugnant emanations of rotting bodies. But for century after century, indeed, for millenia, the techniques of conserving meat were identical with those used for conserving human corpses. We know through Pliny, for instance, that sea salt was used by the Romans both in the preparation of sausages and for the preservation of corpses. To forestall putrefaction honey was also used, as it was also used to conserve the fish that were exported to Rome from distant lands, in scent jars. Fermentation and putrefaction, by rapidly transforming organic compounds, gave substance and smell to the sense of the ephemeral and fear of the transient. Oils, resins, preservative balms, to combat putrescence and fermentation, aromatic woods and the liquids obtained from distillation, such as *cedrium* (extracted from *teda*, a kind of pine) were used to embalm the remains of the dead. The same distillations, oils and ointments (in their multifarious local and cultural variants) were widely used for application on the skins of the living. Even the 'curing' of hams, bacons and meats smoked over the open fire was technically the same as the practice of preserving cadavers by hanging them for the requisite time over a fire and smoke produced by aromatic woods. 'Bresaola' [dried salt beef] and 'speck' [bacon] were smoked using the same technique as that used by the Amerindians for the conservation of the dead and by our apothecaries in the preparation of 'mumia'. The apothecary's laboratory was not complete without a little 'dried human flesh' and the odd desiccated head of a corpse, according to Berengario da Carpi. These appurtenances belonged to the same cultural realm, in which fire and flame were adroitly used, as the instruments of conservation, for the delaying of decomposition, the same world as that in which salted and smoked meats were used to prolong life in the living or tangible presence in the deceased. It was a world in which the dividing line between life and death, between presence and absence was not as well-defined as it is today, where death cancels in one stroke all semblance of life, where the body of the formerly living person is removed, hidden, eliminated, mourning is abolished and funerals have become well-nigh a clandestine matter. The conservation of flesh from deterioration, by the lengthy processes of salting, hanging and smoking, belonged to a culture in which the active presence of the deceased, the prolongation of his memory, the attempt to keep at bay annihilation and pulverization, went hand in hand with a feeling for life's slow unravelling and a collective search for longevity, not only of the flesh, but also of memory and experience. The lives of the living were intertwined with those of the dead in a way unfathomable to our era where the Freudian analysis of dreams has eradicated conversation in favour of nocturnal shadows, broken the fragile network of messages between the dead and the living, destroyed the night's disquieting yet exciting colloquy with the dead, interrupted social memory whereby the past is transmitted orally, verbally, by advice proffered, warnings issued, and messages of foreboding received from household spirits. Family gods and ghosts, penates and hearthside crickets, the lamentations of the dead have all melted away along with the disintegration of the family as the workshop in which the experiences and wisdom of our forebears are recast, moulded and put to general good use.

Even the integumenta, the protective winding sheets, the raiments which enveloped and preserved the body formed part of the logic of congruence and therapeutic consensus. No unseemly or casual dress was permitted, only that dictated by wisdom and forethought: generally speaking, forms of clothing were chosen that

> inclined to warmth and dryness and in winter took the form of sheep, wolf or sable-skin; stockings should be made of hare's skin much benefitting the joints, or of wolf skin which comforts all the limbs. Other clothes should be made in wool, cotton wool, silk, but those of linen are the least worn. The whole body should be covered day and night, most of all the head, which is the home of the reason and on which many a sickness depends . . . [7]

The garments, in their turn, were impregnated with essence of perfume, with 'tannin' or aromatic waters, according to season. It might be thought that this sensitivity to perfume was a form of snobbery, but, no, it was popular and widespread, in a way with which we are unfamiliar today, and it went hand-in-hand with a heightened sense of smell: the sensitivity to taste was aroused by its 'affinity and correlation' with odour.[8]

> Take [in winter] of *Iris Florentina*, or Flower-de-luce, *Zedoary*, Spikenard, *ana* one Ounce, Storax, mastick, Cinnamon, Nutmegs, Cloves, *ana* half an Ounce, Juniper-berries three Drams, Behen, Amber, Musk, *ana* one Scruple: Distill all these things with Wine.[9]

[7]   Ibid. pp. 7–8.
[8]   L. Magalotti, *Lettere sopra i buccheri*, ed. M. Praz, Firenze, 1945, p. 316.
[9]   C. Durante, *A Treasure of Health*, p. 8.

And in summer:

> take of Rose-water, four pounds, of the best Vinegar one pound, of Red Roses one handful and a half, Camphire half a Dram, Musk seven Grains, Spice of *Diambra*, Flower-de-luce, *ana* one Ounce; pound all these, except the Spice, and Musk and the camphire, and dissolve them all in Rose-water, which being put into a Limbeck, cover it nine days under Horse-dung.[10]

As an alternative to the waters, garments might be sprinkled with scented powders dissolved in rosewater: and together with red roses, violets, citron-peel, myrtle, aloes, sandalwood, camphor, amber, musk, behen, the result was a 'most subtle powder'. Aromatic apples, balls and sponges accompanied the powders and waters.

> 'Tis also good to carry Odoriferous things in your Hand, in the Summer-time, a Sponge dipt in Rose-water, or Rose-vinegar, and smell to it often; or carry with you this Odoriferous Ball: Take of Roses one Dram, Red Coral four Scruples, Water-Lillies one Dram and a half, Bole armoniack one Dram, *Storax Calamita* on Dram and a half, *Lignum-Aloes* two Scruples, Mastick one Dram, *Ladanum* two Drams, Amber, Musk, *ana* two Grains; these are pounded, and so made into a Ball.
>
> The winter carry a Sponge infused with Vinegar, wherein steep Cloves and Zedoary: Or else carry in your Hand this Ball of Amber. Take of *Ladanum* half an Ounce, *Storax Calamita* two Drams, *Bezoar*,, Mastick, *ana* one Dram, Cloves, Nutmegs, Crocus, Dyers-Grains, white Wax, *Lignum-aloes*, *ana* one Scruple, Amber half a Scruple, Musk dissolved in Malmsey five Grains; make it into a Ball.[11]

Spicy scents and balms: suave, delicious, beneficial and comforting medicaments: fragrance of musk, gentle yet pungent, fountains of perfume, of amnesic and inebriating essences (laudanum often makes its appearance in enormous doses), household fragrances, 'exhalations gentle and most delightful, vital and ineffable',[12] tablets to be melted in the mouth, others to be burnt on braziers, perfumes, incense, myrrh, aloes, *belzoí*, by the handful, fire tablets and water tablets, *buccheri* [scented jars]. Sprayed mists of fragrant water, jasmin water, orange blossom water, bramble rose water, juniper water, water from damask rose, exhalations, 'invisible breaths', remarkable evaporations to neutralise the 'universal corruption of the world', *buccheri* full of edible,

10   Ibid. p. 9.
11   Ibid. p. 9.
12   L. Magalotti, *Lettere sopra i buccheri*, p. 38.

scented or drinkable ambrosia, ingestible aromatic powders, or pastes of fire and water:

> The first are winter perfumes, the second for the summer; the former sharpen the air, the latter sweeten it; the first invade the head, and the second sooth the heart; the former are not for the healthy, the latter are prescribed to the sick ... [13]

'Daily fumigations', 'perpetual scentedness' '... seemed to be in all the spiceries that the Orient ever produced': a thick blanket of sharp or sweet scent enveloped everything 'from the East to the West Indies ... The East, fiery and exalted in its dryness; the West softened and diluted by humidity'.[14]

The sublime olfactory deliria, states of mystical sublimation, attacks of dizziness, labyrinths full of aromatic vapour, through which generations of 'sensitive odorists' passed, found in Lorenzo Magalotti with his extraordinary responsiveness, a veritable 'hero of the nose':

> ... it sufficeth not to know merely of rose water and catmint. Another treasury of knowledge, another study, is required, of other conserves, another understanding of materials, doses and mixtures. Essential is practice in the arts of smelling, of manipulation, which are learnt through repeated error and repeated deception; of immersion, absorption, of inebriation of the fancy, retained through the years and reawakened across the years in a continuous and ideal bath in abundant aromatic spices, from which the imagination, impregnated and satiated, will rise, baptizing (as it were) and imbuing the soul with vapours purified of every vestige of matter, which when they reach the mind act as a pure spiritual suffumigation, inundating it with so unique a harmony that all plurality is banished, unity reigns, a unity according to the mind's inclination, which is independent of all externally applied ointments; and the latter, the soul being in this condition will act no longer as odours, but as though entranced or, indeed, eclipsed in that abyss of odourous light.[15]

This is none other than the language of mysticism translated into fragrant emanations, olfactory and narcotic quintessences; where subliminal ecstasy takes the form of 'pure spiritual suffumigations', evoking an extrasensory experience which in its turn embraces the Whole and 'rejects all multiplicity'. A perfumed narcosis, a heightened consciousness where, immersed in contemplation, the seeker of cosmic unity

13   Ibid. p. 35.
14   Ibid. p. 116.
15   Ibid. pp. 313–14.

realises his dream. The techniques of asceticism find expression in olfactory sublimation in a society which rose above earthly putrescence by smelling and imagining fragrant dreams. Lorenzo Magalotti was but a rising star in a firmament of mystical odorists, of delirious perfumiers who were capable of experiencing extremes of sublime perversion. Louis William of Aragon, Duke of Montalto, later Cardinal of Moncada (1613–73), 'the virtuoso of the sense of smell' was accustomed to take 'clysters of flower water without salt, so as to retain them all day in his body':[16] without salt to prevent the separation encouraged by enemas which were held to 'stimulate the excretory functions'. Not only the nose but the whole body, too, was to be the glad recipient of this perfumed inundation. Nose culture was so highly developed in the Florence of the Grand Duke Ferdinand II, that a certain inquisitor 'used to roam the streets on a Friday to ascertain, by means of smell, whether or no the faithful had partaken of meat'.[17] In that same period – according to Father Segneri – St Philip Neri exhaled

> from his living body so exquisite a smell, so singular and rare, that everyone called it the odour of virginity: indeed one of his penitents upon smelling it immediately felt every carnal desire vanish from him, as worms die that smell myrrh, vultures that smell amber and snakes that smell citron. He would even tell those who appeared before him affected by gross carnal desires by the smell.

The society of old was widely versed in distillations, quintessences, medicinal waters, perfumed tablets, fragrant pomades, aromatic balsams, with ointments, creams and liniments. In the century into which the Count, such a connoisseur of smells, proudly poked his discerning nose – like an olfactory spy-glass focussed upon worlds inaccessible to the majority – certain religious observances were suggested which read like a handbook of the most attractive and inebriatingly odourous experiences. In his *Alfabetto de' secreti medicinali* Lazaro Grandi, the self-styled 'doctor of medicine', presents the reader with three recipes for 'odiferous and beautiful Pater Nosters', 'scent-bearing Pater Nosters, with another paste that they may shine the better', and 'Pater Nosters of any scent desired, the manner of their making being different from the above'.

> Take two ounces of dragees that have been softened in rose water, some benzoin and laudanum. All these should be crushed

16   L. Magalotti, Letter of 1696 to mons. Leone Strozzi, in *Lettere odorose di Lorenzo Magalotti* (1693–1705), ed. E. Falqui, Milano, 1943, p. 202.
17   G. Imbert, *Seicento fiorentino*, Milano, 1930, pp. 254–5.

together. Then take half an ounce of liquid styrax, two drams of camphor, some carbon of *salix alba* and burned bone, and make a paste with all of these. Work the shapes desired, taking care to add a little sweet-smelling oil, and when they are done they shall be both exquisite and beautiful.[18]

In this society of 'odorists', the nose was the channel through which the mysterious and – in many cultures – divine sneeze was transmitted: a sensitive and refined conduit up which aromatic messages made their way, ascending finally to the brain, the presumed seat of human reason. In treating many cerebral illnesses, particularly epilepsy, among the most common medicaments used were the *medicamenta errhina*, taken nasally, examples of such distillations being the so-called 'capital' waters, the juices of pimpernel, onion, cyclamen, cabbage, bellflower: 'are smeared or inserted in liquid state into the nostrils'; from time to time, Gordonius comments in his *Lilium Medicinae*, one of the most popular medical works of the fourteenth century – 'aromatic oils and spices should be mixed in hot'. However, if the medicine had to be stronger ('valentiora') such as extract of white horehound, pepper, white helle-bore, 'dry ingredients, which are inserted into the nostrils with straw, or mixed with liquid of some kind or wax and applied to the nostrils in a trickle'.[19]

Suffumigationes, 'to create a pleasing perfume', scented suffumi-gations practiced over a low fire (brazier), were greatly favoured in the Middle Ages: powders and mixed aromatic herbs 'were burnt or thrown onto red-hot coal fire'. Sage, rosemary, mace, cinnamon, incense, marjoram, basil, carnations, aloes, myrrh, mastic (lentisk gum) were all recommended by Gordonius, a contemporary of Boccaccio's, and a visitor (guided by the Isidorian *ethimologiae*) to the fragrant garden of Pomona in which:

> you may see a copious shrub of warm and pale-leafed sage, and above it narrow-leafed and serviceable rosemary; beyond, you will find in abundance the valuable betony plant, followed by the fragrant and tiny leaves of marjoram usefully sharing the ground with mint. And in a corner you may find frigid rue and tall-growing senvy, offensive to the nose but useful for purging the head. Here, too, hugging the ground there abound thinly sinuous twigs of wild thyme; and curly basil, imitator, when in

18   L. Grandi, *Alfabetto de' secreti medicinali. . .*, Bologna, 1693, p. 129.
19   B. Gordonius, *Opus, lilium medicinae inscriptum, de morborum prope omnium curatione, septem particulis distributus. . .*, Lugduni, 1574, p. 112.

season, of the carnation's scent ... Here are mallows, nasturtiums, dill, tasty fennel and frigid parsley.[20]

The *hortus sanitatis* [Garden of Health] of mediaeval days was a medicine chest of health and vegetable voluptuousness, a pharmaceutical orchard of pleasure, oblivion, sleep and longevity, so responsive and so sensitive was nature here that it even captured the odourless smell of water.

Gradually awakening to the smell of its meandering waters, the garden put forth the many riches in which it abounded: hyssop, the herb that benefits the lungs and grows in the crevices of rocks, poppy that is born in the plain and induces sleep. Senvy that fills fields and loosens a cold in the head ... Daffodils grow by springs, privet in the hedgerows; roses grace the garden, lilies enhance the valley. Endive shares its ground with soporific lettuce ... mint spreads its scent all around, the stripey iris, delicate mallow alongside suppliant dialtea. Rocket rich in voluptuousness, savoury the flavour for condiments, rag-wort that makes the old young; and the plant that at dusk closes upon itself and opens again with the opening of day and follows the sun like a betrothed. And mother-wort with its blue-green buds, having the power to abolish the ills that women suffer. Sage flourished upon its stalk, ready to heighten the flavour of celebratory fare: man, who is prodigal and loves his pleasures, introduced this plant, more properly medicinal, among the victuals of his kitchen. Fennel, topped with a tuft of fine hairs, is potent to free blind eyes from their darkness: when the serpent casts off, together with his skin, the years which encumber his vigour, he refreshes his weary eyes with fennel. Oregano burrows deeper with its roots, and wild thyme, noted antidote to the viper's offspring, begins to creep across the ground. And there is wild mint, the best medicine to relieve the muscles when articular pains assault the limbs. There is also penny-royal, the correct remedy for one who may have imbibed poison, and chervil, which is a herb of lesser value. Wild nard that gushes up from the earth like a vapour and bugloss that benefits menstrual flow, effective in purging the spleen and mind. And savoury herb

[20] G. Boccaccio, *Comedia delle ninfe fiorentine*, ed. A. Quaglio, Milano, 1964, vol. II, pp. 745–6. Cf. *Le virtù del ramerino*, writing of the XIVth century, ed. G. Chiarini, Livorno, 1868. The first modern and non-magical study on sage is *Sacra herba, seu nobilis salvia, juxta methodum et leges illustris Academiae Naturae Curiosorum descripta, selectisque remediis, et propriis observationibus conspersa*, by Christian Franz Paullini, Augustae Vindelicorum, 1688.

that benefits the kidneys, and lanceolate rib-wort which performs the same function but even better. And there are rue and camomile that pleasantly calm the brain. Dittany with the power to draw foreign bodies that have inserted themselves beneath the flesh, wound-wort to heal the worst wounds. Aniseed, which is by nature warm and hinders the genital conduits and thus impedes the passage of sperm. Wormwood, that through sweat, melts away evil juices; violets, that dispel heat. And here there is milk-weed that lightens a heavy stomach . . . Milk-cap grows that will cause tumult in the belly, a purge full of tempests. Hemlock, Socrates's herb, grows beside henbane which together with the stalk of hemlock, is death's associate. The Earth, mother of a thousand prodigies, has engendered madragora, the herb that imitates the human appearance.[21]

It is as though everyone carried within him a herb garden, in his blood and in the tissues of his body. Medicinal, aromatic, benumbing, stimulant, tranquillizing herbs penetrated the system by all possible routes; they were inhaled, smelled, chewed, pulverized, applied to the skin, sucked up, swallowed and injected with syringes.

The nasal cavity, full of veiny and arterial folds connected to the cranial cavities, was one of the preferred channels. A great range of *odoramenta*, whether of the cold variety like the water-lily, oil of violets, extract of poppy, rose, sandalwood, camphor, mandragora and *populeonis* ointment (as powerful as an immobilizing dart) or of the multifarious *odoramenta calida* species, like aloes, cinnamon, mace, mastic, musk, juniper, cat-mint, broom, marjoram, carnation, opium, lavander and incense, that 'by their mere odour influenced the brain', were burnt, drunk, chopped, distilled in alcohol or spread upon the skin like ointments. Moreover, there was the category of *medicamenta masticatoria* that 'are retained in the mouth, chewed and crushed between the teeth, or they are pounded together with a liquor or even honey and made into masticatable tablets'; hyssop, organs, thyme, penny-royal, capers, senvy, ginger, pepper, pyrethrum, acorus root, were taken particularly in the morning when 'the body expels the remnants of excreta'.[22]

But *loch* and *eclygmata* [sap] (of pine, cabbage and scilla) were consumed at all hours; loch of poppies was on the other hand 'administered in the hours subsequent to dinner'.

21   B. Silvestre, *Cosmografia* in Theodoric of Chartres, Guillaume de Conches and Bernardo Silvestre, *Il divino e il megacosmo. Testi filosofici e scientifici della scuola di Chartres*, ed. E. Maccagnolo, Milano, 1980, p. 487–9.
22   B. Gordonius, *Opus, lilium medicinae. . .* , p. 1112.

If the *confectiones aromaticae* are added to these vegetable distillations: such as infusions, decoctions, clysters, suppositories, liquid and
solid purgatives, the *bolus purgatorius*, syrups and scented waters (each
one designed for a particular part of the body), trochisks (those made
from rhubarb, myrrh or liverwort were used against *febrium horrores*),
and finally the *conservae* of roses, nard, maidenhair, violets, paeony,
lavander, betony, chicory, sage (borrage, bugloss and sorrel were
recommended for the treatment of melancholic palpitations and depress-
ions), to which were sometimes added *pulveres aromaticae*, one will
obtain a vivid picture of the aromatic aura which pervaded the world of
Galenus's man at all hours and in all seasons. These fragrances were
forms of knowledge, they were tools for the identification of reality:
everything passed through the medium of smell. Both sacred modes and
moral codes were intangible versions of the impossible, having a real, not
symbolic, odour of their own.

Where in the pagan world of fragrance heralded a divine presence, in
the later part of the early Christian era, the man of god smelt out a satanic
presence. One day, Hilarion alone among the others smelt a terrible
stench arising from a bunch of green chickpeas placed on the table:

> ... old Hilarion cried that he could not bear the stench and
> asked whence it came. When Hesychius answered that a brother
> had brought the first fruits of the season from his little field as an
> offering to the other brothers, he exclaimed: 'But can you not
> smell a fearful stench? Can you not smell the odour of avarice in
> these chickpeas? Throw them to the oxen, throw them to ugly
> animals and see if they will eat them.' The other, no sooner had
> he heard this, than he placed the peas in the manger; and the
> oxen, lowing fearfully and louder than usual, fled in all direct-
> ions breaking their halters. For old Hilarion had this particular
> gift from heaven, that he could divine from the apparel worn by
> a person or the things he had touched, to which devil or vice he
> was prey.[23]

When several months after his burial, Hilarion's remains were raided
(according to the highly respected St Jerome), those charged with
removing him to a surer burial place noticed that his body was unblemished as though he were still alive, and it exhaled such a fragrance that
it might have been thought he had been embalmed with an ointment.[24]

St Jerome launches into a long series of descriptions of odiferous
exhumations in which holy bodies remained whole and intact, escaping

[23] Hieronimus, *Vita Hilarionis*; Italian version taken from *Vita di Martino Vita di
Ilarione In memoria di Paola*, Milano, 1975, pp. 113–14.

[24] Ibid. p. 143.

the pitiless ravages of time. The *topos* of the odour of sanctity reappears in an overwhelming number of stories about exemplary lives, from the modest hermit to the prestigious saint.

> In Bologna on the night of 23 and 24 May 1233, at the canonization of St Dominic, his coffin was opened before a gathering of Franciscan preachers and a delegation of noblemen and burghers, that his body might be exhumed and transferred. When the coffin lid was opened, a wonderful odour enveloped all those attending.[25]

This evocation of the familiar myth of Western man's acute longing for and journey in search of the 'paradise of delights', filled with pleasures of a sensual kind, with the titillations of the palate, sight, smell, is like a 'transference' of beatitude to the corporeal field, or a perception of spiritual happiness through the less 'spiritual' senses. The enchanted mountain upon which the three monks of the legend, land after a year-long journey, the 'mountain most high ... in Oriental climes', produces 'apples and ravishing fruits delightful to the taste', 'herbs laden with manna', 'trees loaded with the sweetest and most succulent apples', all 'populated with trees full of sweet and fragrant apples, delicious to eat and marvellous to behold; and it was all abundant with marvellously flowering and blessed herbs, emanating marvellous fragrances'.[26] And there the monks dwelt for seven hundred years, returning at the end of these to their monastery, unrecognizable to their brethren, transformed into three youths whose freshness belied their pluricentenarian age: 'How can it be that these men have lived so long and yet appear barely thirty years of age?'[27] The magical herbs of the *locus voluptatis* (the biblical *paradisus voluptatis* where 'gold is born', where 'bdellium and lapis anychinus are found', is a treasure house of herbs, trees, stones, endowed with miraculous properties, it is a gold-mine indeed), and the woods that grow there, the waters that course their way among them prolong human life indefinitely and reverse the passage of time: in its midst 'plays the fountain of life and whoever drinks from it will never grow old, and your old man will become a youth of thirty'.[28] There grows 'a tree whose apple is an antidote to old age'. In this orchard of miracles our monks also beheld:

25   J. Le Goff, *La Civilisation de l'Occident médiéval*, Paris, 1964.
26   *La leggenda dei tre monaci che vanno al Paradiso terrestre*, in G. Battelli, *Le più belle leggende cristiane tratte da codici e da antiche stampe commentate e illustrate*, Milano, 1942, p. 466 *passim*.
27   Ibid. p. 471.
28   Ibid. p. 468.

another tree that whomsoever partook of its fruit never died . . .
And they then saw four springs: from each there flowed a river
which sought the world. And then they espied a fountain five
miles in length and five in breadth, and it was full of fish that sang
both day and night. . . . And they cast their eyes then upon the
tree of glory, so great that its branches thrust into the air for the
span of a mile: and its leaves were of gold, large like the leaves of
a fig, its fruit carved and frosted with sugar as though by miracle:
such joy, delight and sweetness was there in the eating thereof
that it defied description. And this tree was live with tiny birds,
whose red feathers were like so many flaming coals that the tree
seemed full of little lanterns, and they all sang in unison . . . [29]

The carved and sugared fruits of the tree of glory seemed to be a
reflection of the forests of sugar which herbalists and confectioners were
so adept at creating. This caramelized and sugared vegetation was to be
savoured and enjoyed sensually ('such joy, delight and sweetness was
there in the eating thereof . . . '):[30] it was a Land of Cockaigne for the
senses providing spellbinding and intoxicating experiences in a fairyland
ambience, inducing 'highs' or euphoric states similar to those resulting
from the taking of hallucinogens or cocaine [*mama cuca*]. So great is the
perimeter of the fountain that it resembles a lake (spatial realism is lost,
as is temporal realism: seven days have the same value as seven
centuries); the monks gaze at luminous objects as though hallucinated
('they gazed on the cherubic angel and they had so much sweetness and
joy in their hearts that they forgot this world and the next: so great was
the exceeding and miraculous beauty of the angel. And so they remained
on the threshold, lost in contemplation of the angel for five days and five
nights').[31] The fish sing uninterruptedly day and night (dumb creatures
become singing springs and change their nature altogether). All these
phenomena make this enchanted land seem more of an artificial paradise
or a chimera sprouting from some evil toadstool than a 'holy' precinct.
Their very ability to disappear, the ease with which the body dwelling
there dies and is simultaneously turned to ashes ('we will fall dead at the
end of forty days and will at that very moment be nothing but a pile of
ashes'), the way in which they melt away into an odorous nothing, are all
symbols of the visionary excesses which are the stuff that legends,
fairy-tales, dreams, journeys and stories are made of, to be enjoyed as a
supplementary drug: 'And forty days having passed, the three holy
monks became ashes and such was the scent that came from them that it

[29]   Ibid. pp. 468–9.
[30]   Ibid. p. 469.
[31]   Ibid. p. 467.

seemed all the musk and fragrances of the world were united in them . . .'[32]

Saints reduced to perfumed essences, to forgetfulness in an aura of musk, to a fragrant dust, evoke a chain of astonishing metamorphoses, a crazed whirligig where identity, matter, attributes and categories change continuously in their position, size and reality. Basically, Dante's 'holy table-land' where 'any plant/without seed manifest there taketh root',[33] the site of strange apparitions and monstrous metamorphoses:

> Transfigured thus the holy edifice,
>> Thrust forward heads upon the parts of it,
>> Three on the pole and one at either corner.
> The first were horned like oxen; but the four
>> Had but a single horn upon the forehead;
>> A monster such had never yet been seen![34]

All this bears the semblance of a charmed place, of a magic corner where miracles occur in space, of a theatre of illusion and sacramental games, of an allegorical side-show at a fair or of a visionary liturgy performed against a lustral, purificatory backdrop, where the players sink into the arms of oblivion. A cart decked out with feathers and which, transformed in its nature, sprouts three two-horned heads from its shaft, and four single-horned heads at its four corners; the dragon sprung forth from the bowels of the earth, the dream-like procession of ghosts, the tree 'whose wood is sweet to the taste', whose

> . . . tresses which so much the more dilate
> As higher they ascend, had been by Indians
> Among their forests marvelled at for height.[35]

The monstrous vegetation of the Indies looms large, outstripping the allegorism and fanciful engineering derived from the St John Apocalypse, whilst yet seeming to belong to the visionary world of artificially induced delirium.

Despite this complex and mechanistic *mise-en-scène*, despite the awesome and contrived decor, the earthly paradise of Dante is nonetheless a haven of sublimated delights, of remarkable states of grace, of supercharged visionary experience, of super-human awareness, of dilated pupils, of extraordinary occurrences. The dazed and bewildered traveller pursued his journey against a backdrop of incandescence, bright

32   Ibid. p. 472.
33   Dante, *Purgatorio* Canto XXVIII, vv. 117–18. Longfellow's translation quoted here, 118, 116–17.
34   Ibid. XXXII, Longfellow, 142–7.
35   Ibid. XXXII, Longfellow, 44, 40–2.

hues, flashing lights, tastes, fragrances that defy description, 'ineffable delights' (*Purgatory* xxix, 29):

> While 'mid such manifold first-fruits I walked
>> Of the eternal pleasure all enrapt,
>> Still solicitous of more delights.[36]

where the waters offer memory and oblivion at once:

> From whence its name of Lethe on this part;
>> On the other, Eunoe: both of which must first
>> Be tasted, ere it work; the last exceeding
> All flavours else . . . [37]

The magic of the waters, the springs endowed with such extraordinary powers, the sap turgidly abundant in astonishing 'virtues' are, in their algid vitality, enjoyed through the senses of taste and smell, even when they are among those which by tradition sharpen the mind or the memory.

Waters and plants, the freshness of an enchanted, 'magick'd place, where vegetation itself harbours fundamental secrets, where strains unknown to botany take root' (the 'holy table-land/in which thou art is full of every seed/and fruit has in it never gathered there', *Purgatory* xxvii, 116–18); a botanical garden dominated by:

> . . . the loveliest plant
>> of paradise, the happy plant,
>> that preserves life and renewes it.
> This great plant, this great marvel,
>> . . . is the tree of life
>> giving life to all who pluck its fruits.[38]

This miraculous plant, a symbol at once of the subversion of physical laws and the power of heavenly magic, is seen upside-down by Federico Frezzi:

> Up in the sky were locked its roots
>> and down towards earth sprawled its branches,
>> whence came a song, here untold.
> So large and broad was its head
>> that its spread, I'll warrant, from side ·

---

[36]   Ibid. XXIX, Longfellow, 31–3.
[37]   Ibid. XXVIII, Longfellow, 130–3.
[38]   F. Frezzi, *Il Quadriregio*, ed. E. Filippini, Bari, 1914. These and subsequent lines of poetry are taken from book IV, I, 136–50.

> to side outstripped two miles . . .
> Its base is fixed firmly in the sky
>   whence comes that God-given virtue
>   to bestow immortality on men.

This tree (which is none other than the 'holy tree' of the crucifixion) with its roots in the air and its head in the earth, a hallucinatory and inverted image of the vegetable world, a chlorophyllous spectre turned upon its head with its 'gentle fronds' obedient to the exorcistic prayer of the 'ancient fathers', Enoch and Elijah, answering their call, has the power to appease all human yearnings:

> . . . let me taste of the leaves
> that those leaning branches offer me
> and thus placate all my desires.[39]

These 'leaves' which when tasted satisfy all human 'wants' cause the disquieting Andean spectre to gleam in its mantle of exhilarating foliage whose property it was to alleviate hunger and fatigue, sadness and worry in those who ate thereof. There is here a quite fortuitous but genuine parallel with the demand in the Europe of the past, for magical herb 'cordials' to assuage hunger, thirst and melancholy, to induce pleasant and optimistic visions or dreams that eradicated memory, and states of suspended and relaxed consciousness, of intoxication and delirium, swoonings and 'journeys' that might vanquish the dark sense of doom which accompanied every-day living, banish reality for a while, make troubled nights tolerable by populating them with charming dreams, alleviate the sense of precariousness and insecurity of daily life and the brushes with the ephemeral, simplify the complex and triumph over transience, the demand for a tonic that might intensify life artificially raising it above the level of the quagmire of earthly existence, was certainly very prevalent.

These 'agents of oblivion', whether potions or philtres, beverages or ointments, salads or omelets, chickpea purées or powders, tried to satisfy the unceasing social demand for euphoria, pleasure and oblivion. Both the pharmaceutical culture of the lower classes and that of the upper classes, both the herbals of necromancy and the family brands reveal the need for a constant stream of rousing images provided by mesmeric and tranquillizing herbs on the one hand, and narcotic and visionary ones, on the other. The Andean state was the very one unconsciously sought by Western mankind. As yet unknown, *erythroxylon coca* was nevertheless prefigured in other plants. The prescriptions of the past, both classical and mediaeval, against fatigue and lassitude suggested imaginary restor-

[39]   Ibid. IV, II, 10–12.

atives for wayfarers and pilgrims exhausted by the rigours of their journeys. Motherwort, a lunar herb, possibly associated with the cult of Diana, goddess of the night, was used as the magic talisman for the relief of fatigue in walking and the weariness consequent upon travel.

> If a traveller carry some motherwort about his person, he will not feel the fatigue of his journey. And if in the evening he give the juice of motherwort to one who is weary, the fatigue and lassitude will leave the other straightway, and no-one will believe that there could be so much vigour in him.[40]

Before the news started to percolate into Europe of a herb from the 'West Indies called *cacahe*' (Ovidion Montalbani) which 'when carried in the mouth kills hunger and thirst' (Giovanni Maria Bonardo), Europe had fantasized about a plant known to the peoples of the steppe, the Scythians, whose root – called *hipice* – 'merely when held in the mouth for twelve days banished hunger' (Montalbani). The legend was an old one. 'Scythia', recounts the Elder Pliny,

> discovered that [herb] that was called Scythian, which grows around Bochia and is sweet, and another also exceedingly useful, which is known as Spartiana. This last is such that when held in the mouth, neither hunger nor thirst are felt. This very herb is also called Hipice, that is equine because it has the same effect on horses. It is said that the Scythians with these two herbs may ward off hunger and thirst for twelve days.[41]

Hunger, thirst and cold: three forms of discomfort for the long-distance traveller, especially across deserted, barren or uninhabited tracts of land. To combat the first an *itinerantium regimen* (travellers' diet) was recommended which consisted, in the absence of paradisiacal leaves, in a cream that would make a modern gorge rise:

> Take the liver of a pig or some other animal and lard it with cloves – only a few – and an even smaller quantity of lard. When it has been boiled for long enough, cut it up and grind it small; then mix it together with calves' marrow or liquid beef fat, and with sesame oil or sweet almond oil, and gather it together in a single lump like plaster. This lump is to be consumed little by little in times of hunger: it is very nourishing, and takes away desire for food so completely that a person could keep himself alive for a very long time by this means.[42]

40   *Secreti medicinali*, c. 87r. of ms. SC. MS. 97. Rimini, Gambalunghiana.
41   Caius Pliny the Elder, *Naturalis Historia*.
42   B. Gordonius, *Opus, lilium medicinae...*, p. 938.

This shapeless, greasy paste, though an affront to the taste buds, was recommended by a serious, well-known and highly popular late mediaeval treatise, but seems more designed to discourage the appetite than actually to blunt hunger.

As a remedy against thirst, a type of seed was sucked: 'seeds of purselane and acetose should be ground up and mixed together, and held in the mouth'.[43]

There follows, finally, an antidote against cold, with appropriate ointments and equipment:

> Any as will travel through frozen regions should anoint their whole body in the morning with oil of lilies: they should then dress themselves in a fitting manner, in fox-skin clothes, a cape of *filtrum* which overlaps the clothes; their feet should also be well shod with shoes whose soles are made of the wood that pattens are made of; the lacing should not be too tight, so that the feet may be somewhat free to move.[44]

These forms of protection were appropriate for anyone who had to traverse icy parts ('qui iterus est per loca frigida'). But there were other forms suited to other degrees of seasonal cold. Here again ointments were the principal remedy:

> So as to avoid ever feeling the cold [decreed the Pseudo-Fallopius] pluck a nettle and boil it in oil, and with that oil anoint the limb that you would have warm, but this nettle must be removed before sunrise. Pluck now some cummin and wild vine, hypericum and aniseed, pepper, myrrh, spurge and incense, a little of each, chop and bind together with oil and wax; and with this anoint such members as you will, and you will be able to walk through any snow and ice and feel no cold. Again, pluck jequirity and cook it in oil; and with this anoint yourself and you will not be cold; if you but drink this herb with wine, you will never suffer cold.[45]

Surprisingly, the accoutrements recommended for hot journeys were largely the same as those recommended for cold ones. If the ointments changed in their ingredients and antithermal waters and antiparasitical creams were added to them ('take the juice of purselane and mucilage of fleabane, oil of roses and of violets, all well mixed together'),[46] head and

---

[43]   Ibid. p. 939.
[44]   Ibid. p. 940.
[45]   *Secreti diversi et miracolosi racolti dal Falopia, et approbati da altri medici di gran fama...*, Venezia, 1578, pp. 339–40.
[46]   B. Gordonius, *Opus, lilium medicinae...*, p. 919.

hands were nonetheless protected much as in winter time, with berets and gloves: 'the head should be well covered, preferably with a hat made of beaver-skin ... gloves should be worn of deer-skin; and then you should begin your journey in the name of the Lord; for no heat can harm you on that day'.[47]

But in the final analysis, a journey blessed by the Almighty and enlisting the protection of the supernatural powers was the one most likely to succeed without mishap to the traveller, wayfarer, pilgrim or merchant.

However, the ceremony to enlist protection was a complex one, even in the preliminary states prior to reaching the new climes or new atmosphere, and consisted of a series of 'ritual journeys' of the body: 'If you are going to travel from one climate to another, take special care to purify your body through blood-letting, purges and abstinence, in order that the strains of travel and change of air should not cause the humours of the body to boil.'[48]

The journey was fraught with dangers at every corner: even leaving aside the usual adventure and treachery (there is a whole literature on *pericula in itinere* [the dangers of travel]), the body of the itinerant person had first to go through a whole series of therapeutic purificatory rituals in order to exorcise the fear of upsetting the humoural balance of the body, the 'distempering' of the 'bodily constitution'. In addition to the danger of boiling over, there was that of contamination and corruption by contact with the air. With this in mind a special diet was devised for those who had to travel in *loca foetida*:

> But if you will travel through regions that are foul and full of corruption and poison, or a land where there are many rotten fish or corpses, snakes or other poisonous living creatures, you must keep your mouth and nostrils covered as much as possible so as not to take in the air; carry with you a small bag full of roses, violets, nard, camphor, sandalwood and a little of the bark from aloes, musk and amber; keep this close to your mouth and nostrils. When you reach a place where you have to rest, take some oil of cucumber seed, since this is very powerful against poisons ... [49]

We can hardly be surprised if in such a poisonous, contaminated, smelly and excremental world (human and animal dung, both male and female in origin, was often an ingredient in medicines and in cosmetics), ravaged by aposthemous sores, scrofula, leprosy, plagues, tormented by

47   Ibid. p. 939.
48   Ibid. p. 938.
49   Ibid. p. 919.

lice, grubs, ringworm, malaria, dysentry, typhoid, people dreamt of a sheltered, wholesome, healthy refuge, which afforded long life, sweetness, pleasure, enjoyment and delight, where the body would be 'beautiful, robust, healthy and clean',[50] a place where time stood still, where nothing 'was old or new' (idem), where human beings would not be 'troubled by boiling heat and tiny animals' (Petrarch, Prologue in *De Remediis*), where the worrying of 'minute animals' was non-existent. Time standing still, nothing new and nothing old, time standing outside time, ageless and timeless, devoid of dawns and dusks, or of the motion of days and hours. A flight from personal and social time, from the liturgy of consumated, useless and servile:

> Nothing is more flytting then youth, nothing more deceyvable then olde age. Youth stayeth not, but in delighting slyppeth away, olde age immediately folowing after softly in darknesse and silence, striketh men at unwares: and when she is thought to be farre of, then standeth she at the doore.... For Heaven turneth about with perpetuall motion, minutes consume houres, and houres the day. That day thrusteth forth another and that, the next day folowying, and there is never any ceasing.[51]

The 'delician paradise' answered to the yearning to stem 'the fickle passage of time', and to the collective demand for good, pure, fragrant and perpetually warm air: it was a constant, different, sheltered, inaccessible place: 'This Paradise *Terrestre* is inclothed all about with a Wall, and it is covered with Moss, as it seemeth, that Men may see no stone nor nothing else whereof it is...'[52]

Forbidden to mortals after the Fall, there was the danger that the *paradisus voluptatis* might be recreated as a devilish deceit in some remote corner of the world. According to Marco Polo, this might be in an inaccessible mountain valley or some lost eastern isle where a 'crafty old man' had built a counterfeit heaven, where bird song was reproduced by automata. The legend of the 'olde man in the mountain' is a well-known one:

---

50   Lorenzo il Magnifico, *Selve d'amore*, II, 102, Cf. H. Levin, *The Myth of the Golden Age in the Renaissance*, London, 1961; B. Nardi, 'Il mito dell'Eden', in *Saggi di filosofia dantesca*, Firenze, 1967, pp. 311–40.

51   F. Petrarch, *De rimedii dell'una e dell'altra fortuna*. English version from *Phisicke against Fortune, as well prosperous, as adverse* ... by Frauncis Petrarch ... now first Englished by Thomas Twyne, London, 1579. Chap. 1, 'Of flourishing yeeres', c. 1r.

52   Sir John Mandeville, *I viaggi di Gio. da Mandavilla*, ed. F. Zambrini, Bologna, 1870; reprinted, Bologna, 1968, II, p. 195. English version made by A. Wilde as *The travels of Sir John Mandeville*, Chap. CIII.

he had had the whole mountain surrounded by walls and, within these walls, there flourished the finest gardens that there might ever be. There he had planted many good and fragrant plants and many trees that bear the most noble flowers that e'er were seen; and he had playing there many a lovely fountain, beneath which he created sumptuous rooms all painted in gold and azure, and he had built many a deceit: there were mechanical birds that moved and sang as though they were real. This garden was populated by every sort of person and creature, that it might delight and please a man to behold and touch. He had filled it with lovely maidens of fourteen years of age and handsome youths of like age. Their clothes were of golden cloth and he was wont to say, they were angels. He had built three beautiful and noble fountains, all encrusted with precious stones and pearls, with underground conduits so that at will he might cause milk to flow from one, wine from another and honey from the third; he called this place paradise. And when any bold, valiant and courageous youth ventured upon his territory, he would show him his paradise, the divers things and divers delights, the birds that sang, the lovely maidens, the noble fountains of milk, wine and honey, and ordered musical instruments and voices to perform from a high turret, in such a way that those who played might not be seen; and he said that these were God's angels, and that this place was the Paradise that God had promised to all his friends, saying: *Dabo vobis terram fluentem, lac et mel.* Having shown the youth all these wonders, he would give him a drink which straightway made him drunk, and in this condition all these things seemed the more wonderful . . . [53]

'Pleasure and delight', 'to touch and behold', music and colour, 'lovely maidens' and 'noble fountains', bird-automata, adolescent angels, water, wine, milk, honey and finally the 'drink' that knocked you out, a *soma* of hashish, habituation, drug-dependency, conditioning, planned murder. It is as though we had a parable of modern taste, half-way between an allegory and a computer programme, immersed in a bland rhythm of doped and drowsy legend, fragrant and overflowing with honey, in which the sins of angel-boys smell of perfumed blood. Perhaps we are witnessing an x-ray carried out by mediaeval society on itself, or a reflection on the criminal implications of the ideology of all that is sugared, sweet and honeyed (an area of taste which instinct associates with a blessed and

[53] Ibid. II, pp. 160–1. [I have translated this passage from the Italian as the Wilde translation is not close enough to the Italian content for it to serve the author's purpose.]

divine condition). The sugared way is above all an *itinerarium mentis*, with a deep imprint, it is a yearning repressed. The compulsion to keep the glycemic level of the bloodstream high reflects an irresistible desire for beatitude, for massive ingestions of 'divineness' and 'holiness' (the hedonistic and sensual dimension of the delician paradise), for pungent euphoria bordering on extreme neurosis. All this honey, molasses, sugar, scent and balm point to a dream in which the Garden of Eden provided the largest concentration of mental images serving as surrogates for the drudgery of every day existence and the transience of life on earth. Time in the Garden of Eden was protected from the inferno of humoural distemper by a 'nature without blemish'.

> The human body was so well formed,
> So balanced and divided the humours,
> That desire was tempered and held in check:
> No false hope, no envy, anger or distress,
> Or appetite was thrown by nature in its path,
> To assail it through the hairs or pores,
> No superfluity: nor was there anything to spare
> By way of sweet foods or excess.[54]

The Fall was also a tragedy of 'sad humours'.[55] In his *Selve*, Lorenzo the Magnificent saw Adam as a rather inept Prometheus who 'draws fire from his nature'. The fatal mistake was that, happening to coincide with the dawn of Time, History and Technology, 'he deprived the world of its happy state' and 'man [of] his beatitude'. The birth of artifice, the perversion of primordial elements marked the end of the 'pleasant place', the 'pleasant age', the 'pleasant idleness', all 'true delights', the 'pleasant place and lower paradise'. The imbalance caused set in motion the perverse mechanism of history whereby bitterness replaces sweetness. Humoural chaos and war between the elements precipitated mankind's pollution:

> Whence the war was born that rages still
> Between the elements, scornful of each other,
> The world trembles, the sky showers rain and lightning,
> And sets the pattern for intemperance.
>   Lorenzo the Magnificent, *Selve d'amore*, II, 114

The 'holy place' in the Middle Ages, was first and foremost the Kingdom of Sugar, the distant island of sensual happiness, bathed in warmth and sunlight, bright colours and fragrant balm:

---

54   Lorenzo il Magnifico, *Selve d'amore*, II, 101–8.
55   C. Malespini, *Ducento novelle*, Venezia, 1609, c. 210v.

> Sweet idleness returns, untouched by hope or pain,
> Oaks sweat honey, rivers run with milk or nectar,
> All suffering is put to flight, and blissfully
> Our hearts will burn with sweet love.
>
> (ibid. II, 117)

Physical imbalance and humoural discord upset physiological equilibrium: the rhythms of physical bliss once broken, life became prey to all-consuming lust on the one hand or impotent languor on the other. Whilst in the 'sweet age', 'sweet loves' were consumated:

> Oh, life of everlasting passion and serenity!
> Ignorant of the torments of intemperate desire
> Where numbing languor never stills the body.
>
> (ibid. II, 104)

The path of health passed through the Garden of Eden across the green meadows of the Golden Age. The *leitmotiv* of 'sweetness', associated with beatitude, the boulimia which hankered after sugar, are symbols of the hunger for good health, physical equilibrium, humoural harmony, corporeal 'beatitude'. A 'blessed man' was the man of Eden, a vegetal man, antipromethean, divinely savage, well-balanced and of good constitution.

> Too much knowledge and the mind is troubled,
> With his scanty knowledge, our foolish brother released
> Death, and the multitude of disease.
>
> (ibid. II, 113)

The sweetness of paradise – as the legend of the 'olde man' would suggest – the pleasure of refuge in honeyed delights and drugs, is enough even to justify the odd crime. Abstinence from the pleasures afforded by this haven is so unbearable as to push the abstainer to extremes. Nonetheless, the artificial paradise, simulated by the crafty old man, this sugared heaven beckoning with its opiate delights, receives no condemnation either at the hands of Marco Polo nor at those of Sir John Mandeville. This perverted *paradisus voluptatis*, this paradise of hashish and honey, blood and crime, is regarded more or less in the same light as that which awaits the man of unblemished heart (*cor crimine mundum*). We have to wait until the eighteenth century before the 'canny old man' is actually found guilty. Already in the seventeenth century (see the writings of imposter and adventurer, Celio Malespini), he is branded an 'old rascal', while his necromantic garden becomes an execrable 'Paradise of Satan' overflowing (in the language of the Inquisition) with 'a thousand diabolical superstitions'. In this atmosphere of sombre *refoulement*, characteristic of the Counter-Reformation, the adorable young misses who, like the fountains and flowing waters, embody the freshness and gaiety of youth, are demoted to become mere symbols of raw sexuality, of lust in an erotic orgy, the youths seeking only to 'embrace them, kiss them and disport with them, and enjoy their favours'.[56]

In fact, the earthly haven which Mandeville places 'beyond the land and islands of John the Priest, in an easterly direction', belongs to the *mirabilia Indiae* where all of mankind's repressed desires flow to a head, and was seen as an *hortus sanitatis* in the early part of the mediaeval era. Its herbs, woods, so sweet to the taste and fragrant in the smelling, harboured properties capable of prolonging life miraculously. The age of brevity toyed dangerously with the ghost of longevity. Trees shot up in the Orient which prophesied long life to the avid seeker, botanic oracles such as

> the trees of the sun and the moon, which spoke to King Alexander and foretold his death. And it is said that John the priest and others who guard these trees, and eat their fruit and their balm, which grows upon them, live four to five hundred years by virtue of this balm.[57]

On another heavenly island of the East, the natives (each era cultivates its own mythology about primitivism and the theory of the noble savage was born a good while before Europe and the New World even crossed paths), 'are not only most reasonable but also quite simple and like animals' – they live only on odours:

> The people of this island neither cultivate nor till the soil, and though they eat nought, they are yet of a healthy colour and build. Though small, they are not as pigmies. They live off the scent of wild apples; and when they make long journeys, they carry with them these apples, for if they smelt evil smells and had not these apples with them, they would die . . .[58]

These ethereal and aromatically-nourished savages are as if born out of the balm-ridden mythology of the Europeans who, living perpetually in the foul air of their townships and villages, surrounded by stench, dreamed of islands in which survival was a function of sweet smells. The pomanders and aromatic sponges carried by people in the West were transformed into the green 'wild apples' of these scented havens.

Basically, we are dealing with the same mental association as that

---

[56]   Sir John Mandeville, *I viaggi. . .* , II, p. 194.
[57]   Ibid. II, p. 188.
[58]   Ibid. p. 187.

made by modern man, drawn to the world of exotic oriental cultures which offer patterns and models different if not indeed, opposed, to those of the West. Zen, yoga, acupuncture, shiatzu, vegetarian animism, 'philosophical' diets, naturistic cuisine, biological agriculture, are offerings of the Indian Orient and the modern answer to the wonders of India, and the mysterious East. Whilst the enigmatic and elusive Orient was held in terror by the ancient Romans, with a terror often inspired by remote and far-flung lands, uncanny regions on the fringes of the world, seen as at once monstrous and prodigious (from this same perception arose the dichotomy centre-versus-periphery whereby monsters were more apt to proliferate in distant ghettos and outlying kasbahs) – the early twentieth-century concept of a 'yellow peril' was a political and militaristic version which replaced the ill-defined terror felt for the people of the steppes and islands with an awed admiration of them.

The way to the 'complete life', or macrobiotics, is none other than the unrecognized yearnings of the West returning in a transformed and renewed guise; an old mythological phantom going back to Pliny's days and imprisoned between the monsters of the infinite borders of the non-Roman ecumene, the Ethiopian *Macrobii* who, like the *Cimi* of India, were supposed to have had an average life-span of a hundred and forty years. And, indeed, the author of *Naturalis historia* wrote that 'in India and Ethiopia miracles do proliferate'. The belief is hardly surprising that:

> in the parts of India where there are no shadows there are men five cubits and two spans high, and people live a hundred and thirty years, and do not grow old but die middle-aged. Crates of Pergamum tells of Indians who exceed one hundred years, whom he calls Gymnetae, though many call them 'Long-livers'. Ctesias says that a tribe among them called the Pandae, dwelling in the mountain valleys, live two hundred years, and have white hairs in their youth that grows black in old age; whereas others do not exceed forty years . . . Artemidorus says that on the Island of Ceylon the people live very long lives without any loss of bodily activity . . . [59]

Lives that are longer, others that are cut short before their time, young men with white locks, old men with black ones: death at a hundred and thirty years of age attended though neither by decrepitude nor the sufferings of old age, sheltered precincts (Eden) untainted by the myriad of human ailments with which we are familiar. Paradigms of paradoxical existences, of upside-down, suspended worlds, of oxymoric beings

[59] Caius Pliny the Elder, *Naturalis Historia*. English translation by H. Rekham, *Natural History*, London, 1942, book VII, II, 28–30.

dominated by the phantom of the 'complete life'. A recurrent dream: the Macrobii seem imaginary archetypes, the dream inducers of present day macrobiotics, which draws in its wake all manner of tranquillizing and propitiatory formulae, dietary plans and eubiotic slogans of the 'stay young and live long' kind, modern health programmes (*regimen sanitatis*) hailing from the Orient and promising 'protracted youth and long life' or 'eat healthy and you'll live healthy'. Dosed now with a high level of oriental mercury, the old belief that health went hand-in-hand with diet has re-established its hold on today's ultra-polluted Europe.

Fifteen to twenty years ago the mysterious Chinese mushroom appeared on the scene, silently bestowing life and health. It was succeeded by another invasion from the East, the new and anthropomorphic root, ginseng. The thirties in America were inundated with 'Mandrake pills'. Formerly the queen of mediaeval herbals, this anthropomorphic sex root, this wound-proof amulet which graced Emperor Rudolf II's shield, had now widened its market to reach the masses as an aphrodisiac and tonic. Indeed, North American Superman Mandrake was even baptized using the root itself, the *matryguna* used by Rumanian sorcerers in the preparation of their philtres.

In the early years of this century (leaving aside sera of Rumanian origin, *gerovital* and Voronoff), the basic diet of the inhabitants of the Caucasus excited great interest among Italians. By its consumers it was considered a diet of 'divine origin and worthy of religious cult', while practically speaking it enabled these tribes to know 'extraordinary longevity'.[60] There was also *kéfir*, a close relation of yoghurt, obtained from 'whole milk: it was fresh, absolutely pure, clotted and artificially fermented by vegetable agents, especially the Caucasian mushroom. In this mushroom there reign benign bacteria who find coagulated milk to be the best host for their development . . .'.[61]

Milk turned by means of vegetable enzymes, with the aid of the 'benign bacteria' of a Caucasian mushroom. In 1915, the buried nucleus of bygone beliefs to do with agrarian and pastoral magic re-entered the Italian collective unconscious. The 'benign bacteria' were but the updated reincarnation of the will-o'-the-wisp enzymes that were held responsible in the agricultural lore of the past for the leavening of bread, the fermentation of wine, the clotting of milk; micro-demons of transformatory growth, of transmogrified matter, of controlled (and benevolent) reproduction *ex putri*, of new forms of autogenesis, of consolidation and leavening. Will-o'-the-wisps whose habitual lair was a dung-heap, a barrel in a darkened vault, or the moist and frothy warmth of manure. The 'benign bacteria' of the Caucasian mushroom are merely a

60   · *Almanacco gastronomico di Jarro* (G. Piccini) 1915, Firenze, 1914, p. 121.
61 .   Ibid. p. 121.

translation into the hybrid scientific terminology of the early twentieth century of the hidden 'virtues' of roots and herbs, of the vegetable spirits and green demons of chlorophyll that never ceased to amaze the societies of old.

A full eighteen hundred years after the chimeras collected by Pliny the Elder, Riley, the English traveller, in a 'travelogue which has now become a bibliographical rarity, reminisces how the nomadic Arabs of the desert feed almost exclusively on camel's milk, both sweet and sour. This regimen assures them strength and longevity. Riley even attributes to some the age of 200 or even 300 years . . . '.[62]

Of the kingdom of John the Priest no trace remains, the years roll by and there is no mention of the delician paradise. The Ethiopian Macrobii, however, in their flowing nomadic robes, seemed to emulate Methuselah.[63]

'Have we found the secret of longevity?' Jarro asks himself. The polygraph and popular novelist, writing at the turn of our century talks in his *Almanacco gastronomico* (1915) of 'two substances with a prodigious effect', which 'should be substituted for the many harmful and quackish drugs, that benefit only those who invent them':

> These two natural substances recommended to everyone by eminent scientists such as Metchnikov, director of the Institut Pasteur in Paris, Podwyssotsky, professor of general pathology at Odessa, Professor May at Munich, Hallion and Carrion at Paris, Monti at Vienna, are *Kéfir* and *Yoghurt*.
>
> The names themselves are certainly unattractive; and part of our public is not as yet familiar with them. It may be noted, however, that quite apart from verdict of the above-mentioned scientists, Kéfir and Yoghurt have, after due study of their beneficial effects, been recommended also by Doctors Maragliano, Dujardin-Beaumetz, Dimitrieu, Lepine, Hayem, Poten, Hirsch, Nilke, Dresler, Maydel, Gebhard, Loebel, and Mandrowsky. All these sovreigns of science . . . have written scientific reports on the applications of these two substances, recommend their use and testify to the remarkable recoveries attributable to their use.[64]

On the back cover of the *Almanacco* a full-page display in capitals reads:

> KEFIR: THE KING OF TONICS. YOGHURT: CURES AILMENTS OF THE STOMACH. STRENGTHENS. REVITALIZES. PROLONGS LIFE — AS

62   Ibid. p. 122.
63   Ibid. p. 119.
64   Ibid. p. 120.

SCIENTIFICALLY PROVEN BY THE EMINENT PROFESSOR METCHNI-
KOV, DIRECTOR OF THE INSTITUTE PASTEUR OF PARIS. FLOR-
ENCE, VIA PESCIONI.

The age of medico-pharmaceutical pick-me-ups, tonics, restoratives
was in full swing and 'restorative' gastronomy was more popular then
ever before, injecting strength and 'revivifying the stomach'. The
stomach continued to be (as it had been in Fioravanti's day) a most
alarming place, perpetually a host to things that should not be there, that
cannot be assimilated or digested, the seat of dark resentment, rejects,
sickness and residual encumbrances. It seemed to operate in the shadow
of evil, as though infiltrated by a malignant spirit about to attack the core
of the digestive system or undermine the source of vital energy (the oven,
as it were, of life), a spirit that still refuses to dissipate itself.

On the inside flap of the back cover there appeared the further
recommendation:

> STENOGENOL – a restorative cure by De-Marchi di Saluzzo.
> Proclaimed the best restorative for the organism and nerves by
> thousands of Doctors. It is a first-rate tonic and restorative,
> boosts energy and facilitates digestion.
>
> It is prescribed by the most illustrious Clinicians and is
> regarded as highly effective in treating pale and weak babies;
> young people who are anaemic, melancholic, weak and ema-
> ciated; people extenuated by the effort of work, at times
> excessive, illness and abuse, the elderly of both sexes in a
> weakened condition; it is delicious to taste: very much appreci-
> ated by Ladies and children.

The wan and frail creatures in this barely sketched portrait are the
twentieth-century shadows of the teeming sufferers and hypochondriacs
of the past.

A couple of lines lower down on the cover, in smaller print as if trying
almost to avoid attention, there appears the following advertisement:

> Among the most delectable aperitives for consumption before a
> meal none is as good as PERUVIAN QUINA LIQUEUR by
> De-Marchi of Saluzzo. Sample at home by sending L0.50.

This would have eluded our attention had we not remembered that at
that very time (according at least to the account given by W. Golden
Mortimer in *Peru: History of Coca*),[65] Pope Leo XIII 'was in the habit of

[65]   R. Byck, 'Sigmund Freud e la cocaina', in S. Freud, *Sulla cocaina*, 1979, p. 77.
Cf. R. Romano, *Cocamania e cocainomania* in *Belfagor*, 1982, XXXVII, 6,
pp. 661–74.

finding sustenance during his spiritual retreats in a preparation of Coca Mariani'. 'Mariani wine', a sort of infusion consisting of 'wine and coca' prepared in Paris ('tonic wine with Mariani coca from Peru'), 'feeds' – proclaims an old English advertisement – 'fortifies, refreshes, aids the digestion, strengthens the nerves'.

This was the era of 'nerve tonics', like the popular 'Okasa', and virility creams such as the hardly less famous 'Casanova Pomade'. It is highly likely that the *quina* liqueur from Peru prepared in the distillery at Saluzzo was also an ingredient in the tonic designed for 'people extenuated by the effort of work, at times excessive'. In those days people worked so hard, that whether popes or metalworkers, Catholic or no, they had to seek respite in a provincial acquavite which contained a modicum of the 'divine plant' of the Incas, appearing in 'Peruvian quina', to restore their languishing strength. The climb to the top of the ladder was easy neither for the bosses nor for rank and file.

12

FORBIDDEN GAMES

The widespread sensitivity to smell, whether aromatic, pungent or balsamic, found its formal expression in a culture of effluvia which set great store by the therapeutic messages or, contrariwise, noxious messages which fermented in the air and presaged disaster.

The emanations of plants, bodies, human excrement and animal dung, were carefully evaluated and utilized. The observations of Paolo Boccone (who enjoyed a 'universal fame as the pre-eminent botanist of Italy')[1] are invaluable instruments for assessing the then prevailing mentality and scientific approach, which admitted the free exchange of information between peasant lore, magical/alchemic 'experimentation', medical doctrine, the practical empiricism of rural healers, of barbers, pork butchers, surgeons and midwives, against a common cultural background.

> Having left upon the table a certain quantity of fresh hazelwort with roots, purposing that cats should urinate upon it, I found the whole room impregnated with a pungent smell that resembled ammoniac acid or volatile salt of deer horn. This animal likewise enjoys the smell of valerian root, as it does that of ordinary catmint. I observed the same odour was produced by placing a burning ember in a pit in which human urine has been left for some time: and so strong and stimulating did the vapours of the urine seem at the first experiment I made that I straightway decided to produce the aforementioned vapour by means of ash from the fronds of trees.
>
> This odour when inhaled through the nostrils by women suffering from uterine vapours or headache, has provided them with much solace and relief . . .[2]

The medical empiricism of shepherds and peasants excited the interest of the indefatigable observer of culture and folklore in Paolo Boccone, botanist and physician to the Grand Duchy of Tuscany, providing him with food for speculation and enquiry. Rural healers, village mothers and grandmothers, shepherds, livestock farmers, all come under his careful

[1] A. Cocchi, *Elogio di Pietro Antonio Micheli*, in *Opere*, I: *Discorsi e lettere di A.C.*, p. 109.

[2] P. Boccone, *Museo di fisica. . .*, pp. 144–5.

consideration. The 'doctrine of peasants' (the expression is his own), their 'empirical medicaments', their knowledge of 'the capacity of certain plants to cure various ailments in quadrupeds', the therapeutic techniques and intuitions of 'practical shepherds', the 'observation of shepherds', the empirical know-how of the women and charlatans of Pieve di Quero (Venetian territory), of the province of Ancona, of Corsica and Sicily; the extraordinary picture drawn of one Menigo Donadon of the 'village of Combai' in the Province of Treviso, his 'wonderful cures', his 'external panacea', his 'external' remedy used by him to such beneficial effect ('he would crush the aforesaid leaves [of "yellow male wild-leaved mullein C.B."] and mixed with a little of the saliva of one who had not eaten, he applied it to the part of the body corresponding to the affliction, whether in the form of fluxions, inflammations, catarrh, pains and swellings')[3] aroused the profound interest of this inquisitive doctor, if not at times his disenchantment, or astonishment, his professional eye sometimes dwelling with admiration on the natural magic of an illiterate world that experimented with its pragmatically tested knowledge and passed it on, gathering together in the process a veritable *thesaurus* of empirical cures and wise measures based on hard experience and on the incontrovertible need to care for the health not only of its children, women and men, but also of its beasts which represented, at least in poor communities, a kind of second body or extension of itself. This familiarity with the afflictions that assailed 'dumb beasts' demonstrated – if there were need of such a demonstration – how bound was, and is still, man's destiny with that of animals and how human science can hardly dispense with the presence of the animal world. Cattle plague and swine fever represented social catastrophes, all but obliterated now by a mountain of literature concerning the diseases afflicting that bipedal species, *homo sapiens*. The literate culture of the towns has virtually ignored these catastrophes or, at most, has regarded them in the light solely of economic loss.

The prominent rôle played by the nose in societies of the past together with its function as an organ of sense (and its prestige has now plunged to infamous depths, amidst a sensory hierarchy much changed in character, not to say, challenged to the core for the supposed precariousness of its perceptions, indeed, attacked as too imprecise and deceptive to be deemed useful by a culture that presumes to know the world solely through an abstract and absolutely intellectual cognitive methodology), can be appreciated quite clearly if one considers that one of the four elements on which worldly order rested was that of air. Not only was air the sublunar space where cosmic miracles took place, in which prophetic

---

[3]   P. Boccone, *Osservazioni naturali...*, p. 133.

warnings and signals were to be read, it being a subtle medium of communication in which aerial spirits, the intermediaries between man and the divine cosmos, floated like fish in water in order to appear with disquieting phosphorescence before human beings; a place where angels, demons, monsters, giants, fiery brands, aerial battles, visions of blood and death, portentous comets, falling stars, a whole host of signs portending an awesome, mysterious and impenetrable future; the shadowy chessboard upon which invisible players pass indecipherable and troubled messages from the dead to the living; but it was also the element through which there floated volatile perfumes, the aromatic essence of an object, accompanied by a whole range of 'effluvia' and odorous 'impressions' emitted by the mysterious particles that spread foul and fatal contagion. A vehicle of arcane and elusive contagion, air was an element mankind had always to reckon with. The mysterious 'particles' could carry messages of decay and death.

Even plants were players in a complicated game of odiferous affinity and antipathy:

> If a dittany flower (*dictamum album*) be recently plucked from its plant and with it we touch other flowers like a rose, violet, carnation, orange bloom and so forth, that bear a scent, they will immediately lose their natural scent and assume that of the dittany. It is the effluvia and volatile parts of this flower that penetrate straightway and make a speedy impression upon the scent of the other flowers, provided these are scented.[4]

It was especially at times of contagion that the system of smells, with their exchanges of effluvia and counter-effluvia, entered a state of suspended alarm. The network of 'preservatives' (in daily use even at times of no apparent emergency) constituted a kind of preventive medicine against pestilential emanations.

> In times of plague, it is the custom to form a pomander with laudanum and divers other aromas in order to thwart contagion, frequently inhaling the said pomander. Others may be made of camphor, laudanum and garlic juice, which are simpler; to the latter I would add tincture from a dittany flower, from valerian root and that of hazelwort, boiled with spirit of wine, and evaporated to the consistency of a glutinous liqueur. In the absence of spirit or wine, these three plants may be reduced to a powder and mixed with garlic juice, camphor and laudanum and will fulfil the function of a preservative, such plants being

[4]   P. Boccone, *Museo di fisica . . .* , pp. 142–3.

extremely active and strengthening, and full of balsamic effluvia, which oppose decay and putrefaction.[5]

Before the bacteriological revolution, when the mechanics of contagious infection were as yet unknown, air was considered to be insidious and dangerous. There loomed perpetually the threat of 'corrupted air', of 'infected air' (Alessandro Tassoni: *De' pensieri diversi*, I, 14), the fear of the intangible and invisible, which hung like a sword of Damocles over people's heads. Corruption and putrefaction could appear suddenly, ubiquitously and in volatile form. Aerial death made the invisible sublunar world appear like some continent harbouring vague perils which prophets, soothsayers, fortune-tellers and visionary diviners of the future set out to foretell with a kind of desperate certainty, and witchdoctors and doctors to exorcise.

Against the 'contagious air' and 'lethal effluvia' that used to stagnate in 'infected or suspect' rooms, 'surgeons who have spent much time in Turkey' 'fashion for inhalation a ball of rubber, made with laudanum, spikenard, or lavender, they bore a hole in it through which they thread a ribbon with which they carry it hanging from their wrist'.[6]

This aromatic pomander was recommended against the particular threat posed by insects, both visible and invisible, against poisoning and contagion transmitted by 'small animals'.

> This preservative must act as a curative and expellant to rid the body of poisonous insects that roam the air and are admitted by it in times of plague; for though almost invisible to our eyes, once they are killed or chased out, man may breath and inhale an air that is untainted. That in the air, in sage leaves, in fennel flowers, in radish roots, in the rottenness of sores and boils there may be insects, worms and minute little animals, which germinate with the body's effluvia and burrow their way into one place or another, we cannot deny . . .[7]

But those very same poisonous 'little' animals could, if treated by chemical and pharmaceutical procedures, be pulverized, turned to salt or oil, to beneficial and curative effect:

> Collect . . . a great abundance of volatile salt from insects, such as earthworms, millipedes, ants . . . toads, frogs and also the excrement thereof. The strength and efficacy of the effluvia of these insects, of the Spanish fly, of bedbugs, of scorpions is common knowledge.[8]

5   Ibid. p. 143.
6   P. Boccone, *Osservazioni naturali. . .* , p. 60.
7   Ibid. pp. 61–2.
8   Ibid. pp. 78–9.

The vegetable and mineral worlds likewise participated in this merry-go-round of mysterious emanations, in this nature that exhaled disconcerting powers.

> Plants and mineral substances have also most potent effluvia, as proven by the crocus, opium, the thorn apple, sympathetic ink or powder, which may cause apparently supernatural or magical effects . . .
>
> In Lyon in France, experiments were carried out using effluvia of *Tanacetum crispum* in the following manner. To revive and comfort a person that is weary and languid from a long journey or some other strenuous motion, having rubbed the palms of his hands lightly with seven to eight tansy leaves, they placed these between the patient's hat and his head and this much benefited him . . . . Moreover, it is the custom among the Jesuit fathers of Lyon, that when they are ill they request to be made to sweat, which is done by closing well every door and window, and scattering not only all the corners and the whole floor of the room, but also the bedcovers of the invalid with tansy leaves, which induces sweating after a short time, without the aid of fire.
>
> Because of these principles and applications, it must be accepted that not only in insects, but also in the excreta of animals and other creatures, too, there is a proportion of volatile salt and highly potent effluvia. And as we have found, with a deer's horns, the hooves of asses and mules, with hair, with the feathers and claws of rostra, hens, pigeons, cocks and other feathered species, so is it also true of the hooves of horses.[9]

While Boccone broadened the basis of his observations, the magical-therapeutic intuition of *transplantatio morbi* was widespread and practiced everywhere a little: a live tench was applied to a patient's stomach to cure jaundice, until the fish dies; or indeed, omelettes made from flour mixed with the invalid's urine, 'which fed to the dog, free the patient of his illness and infect the dog'.[10] Meanwhile

> if a horse suffer from stomach ache, take a live mole and hold it and squeeze it between the hands till it die; the horse must then be stroked with the infected hands from his neck down to his belly several times, to ease and free him from his pain.[11]

[9]   Ibid. pp. 79–81.
[10]   P. Boccone, *Museo di fisica...*, p. 149.
[11]   Ibid. p. 149.

In this system of sympathetic magic in which both effluvia and morphology and 'marks' (external signs) played a role of prime importance, magical and hallucinative plants with their 'extraordinary effects' dominated the scene. 'Clysters' of hypericum (the anti-devil plant used by exorcists also as a liberating evacuant), the root or bulb of Colchicum tied to the neck as an 'amulet' to preserve health during times of plague, the leaves of a hellebore which peasants would lay upon animal sores, 'narcotic effluvia' released by bunches of *solanum hortense* placed around a baby's cot to send him to sleep and quieten him, laudanum and poppy in milk to calm and tranquillize him, narcotic poultices on the 'pores' (orifices of the body) of a young baby to influence his dreams and keep away hob-goblins at night, special diets based on soporifics and stimulants for the women who were breast-feeding them; all these are indices of the close ties between the world of herbal magic and that of educated society. The human body was to experience such far-fetched 'vegetable' treatments that they sometimes bordered on the absurdly paroxistic, or grotesque or even ended in tragedy.

> Around the year 1674 [so wrote the devout and God-fearing Paolo Boccone] in Corsica, in the village of Bastelica, under the jurisdiction of Aiaccio, some roots of parsnip were given to the lady of one of the leading families in that place, in the midst of which there chanced to be a root of hemlock, which when the lady ingested caused her to go out of her mind and rave. Among her lunatic deeds it is reported that she stood naked for twenty-four hours and solicited both men and women to the act of fornication. Whether mandragora which was so eagerly sought after by the two women of the Holy Scriptures, leading one of them to yield her bed to the other for one night, does in effect awaken her venereal desires, I have been unable to reconcile physical evidence with historical hearsay.[12]

While not wishing to discount that this scriptural account of bed-sharing may have directly provoked Machiavelli's biblical-cum-botanical fantasies, it is certain that his *Mandragora* was engendered in the general context of a mentality steeped in vegetable mythology. The heavy preponderance of herbs together with their magical properties made itself felt on a society immersed both figuratively and physically in a great sea of forests, essences, and 'simples'.

In this vegetal chaos, controlling the quality of the herbs was difficult and their frequently uncertain, not to say variable, classification, increased the probability of confusion and danger. The herbs themselves

---

[12]   Ibid. p. 146.

could be sources of anxiety and fear, as were insects. It could happen, for instance, that apothecaries and charlatans might buy products from an unknown provenance, sometimes so 'bad' as to precipitate fatal results. Adulteration on a large scale of medicinal herb products was a booming industry for unscrupulous quack-herbalists and professional swindlers devoted to this dubious pastime.

Many others, however, died by their own hand. The uncontrolled mania for slimming diets, sometimes with fatal effcts then, as indeed now, was responsible for this form of self-poisoning. Obesity, as we have seen in a previous section of the book, was the scourge of the rich, the diabetic and the gouty, whom crafty preachers wooed by offering glimpses of remarkable havens of agility, mobility and 'dryness'.

> The signor Antonietto Pallavicino, a Genoese gentleman, who lived in San Pietro d'Arena, desirous of a medicament that would make him thin, drank some broths in which he had cooked roots of *Tithimala Epithimi Fructu*, known by the common folk of Sestri di Ponente as 'erba varego', with which medicine he became cruelly ill and died in the term of twenty hours.[13]

If hunger killed the poor, fat and excessive abundance took its toll of the rich directly or by the agency of some remedial herb.

The hallucinations evoked by herbs could also result in extraordinary comedies of (vegetable) error.

> The herb thorn apple is called opium by the Corsicans and the experience of it that the villagers of Pieve di Talao have is this: certain pigs who had eaten of thorn apple became dazed, and drunk for a term of twelve hours; and in walking they fell down and would drag their legs behind them as though they had lost all their strength. The seeds of this same plant were crushed, allowed to stand in wine and administered to some bum-bailiffs by a mischievous peasant. So excited and confused did the brains of these bailiffs become that entering into an argument, one of them maintained that a hen (who chanced to pass the table where they ate) was a goat, and they came to blows, the quarrel ending in a torn moustache.[14]

Such events were predictable. The society of the past enjoyed playing with fire when it joked. Games with hallucinogens, with seeds and philtres, which induced temporary lunacy, deliria, split personality

---

13   Ibid. p. 146.
14   Ibid. p. 146.

syndromes, 'crude, contorted, distorted and gruesome phantoms',[15] were part and parcel of its life-style, with its urge to experiment with new forms of comedy, to probe the mechanism of laughter, to experience unusual thrills on the threshold of danger. Risk was exciting. Vegetable poisons belonged in an overall atmosphere of use and abuse of nature's secrets, of forced and nervous confidence with dream-herbs, of escapism, of artificial madness. Black henbane, when drunk or eaten brought on a kind of drunken forgetfulness, or 'aberrant behaviour akin to drunkenness'.[16] Relish at the spectacle of temporary lunacy was but another facet of an outlook on life which expressed itself in the theatre of 'ingenious machines', of make-believe toys, of dance, games, intermezzi, and disconcertingly grotesque peformances. So subtle, so strong was the taste for theatrical spells that it even lead to the staging of scenes of witchcraft bordering on catastrophe. The attraction of the forbidden, of controlling the forces of magic and of sin (the ointments of sorceresses reached their high point in the sixteenth and seventeenth centuries, in a thoroughly 'bewitched' and 'spell-bound' world), finds corroboration in the irrisistible urge to penetrate the barriers of the unknown, dark territories, on the frontiers of reason. Forbidden games with hallucinative herbs belong to a theatre of frenzied and distorted images:

> with Stramonium, to Solanum Manicum: the Seeds of which, being dried and macerated in Wine, the space of a night, and a Drachm of it drank in a Glass of Wine, (but rightly given, lest it hurt the man) after a few hours will make one mad, and present strange visions, both pleasant and horrible .... We may also infect any kind of meat with it, by strowing thereon: three fingers full of the Root reduced into powder, it causeth a pleasant kinde of madness for a day; but the poysonous quality is allayed by sleep, or by washing the Temples and pulses with Vinegar, or juice of Lemon. We may also do the same with another kind of Solanum called *Bella Donna* [witches' herb], A Drachm of the Root of which, amongst other properties, hath this; that it will make men mad without any hurt: so that it is a most pleasant spectacle to behold such mad whimsies and visions; which also is cured by sleep: but sometimes they refuse to eat. Nevertheless, we give this precaution, That all those Roots or Seeds which cause the Takers of them to see delightful

15   G. B. Della Porta, *Della magia naturale libri XX*, p. 281. English version, *Natural Magick* (Young & Speed), chap. 12, p. 219.
16   I. J. Wecker, *Antidotarium generale a Iacobo Wuechero ... digestum*, Basileae, 1580, p. 133.

visions, if their Dose is increased, will continue this alienation of mind for three days: but if it be quadrupled, it brings death.[17]

This metamorphosis of man into a madman, lunatic or idiot threatened by a nasty end, is another illustration of the cynicism and cruelty typical of those days, especially among the upper classes, who used their servants as puppets in dehumanizing humiliating games bordering on bestiality. This attitude vis-à-vis one's inferiors testifies to the high degree of indifference and insensibility then prevailing towards the serving class [the English translation quoted differs from the Italian in referring to the subject as a 'friend' rather than as a 'servant']. During the years when Della Porta was carrying out such 'experiments', Torquato Tasso was theorizing in *Il padre di famiglia* about a rigid slave-like discipline for beast-servants.

Certain of Della Porta's accounts are nothing if not astonishing:

> I had a Friend, who, as oft as he pleased, knew how *To make a man believe he was changed* into a Bird or Beast; and cause madness at his pleasure. For by drinking a certain Potion, the man would seem sometimes changed into a Fish; and fling out his arms, and swim on the Ground; sometimes he would seem to skip up, and then dive down again. Another would believe himself turned into a Goose, and would eat Grass, and beat the Ground with his Teeth, like a Goose: now and then sing, and endeavour to clap his Wings. And this he did with the aforenamed Plants: neither did he exclude Henbane among his Ingredients: extracting the essences by their Menstruum, and mix'd some of their Brain, Heart, Limbs, and other parts with them.
>
> I remember when I was a young man, I tried these things on my Chamber-Fellows [in Italian original 'slaves']: and their madness still fixed upon something they had eaten, and their fancy worked according to the quality of their meat. One, who had fed lustily upon Beef, saw nothing but the formes of Bulls in his imagination, and them running at him with their horns; and such-like things. Another man also by drinking a Potion, flung himself upon the earth, and like one ready to be drowned, struck forth his legs and arms, endeavouring as it were to swim for life: but when the strength of the Medicament began to decay, like a Ship-wrack'd person, who had escaped out of the Sea, he wrung his hair and his Clothes to strain the Water out of them; and drew his breath, as though he took such pains to escape the danger . . .[18]

[17]   G. B. Della Porta, *Natural Magick*, p. 220.
[18]   Ibid. pp. 219–20.

The experiments of the young Della Porta (an extraordinarily gifted child prodigy who, aged fifteen, wrote his *Magia naturalis* in Latin), seems to be closely related to his studies of physiognomy, with his identification of the morpho-somatic relations between man and animal (the latent figural archetype), with his exploration of the dark origins of human flesh. It almost seems as if this 'magician of Naples' was attempting to create some theatrically avant-garde laboratory in which to test the techniques of artificially induced madness, to explore the dramatic potential of mental alienation and delirium in man-beast. We are witnesses to an obvious cycle of experimental tests in which theatre and science are inextricably bound: identifying the theatrical behaviour of man-beast (the 'slave') was useful not only for the purposes of creating a gallery of faces, of studies of physiognomy, but also to fill a cupboard with dummies for his clowning and theatrical-cum-scientific pastimes. Physiognomy was at the service of theatre and vice-versa.

The insomniac and delirious bachelor of Ferrara became a wise *pater familias*, and in his laboratory of lunatic phantoms, he theorized in North-East Italy in the style of Hesiod, Aristotle and others, with the impassive coldness of the dissector of cadavers:

> when it so happens that one is found servile not only by birth and family but also by nature and spirit, he is so absolutely a servant, that with him and his likes will the master of the house, who desires his servants to be such that they may be easily commanded, accommodate his whole family; nor will he require of them more intelligence than that necessary for them to understand and execute the orders they receive. In this respect they differ from horses and other beasts whose nature is docile and tameable, only in that when out of the presence of their master they yet retain orders in their memory and can execute them, which is not the case with beasts. The servant is therefore an animal endowed with reason . . .[19]

A cold, impersonal judgement. Even in Tasso's laboratory at Ferrara, then, social physiognomy was permeated with negative projections and dichotomies such as ox/man, horse/servant, toy/servant, guinea pig/servant, martinet/servant, animal/servant. Not only was the world a dream, it was also a bestiary and a stable:

> It will much help too, to anoynt the Liver: for the Blood passeth upward out of the Stomack by evaporation, and runneth to the Liver; from the Liver to the Heart. Thus the circulating vapours

[19]   T. Tasso, *Il padre di famiglia in Dialoghi*, ed. E. Raimondi, Firenze, 1958, vol. II, I, p. 365.

are infected, and represent species of the same colour. That we may not please the sleepers onely, but also the Waking, behold *A way to cause merry dreams*.[20]

'The Heart, the principal seat of the senses,'[21] beats in close association with the liver; and anointings, especially those carried out with an ointment called 'populeon' conjure up happy dreams, images of serenity: 'Fruit, Gardens, Trees, Flowers, Meadows, and all the Ground of pleasant Green, and covered with shady Bowers: wheresoever you cast your eyes, the whole World will appear pleasant and green.'[22] Torquato Tasso was an avid consumer of 'populeon' ointment, but he never discloses to us the sublime visions of a rural Eden that resulted from anointings of the liver. His 'troubled spirit' continued to be tormented by 'deceitful shadows' and 'sombre and tumultuous' dreams on the nights of St Anne (Della Porta).

> . . . oft pois'd o'er me,
> Lion-like, my enemy roars,
> Sucks my blood like a poisonous dragon,
> Hisses through my bewildered mind.
> Bares his angry teeth, and like a wolf
> Hounds me or steals away to persecute
> Devour destroy another hapless soul;
> I tremble, sure that he intends my death.
> Tame and innocent as a lamb
> (Who would believe th'insidious disguise?)
> Bright and lucent as an angel . . .
> Deceit's master, vile trickster, juggler,
> Father of all primordial and original sin
> By cunning art he harms me in manifold ways.[23]

Della Porta's phytonomy proposed preparation techniques and dream conditioning based on vegetal treatment. Plangent and weary are Tasso's lines dedicated to narcotic herbs, stimulants and inducers of madness. After dwelling on hemlock and hellebore, beloved of birds, he continues his list of botanical hallucinogens:

> The mandrake and the poppy give us sleep
> but also aid the now abating worth
> of famous women, and of heroes, won

20   G. B. Della Porta, *Natural Magick*, p. 220.
21   Ibid. p. 220.
22   Ibid. p. 220.
23   A. Solerti, *Vita di Torquato Tasso*, Torino-Roma, 1895, I, p. 409. [This being a Sonnet to Father Francesco Panigarola.]

by illness and not yet by mighty arms.
The hellebore's medicinal effect
is still praised highly by philosophers,
because it pricks and prods the intellect
accustomed to profound enquiries,
as Proteus' daughters understood and knew,
together with mad Hercules and him
who taught and counselled, dear, old Pericles.
With its repressing qualities the hemlock
can sate man's rabid hunger . . .[24]

Whilst we see the 'family' of servants reduced to an animal farce by vegetable-based drugs, the philosophic 'family' illumines on the other hand the 'profound question' of the hellebore. Two conditionings and two different relationships with 'nature, that wearing and wearied mother'. This, against a background or myth of perpetual renewal of the 'unequalled bird',[25] the 'immortal phoenix' who:

. . . heavenly dews she in the meantime drinks,
fallen from golden stars and silver moon
in a more soothing, crystal-lustrous shower
                                        (verses 1410–12)

'immersed in countless fragrances'; a disturbing solar image of renewal and reintegration which 'restores life's fading energy'. 'Father to herself as well as son/the bird will perish and once more have life' (verses 1352–3). A disquieting portrayal of eternal cyclicity, the phoenix born, dying and reborn in her cot/grave, embodies a desire to return and yearning for immortality diametrically opposed to the other, ephemeral, ugly, slimy, dark and shapeless world: the world of putrefaction whose bowels throw up tormenting and murderous worms like putrefying entrails, creatures of darkness and death, epitomes of organic, animal and vegetable disintegration. This mythological incarnation of security, protector from obscure fears and anxieties, this luminous, sun-like expression acts as a foil to the poisonous and voracious monsters spewed out by the dark belly of night and death.

From the luxuriant wood she gathers all
the sweetest juices, the most balmy scents,
such as no Tyrian or Arab owns,
no fabled Pigmy or sun-beaten Hindu
or fortunate Sabean ever finds

---

[24]   T. Tasso, *Il mondo creato*, III, vv., 1080–92. Translation, *The Creation of the World*, 3rd day, pp. 65–6, vv. 1074–86.
[25]   Ibid. Tr., 5th day, vv. 1223, 1410, 1413, 1330, 1353.

in the soft bosom of his sunlit land.
The balsam there absorbs in all its reeds
the air that breathes amomum ceaselessly,
and cassia and acanthus also bloom,
and tearful drops of fragrant incense fall,
and ever younger sprouts of nard appear,
and, all around, wide fields of costly myrrh.[26]

This Eden of sweet smells, full of the perfumed symbols of life and renewal, far from death's stench, from cadaveric odours, the fetor of excreta, the pestilence of bedbugs, eliminated the image of man/lice as a factory or laboratory of worms and mouldering juice, of rotting sperm and infected blood, far from the world's corruption; in its midst the immortal phoenix rises as an incorruptible image out of ashes and destruction, as a projection of happiness and odourous perfection. Balm becomes an antidote to death by corruption and fetid annihilation. Like a visionary reversal or transcendence of birth from putrescence, the phoenix is born and reborn from sweetness, scent and balm. The Bird of Paradise is the symbol of divine immortality.

[26]   Ibid. Tr. 5th day, vv. 1354–65.

PART IV

13

THE 'FLESH OF GOD'

The island of bliss is the dreamland version of a safe, warm and bright region unassailable by death or sickness, by sorrow, darkness or fear, where

> there is no need to eat, drink or clothe oneself; and this is the truth that I relate: there is no hunger here, no thirst, no sleep, no clothes. And for a year have you journeyed with your brothers, your companions, and you have known no night upon this island but only limpid days and it has been forty days since you last ate or drank or wished to sleep; there ne'er was cloud, or rain or turbulence in the air or sky, neither was their sickness, boredom or sorrow, nor colour or death. And so brilliant [is] the light it comes not from sun, moon or stars, but from God, our treasured Lord . . .[1]

The paradise of delight answers to the widespread demand for a different life, the search, common to all men, for euphoria, security, light, warmth, health and food.

In those very years, filled with the cries of famine, with climatic upheavals, with nature's calamities, unending rains, raging poverty, atrocities committed on wayfarers and children, cannibalistic excesses, there grew apace, across a web of forbidden dreams, descriptions of a sweet and beatifically serene life, ecstatic images of havens so scented as to stun the brain; of aromatic baths in celestial spiceries, of countries in which there is no need to eat, where 'sweet and celestial food' trickles in a dew down gummy, resinous, honeyed and sweating trees, bestowing comfort and ineffable delight upon the privileged occupants of the sacred precinct.

The paradisiacal legends of the Saints Brendan, Patrick and Macarius, not to mention the writings of St Peter Damian, Ernaud de Bonneval and Honorius of Autun are all contemporary and share the same mental outlook evident in the stories told by Raoul Glaber, the Cluniac monk who, writing in the first century of this millenium, was able to observe the Babylonian horrors perpetrated on earth, the 'inferno' to which the living were condemned:

[1] *Navigatio Sancti Brendani. La navigazione di San Brendano*, ed. M. A. Grignani, Milano, 1975, p. 41.

Want brought devastation and it was feared that the whole human species might vanish. Atmospheric conditions became so unfavourable that there was no appropriate time to sow seed and particularly because of flooding, it became impossible to harvest .... Continuous rain had soaked the ground so thoroughly that for three years it was not possible to dig furrows capable of holding seed. At harvest time, wild grasses and the harmful bearded darnel had overlaid the whole surface of the fields .... In the meantime, when they had eaten wild animals and fowls, driven by terrible hunger, the people began to scour the land and eat all sorts of carcasses and things too horrible to describe. To flee starvation some had recourse to woodland roots and river weeds. Indeed, we were struck by the malice of the human species at the time. Ah me! What horror! and almost unprecedented, that men should be so driven by hunger as to devour human flesh. Travellers were abducted by people stronger than themselves, they were dismembered, roasted and eaten. Many for instance who fled from place to place to avoid famine and had found hospitality, had their throats cut during the night and were consumed by their hosts. Others, luring children with fruits or an egg, would take them to a remote spot, massacre them and devour them. The bodies of the dead were frequently torn from the earth so that by eating them starvation should be avoided.[2]

Whilst nature rebelled against the order of the seasons, health-giving herbs, the vegetable agents of survival, became perfidious enemies of mankind (evidence of the dull fear, the ambiguous ambivalence felt by mankind towards the vegetable world, reservoir of health and pleasure, on the one hand, or poison and death, on the other), murderous instincts were unleashed, sins committed against life and children massacred.

The recurrent, inexorable, ineradicable and unfathomable anxiety that nature might have rebelled, that the elements might be about to melt (a kind of pre-atomic 'China syndrome') or that time's logic or the seasons' rhythm might be upset, had again returned: 'It was feared [wrote Raoul Glaber] that the succession of the seasons and the order of the elements, that from the beginning of time had regulated the passing of the centuries, were fallen into everlasting chaos thus signalling the end of the human race.'[3] The seasons all topsy-turvy was the sure sign of

---

[2]   J. Le Goff, *La Civilisation de l'Occident médiéval*, p. 257 in Italian translation
[3]   Raoul Le Glavre, *Storie dell'anno Mille, I cinque libre delle storie, Vita dell'abate Guglielmo*, ed. G. Andenna & D. Tuniz, Milano, 1982, p. 141.

the imminence of man's last hour, of the world's return to chaos, to total and final disorder.

The belief that ultimate catastrophe would follow upon *senectus mundi*, when the world became old and weary, was deeply rooted in Europe in AD 1000, much as it had been at the decline of the Roman Empire in the late Classical era. The oecumenacy was assailed periodically by a sense of cosmic exhaustion, of fear and yearning for the end.

> 'I have devoured too many corpses [murmured the Earth, in the Guarany myth], I am satiated and exhausted. Father, cause me to end.' The water for its part pleads with the Creator to grant it rest and to release it from all trouble; so too the trees . . . and all of nature.[4]

From the skirts of the Amazonian forest to the sculptures of Imperial Rome, there flowed the same *taedium vitae*.

Against the coruscating backcloth of *de postremis temporibus*, Lactantius Firmianus etched a landscape of profound jadedness and abomination: 'Then there will be an unspeakable and accursed time, when no-one will be pleased to be alive.'[5]

This horrible, indescribable and sadistic age bore within it the sinister and premonitory cancer of *vitae brevitas*. Man's unstoppable descent into old age was a clear reflection of the state of the cosmos: upturned, arid and increasingly drained; where even the living envied the dead: '. . . the world will reach the point where the living will be attended by mourning and the dead by congratulations'.

> The city and towns will be destroyed, sometimes by fire and the sword, sometimes by frequent earthquakes, sometimes by torrents of water, sometimes by plague and famine. The earth will bring forth no produce, made sterile either by excessive cold or by too great a heat.[6]

The elements would change their basic nature, lose their identity. Water would turn to blood or at the very least become bitter and repellent: 'Some stream water will be turned into blood; the rest will be spoiled by a bitter taste: it will be neither good for growing food nor healthy to drink.'[7]

Cosmic miracles would provoke anxiety and terror, comets multiply their appearances, while the sun (reminding mankind of its age-old fear

---

[4] M. Eliade, *Myth and Reality*, New York, 1966.
[5] L. Coelius Firmianus Lactantius, *Epitome Divinarum Institutionum*, Lugduni, 1541, p. 605.
[6] Ibid. p. 605.
[7] Ibid. p. 605.

of losing heat or light) 'darkened by everlasting mourning', would slowly lose the heat of its fire. While the stars plunged to earth one by one, the moon, for its part, would become enveloped in a blood-like mist ('lunam color sanguinis obumbrabit'), Time would grind to a halt, the seasons merge, their sequence upset, the days grow shorter:

> All the stars will fall, nor will the seasons keep their courses, but winter and summer will be confused. In that time the year and the month and the day will be shortened: this will be the old age and infirmity of the universe . . . . Trismegistus has spoken.[8]

Epidemics, hunger, interminable rains, pitilessly ravaged man's world, animals and fields ('hunger rages . . . deluges and rains long delay fair weather').[9] All things wane and the old world creaks upon its axis. 'The world has already grown old', as St Cyprian put it bluntly in his treatise, *Contra Demetrianum*:

> The man who has been incited to mischief by means of false-hood, will more easily be led to what is good, when truth exercises its strength upon him. . . . still the world itself declares it, and attests its own ruin in the tottering estate of things: the showers of winter failing to nourish our seeds, the sun's heat in summer to ripen our corn; nor will the springtide fields display their customary growth, and the trees of autumn will be barren of their accustomed issue. . . . Needful is it that that must wax weak, which is now drawing near its end, and verges downward to the close. It is thus that the descending sun darts his rays with an obscured and impeded lustre, and that the moon, as her course declines, contracts her exhausted horns; thus that the tree once green and fertile puts on the graceless barrenness of the sere boughs in age, and the fountain which once poured out the large effluence of its overflow-ing veins, worn out by time, scarcely trickles with an insufficient moisture.[10]

The tree deformed by premature senility, with dry, barren, sapless boughs, stands as a desolate symbol of a world in its dotage, increasingly sterile, productive of nothing, inhospitable to life:

> It is a sentence passed upon the world, it is God's law, that as things rose so they should fall, as they waxed so should wane, the

8   Ibid. p. 605.
9   St Cyprian of Carthage, *Contra Demetrianum*, in *Opera*, Venezia, 1547. English translation by C. Thornton, *The Treatises of St Cyprian*, London, 1839.
10   Ibid. pp. 200–1.

strong become weak, and the great become little; and weak and little when they ate, then should they gain their end.[11]

Gone were the vigour and perfection of the senses, limbs, internal organs, the mythical longevity of the patriarchs. Now, while the world, a prey to fatigue, exhausted the last of its energy and abandoned itself to the overturning of nature's laws and to the biological chaos, babies were born old, the beginning became identified with the end, birth with senility:

> Boyhood betrays hoariness, the hair falls away before it grows, and life instead of closing, begins with old age. Thus life at its very infancy makes haste to its end, and all that now has birth, deteriorates in this old age of the world itself. Let no one wonder that the things of the world are one by one failing, when the whole world itself is already in its failing time and end.[12]

This mournful feeling of impending doom, of a threatened end, continued to oppress the melancholy dreams of the Middle Ages when:

> it will seem to some that God has grown old, and to others that the angel who moves the globe has become tired and is running away all the time so that heaven cannot hold itself together. Others are afraid that they are being drawn downwards . . .[13]

Worry, dread and insomnia, anxiety and insecurity, terror of an unfathomable end, miniature apocalypses wrought by famine and epidemic; these key words, recalled in a memorable page of Lactantius's *Divinae Institutiones* (he was active in the reign of Constantine), continued to haunt mediaeval man day and night, much enriching his basic vocabulary of terror:

> There will rage war, fire, famine and plague, and over all of them fear will hang continuously. Then will they pray to God and he will not hear; they will hope for death and it will not come; nor will night bring an end to fear, but loneliness and wakefulness will gnaw at men's spirits.[14]

In the great insomnia of the Dark Ages, night is endless, troubled and evil. The gloom of darkness casts its pall so oppressively upon the frustrated sleeper that to dispel it every remedy is tried (drugged wine, sleeping draughts, sleep-inducing ointments: sponges dipped in opium,

11   Ibid. p. 201.
12   Ibid. pp. 201–2.
13   B. Gordonius, *Opus, lilium medicinae. . .* , p. 211.
14   L. C. F. Lactantius, *Epitome Divinarum Institutionum*, p. 470.

seeds and purées, the more desperate even resorting to poisonous mushrooms and plants) to soften the rigours of the night and thwart its monstrous intruders.

Loss of sleep inexorably accompanies the reversal of natural order. Fear of a return to chaos contains a sad presage of doomsday, premonitions of cosmic catastrophe:

> They will weep and groan and gnash their teeth: they will say that the dead are fortunate and lament the living. Through these and many other disasters there will be desolation on earth and the globe will be defiled and deserted.[15]

A weary God, an ageing universe, an infertile and empty plain stretching across a shapeless world, continued to haunt men's dreams until well after the year AD 1000.

The terrors that night held, the fear of long shadows, of 'divers, terrible phantoms' (Gordonius), of dark and terrifying dreams ('... because it seems to him that in his sleep he sees demons, or black monks, or hanged men, or dead people'), added momentum to the search for control over these ghosts, stimulated the demand for euphoria, for 'jovial', 'cordial' and soothing potions. Laughter was universally recognized as a tonic which could detoxify the blood and humours, and renew life, *hilaritas animae, exhilaratio* quickens the pulse, rejuvenates, purifies the blood, making it course faster through the veins, while *tristitia* 'desiccates the bones, eats away at the flesh, troubles the spirit and wrinkles the skin'.[16] To induce a state of happiness and banish melancholy, Arnaldo di Villanova prescribed 'crocus wine' (i.e. saffron wine) and 'bugloss wine'. Foremost among these gentle providers of mild and moderate comfort was borage: 'Borage am I, who bring joy I cry'. Borage 'has a predominant quality over the Passions of the heart', 'When being infused into Wine it causes chearfulness of Mind, and wonderfully comforts the Heart, taking thence all Melancholy Thoughts, instead thereof introducing Joy and gladness.'[17] Macer Floridus (Aemilio Macro) is full of praise for verbena: '[Verbena] when scattered among the party, is said to make the guests cheerful, as was the bugloss recommended before'.[18] The seed of cold lettuce that extinguished excess heat 'restrains worthless dreams' particularly 'Veneris somnia'.[19]

Magic stones were used as 'protective amulets' against nightmares. Macro (*De natura lapidum*) tells us that chrysolite or topaz counteracted

[15]   Ibid. p. 470.
[16]   A. de Villanova, *De conservanda iuventute et retardanda senectute*, vol. I, col. 819.
[17]   C. Durante, *A Treasure of Health* (translation by John Chamberlayne).
[18]   Macer Floridus, *De materia medica libri V*, Francofurti, 1540, c. 65r.
[19]   Ibid. c. 13r.

'nocturnal fears ... it frightens devils away and harries them'.[20] While black, shiny and light jet: 'is thought to be effective against demons ... It overcomes spells and undoes harmful incantations'.[21]

'Just as melancholy weakens the digestion, so does happiness fortify it'. Fears, fretting and unwholesome thoughts provoke 'crudities and putrefactions':

> For Fear withdraws the Spirits and the Blood, attracting them inwardly to the Heart, whence the Members grow cold, the Body pale, causing tremblings, the Voice is interrupted, and the whole force of the Body is deficient; for Fear, whilest the Evil feared is expected, causes a beating of the Heart, which causes a commotion of the Spirits, the which being moved, disturb all the Blood; whence afterwards are occasioned Crudities and Putrefactions.[22]

That Torquato Tasso should be visited by 'manifold terrors of the night' was not a phenomenon unique or peculiar to him: the 'errors', 'delusions', 'shadows' of his interminable nights, of his 'tormented spirit' 'immersed in sleep and deep oblivion', were common states in the sleeping life of many people, of generations of people prey to attacks by Ephialtes ('ab insiliendo' i.e. 'by springing attack'), to nightmares ('ab incubendo') which 'impeded movement and numbed the senses in sleep', whilst 'suffocating the mind and oppressing it'. 'Aggressions', 'nocturnal invasions', 'nocturnal suffocations', 'fearful panic', 'mocking fauns and satyrs': such were the outrages perpetrated by the 'strangler' of the night who laid with his full weight upon the sleeper's body:

> ... oft above me
> Like a lion doth mine enemy roar:
> As a dragon, infect and suck my blood,
> Screaming at my bewildered mind.

Father Angelo Grillo's exorcistic advice was of little use, however:

> And if grim shapes or shadows, your sleep
> Torment, then may you quell or banish them
> By your high flame ...

It was of little use because the Evil One;

> A master of deceit, an evil sophist, a sorcerer
> The father of every sin, both old and new,
> By every artifice he harms me in every way.

20   Ibid. c. 105r.
21   Ibid. c. 109v.
22   C. Durante, *A Treasure of Health*, p. 41.

'Nervous people easily dream up apparitions, with the result that some believe a hag is sitting on their chest, or some kind of animal, a monster or a demon, although these things are pure foolishness, delusions, the frail imaginings of sleep.'[23] Every humour had its corresponding vision or nightmare, in full colour. According to Avicenna: 'Each and every humour causes visions with a corresponding colour'.

> All melancholy thought and everything that may weigh upon the spirit should be avoided by every means possible [exhorted the doctors]; hope should always be entertained, for a jovial frame of mind is good in sickness, whilst the opposite is bad; nor should one remain too long with the imagination, for what is in the imagination may become true.[24]

'Glorious pills' made out of pimpernel, widow wail, myrrh, aloes, saffron, mixed with mandragora oil 'delay old age and hoary locks, make you merry and excite the intellect ... cleanse the heart, stomach and intestines of all superfluities ...'[25]

'Small dragons', pimpernel and rosemary all had a soothing effect. Saffron was particularly 'calming to the stomach and bowels, conducive to sleep, coitus and good cheer', but taken in massive doses, 'it causes instant death by laughter'. In winter it was like a manna for 'the old, the phlegmatic and the melancholy'.[26]

In cases of insomnia caused by a 'bad constitution', the following procedures were recommended;

> small dragons, or poppy syrup, or crushed poppy seeds should be taken before going to sleep .... And both the head and the legs should be anointed with decoctions of white poppy heads, violets, willow leaves and white vineleaves. And similarly it is greatly beneficial to anoint the body internally with nenufar oil, and likewise to rub the forehead, temples, palms of the hands, soles of the feet and inside of the wrist with populeon ointment, or to take a purge of violet oil and women's milk. And much benefit will be derived from smelling the sleep-inducing sponge described by Nicolao da Salerno in his antidotary. Herb balm sprinkled upon the head will induce deep sleep: in the Sahara it is used as a suffimigant for the same purpose. Roses, violets, willow leaves, sandalwood, nenufar flowers, poppy husks, should all be placed in a glass flask with rose water and, the jar

23   J. F. Löw ab Erlsfeld, *Universa Medicina practica juxta veterum et recentiorum mentem efformata et aucta...*, Norimbergae, 1724.

24   Ibid. p. 43.

25   F. Canale, *De' secreti universali...*, p. 10.

26   C. Durante, *A Treasure of Health*, p. 303.

being sealed, be boiled until they have reduced by a third; the stopper is then removed and the contents inhaled.[27]

Poppy syrup, ointments, anointings, baths, inhalations, powders suffumigations . . ., the so-called *requies magna* [great repose] and powerful *spongia somnifera* [sleep-inducing sponge] of the *Antidotarium Nicolai* (a sea sponge soaked in the juices of opium, henbane, hemlock and mandragora which was applied to the nostrils) were all drawn from the armoury of remedies in the long and arduous battle against insecurity, pain, insomnia, bad dreams, or, as Mesue said: 'provided the consolation of a pure medicine'.

In that tortured, harassed, fumigated and oiled world, many of life's important moments, especially the most delicate and secret of these, were attended by suffumigations and anointings. Women wishing to be fertilized underwent a special suffumigatory procedure or ritual (whether of a magical or liturgical kind) which favoured conception:

> Take incense, mastic laudanum, myrrh, cyprus kernels and leaves, aloe wood, leaves, powdered moths, acorn cupules, ground ivory . . . and mix with fresh goose fat to form a paste, from which flat pills shall be made to the shape of lupin flowers. One or two shall be placed upon a brazier beneath a perforated chair and by means of a funnel shall the fumes be made to reach the mouth of the womb.[28]

This additional device in the strategic armoury of the gynaecological medicine of the time, a kind of surrealistic chair with a funnel and stove arrangement designed to 'facilitate conception', provides yet another proof of the deep scrutiny which that mysterious, moist, magical vessel (as Hippocrates put it: 'That fountain of six-hundred calamities') the womb, came in for. The vast and imponderable problem of reproduction, reflected in Latin countries in their cult of the Virgin as queen of the waters (*Mysterium magnum*), is probably unconsciously felt at the etymological level in the association between 'matter' and 'maternity' pointed out by Freud.

The ritual leading to fertile coitus, in a highly corrupt, insanitary environment, required not only the 'correct living habits', but also a 'general purge', a 'purging of the womb':

> place in the nature [that is the female pudenda] some finely ground mercury herb, in a small bag measuring two inches in length and tied to the thigh by means of a thread . . .; it should be kept inside for three days, after which a bath should be taken as

27   P. Bairo, *Secreti medicinali*, Venezia, 1602, c. 21r.
28   Ibid. c. 193v.

> described hereunder: Take feverfew, wormwood, oregon, wild
> mint, motherwort, camomile flowers, cloves, wild rue, storax,
> wood of a balsam tree, costmary, fruit of balsam, madder, a
> good red colour .... These should be cooked in water at a
> comfortable temperature and of sufficient quantity so that the
> subject may sit in it up to her navel.[29]

This purificatory and exorcistic ritual highlights once again the equation vagina = hell, infested by rotten miasma and vicious spirits.

Tainted though it was by implication, conception was nonetheless to be attended by immaculate conditions, by the utmost purity. Among the things that 'assist a person to conceive', 'some are given before coitus, some during, and some after coitus'. Prior to intercourse, for instance, for three successive days a 'tampon or pessary' was placed in the 'natura' and 'kept there for three hours, water having first been passed and the body purged'. 'Take mastic of frankincense, the kernel of a cypress, liquid storax, borax, amber and musk; mix these with some good malmsey and place them in the neck of the womb with a tampon of wool or cotton wool.'[30]

The evenings were set aside for the fumigatory ritual of the funnel-chair. Among the various measures preparatory to sexual intercourse was the making and taking of Arnaldo di Villanova's 'tried and tested' electuary:

> Take the testicles of a fox (that is the animal known by this
> name), and the root of the herbs named fox's testicles [trefoil],
> the right testicle of a boar or male pig, dried in the shade, ground
> ivory, *sesoleos*, the wombs of some female hares and rennet ...
> and sugar to half the weight of the rest: make the whole into a
> powder, which should then be taken upon an empty stomach.[31]

Another preparatory treatment favoured by the *ars procreandi* of the epoch, and which 'aided procreation', was to 'anoint the umbilicum and the kidneys from beneath with an oil made from ivy-wood, because it sooths the womb and consumes the humidity that impedes conception'.[32]

> There follow now those things that are to be done during the act
> of copulation, because sometimes it happens that women are
> later than men, or the contrary, and for conception to take place
> it is necessary that the man's seed and that of the woman flow
> together at the same time and moment. From which it follows

29   Ibid. c. 193r–v.
30   Ibid. c. 193r–v.
31   Ibid. c. 914r.
32   Ibid. c. 194r.

that the one who is slower should, by means of stroking touching and like actions, be induced to send forth his or her seed at the same moment.[33]

And after coitus:

the woman should rest for an hour, keeping her thighs together and anoint her vagina with liquid tar, frankincense and oil for two or three days. If in that time the seed does not flow out, it is a sign of conception. But if there are no signs of conception yet, then the above-mentioned methods should again be tried, using among other things the following tampon or pessary: Take two leaves of hypericum, some ground ivory, musk, oriental amber ... with wax made from catmint juice and a *polenta* made from chickweed. Make a soft tampon wrapped in silk dyed in carmine grain dye, place it in the vagina and keep it within for a long time.[34]

Both the moist womb and dead waters wherein lay the black, stagnant and sinful humours contaminated by witchcraft, called for a total purging, a lustral bath, suffumigations with the same herbs. The exorcism of the womb and that of the soul (and polluted blood) had many points in common.

Obviously, it is not just for gratuitous theatrical effect that we choose to offset the harsh reality of those times (together with the anguish-filled pages of great literature) with the islands of peace, kingdoms of bliss and gardens of voluptuousness created by them; rather is it out of a desire to reflect upon the arcane relationship seen to exist between hell on earth and bliss in death, between the hardship and horror of life on earth and the inexhaustible sweetness of the delician paradise, of elusive oases, of lost islands, of enchanted mountains, inaccessible to the living. This journey to blissful lands transcends the Jewish/Christian tradition and the ancient hedonistic mythologies common to all cultures: it expresses both the forlorn striving for a different life and the hidden desire for death, an unconfessed yearning for the end. It is hard to say which was stronger: the fear of doomsday or the hope that it would arrive as soon as possible. The evil weeds that suffocated harvests mentioned by Raoul Glaber are diametrically opposed to the 'milk-white and honey-sweet herbs in the eating of which' the friars who set off in search of St Macarius found comfort and sustenance, insensible to the 'long duration' of their walk and to the weariness of travel. The stench of corpses and 'horrible things' was quite another matter from the 'gentle odour as of an exquisite

33   Ibid. c. 194r–v.
34   Ibid. c. 194v.

balm', or from 'a sweetness upon the palate as of honey',[35] the fragrances and sweetness that induce sleep, oblivion, inebriation, forgetfulness and visions:

> Through all these things, almost as though inebriated, we fell asleep, and arising after a little while, we beheld a remarkably beautiful and ornate church, which seemed as of crystal, having in its midst a magnificent altar, from which there gushed a stream as white as milk ... and this church where it faced noontide resembled a precious stone, to the south the colour of blood, to the west as white as snow, and over it there sparkled many a star, so far brighter than a normal star, and like our sun there shone seven much more resplendent and hotter suns; the alps and mountains were higher; the trees and fruits larger, finer and better; the birds were prettier and sang more sweetly; in a word, whatsoever we rested our eyes upon was lovelier, more fruitful and noble than their counterparts in this world. That world was itself white like snow upon one side and pink upon the other.[36]

White herbs, milk-white water, a pink and white world, taller mountains, sweeter fruits. Heightened perspectives, over-blown dimensions, haunting colours. Visionary images of a precious and improbable place (water gushing from an altar, life from the sacrificial site): sweet forgetfulness and intoxication, dreams and landscapes, proud and magnificent geometries.

From the unfolding of such legends, evoked in the imagery of the great visionary apocalyptic literature (like a church with variegated walls), we again receive the ineluctible impression that the 'Aztec condition', or ritual 'visionary receptiveness' obtained from masticating and swallowing 'the flesh of God' (identified with the holy and hallucinogenic mushroom) was somehow, and in some immeasurable degree, making itself felt in the monastic life of the West, macerated by fasting, tortured by self-flagellation, intoxicated by berries, roots, herbs, and mushrooms – noted these last by Baldassarre Pisanelli, a late sixteenth-century physician, for their property of causing a 'stupor'.[37] These 'fruits engendered from the earth's excrements', 'being fatty, slimy, cold and moist in nature, become like blood in quality'. Toxic and harmful while not actually poisonous, they were regarded with terror and suspicion by medical literature as corruptors of blood, associated with the underworld, with darkness and death, and adverse to a good 'constitution' and to self-control. They were impure and felt to be dangerous and insidious.

---

35   *La leggenda di S. Macario*, in G. Battelli, *Le più belle leggende cristiane*, p. 438.
36   Ibid. p. 438.
37   B. Pisanelli, *Trattato della natura de'cibi e del bere*, Bergamo, 1587, p. 26.

> Cooked and boiled, mushroom, I know you well,
> But if I eat you I fear to die
> And therefore I condemn you to a cesspit.[38]

While deemed 'food for the gods' by Nero, who had an extraordinary penchant for mushrooms, or 'flesh of God' according to the clergy of the New World, in other cultural contexts the association of the mushroom with the supernatural world was a pejorative one, it being seen as a corrupt (born of putrefaction) transmitter of celestial phantoms and solar visions. Choreic frenzies and mass hysteria could be brought on by a fungus that attacked rye (cocks' spur or ergot) and caused devastation during the mediaeval era. Almost nothing, however, is known about the consumption of the 'normal' edible mushroom. Physicians maintained that every fungus is 'by its very nature' 'almost poisonous', 'fermenting earth', a 'pituitous tree'.[39] It was certainly regarded as a 'depraved' substance, full of death-dealing 'iniquity', of voluptuous temptations. It is, however, impossible to ignore the existence of a certain strange affinity between mediaeval visionary literature and the fantastic constructs appearing in certain reports by today's experimenters inspired by the idea of the sacred mushroom. The ethnologist, Robert Gordon Wasson, who personally experienced the effects of *teonanacall* (a mixture of 'God's flesh' based on the *Psylocybe* and *Stropharia* mushrooms, rich in alkaloids of like name and psylocyne with a strong psychotropic action), reported seeing

> geometric, angular, strongly coloured shapes, reminiscent of architectural structures, with columns and architraves, princely courtyards, brightly-coloured edifices, adorned with gold, onyx, ebony exceeding the human imagination in magnificence. One gains the impression that the walls of a simple dwelling (where the ritual takes place) disappear and that one's soul floats unfettered in space.

We have a paradisiacal structure here of dazzling, brightly-coloured and variegated intensity: an architectural set in the full apocalyptic tradition, reminiscent of that envisaged by mediaeval monks and 'men of God' (great consumers of herbs, roots and tubers), by the Counter-reformation, by Giuseppe di Copertino in the throes of his 'abstractions'. The 'gallery of beautiful things' which he visited during his ecstasies belonged to an unstable world in which celestial components were easily changed.

[38]   S. Mercuri, *De gli errori popolari d'Italia*, p. 508.
[39]   G. Mercuriali, 'De venenis et morbis venenosis', in *Opuscula aurea selectiora*, Venezia, 1644, p. 100.

J. Gottlieb Georg, a German traveller in the eighteenth century, saw, when he crossed Kamschatka, that:

> the Ostiachs, Samoyeds and Tungusis immersed this mushroom [*Agaricus muscarius*] in *Epilobium* juice and then drank the liquid thus obtained to experience a pleasant feeling of inebriation, and indeed, so as to renew this cheaply, they would drink their own urine by means of which the active substance was expelled.[40]

But even if we discount additives of this kind, the efficacy of fasting for the purposes of producing a visionary experience cannot be underestimated, or of restricted diets in unleashing hallucinatory 'highs' in a controlled and secret environment. The combination of cell and fasting was a melting pot for the visionary experience.

When in *The Purgatory of St Patrick*, the knight Owain approached the delician paradise, he was still half a mile away when a 'great and gentle scent reached his nostrils'; it was 'as though the whole world were populated with spiceries. The Knight had known no scent surpassing this one and he was greatly comforted and fortified by the sweetness thereof, which he deemed sufficient to enable him to bear all the pains and torments he had borne till then'.[41] These invigorating and strengthening aromas, sustaining a man through fatigue and hardship, reminiscent of the tonics intended to fortify the body's natural defences, instilling courage and stimulating potency, far surpassed any desperate spells in effectiveness, such as the suggested mingling of two milks in Maestro Pietro Veneto's recipe (sixteenth century), which attempted to mitigate the pangs of suffering: 'take the milk of a woman who is a mother, and the milk of the daughter of the aforesaid mother, mix these two milks together and give them at once as a drink to the person who is about to be tortured.'

Surrounded by 'lovely meadows', 'lusciously green, sweet-smelling and enticing herbs, many-coloured flowers, delicious fruits hanging from

[40]   Quoted in A. Benedicenti, *Malati medici e farmacisti. Storia dei rimedi traverso i secoli e delle teorie che ne spiegano l'azione sull'organismo*, Milano, 1925, vol. II, p. 1222. The French translation of Georgi's work, *Description de toutes les nations de l'empire de Russie*, was published in St Petersburg in 1776–7. For the ritual use of *Amanita muscaria* among the 'Iacute, Samoied & Tanguse' peoples see Philip Johann von Strahlemberg, *An Historial and Geographical Description of the North and Eastern Parts of Europe and Asia, particularly of Russia, Siberia and Tartary*, English translation, London 1736. For the particular hallmarks of *ivresse amanitique* and the use of inebriating urine, see Louis Lewin, *Phantastica*, Paris, 1970, pp. 140–5. For the 'dance of the Peyotl' see A. Artaud, *Les Tarahumaras*, Paris, 1971.

[41]   *Il Purgatorio di S. Patrizio*, in G. Battelli, *Le più belle leggende cristiane*, p. 494.

the trees, from all of which there sprung a wondrous fragrance',[42] the 'blessed multitude' waited every day for its 'heavenly and exquisite food ... which charmed and filled with great delight'. This 'substance', which was as indescribably nutritious as a cosmic manna, penetrated the body like a golden rain and had an immediately intoxicating effect upon the consumer, reminiscent of narcotic alienation, filling him with indescribable peace and superhuman sensations. One single ration of this 'celestial food' had an overwhelming effect: like an abrupt (and therefore sadly short) dive into an unexplored and traumatic experience. This *rite d'anéantissement* [rite of annihilation] leads, through disintegration and submersion of the Ego, to reabsorption and involvement in the Whole, as in the *Ciguri* of the *Tarahumaras* examined by Antonin Artaud. Like an instant journey to the source of all delight, like a sinking into oblivion and bliss:

> ... suddenly a shining object fell from the sky almost like a flame, and covered the whole land, so that its rays spread and appeared upon each person's head, then filling the whole of his body. So overwhelmed by this was the knight, so brimming his heart and head with sweetness that he almost felt outside himself, neither alive nor dead. But this sweetness and charm passed away and in their place he felt invaded by the comfort of a new sweetness and delight.[43]

The temporary 'comfort' derived from a single daily dose was transformed into boundless joy for those destined for the heavenly paradise, an uninterrupted state of intoxication, an unbroken contact with the sublimely celestial Mushroom:

> ... those who are brought from this place to the glory of the eternal life are fed upon this food not once daily but as often as their souls desire. But since this succulent and celestial food is ever to hand, they may taste of the solace it affords as often as it may please them to do so ...[44]

Divine presence, enjoyment of heavenly bliss, the last stage of the journey towards ultimate sublimity were part and parcel of the state of hallucinatory ecstasy. It was like a tangible and limitless absorption of divine essence, like a quintessential sugar, the 'sum-total' of indescribably delicious, balmily devastating and wholly unprecedented sweetness. This harping on sweetly ecstatic substances in the early history of the Christian West, points to an idea of paradise (the delician and celestial

[42]   Ibid. p. 496.
[43]   Ibid. p. 500.
[44]   Ibid. pp. 500–1.

versions seemingly confused and mingling with each other, say, up to the Dantean age) which finds its inspiration in an exotic primitivism of a kind. Divine-ness was perceived sensually, it was inhaled in the form of essence of perfume, it was tasted, it was absorbed by the intestine, it was touched, smelled, drunk, eaten, digested. The ritual drugs opened the door to a whole range of comforting intoxications.

At the popular level, the inaccessible peak of paradise on earth was dimly perceived in a sort of land of Bengodi – the sublimated version of a Land of Cockaigne, enjoying a monstrous abundance – in which food passed through other channels: the nose as well as the mouth, and not least the eyes. It was a land of scents, sound, lights, intoxicating fluids, a land of youth and beauty, of endless festivity. Even the strictest and most ascetic of the Church fathers, like the austere, steely and intransigent St Peter Damian, had a lasting notion of blessedness as being founded on physicality and earthliness. Once fear of the future, historical anxiety and insecurity were overcome ('with a quiet mind ... future adversity will never ... burden us')[45], cleansed of all 'corruption' (*corruptela*), detoxified of vices and passions, freed of earthly dross, the human condition attained to perfect 'cleanliness' (*munditia*), no longer in the thrall of human passions (although the saint of Ravenna, drawing upon the vocabulary of visceral earthiness and with an unexpected deviation into the rustic style, writes: 'she dances about, besmirched with the defilements of all the passions with intense physiological and expressionistic fervour'); Death is put to rout ('and then is Death absorbed in victory'), Hope entertained, feasting endless, but in a different way from on earth: 'among us [the living], when one feast is celebrated, no other is celebrated at the same time; there [among the blessed dead], however, the joy of all the great feasts together is combined at all times'.[46]

His holy land was the Celtic land of legend and youth, of beauty, health, strength and life everlasting:

> Here is the never-ending greenness of flourishing youth, here is the charm of beauty and the unfailing strength of good health. They draw water from the spring of eternity so that they may live forever and be indescribably happy .... There the sweetness of the perfume surpasses the power of all scents, outdoes the fragrance of all unguents. There musical instruments of delight charm the ears of the Blessed. There in meadows which are green and of superlative beauty, the gleaming white lilies never

45   St Peter Damian, *Institutio monialis*, col. 784.
46   Ibid. col. 785.

fall, and the purple roses and yellow crocus flowers never wither.[47]

In this land of incorruptibility and eternity where nothing fades, putrescence is unknown; here all vegetation is evergreen, beauty undying and vigour ever present. The analogy with the world of plants and the adoption itself of a horticultural vocabulary themselves are token enough of an image of man as eternally blessed. We need only to look at the symbolism of the Garden of Eden: the reproductive tree (tree/ phallus, tree of life), the tree of the Cross (the tree of Christ's passion and blood, of the pagan vegetal myths of death and rebirth), the tree of regeneration. The branches of the tree of sensuous pleasure mingle with those of the tree of wisdom; knowledge (*cognoscere*) is at once abandonment to and control of bodily awareness, it is an interlocking of bodies, it is copulation, multiplication, ramification, it is the birth of new shoots, shrubs, leaves, new families. This anthropogenic, life-engendering tree is an emblem of man's meditation upon himself, as he meditates upon the essence of trees and vegetation, and on the mute yet sensitive spirits who hear, remember and record life's secrets. It is no mere coincidence that the oldest manifestations of religiosity take the form of vegetal apparitions and tree cults, at once sublime interpreters of human aspirations, and kindly presences or silently nurturing friends. Nor is it mere chance that one of the great mediaeval popes, Innocent III, paints a horrifying picture of the human condition in which man is seen as a failed, dirty and imperfect vegetable, smelly to boot and devoid of all human dignity, a defecator, producer of lice, grubs, no better in short than an abortion of a grotesque and puny up-ended tree:

> What kind of fruit does man bring forth? The worthless shame of the human condition, the shameful condition of human worthlessness! Look at the plants and trees: from themselves they bring forth flowers, leaves and fruit, while you bring forth fleas and lice and worms. They pour forth from themselves oil, wine and balm, while you pour forth spittle, urine and shit. They breathe forth the sweetness of perfume, and you give forth from yourself an abomination of putrescence. As the tree, so the fruit: for a bad tree cannot bear good fruit, nor a good tree bad fruit. For what is man, to judge by his shape, but a kind of upside-down tree? His roots are his hair, his trunk his head and neck, his stem his chest and belly, his branches his shoulders and arms, his leaves his fingers and their joints.[48]

[47]   Ibid. cols. 784–6.
[48]   Cardinal Lotharius, *De miseria humanae conditionis*, pp. 14–15.

People's imagination fled from the crush of the cities, from the dirty, miry, unsewered, polluted villages of Europe, where pigs peacefully rooted among the refuse that was thrown out of windows, among the fermenting excrement that flowed freely down the streets. Men's fancies soared above urban overcrowding where, as well as the prevailing odour of sulphur, unwashed bodies and rotting skin, lice, vermin, scabies, scrofula, ulcers, apostemes, tumours, chilblains and sores proliferated. Their fantasy sought refuge in distant, uncontaminated lands, 'lands full of wonder', unsullied and 'miraculous islands', in archipelagoes whose mountains provided comfort and refreshment to the jaded senses:

> The fourth mountain . . . is entirely made out of sugar, covered with grasses, woods and copses. It is somewhat smaller than the first, its fruits are sweetmeats, its flowers, the leaves, bark, trunks, roots of its trees have miraculous properties: notch or flake away their bark, and an abundance of sweet-tasting and bright-coloured syrup will issue forth smelling of the wood itself: there may you see forests of cinnamon, of green ginger and nutmeg, cloves and shrubs of balsam, spices, mirabolans, citruses, lemons, oranges, apples, muscat pears and all manner of fruits, also almonds and walnuts, peaches and plums, cherries, pumpkins, water-melons, cucumbers and melons.[49]

This forest candied down to its roots, these sickly, perfumed and coloured syrups, this obsessive yearning for sugar, balm and fruit are but another manifestation of the fixation with scented journeys, aromatic experiences, olfactory 'highs', with waters, streams, pools, grottoes and caves exuding soothing oils and precious ointments, with mountains riddled with underground passages bursting with intoxicating liquids:

> The fifth mountain . . . ., a mountain that would seem to touch the sky, full of fountains, streams and brooks, home of transparent waters and sweet odours, lakes of civet musk and other unguents; here are countless grottoes and caverns, where the soil is as musk to the taste, some being of ambergris; here are mountains of benzoin, storax, woods and copses all around, and on the summit, aloes and plants of like nature, whose perfume defies all description.[50]

On the one hand aphrodisiac and hedonistic, these essences of perfume were at the same time used to embalm, to defeat the process of

[49]   *Opera nuova molto utile e piacevole, ove si contiene quattro dialogi, composti per l'eccellentissimo dottor delle arti et medico Messer Angelo de Forte*, Venezia, 1532, c. 32v.
[50]   Ibid. c. 33r.

putrefaction. They were agents, it could be said, in the desperate battle to survive in a transient, ephemeral world, to rescue the putrescent body, to staunch 'sanies' and mend fraying parenchymata. In his dreams, Angelo de Forte, doctor and charlatan, was not far from the physiological treatises which purposed to gloss upon all the great problems of Aristotelian physic. The *Tractatus de putredine* (Venice, 1534) by Gerolamo Accoramboni, Antonio Bergia's *Paraphrasis*, the *De simplici generatione, putredine, coctione, concretione et liquefactione mistorum corporum et perfectorum* (Mondovì, 1565) by Mario Sanbarolitano and his *Degressio de putredine . . . super foen tertia quarti Avicennae descriptio* (Venice, 1535); Giovanni Bravo Patrasitano's treatise, *De saporum et odorum differentiis, causis, et affectionibus* (Venice, 1592), and that of Stefano Lorenzini, *Dell'organo dell'odorato [Of the Organ of Smell]*, are cases in point.

And finally, there was the dream of the mountain that hid the secret of life, the province of 'Verity', the magic fountain from which there the water bubbles out that when drunk reveals new (and lost) paths of consciousness and communications between men, herbs, animals and plants. It was like a rediscovery of the secret code to universal communication, occult languages, silent channels through which the great dialogue between things, whether animate or inanimate, but all feeling, alive and memorable, weaves its way. This lost, celestial language, with its universal and arcane code for all created things and elements is

> . . . the province of Verity. This surmounts the topmost brow of a hill. It is flat and circular and around it grow shady pine woods which, while not great, yet abound in wondrous things. In the midst of these there gurgles a living fountain, remarkable in its qualities, because whomsoever drinks of this fountain divines what its stone, metals, its herbs, trees and animals have mutely told him . . .[51]

All these occult 'secrets', unknown formulae, lost keys, dawned in the consciousness as a result of drinking a miraculous water: all kinds of impossible metamorphoses, forbidden transformations, dreamed-of reversals, could now be enacted.

> . . . at first our minds were dazed, but when we were grown accustomed, we were well pleased. We heard of things there that transform a man's nature: the elderly become young, beautiful and strong; the poor, rich; the ignorant, knowledgeable; the

51   Ibid. c. 35v.

lazy, fortunate; the mad, sane; the idle, swift and light; the cowardly and foolish, famed people; the dumb, eloquent; the sterile, fecund; the ugly, handsome; and other similar wonders.[52]

[52]   Ibid. cc. 35v.–36r.

14

'PARADISUS VOLUPTATIS'

The 'bless'd' place radiated clarity, an extraordinary and artificial light, emanating from 'God's countenance', from the divine but immobile engine, an 'immeasurable' magnet that cast a shadow on sun and moon, ordained changes in nature and its *vis genitiva*, transformed climatic laws, time's pattern and death itself. The 'heavenly Jerusalem' dreamed of by Giacomino da Verona is the urban variant of the *paradisus voluptatis*: a city full of water and herbs, of fountains, of scented and gustatory delights. The 'clarity' implicit in these symbols is synonymous with beauty, purity and holiness: God is a shining, unexhausted and inexhaustible fountain; night and murky darkness are symbols of contamination and demoniacal forces. The 'man of God' benefits from the divine light, he is handsome and luminous, like the saintly hermit whom the adventurous monks in the *Navigatio Sancti Brendani* meet on an island 'full of precious herbs, flowers and fruits . . . and precious stones'; he is a 'very handsome man who [shines] all over'.[1]

On the 'precious island' called also 'the promised land of saints'

> there are flowers of many kinds and the trees are always laden with flowers and fruit, and the birds always sing merrily. There is no night on this island, but only clear daylight shining with an intense light; the air is calm. Hunger, thirst, the need for sleep, pain, sorrow and worry are unknown.[2]

In this 'precious place', the normal physiological processes become irrelevant. The 'promised land of saints' was a charmed limbo where the human condition no longer continued in its struggling and precarious physical mode, in its awkward animal rhythms. It was a place of rebellion, of glorious freedom, where the shackles of life's drudgery were thrown off and mortals were no longer slaves to the demands of their bodies. In this land, the problem of *de conservanda valetudine* [the preservation of good health] was resolved, physiological time, metabolic rhythm, life's vicissitudes, the irrepressible needs of mind and body ('food and drink, movement and stillness, sleep and waking, hunger and surfeit, the passions of the mind') were banished, put to rout. This heavenly retreat, rather than an ethereal and sublimated Land of

[1]   *Navigatio Sancti Brendani*, p. 39.
[2]   Ibid. pp. 43–5.

Cockaigne, had become an exclusive retreat for the pure and the blessed where their survival was a function of light and smell. In this place, saints lived a quasi-vegetal existence, feeding as plants do, off light, clean air, pure water, becoming scented like flowers:

> 'Can you not tell from the odour of our garments that we have been in Paradise?' Whereupon the bretheren answered: 'Abbot, we did indeed smell a great perfume, and we therefore believe that you have been in a fine place; we would gladly know where this Paradise is which we do not know, for we have noted that for a full forty days since your return here the scent has been about your garments.'[3]

Indeed, practically all the islands of the Celtic West known to Irish seafarers belonged to a great archipelago famed for its miracles and apparitions: where ships were sighted propelled by invisible forces, bells rang of their own accord, lamps lit up mysteriously, where hunger and thirst were reduced to vague memories:

> And in this island, I have to tell you, we were never hungry, nor did we eat cooked meats; nor did we suffer excess heat or chaffing cold, for the air is always warm; and when it was time to sing mass in the morning or vespers in the evening, the lamps had been lit in the church we knew not by whom or how, and lit they remained throughout the service and never lacked oil.[4]

These fragrant islands form part of a heavenly sphere whose aromatic emissions stunned the senses, producing a sort of pungent, benumbing, and narcotic nirvana. The ecstasies and deliriums highlight the importance of the olfactory sense. The nose was a prime instrument of knowledge (or loss of knowledge, too), it was a gnosiologist in fact, an open door onto the world of smells where everything had its place and its scented identity. Aided by the balsamic decodifier present in the nasal ducts, this information system was capable of sorting and analysing all manner of incoming aromatic data:

> ... there flourished trees laden with precious stones; silver and golden were their leaves and bejewelled their boughs, and they seemed to burn upon one side, whence there came a scent so sweet as almost to overwhelm the senses, and it seemed as of aloes, incense, musk, balm, amber, rosemary, sage, roses and jasmin.[5]

3   Ibid. p. 45.
4   Ibid. p. 97.
5   Ibid. p. 244.

Even clouds emanated a 'very great and sweet scent', a palliative to body and soul. 'So aromatic an aroma' is incontrovertible proof of blessedness, of the proximity of divine-ness:

> The weeds of the river were so lovely and so scented, that they surpassed all our own scented weeds in beauty and fragrance: sage, rosemary, mint, violet, roses, cumin and orange-blossom are nothing in comparison. The trees in this place were so tall and fine, that no finer flowers, no brighter fruits might be found adorning our trees; every branch was weighed down with ripe and unripe, half-ripe, half-unripe fruit: dates, pineapples, pears, chestnuts, plums, persicums, citrons, cinnamon and carob. We saw sugar cane and many rare fruit trees, which cannot be found in Italy, that it would be impossible to describe them all.[6]

The blessed who inhabited this promised land, lived off aromas, just as the mouthless *astomi* of legend, fed off the smell of roots, flowers and wild fruits. In some of the stories about Alexander, as recalled by Arturo Graf, rumour had it that there existed peoples who were nourished from the smell of spices. The belief that there was a people living in the East who survived solely on the fragrance of an apple finds a distant echo in some Gaelic (therefore Western) seafaring tales:

> He would that apple have,
> Whose scent alone gives life
> To distant peoples, who meat
> Nor other food do taste.
> (Il mare amoroso. Ed. Monaci, 223–6)

The far Eastern *mare amoroso* [amorous sea] lapped the shores of the *imrama* of the far West.

Carnivorous Europe, in whose larders, slaughter-houses and kitchens, meat succumbed to the same processes of putrefaction as those which overtook the bodies of dead human beings (and let it be said that in mediaeval times they existed almost in a state of cohabitation with their living colleagues and were buried by them in city cemetries, which in their turn acted as social meeting places, settings for merry-making, market-places for foodstuffs – the Franciscan cemetery at Cesena doubled as a fish-market in the fifteenth century), met with a radically different physiological state of affairs in the East, where smell predominated over taste, scent over stench.

In adopting the life of the 'homo sylvester . . . et practicus rusticanus' [man of the woodland and practicing rustic] (as a famous contemporary

[6]   Ibid. p. 210.

of his, Arnaldo di Villanova, was fond of describing himself), the great canon of Laura, who watched over the growth and development of his plants and respected the lunar calendar as only an expert rustic would,[7] found in his garden the solace and charm which the nomadic life of the professional man at the courts of the powerful (*peregrinus ubique*), was unable to afford him; deeming the 'odour of women's creams and that of meats . . . unwholesome when compared with the scent of flowers and apples,',[8] he would create oriental scenes which were the reverse of Western ones.

> It is known and absolutely true, as testified by great and eminent doctors, that a certain people living near the source of the Ganges feed not on solid foods but only on the scent of wild apples; and, if they journey, they take with them no other nourishment than these apples, which give them life; they are so little tolerant of foul smells, that as good odours nourish them, so are they killed by evil ones. So delicate a constitution, which lives and dies thus, is excellent. When it is that all peoples living in the Orient are dissolved by the quality or mildness of the air; the less their need for food, the greater their need for fragrances . . . [9]

Aromatic *transfert* lead to that inaccessible retreat: the earthly paradise, to the 'dense, living and divine forest' to the 'soil that exudes fragrance from every pore', to the 'sweet air', the 'gentle wind', to the 'holy countryside', to nectar, to the balmy heart of a cosmos that bestows immortality upon the dead, manufacturing forbidden elixirs and humanly unattainable perfumes in hidden laboratories. Such perfumes were beyond the distilling prowess of alchemists, who had to content themselves with natural balsam (or, in the absence of this, with 'artificial' balsam, a 'liqueur which resembled balsam as far as possible'); they were 'very hot, penetrating, desiccating, with the property of preserving dead flesh from putrefaction and of maintaining youth in a living person and delaying old age'.[10] Myrrh, aloes, and incense were also prized as aromatic sources, and when mixed with turpentine or other essences, and distilled in a retort produced the mysterious ointment which preserved life and 'truly seems of God's own making'.[11] This 'precious jewel', this miraculous 'liquor', this *elixir vitae* that 'preserves dead bodies from decay

7   Cf. P. De Nolhac, 'Petrarque dans son jardin de Parme', in *Archivio storico per le Province Parmensi*, N.S. XXXIV (1934), pp. 37–40.

8   F. Petrarch, *De rimedii dell'una e dell'altra fortuna*, II, p. 126.

9   Ibid. p. 126.

10   L. Fioravanti, *De' capricci medicinali*, c. 90v.

11   Ibid. c. 92r.

and living ones from change',[12] this 'glorious elixir' for embalming dead flesh and fixing in time living flesh, is basically an odiferous talisman or cocktail of volatile essences transformed into miraculous water.

'The finest turpentine, oil of bay leaves, galbanum, gum arabic, incense, myrrh, ivy gum, aloes, galangal, clove, *consolida minore*, cinnamon, nutmeg, zedoary, ginger, white dittany, musk, amber',[13] the *res odiferae* that Arnaldo di Villanova recommended as the best remedy for the cure of putrid phlegm, to ward off 'corrugatio' *[wrinkling]* and 'senectus' *[ageing]*, to promote 'reiuvenescentia':[14] a paradise in miniature, captured in an alembic and translated into distillation.

This was heat and humidity triumphing over dryness and cold, sweet effluvia over rank ones, *conservatio* over *corruptio*, according to the medical precept that stated that:

> this is physical wholeness, and nature maintained in an intermediate position between warm and damp, from which elements perfection is blended, together with nature. For this reason those who have the most heat and moisture in the constitution are the longest lived. But those who are of the opposite disposition, cold and dry, grow old and die more quickly.[15]

Clean air was victorious; 'mild, calm, pure, fine, enduring and free air, free of foetor, devoid of putrid infection', reigned supreme; the atmosphere was protected, padded, untroubled by winds, the absolute opposite of *aeris malitia*, or 'harmful and noxious, turbid and cloudy, impure and fetid, gloomy, rotting and close air'. This paradise was made to mankind's specifications, the plans could be 'found in manuals holding the secret of life and longevity, showing the road to the perfect *regimen sanitatis* which looked ahead to man's decline by providing a *regimen senum*. Gentle and healthy breezes wafted through this paradise ensuring an atmosphere immune to 'all rank smells' (Arnaldo di Villanova), refreshing it and conditioning it with bursts of fragrance:

> In the matter of perfumes, the spirit is constantly nourished in one way or other by the air, by swift and true perfumes: the heart and brain are strengthened, the spirit restored, whereby thus renewed, the body feels both pleasure and new vigour. Rank and unhealthy air is improved and corrected by scents and suffumigations. No sooner have we imbibed the scents than it [the air] is lost. And so does the spirit in us escape . . .[16]

12   Ibid. c. 90v.
13   Ibid. c. 91v.
14   *De conservanda iuventute et retardanda senectute*, I, p. 816.
15   Heinrich Rantzau, *De conservanda valetudine liber*, Antuerpiae, 1580, p. 24.
16   Ibid. p. 26.

The odiferous system had to be carefully measured so as to achieve the right balance within the cranium mixing cold with hot:

> When the disposition of the brain is intermediate between hot and cold, it is pleased by moderation and conversely is thrown into great confusion and damaged by anything else. For this reason, perfumes should be mixed and varied from time to time; for example, if cold is dominant, those scents which tend towards heat should be introduced, and if heat is prominent, those which are close to coolness.
>
> The perfume to be inhaled should be of roses, violets, myrtle, camphor, sandalwood and rose-water, which are cool, and also of cinnamon, lemon, orange, aloes, amber and musk, which are warm, according to what is appropriate, and they should be applied not only to the nostrils, but also to the chest and belly . . . [17]

So we have an image of the body inhaling a variety of fragrances through all the channels available to it, in a constant state of aromatic receptiveness, finding ultimate consumation in the scented orchard, where the sensory system can let itself go with joyous abandon to a perfect mixture of perfumed essences which revitalize the spirit:

> It will bring no little improvement and restore your spirits to walk about frequently in the garden, where many good fragrances waft among flourishing and sweetly scented plants; and to set out in your house, flowers and grasses according to the season, chosen according to the requirements of your own physical condition; to scatter the area with leaves of willow, roses, violets, young vines, oregan, wild thyme, thyme, lavender, myrtle, quince, pear, orange pomegranate and similar shrubs, or with rose-water, or orange-blossom water, or alternatively with vinegar. And from time to time burn fragrant incense in your room. [18]

Rooms were imbued with the scent of suffumigations and fragrant braziers which imitated the natural perfumes of the orchard. They must necessarily be heated by 'dry and odiferous woods'[19] mixed with aromatic essences: 'Use a crucible over a moderate heat and burn in it juniper, myrtle, turpentine, laurel, sage, rosemary, lavender, wood of ash, oak and beech tree.'[20] 'Sweet-smelling things are witness to a

17   Ibid. p. 26.
18   Ibid. pp. 26–7.
19   Ibid. p. 32.
20   Ibid. p. 33.

sound humoural condition';[21] distemper was conversely brought on by evil odours.

So deep was the obsession with the *hortus deliciarum* that attempts were made to reproduce its scented effluvia artificially. The image of a simulated and domestic paradise in miniature was based on the ghost of *Gramisio* which Bernardo Silvestre conjures up in his *Cosmografia*:

> Gramisio is a distant and solitary place, to the East: having enjoyed the warm rays of the Sun in its infancy, its climate is mild and favourable, nature flourishes and sprouts anew. This place is called Gramisio because it is perpetually covered in verdure of every kind.
>
> Its hidden womb provides all that is necessary to the cure of illness, to the benefit of good health, and to the creation of pleasurable and voluptuous sensations: plants, herbs, scents, spices. . . .
>
> This place, so splendid in itself, waxed in beauty: for it seemed as if prepared for Nature's own arrival, as the mother of all things. Earth, then, having conceived from the Spirit of Nature, suddenly became swollen and began to put forth buds with renewed vigour. The forest of the Eliad exuded a greater abundance of ointments, incense was used to distil new fragrances, amomum and cinnamon filled the surrounding air, the first with a delicate aura, the second with a heavier air. All the burgeoning delights of the Orient seemed to welcome Nature's arrival with joyous countenance.[22]

A fecund and germinating womb, a warm and moist nest, a greenhouse full of inexhaustible self-renewal, a warm incubator ('by moisture we live, by dryness we die'), this naturalistic and pagan paradise reappeared in the day-dreams of theologians and visionaries in all its sumptuously exotic apparel. It became a place outside the life we know, a retreat where the bodies of the blessed would find eternal repose, where everyday life survives only in terms of discarded symbols, it was a sanctuary for *vis generandi*, a remote island where life was to be enjoyed to the full. Moreover, the divarication between divine genesis and molecular self-reproduction, between generating and generated matter seemed disquietingly challenged by these bizarre Christian havens.

Out of the mists of the biological past there re-emerged the pale remembrance of primordial, random and spontaneous forms of life, on their way from ephemeral creation to the warm lap of immortality. The journey begins with the appearance of the first living organisms and

---

21   Ibid. p. 56.
22   B. Silvestre, *Cosmografia*, II, IX, 2–4, pp. 528–9.

finishes upon the furthest shore of the island of the perfect life, touching in passing upon the experience of death. The regeneration of the dead follows the same pattern as the procreation of the living. The journey ends in another 'bosom' overflowing with latex (the symbol of divine motherhood) in the heart of total renewal, in the green bower populated with health-giving and pleasure-giving herbs, in the house of light (the 'claritas permaxima'[23] of the blessed), where as well as the properties of *agilitas* and *impassibilitas*, the 'dos corporum' *[endowments of the body]* are multiplied and sublimated to correspond with the four elements, the 'quattuor proprietates'. Thus the good Dr Serafico dreams of the 'gifts of the body quadrupled and the body returning to its perfect state' to imbibe 'sweet plenitude and divine intoxication'.[24]

In this Christian paradise, the 'blessings of the body' (*bona corporis*) seemed to outweigh the 'blessings of the soul' (*bona animae*):

> If beauty favours them the righteous will be radiant as the sun; if speed and strength and nobility, they will be like your angels, O God, because the living body is sown as the seed, and the spiritual body springs up from it, in potentiality, that is, not in nature. If they have been blessed with long life and good health, they will live forever, and their health is from the Lord. If they have been blessed with affluence, they will be fulfilled when the glory of the Lord is revealed; if with drunkenness, they will be made ecstatically drunk on the bounty of the house of God; if they have enjoyed pleasures which are not gross, but decent, you will give them to drink deeply from a flood of pleasure in you, O God . . .[25]

The 'house of God' is seen as the genetic centre of the universe, the vessel of abundance and fecundity, a hollow brimming with juice, revitalizing fluids, sacred honeys, dripping unguent, like a gigantic breast (*ubertas* [fruitfulness] and *uber* [breast, teat] share the same stem), evocative images of 'great goddesses', fertile liquids and waters, of 'tonic and immortalizing drinks: white *hom or soma*, the divine honey of the Finns, etc.'[26]

To this personage: father and god, destroyer and creator, this phallic tree of life, lord of the vegetable kingdom and the kingdom of light, this embodiment of fertility and prince of annihilation, the men of past ages,

23   S. Bonaventura, *Breviloquium Theologiae*, Patavii, 1562, c.104r.
24   Ibid. c. 104f.
25   Ibid. c. 105r.
26   M. Eliade, *Trattato di storia delle religioni*, Torino, 1954, p. 292. Cf. A. De Gubernatis, *La mythologie des plantes ou les légendes du règne végétal*, Paris, 1878–82, 2 vols.

terrified by 'the change, decay and corruption of our bodies', the 'the ruin and decay which we suffer in our bodies, by old age, death and all the ills of this calamitous life', offered up their prayers, imploring that their lives might be lengthened by at least a few years, were it only for the fifteen years that King Sedechiah obtained for himself:

> Therefore, this God, the everliving and most merciful father of our Lord Jesus Christ, the God who extended the life of King Sedechiah, a sinner, for fifteen years, should be begged in our prayers above all to grant us a long life, with a physical constitution free from weakness, and in good health; and to preserve both our physical and mental faculties intact and sound.[27]

This request for a small respite, less to do with the desire for sound health and unimpaired strength than with the wish to delay the inexorable (*longitudo vitae* seems an absurdly excessive demand to make when compared with the modest request for the odd extra year or two) is the more revealing as a measure of man's evident insecurity in aspiring to *vera securitas* (St Bonaventura) when it comes to us in the form of a bitter admission of impotence by this sixteenth-century physician to his sons, in a series of private letters or 'reminiscences' published, as often happened in such cases, posthumously.

The *hortus deliciarum*, the Garden of Eden ('here reigns voluptuousness') was above all an orchard of health, a mild place sheltered from illness and decay, a gentle clinic in the open air, an aromatic apothecary's shop oozing with dew, elixirs, balms, oils, gums, dripping with miraculous resins, rarefied honeys, where the air exudes aromas of delicate unguents, precious woods exhale vegetable inebriants which prepare the body for beatitude, soft fattiness, and the total amnesia of the ecstatic condition. Ernaud de Bonneval's orchard (described in his *Hexaemeron*) was a place immune to putrefaction, where neither human beings nor the fruits of the earth suffered degeneration. It was rather like a warm refrigerator or an enchanted embalming laboratory, where matter that would normally perish, survived intact from year to year. Both body and fruit are as though 'fixed' in eternity, time stands still for ever. Dewy, honeyed and redolent with aromatic balms, the saint was equipped to survive, mummy-like, in a timeless world. His flesh was treated against the contamination of the years, packaged to last through all infinity. The most striking feature of the mediaeval fantasies about paradise was their desperate fixation with good health, their striving for beatitude (particularly physical), unobtainable on earth.

[27]   Heinrich Rantzau, *De conservanda valetudine*, pp. 20–1.

The fountain of paradise that 'cools and cleanses the body's veins',[28] maintaining the body at its correct internal temperature, perfectly regulated, purified the now immortal blood that flowed through it. No sickness could penetrate. Every possible therapy was kept at the ready for use: 'there was no fever, but already there was a cure for it; there was as yet no infirmity in nature, but already the medicines for disease were sprouting'.[29] We may be surprised at finding these images of physical contentment and fitness, not to mention the medical precepts intended to ensure the continuance of good health (correct temperature, purified blood), applied both to living patients and to those who had passed to eternal beatitude. Yet the whole artificial and paradisiacal apparatus was geared to 'conserve human nature in its integral state'; in wholeness, happiness, longevity.

> There were fruit trees there which did service to the taste and to the sight, being fair to see and pleasant to smell, and sweet to every delighted sense. Everything was to hand which not only necessity but also pleasure might want. The splendour of the trees was of one kind, of the fruit of another; and nothing there was without use or unnecessary: the tree-trunks yielded sap and their branches shade, and their fruit provided food. There were to hand medicinal gums for illness, shade against the heat and food for weakness. But these pleasures were beyond our own experiences, not outside them . . .[30]

Dulcedo and *pinguedo*, sugar and fats: the aesthetic ideal of the paradise of the early part of this millenium, contrast with today's cultivation of the slim, nervous, exiguous shape and the dietetics of lightness. It was different, too, from the paradise of the rich, from baroque gastronomy, from the sixteenth-century infatuation with movement, flux and flight. Greasy rotundity, an immobile sphere, *satietas quietissima*, are all associated with the notion of bodily incorruptibility and immortality. Everywhere in the orchard there grew 'apples which do not wither', 'wood which does not rot', 'fruit which does not decay', which by their mere smell and taste were able to satisfy 'to repletion all tastes whether olfactory or of the appetite'. 'Could there be anything missing from that unique feast, when the eyes were filled with beauty and the taste with sweetness, and the sense of smell with a choice?'[31] Sight, taste, smell, colour, sense of smell: all found their

28   Ernaud de Bonneval, *Hexaemeron*, in Migne, *Patrologia latina*, vol. 189, col. 1537.
29   Ibid. col. 1536.
30   Ibid. col. 1536.
31   Ibid. col. 1537.

requirements fulfilled. 'Desire could solicit nothing different or greater than what was within sight and reach. Everything was to hand which not only necessity but also pleasure might want.'[32]

Sheltered from 'the horrors of winter', the delician paradise was imagined and planned as a greenhouse oozing ointments in which pinguid and placid saints experienced a celestial state of inebriation, whilst their 'soul's passions' were simultaneously abated and suspended between ecstasy and fragrance, their senses drugged by scents and colours, in a place 'where there is no sorrow ... nothing is corrupt, nothing lugubrious':

> there was a sweet-smelling shower from the fruit and from the very branches of the trees, and perfumed sap burst forth from their trunks. A scented gum dripped down, and liquid balsam flowed from the split bark and soaked far and wide into the stonework of the pavement. Scented ointments flowed through fields of nard, and, as gum dripped forth ignorant of the violence of the press, that whole region was flooded with countless perfumes. There was nothing grim there, nothing rotten to corrupt the rest, since every nursery-bed in that garden was scented with the virtue of its gardener, and foreshadowed the joy of heavenly glory. The wood sweated rich sap, as the love of the saints would send out purity; in the sweetness of that perfume there was revealed the truthfulness of the foreshadowing as much as the wild joy of eternal bliss. The fragrance which pushed the senses of the flesh to their limit was like a kind of ecstasy. Cinnamon juice and myrrh, caramom, ears of corn and medicinal seeds fell of their own accord and enriched the fertile soil . . . [33]

A restful garden like an exclusive clinic, a peaceful and temperate refuge where physical solace of a measured and programmed kind was the order of the day ('corporalis haec erat consolatio'), where bodily contentment was enhanced by a perfect serenity of mind, untroubled by the immoderate demands of the senses:

> No vicious sensuality lulled the dissipated spirits into wantonness, nor did an excessive stimulation of the flesh transgress the legitimate bounds of feeling, but feeling kept itself within the prescribed limit. And an act of will kept the form of all things, which the Creator had circumscribed within fixed rules, inside the determined limits; the will was docile and, abounding in all

32 Ibid. col. 1536.
33 Ibid. col. 1535.

that was necessary to reason, did not become corrupted by wallowing in unlimited indulgence. Every immoderate action is, of course, shameful and a vile abuse . . . [34]

In this zone of temperance and sobriety, of measured equilibrium, the stones and trees distribute supernatural 'virtues':

> We have discovered by experience that there is much power in those gemstones which are washed among the gravel of that central spring, and which reach us carried down and deposited by rivers. Who would doubt that in those trees, which outstrip the range of our senses with their scents and flavours, there is to be found unique benefit and antidotes to many kinds of ills? Hence, the wood of life might forestall the ills of old age, and the wood of moderation quench the fire of greed; the wood of chastity was, without doubt, so far able to control nature that the sexual organs were no more aroused for sexual intercourse than any other part of the body. Each of these perform its proper function in due course without any need for the prick of stimulation. This can also be brought about by camphor in illnesses of the kind where the reactions have already become sluggish and etiolated; if camphor is smelt or inhaled often it dries up the vessels which contain sperm, and it chills and shrivels up the tools of that trade . . . [35]

A perfect example of balanced botanical intervention, the tree of life annuls the scourge of age, the tree of temperance extinguishes gluttony, whilst that of chastity cools and restrains carnal desire.

The *libido* once checked, histrionic excess will find no place in heaven. Mimes and masques will be banned. Comic impropriety, deceiving artifice, masked games were forbidden from disturbing the orderly process of human interaction, the network of gentle and simple communications: 'In paradise there was no mime or actor. All things referred simply to themselves, and there was no impersonation of characters to bring forth the comic stage with its deceitful illusions.'[36]

Old age, gluttony, lust: the great fear of the last journey (old age to death), and the two worst temptations of the flesh that afflicted the mediaeval clergy and monastic orders (gluttony-lust). There was fear and weakness, dizziness and guilt on the one hand, and on the other, the yearning for warmth, plenty, good health, and most of all for well-being and the body's safety. The delician paradise was a great votive casket full

34   Ibid. col. 1538.
35   Ibid. col. 1539.
36   Ibid. col. 1538.

of dreams, desires and hidden fears. It was an emporium of wise pleasures where the repressed and prohibited, or simply denied, expression of mediaeval carnal spirituality accumulated. The nostalgia for the lost Eden kindled the desire for what was missing: above all for the body's permanence, the total efficiency of its working parts: eyes without their worldly spark, strong teeth, an abundance of years. In Honorius d'Autun's *Elucidarium*, when there is talk of *de corporum dotibus in beatis*, the pupil hearing from his master of the delights of corporeal perfection enjoyed by the chosen, rapturously exclaims at their physical excellence:

> *Pupil*: Oh the sweetness!
> *Master*: What if, along with these five, you were as healthy as Moses, who never lost a tooth, whose vision was never clouded over?
> *Pupil*: Oh health!
> *Master*: What if you had all these things, and were also as long-lived as Methuselah, who lived almost a thousand years?[37]

This youth's exclamations are another testimony of the avid desire for health and long life, of a dream forbidden not only to hermits and ascetes but also to any who may simply have wished to live a 'normal', balanced life, without sinking into abysses of lust ('abnormal carnal itch'), or chasms of intemperance, or succumbing to excessive histrionic mirth.

The blessings of the delician paradise tended to mingle with those of God's kingdom, the boundaries between the *paradisus voluptatis* and the city of saints, angels, patriarchs, martyrs, virgins and apostles become blurred. The two degrees of beatitude ('there are two kinds of blessedness: the lesser one of paradise and the greater one of the Kingdom of Heaven') merge one with the other.

The Jerusalem of the blessed was a city of waters, herbs, precious stones, a scented and therapeutic city of immortal people, where death and pain were unknown ('they death and pain flee, because they live forever'). 'Health', 'length of life', 'pleasure for the sight', 'pleasure for the touch', 'pleasure for the taste', 'scent', 'courage', 'strength': these were the 'bodily goods' that would reward the blessed. This body, sublimated in every sense, participated in the infinite strength of the divine, which had become indestructible, luminous, perfumed and swift like light.

> The waters and fountains that flow in the town,
> Far excel in beauty both silver and molten gold;

---

[37] Honorius Augustoduniensis, *Elucidarium*, in Migne, *Patrologia latina*, vol. 172, col. 1170.

> Full certain am I, Death shall ne'er visit
> Any that may chose to drink thereof.
>
> And through the city, too, a beauteous river flows
> Upon whose banks a luscious verdure grows,
> Trees wax and lilies sprout, a host of lovely flowers,
> The rose and the violet their matchless scent they waft.
>
> Crystal are its waves, clearer than sparkling sun,
> Upon their crest they carry pearls of pure gold and silver
> And precious stones that, glowing all the time,
> Remind us of the stars that grace the holy firmament.
>
> Each and every star in virtues so abounds
> That it bestows youth upon those that aged are;
> Any who beneath their monument a thousand years have lain,
> On touching such a star, will live and walk anew.[38]

Precious stones are like magic talismans that make the old young again and cause age-old rotting cadavers to rise from their graves. The fruits of the trees and plants washed by these waters restore the sick to health:

> The fruits of the trees and meadows that border
> The river, the plants that grow upon its banks,
> So much sweeter than honey or any other food,
> When tasted by the sick, restore them to their health.
>
> Of gold and of silver are the leaves and trunks
> Of the trees that bear these many sweet fruits,
> Their flowers they flower a dozen times a year,
> They never lose a single leaf, nor ever do they fade.
>
> So redolent is each and every lovely tree
> That for a thousand miles, nay more, the perfume reaches,
> Whence the whole city, within its walls and out,
> Seems filled with the scent of cedar and of mint.[39]

The city of the blessed betokens the removal of a perfect earthly city to an inexhaustible domain in space: a utopia based on a rational and artificial city, where worldly pleasures are enjoyed in sublime perfection, to an unsurpassed degree: a veritable consumer's paradise:

> Here, that is, in this world, it is pleasurable to see many beautiful
> men and women, to wear fine clothes, to look at great buildings,
> to hear sweet singing, charming conversation, organs, lyres,

[38]   Giacomino da Verona, *The 'De Jerusalem celesti' and the 'De Babilonia infernali'*, ed. E. Isopel May, London, 1930, p. 26, vv. 85–100.
[39]   Ibid. p. 76, vv. 101–12.

citharas and the like; to smell incense and various other kinds of perfume, to enjoy food of different kinds and to spend one's time in comfort and enjoyment; and to have much property and all kinds of furniture; all these things will be available in abundance to the saints.[40]

40   Honorius Augustoduniensis, *Elucidarium*, coll. 1171–72.

15

FOOD SANCTUARIES

The holy temple of Jerusalem, undefiled by iron, forbidden ground to the impure, to menstruating women, to sufferers from gonorrhea and leprosy, in which there wafted thirteen holy perfumes sprinkled upon the altar of incense, 'inaccessible, inviolable, and invisible to all' (the 'holy of holies' where there was 'absolute nothingness'), housed, in its innermost sanctum, a great number of victuals of holy foodstuffs, of 'the holy first fruits deposited in the temple'.[1]

In the ancient world and in mediaeval Europe, centres of faith have a history closely bound with that of food-stores.

Recently, in developing an observation made by Bronislaw Malinowski, Claude Lévi-Strauss has brought to our attention the village of Omarakana in the Trobriand Islands, where the barns in which yams are kept (a staple food-stuff of the people of this country) 'are pregnant with all kinds of taboo',[2] and are 'holy in character'.

The systematic preservation of food-stuffs, upon which the survival of the group depends, gives rise to the complex notion of the 'food sanctuary', a holy place dedicated to survival, a reservoir of life and a repository of continued progeniture, and as such it is protected by a respected and feared network of invisible threads. The terror of sinning against cosmic order, is closely connected with natural equilibrium (ecological order) and is at the heart of alimentary taboo.

Once again, we see strongly emerging the relation between the concept of 'regular diet' and 'regular religious observance'. The dividing line between the pure and the impure is even more clearly defined when applied to 'the culture of matter', where food that has been well preserved, is fresh, incorrupt, uncontaminated, not debased, the food that bestows energy, life, health, inculpates (and 'prosecutes', in the current penal sense) the deteriorating, manhandled, badly preserved, sullied, suspect or fraudulent, sophisticated or 'adulterated' product, deeply reflected in the collective unconscious of language as a sin against a social taboo or, conversely, in other cultures against divine nature.

The opposition of healthy and sick, pure and contaminated is interpreted in olfactory terms even before it reaches the gustatory system, and

---

[1]   Flavius Josephus, *La guerra giudaica*, ed. G. Vitucci, Milano, 1982, p. 341.
[2]   C. Lévi-Strauss, *Structural anthropology*, NY and London, 1963, p. 137.

lies somewhere along the axis that runs between balsamic/aromatic on the one hand and rotten/revolting on the other.

What had been regarded and feared as the 'immortal worm', the invincible enemy, was now on the way to being enlisted as a likely partner in a close collaboration. Once again the earthworm is interacting with man, not to bring about his ruin and death, but actually to promote his survival. It seems inevitable now that our agricultural and alimentary future is shortly to be again in the hands of the perforating and drilling *animalculum*, the busy miner of a land which is fast becoming exhausted, contaminated and profoundly poisonous. His is the task of ventilating, renewing and rejuvenating this land. Perhaps, and soon perhaps, we shall understand better how the Jewish-Talmudic legends considered as divine/demonic the worm, Shamir, who with his natural drill, and his extraordinary perforating apparatus, traversed the hardest stones. The sublimation of the worm (a special place is due to the 'Indian worm', the knight of silk, the silkworm who enjoyed admiring and religious cults both in the holy language – Latin – and in the vernacular) has links with the divinization of the place in which basic food stuffs are kept, vital food stuffs, the sanctum of continuance and physical duration.

The devouring monster, the killer earthworm, has done a *volte-face* and become our monster-saviour. We have not progressed much along the path of intellectual subtlety. We have only to think how today the supposedly primitive and archaic binary interpretations of the world have ultimately triumphed over the trinary (triadic, trinitarian) ones; for trifurcations (such as the third space) and alternative solutions (in political language, we know that 'alternation' is quite another thing from 'alternative') do not long survive the gross simplification wrought by the collective unconscious, with its own brand of rationale. This has also happened to the 'third space', Purgatory, whose slow and tortuous birth has been admirably traced by Jacques Le Goff. This mediating place between Heaven and Hell, of relatively recent genesis, in the twelfth century, is largely forgotten, along with the prayers and intercessions on behalf of expiating souls in purificatory fire, whilst something has still survived of the ancient binary structure of punishment/beatification, isomorphic to the gustatory dichotomy sweet/sour (the dramatic play of paradise/hell). The waning of the taste for sweet-and-sour seems, in allegory of the weakening hold on Western culture of intermediaries, doomed to die in the prolonged agonies of all that is transient. And it befell Purgatory, alternately a very hellish place and one so close to Heaven that it became a sort of sweet-and-sour antechamber to it. It is no mere chance if the myth of longevity in the earthly paradise as a foil to the kingdom of darkness, of privation, of sorrow (not to mention the torment and paraphernalia of punishment in the Christian/Catholic hell) has fascinated the European (and oecumenical) imagination in a much deeper and more lasting fashion than the myths of purgatorial mediation.

If – as one authority has proposed by way of an 'alternative' –, the family's weekly food budget should in future be extended to include the seeds and leaves of the amaranth, a food which, while dear to the Aztecs and the object of their special care and of religious taboo, was banned from the tables of the *conquistadores* precisely for religious reasons rather than for economic or dietary ones because to eat of it would seem a parody of the sacrament of the Holy Eucharist. Indeed in Mexico, the seeds of the amaranth were toasted and soaked in blood. Excommunicated cuisine is one which sins against the religious taboos of the dominant group, which consequently banishes it from all prescriptions, prayers, observances and ceremonies at the altar and at table, it seems not unreasonable to ask why the worm should not be reinstated in today's cuisine, grilled, garnished, pulverized or made into a pâté. After all, are we not currently witnessing the resurgence of that sometime scorned sister of conventional dietetics and pharmacology: herbal medicine, tried and tested across the millenia? This medicine was traditional indeed, inasmuch as the worlds of gastronomy and herbal-pharmacology, rather than bordering on each other, were interdependent, like small oratories (almost sanctuaries) where the frontier between drugs and food was virtually non-existent. Everything that could be ingested had a dual purpose: as a medicament and as a pick-me-up, for body and mind indifferently.

Prohibitions of a vegetal kind never seem to end. Indeed, even the leaves of the 'Erytroxylon Coca' will be outlawed and entire plantations in Peru are to be uprooted *ab imis* – a severe blow to the culture and lifestyle of the Andes. Already in 1567, when the Council of Lima condemned their use as another instance of the 'superstitiones et vanitates' with which the Amerindian 'coqueros' used to surround the excommunicated leaves – despite frequent bans – and the bracing, euphoric and socializing effects of the 'borrachera' ('state of drunkenness'). In the sixteenth century, the Viceroy of Toledo observed that 'all the idolatries they perform are drunken sessions, and no drunken session goes by without superstitions and sorcery'.[3] Yet in that same century, the first bishop of America, Fray Bartolomé de las Casas regarded this herbal witchcraft in a much more liberal light: '. . . the Indians hold *coca* in their mouths for the good it does them; and those who did not believe in the benefits to themselves, still believed that it was not through habit but rather for its usefulness that the others took it'.[4]

---

[3]   Quoted by R. Romano, 'Problemi della coca nel Perù del secolo XX', in *Nova Americana*, vol. 4, 1981, pp. 95–6.

[4]   Fray Bartolomé de las Casas, *Apologética Historia*. Translation taken from Italian version, *La leggenda nera*, Milan, 1959, p. 147.

Even in Christian places of worship, priests had instituted food sanctuaries, granaries (besides wine-cellars and larders), which they tried to protect from attacking worms often by heterodox means. In the monastery of 'Maziers, of the Cistercian Order of Burgundy, the monks are in the habit of protecting their grain from cockroaches, moths and woodworms by placing a handful of savine leaves in the middle of a heap of grain'.[5] Right at the nerve centres of Catholic ritual, it seems that the clergy had more faith in natural magic than in the exorcistic formulae which were not only authorized but even recommended by the Church of Rome.

It is one of the many cases of perfect mingling between the culture of the clergy and that of the illiterate classes, who had worked out, through observation and experience, their own empirical defence system, and it certainly did not lack for logic or valid pragmatism, when it came to combatting the 'ills' derived from animals:

> In Corsica, the merits of a species of 'Gnaphalium minimum supinum polygalae argenteo folio' are well-known among the peasants of Ornano, whose efficiency they illustrate with two examples. In the first, they gather and form a small bunch of this herb, 'gnaphalium', with which they touch several times the recently butchered meat, or they leave this bunch on the iron hook from which the fresh meat generally hangs and with this antidote it is preserved from worms, the eggs of insects and from flies. In the second, the self-same 'gnaphalio', placed in a heap of grain, has the power to preserve and protect the grain effectively from moths and woodworms.[6]

This plant, both 'hairy' and 'hoary' (Mattioli), and also called 'impious, because its offspring (the highest sprigs, that is) tower above their mother's and father's heads', so depicted, according to other sources, 'because there is no animal that will touch it to feed thereof'[7] (even pigs, it was said, preferred to die of hunger rather than eat it), was used as a preservative both of meat and of grain.

Other villages and farms preferred a variant of the same herb:

> Instead of this 'gnaphalio polygalae, argento folio', some inhabitants of the lands of Corte in Corsica use 'gnaphalium vulgare' described and illustrated by Mattioli and Durante, who recommend it be picked before sunbreak on the Feast of John

5   P. Boccone, *Museo di fisica e di esperienze*, p. 148.
6   Ibid. p. 148.
7   P. A. Mattioli, *Discorsi . . . ne' sei libri di Pedacio Dioscoride Anazarbeo della materia medicinale*, Venezia, 1744, p. 503.

the Baptist. They report the same effects as those of the previous plant. This last account corresponds to the experiences
reported by peasants of the lands around Gualdo in Umbria,
who call this herb 'verminary herb', for they treat their bovine
beasts and sheep when they suffer earthworms inside and grubs
outside, which breed in their wounds, tying a bunch of 'gna-
phalio vulgare' to their necks.

From some I have understood that the herb called 'agri-
mony', that is the 'liverwort' of the ancient Romans, when tied
to the neck of the above-mentioned animals, acts both as a
medicine and a defence against earthworms, and it must be
mentioned that all these good effects are produced by the effluvia of these plants.[8]

Where there is an economy of subsistence, the preservation of all
products indispensable to social survival constitutes a dramatic
problem, a source of perennial anxiety even after a satisfactory harvest.
A double fear (the loss of livestock was another fearful unknown)
gnawed at the heart of agrarian communities, a kind of oratory,
common-or-garden fear, we might say, which had no additional or
extraordinary component such as the anxiety produced by war, bandits
or plagues . . .

The feast of St John took the form of a gigantic ritual of preservation.
It was a multi-purpose social tranquillizer aimed at exorcising disease
and vermin in grain, clothes moths, and the thousands of nefarious ills
that attacked men's fields and their existence from all sides. It was a
feast in which the bath in the early morning dew and the harvesting of
magic played two of the most subtle roles.

The agricultural literature of the eighteenth century is full of the
socio-economic scourges of the period. The noble Francesco Ginanni of
Ravenna gives, in his *Della malattie del grano in erba. Trattato storico-
fisico* (Pesaro, 1759) *[Of the diseases in wheat in herbs; an historic-
physical treatise]*, a penetrating and comprehensive account. Bonaventura Corti, Spallanzani's contemporary, born in Corte in the province of
Reggio, in 1729, re-evokes, in his *Osservazioni meteorologiche e
botanico-mediche [Metereological and botanical-medical observations]*
(for the years 1772, 1773, and 1775), the desolation wrought to the
countryside 'by worms in spite of the drought and the cold'.[9]

In agrarian magic, there was room not only for those who 'cast spells

8   P. Boccone, *Museo di fisica e di esperienze*, p. 148.
9   Quoted by L. Serra, 'Bonaventura Corti scienziato e scrittore', in *Il territorio
     querciolese e la valle del Tresinaro*, 'Atti del Convegno di studi storici', Viano,
     24–5 May 1981, Vol. 2, 1982, p. 182.

on worms, blood and headaches', but also for those who 'cast spells on mice so that they will not eat cheese or other foodstuffs'.[10]

Others laid 'ears of corn in bundles on the ground, uttering these words: "little worms, little wormlets, steal so much of my toil as the priest's housekeeper steals of the Mass"'. In households, as a means of warding off invasions by ants, 'the women . . . take a sheaf of corn and, together with the men, surround the threshing ground cursing the ants, so that they should not steal the corn, chanting: "may my toil profit me as the labourer's hire profiteth the master"'.

The dream of overflowing barns and stores impelled women to 'sow the earth floors in their houses on Twelfth Night to ensure bounty', or to take 'on New Year's morning a great stone upon their heads to the fountain, chanting: "may our cheese be as large as this stone"'.

In illiterate cultures, the wisdom of the human world passed through people's relations with animals and their observation of their habits. The well or spring in which they had watched their oxen and pigs bathe were adopted as spas, or 'hydro-sanctuaries', to benefit human health. On New Year's day, 'women . . . vie with each other to be the first to reach the fountain and take with them an olive branch, or branch of some other tree, they salute the fountain and ask favours of it'.

Water held a particular fascination. Certain witch-doctors of the countryside 'intoning foolish words the while, carry the sick to a tank of water, lay a spear by their side and a rod upon their neck to cure them'. And women, 'to have back their health lost, as they believe, through sorcery, taking a knife repair to a spring and cut the waters three times with it'. On 'the first Thursday that hath a new moon, they pick herbs to wear them, believing them to contain certain virtues'.

The spirits of the night would invade stables, assail their inmates and cause them slowly to sicken. Certain procedures were adopted to guard animals from such nightmares and, like children's cots, to immunize stables from dangerous diabolical infiltrations. In the daytime, the evil eye might strike people, harvests or herds. The recipe for the protection was as follows: 'place [within the stable] an onion, and of the "canine" kind, impaled upon a pole, in the belief that the livestock and their fodder will escape the evil eye'. And for human beings: 'collect the scraps, or as they say, the wood chips remaining in kitchens, ovens and other such places, and with a little brimstone in a beaker or with a candle that has previously been blessed, cure the patient stricken by the evil eye with the smoke thereof'. Suffumigations cured human beings, smoke protected the fields against 'little animals'. In the belief that 'they would kill or chase away the animals that harmed their fields', farmers would

[10]   P. D. Maroni, *Decisiones prudentiales casuum, et quaesitorum conscientiae* . . ., Forlì, 1702, p. 318ff.

burn 'the leaves of trees and raising their scythes, and calling to each other with this phrse: "Tom (as it were), who eats the corn?", another would reply: "This animal or that"'.

Against parasites, 'women . . . on Easter Saturday clean their beds and clear their mattresses of bedbugs whilst saying: "may the vermin die, may it die for God's Son is arisen" or like words'.

The symbiosis with animals lead to rituals in which women and animals took part in the same game:

> . . . a mother having lost her milk, milk is taken from her who has suckled the child and the aforementioned milk is placed upon the shoulders of the mother so that she may again have milk, or indeed, they take milk from beasts and place this instead upon the shoulders of the mother who bore the child so that she is again with milk.[11]

Cattle plague or swine fever (both of which were the subject of Bernardino Ramazzini's study) were real catastrophes, striking at the core of a community, much as the bubonic plague did in cities. Among country dwellers, the care of animals (the 'mulomedicine' of the ancient world) was unqualifiably part of mainstream medicine. For them, veterinary medicine was undoubtedly a science of the mind, a 'human' science.

In the protection of the granary, use was also made of the leaves and roots of the black hellebore 'buried inside a heap of grain' (Paolo Boccone). From the moment of harvesting, there had always fallen upon this plant, *ab antiquo*, a formidable taboo. This prince among pharmacological plants, central to the cure of human madness on the one hand and a powerful hallucinogen and violent emetic on the other, had also to perform the task of preventing bugs from attacking grain, vegetal disorderliness, curing barns infested (this verb was used also to describe a house haunted by ghosts) by grubs.

Deterrence took a multiplicity of forms. Garlic, the 'countryman's physic', also played its part:

> . . . rub it upon the floorboards or on the baskets wherein the corn is placed and upon the poles with which the corn and oats are winnowed and threshed, so that the grain may not rot; the effluvia of both these plants [black hellebore and garlic] can keep away and put flight to insects and moths.[12]

The corruption of the flesh and of grain formed part of the same mental and therapeutic system.

[11]   Ibid. p. 315
[12]   P. Boccone, *Museo di fisica e di esperienze*, p. 148.

16

THE 'PLAGUES OF AFRICA'. 'DARKNESS OVER EGYPT'

Ra, the Egyptian god of the sun, fell ill because of a worm which formed suddenly and mysteriously out of his spittle and bit him in the heel. Our minds immediately and spontaneously make the association with Achilles' heel, though in the case of Ra it seems the more menacing because the poisonous attacker issues from the very body of the attacked, like an uncontrolled putrefaction, a nocturnal projection of indecipherable dangers that threaten the solar deity. If even an uranian divinity is not immune to the assaults of the supernatural, accursed worm, this myth could imply that as a cosmic enactment of evil, it portrays all the anxieties, fears aroused and tribulations caused by 'little animals' in that collective unconscious. Egypt, a terrain full of everything that creeps, crawls and ferments (images of worms and scorpions abound in the archeological finds of this territory), land of wizards and miracles, lived in the terror of visible and invisible worms. In this classical breeding-ground of parasites and importunate insects, as indeed in other parts of the African Mediterranean, evil and sickness come both to be identified with the nastier side of the animal kingdom, with the 'worm' that stings and poisons, silently and unforeseeably.

As with the solar gods, so did the Christian virgins of the land of the Pharaohs produce verminous creatures from their orifices and 'excrements'. One day they brought to the Abbot St Anthony, who lived, a strict and dedicated hermit, combatting evil, in the remotest solitude and in the tombs of Egypt, a virgin who produced worms from all over her body: from the mucous membrane, from her tears, from the putrid wax in her ears:

> A virgin who moreover was of the town named Busiris in Tripoli was prey to the most terrible and wretched suffering: for from her eyes and mucous membrane and from her ears there exuded bloody matter that, falling upon the ground, continually became worms.[1]

Even Horus, son to Isis and Osiris, was stung by a scorpion. All sorts of charms, spells, exorcisms, the entire repertory of Nilotic sorcery (reappearing in Christian exorcistic practice and in agrarian witchcraft)

[1]   Athanasius, *Vita Antonii*, in *Vite dei santi*, ed. C. Morrmann, Milano, 1974, p. 116.

were brought to bear against the invaders. The Mesapotamian and Jewish cultures entertained the same ambiguously ambivalent relationship with the abominable, at times demonized, at times divinized.

Solomon – so it is recounted in an episode of the Jewish saga named after him – made use of a magic assistant, a worm, in the building of the Temple dedicated to 'Him Whose Name is Unpronounceable', around whom there exists the taboo against *nominatio*, a choleric, threatening and vengeful Almighty, who – according to Old Testament tradition – embodied the ambivalent powers of an invisible bestower of good and bad, a double-faced uranian simulacrum, God and Satan in one, at once lord of temptation and of healing purification, the occult spring of enigmatic and divalent water that, as it was rumoured about certain incomprehensible fountains of the East, changed colour and level according to the flux of time and the changing hours of the day.

According to other cultures, unconnected with those of the Middle East, like that of Araucan Chile for instance, the worm was possessed of evil powers (in Europe, too, there was thought to be a relationship between verminosity and pestilence):

> Their principle technique [of the *vileu*, the 'methodical' doctors of the 'Chilesi'] is based upon the express belief that all infectious diseases are derived from insects, an opinion shared by many physicians in Europe. They therefore have dubbed all epidemics with the name of *cuthanpiru*, which amounts to saying verminous diseases.[2]

In Andean cultures, too, 'soothsayers, in other words the charlatans of the future' and witches, counted among their other powers, that of casting spells on worms:

> Some boasted of being *genguenu, genpugnu* or *genpiru*, which is to say: the masters of Heaven, of epidemics and worms, because they claim like the *Lamas* of Tibet to be able to make rain to fall and prevent the sad effects of diseases and the worms that destroy grain. They are fearful of the *calcu*, who are self-styled witch-doctors who, according to hearsay, live by day in their caves with their disciples, called *ivunce* (man/animals), and at night become nocturnal birds and skimming through the air, let fly their invisible darts against the enemy.[3]

Among the Azande, it is said that 'if maggots come out of the apertures

<hr/>

[2]   G. I. Molina, *Saggio sulla storia civile del Chili*, Bologna, 1787, p. 97.
[3]   Ibid. p. 82.

of a dead man's body before burial it is a sign that he is a witch'.[4] The special relationship between the world of occult power and the worm is brought into the limelight by this African belief.

The mysteries of Egypt, of 'fable-rich Egypt' (Torquato Tasso) and the Middle Eastern cultures filtered through to the delicate core of (Western) Christian religious sensibility. The symbol of holy time, emblazoned upon the facades of mediaeval churches in the form of rose-windows or the wheel of time, is born of the wheel of life and death, from the so-called 'sphere of Biante', a talisman for divination devised in the Near East. So this symbol lifted from the very cultures demonized by Christianity had pride of place upon the brow of the house of God the Lamb. The wheel of life – as a great Jesuit intellectual of the seventeenth century, to whom all too easily and unjustly even today a certain 'fantasticalness' is imputed, a master of the Collegio Romano which acted as collector-cum-promoter of a high-tension culture poised between the sacred and the profane, pointed out – 'seems to have been produced by a diabolical craftsmanship'.[5]

So far from creating a conflict, there was a crossing of paths, an interlacing, a mingling, an interaction, which seemed to characterize the relationship between cultures that are apparently so diverse and far apart. Egypt and its *magia hieroglyphica*, the Nilotic/Babilonian ideo-grams, taking us down roads that are often hard to unravel, have left a profound mark on Western religious consciousness and culture, haunting them with enigmatic hieroglyphic messages.

Blood, excrement, the human body, unguents, aromas, herbs: Egypt-ian pharmacy which had known 'wondrous and quasi-miraculous effects', pursued its course through the Middle Ages and the modern age when it came to exercise a notable influence on pre-industrial Europe. *Medicina hieroglyphica*, purposing to cull the curative potential inherent in organic matter and in the various parts of the human body, cast its powerful influence over the 'necromantic' herbalism of Europe, which long remained the pharmacological model. The human body, both living and dead, was held a source of life and health. It was a principle that Christianity made its own, in recognizing the extraordinary thaumaturgi-cal and curative powers of saints' bodies, after death.

Central to the Egyptian therapeutic code was the panacea, a universal remedy, for which the human body was the principal source:

4   E. E. Evans-Pritchard, *Witchcraft, Oracles and Magic among the Azande*, London, 1937, p. 23. Worms and grubs are among the various 'things of witchcraft' (*ahu mangu*) used by the Azande witchdoctors to strike their bewitched patients. It takes the ministrations of an anti-witchdoctor (an exorcist) to neutralize these 'missiles' (ibid. p. 38).

5   Athanasius Kircher, *Oedipi Aegyptiaci*, vol. 2, Roma, 1653, p. 419.

> The corpses (called *mummies* by them), which were properly
> preserved beforehand with balsam, myrrh, asphalt and other
> ingredients, they cut up into small pieces and added corn, wine,
> palm-fruits, gold-leaf and other universal medicines; the whole
> lot were mixed together and placed in a retort, from which they
> drew off either a salt or a liquid, which they called a cure-all,
> effective against all diseases. For since, in the aforementioned
> body, each part has its latent potency, and different parts a
> natural sympathetic tendency towards one another . . .[6]

The author himself of these remarks, the 'egyptologist', Athanasius
Kircher, was taken aback when, on examining under a microscope the
blood of some victims of the plague, he noticed (perhaps the first to do
so) 'innumerable knots of worms, not visible to the human eye'.[7] Whilst
he probably saw clusters of blood corpuscles and not bacteria (his microscope would not have had the power to pick out the latter) it is
nonetheless significant that this versatile Jesuit should have thought in
the 'Egyptian' manner, as indeed a protoparasitologist would, of
maggots, of imperceptible worms, even if, as is probable, he was not
aware of transmission via bacterial contagion.

The principle according to which *homo homini salus* where man's
health comes from himself and his body's products, which was taken for
granted by Ulisse Aldrovandi, had placed the organs of the human body
('Man and his parts' as Ottavio Scarlatini expressed it following in
Adrovandi's footsteps) at the centre of Egyptian therapeutic thinking,
founded as it was on similarities, formal and morphological correspon-
dences, those identities of sign which in Europe were known as 'sig-
naturae':

> In order to fortify the vital spirit, they remove the heart of
> someone who has recently died and is still warm, or the liver, or
> the lungs, or the brain, or whatever other organ is required.
> They pound it into small pieces with assorted herbs; if it is a
> heart, with herbs appropriate to the heart, if a liver to the liver, if
> a stomach to the stomach, and they include other ingredients
> appropriate to the chosen organ, and likewise with the other
> organs. They put it in a retort and distil it over a slow heat: for
> the distillate which results from this process was their prescribed
> medicine for treatment of the part of the body from which it was
> made . . .[8]

[6]   Ibid. p. 374.
[7]   Quoted from D. Guthrie, *A History of Medicine*.
[8]   Athanasius Kircher, *Oedipi Aegyptiaci*, p. 374.

It is not easy to find out to what extent Kircher necromanticized Egyptian medical wisdom, according to European therapeutical beliefs, or vice versa. But one thing is certain: that his exploration of the Nilotic mentality and his identification of 'sympathetic' medicine, described as *hyperphysica et astrea, seu characteristica aut amuletaria* bears a very close affinity with the nosological wizardry of his time: amulets, astrology, bewitching herbs.

Modern examination of papyruses has confirmed what to Kircher and, prior to him, Prospero Alpino, author of *De medicina Aegyptorum* (1591) and *De plantis Aegyptii* (1592) was already apparent: an extensive empirical knowledge and a high level of specialization. At the 'court of the Pharaoh there was a "doctor of the eyes" and a "doctor of the nose" and others too: our occulists and ear, nose and throat specialists may find their most ancient forerunners here', according to the eminent Orientalist, S. Moscati.[9] And the learned old man of the Collegio Romano had drawn the same conclusions:

> Hence [wrote the author of the Egyptian Oedipus], eye doctors sought out the means appropriate only to curing diseases of the eyes. Head doctors studied diseases of the head and sought their proper remedies. In the same way heart doctors treated the heart, spleen doctors the spleen, liver doctors the liver, stomach doctors the stomach; chest doctors the chest, and lung doctors the lungs. Thus it happened that they were successful and made great progress in specific treatments.[10]

The way to specialization had been opened by the practice of using parts of the human body in medical applications, and by the theory of sympathetic affinities and the consensus of the parts. An approach that today would be judged totally unscientific contained a foretaste of the realistic treatment of illness. Sympathetic medicine – the belief, that is, that every organ of the human body possessed a 'virtue' of its own, a therapeutic power of its own – had pointed the way to scientific specialization.

The fact that excreta played no mere secondary role in the hierarchy of medicinal substances during our protracted mediaeval era, testifies to a learning that set great store by all (such as spittle, urine, sperm and other 'sordid' dejecta, not to mention a woman's milk) that the great distillery of the human body processed and put forth. In its dreams the popular imagination, both past, and present probably, has always associated dung with gold, wealth and fortune, the dead man with life. Bird droppings that have landed upon the head of the passer-by (in reality, not

9   S. Moscati, *Vita di ieri vita di oggi*, Milano, 1978, p. 158.
10   Athanasius Kircher, *Oedipi Aegyptiaci*, p. 356.

in dreams) were (and to some extent still are) believed to be a sign of good luck and prosperity.

It is unnecessary to reopen the discussion on 'excrement and civilization', particularly as regards the varying uses to which *stercoratio*, one of the structural elements of the carnival *réjouissances* and *charivaris*, was put. Nor do we need to dwell at length on the custom of throwing rice at newly-weds, which has its origins in the 'barbarian' practice of bespattering the young couple with excremental missiles, as carriers of good luck. Suffice it to recall, so as to avoid offending excessively the more sensitive among our readers, that the cure for trachoma practiced by Egyptian experts, based on bird droppings and those of reptiles (and other associated substances), has been amply justified by modern pharmacological research. 'When aureomycin was discovered ... it was noticed that the latter came from land especially rich in excremental waste, which is itself endowed with particular antibiotic properties.'[11]

In that great portion of the Bible devoted to the battle between the rival yet parallel magical systems of Aaron and Moses and those of the Pharaoh's magicians, the plagues that ravage that land of 'wonders' have as protagonists *animalcula* and putrescence. The first scourge falls upon the waters that in putrefying become a bloody corruption; the second scourge is the plague of 'stinking and obscene frogs';[12] the third scourge of '*cyniphum*, that is lice',[13] sees in these creatures (according to a Jewish tradition going back to Philo) a swarming engine of divine wrath:

> This little monster is, in spite of its small size, very often extremely dangerous: not only does it scratch the surface of the skin and cause an unpleasant itch, it also enters further inside the body through the nostrils and ears; it even attacks the eyes if you are not careful.[14]

It appears that the almighty entrusted *pedicularis morbus* or pediculosis with punitive missions of a particular nastiness and destructiveness. Wickedness was punished thus:

> There are born in the blood of man, creatures which will eat through his body ... these creatures will be the instrument of divine retribution for many a man on account of his sins both against God and against his neighbour.[15]

11   S. Moscati, *Vita di ieri* ..., p. 159.
12   I. de Pineda, S. I., *Commentariorum in Job libri tredicim*, Venetiis, 1705, p. 81.
13   Ibid. p. 81.
14   Ibid. p. 81.
15   U. Aldrovandi, *De animalibus insectis*, p. 552.

The finger of God had unleashed this 'new pestilence' that 'miserably and universally afflicted men and beasts in Egypt . . . of lice that teemed with great force, indeed, all over the bodies of the Egyptians'.[16]

Grubs and bugs (*animalia tetra*)[17] infested Job's flesh and it was thought that 'in those grubs there hid devils':[18] these demon/worms lacerated and sullied his flesh. The *verminatio* and *pedicularis morbus* were often associated with occult or supernatural powers, whether positive or negative in kind. God's wrath struck the wicked with such sordid calamities. Divine pediculosis (*morbus omnium teterrimus*[19] – a most foul disease), demolished by horrendous putrefaction the living body of Herod, who had caused so much blood to flow. Harsh, indeed, was the punishment inflicted upon the murderer of infants by the diminutive executioners who fed on his blood:

> According to Flavius Josephus, Herod of Ascalon, who was King of Judaea and son of Herod Antipater, after the deaths of his sons Alexander, Aristobolus and Antipater and the slaughter of the innocents, by which he intended to destroy the Virgin's holy Offspring, died with worms infesting his whole body. He was tormented by a slow heat which could not be felt by touch outside him, but which ravaged his guts inside him; he also had a furious hunger which made it necessary to bring him food continuously, while at the same time he suffered from ulcerations in the bowels and colic pains. His feet swelled with a hot transparent phlegm, and his groin likewise. His private parts were rotten and crawled with worms, while at the same time he suffered from a gross and painful erection, accompanied by a disgusting emission: as well as all this, he suffered from cramps and had difficulty in breathing.[20]

To this 'severe and depraved'[21] ailment, there was added the 'Egyptian malady' of *cynomia* or 'dog-fly'[22] (the fourth plague), followed by a 'grievous murrain' affecting all animals (even Apollo, the uranian deity, punished the Greeks initially with this animal pestilence) 'with malignant ulcers and swelling blood-vessels'.[23]

These horrendous and repugnant scourges reflect (at least to some extent) how far the Nilotic-Mesopotamian cultures were immersed in an

16   Ibid. p. 553.
17   I. De Pineda, *Commentariorum in Job*, p. 76.
18   Ibid. p. 76.
19   U. Aldrovandi, *De animalibus insectis*, p. 552.
20   Ibid. p. 552.
21   Ibid. p. 551.
22   I. De Pineda, *Commentariorum in Job*, p. 81.
23   Ibid. p. 81.

epidemiological and parasitological frame of reference, a tradition which lasted well into the late classical period, even so far as to influence a father of the Church, St Augustine of Hippo. The relationship of the worm with the divine was still in strong evidence in his writings and troubled the popular imagination and conscience (and unconscious) for many centuries to come. The implacable and silent gnawing worm is visible/occult, celestial/terrestrial, internal/external, cutaneous/intestinal, demonic/angelic, and finally, immortal. 'And from worms,' wrote St Augustine, 'God makes angels'.

Egypt was also the classic land of fermentations, where the levitational/rising powers of 'yeast', the magic stimulus that makes bread rise and the occult energy that transforms barley into beer, were supposed to have been first discovered. We do not know whether the curdling of milk, which is precipitated by the putrefaction of a particle of the animal's intestine, was also part of Egyptian 'magical' legacy. Perhaps we do not have to climb as far as the Ural-Altaic plateau among the wandering shepherds of Asia in order to discover obscure cosmogonies that speak of milk and fermentation, of angels and worms. It seems that merely by adopting the Augustinian highroad, the signs (if not the track itself) will point us towards the Jewish/Egyptian/Mesopotamian Orient.

Towards the 'African plagues'[24] of 'sombre Egypt,'[25] where Tasso the 'Egyptologist'[26] placed the worm, alongside the snake and dragon, in the 'arid, parched and fearful sands' where alongside 'frightful armies' of locusts, there pullulated 'foul monsters' vomited by spontaneous reproduction, and hosts of insects and flies:

> Oh, but a large, odd throng of fearful monsters
> seems to retard my eager journey still.
> It is a herd of flying animals
> born of the foul corruption of dead limbs
> or generated with no parent's seed
> from the old mothers' warm and humid womb.
> Such creatures, ever flying numberless,
> instead of terrifying, much annoy.
> How many, oh, how many I can see

[24]　　T. Tasso, *Il mondo creato*, VI, 1218.
[25]　　Ibid. II, 342.
[26]　　Cf. B. Basile, 'Tasso egittologo: Gerolifici, obelischi e faraoni ne "Il Conte overo de le impresse"', in *Filologia e critica*, 1979, vol. 1, pp. 21–72. The works of Prospero Alpino were persistently ignored by the more diehard 'Egyptologists'. This physician and naturalist, a contemporary of Tasso's, embarked for Africa in 1580 and remained there for a long time to study men, animals and plants. Also Pierio Valeriano's uncle, Bolzanio, doctor to Leo X, had more than second hand knowledge of the land of the Pharaohs.

swarming around me, darkening the sky
as with a cloud of thick and dismal hue!
Who will dispel and banish such a cloud?
Your light, eternal Father, I invoke
your light in which in part one Saint appears
to differ from another, if you were
also the maker of these flying flies.[27]

'And there was total chaos ... and that volume moving forward thus became a mass, exactly as milk becomes cheese, whereupon they became worms and these were angels; and in their holy majesty they were no other than God and his angels.'[28] Cheese, worms, angels ...: the miller, Domenico Scandella's chain, even in its variant form: cheese, worms, men (omitting the ultimate product, God), is strongly reminiscent of the Augustinian metaphorical sequence which reads: worms, men, angels, God. 'All men,' wrote the Bishop of Hippo, 'born of the flesh, are they not also worms? And from worms did he [God] fashion the angels.'[29] Even the Dantean worm-man, born to the 'shape of the angelic butterfly' evolves out of this Augustinian prototype. For Scandella [also known as Menochio], as for all the agrarian cultures of the old world, the experience of fermentation was associated with the Augustinian/Biblical yeast/leaven. Religious culture (a key without which it is impossible to

---

[27]   T. Tasso, *Il mondo creato*. Tr., 5th day, p. 173, vv. 1219–34. In St Augustine's polemical writing against the Manichaeans, the theological battle is fought upon the rubbish dump of bodily decay. The 'animalcula' play a principal rôle in the unfolding of the argument, as we may see from the passage quoted below, to which Tasso may well refer: 'Will no-one therefore deceive you when you happen to be tormented by flies? For some are mocked by the devil and lured to the flies. Bird-catchers put flies in their traps to deceive hungry birds: thus are such people lured by the devil to the flies. A man was once annoyed by flies: a Manichaean came upon him suffering in this way; when the man told him that he could not endure flies and hated them violently, the Manichaean asked him at once, "who made the flies?" "Obviously," said the man, "I think that the devil made flies." "If the devil made flies, as I see you believe, because you are a clever man, who made the bee, which is larger than a fly?" The man could not bring himself to say that God made the bee and not the fly, since the case with both was almost the same. From the bee the Manichaean led him to the locust, from the locust to the lizard, from the lizard to the bird, from the bird to the sheep, and then to the cow, the elephant, and finally, to man; and he convinced the man that mankind was not made by God. So that wretch, who was pestered by flies was made into a fly himself, since he was the property of the devil. The name Beelzebub is said to mean "lord of the flies": about which it is written, *Flies destroy the perfume of sweetness* (Eccl. X, 1).' From *Sermones de scripturis* in Migne, *Patrologia latina*, XXXV, col. 1386.

[28]   C. Ginzburg, *Il formaggio e i vermi*, Torino, 1976, p. 63.

[29]   St Augustine, *In Joannis Evangelium tractatus*, in Migne, *Patrologia latina*, XXXV, col. 1385.

get to the core of the pre-modern mentality) cast its light upon secular culture (even the technical aspects) and viceversa, both mingling in turn with the worlds of the professions and arts. Even Menochio's vocabulary is strongly biblical. And biblical, too, was the 'foam' that 'coagulated into a cheese, from which a great multitude of worms were born, and these worms became men, of whom the mightiest and most wise was God'.[30] Even certain maxims of ecclesiastical origin ('nought else is the flesh ...' wrote St Bernard) take us to a confluence of languages and cultures which, whilst differentiated between themselves, are nonetheless all immersed in a mental atmosphere charged with swarming and spontaneous reproduction, of uncontrolled birth from putrefaction and fermentation: water, mud, must, milk, excreta, blood ('man is liquid humour'). Whether from Gerolamo Accoramboni's *Tractatus de lacte (Treatise on milk)* (Venice, 1536), reprinted two years later in Nuremberg as *De natura et usu lactis [Of the nature and use of milk]*, the same year that saw the publication in Venice of his *Tractatus de putredine* or from Jérome Cardan's observations that in order to avoid self-putrefaction in cheese it was necessary to wrap it in 'small dragons' because being 'sour, strong and somewhat bitter, the putrefaction of worm be prevented',[31] or from Fortunius Licetus's *De spontaneo viventium ortu [On the spontaneous generation of living things]* (1618), the culture of 'physics' had unceasingly meditated on the 'mystery of cheese' (Paracelsus) with the same mental approach to the matter as that of illiterate cultures. Even more enigmatic is the 'mystery' of cheese obtained from a woman's milk, there being still traces of this at least until the time of Francesco Redi:

> The Sun is Father and the Earth Mother ... and the sea the earth's sweat liquefied by the sun, uniting the air with the earth, as our blood unites the spirit with the body; and the world is a great animal, and we are inside him, as the worms are within us.[32]

These words in the mouth of a heterodox Dominican could well have been uttered by a master craftsman, whether miller or carpenter, and even more so by a shepherd or herdsman. Friar Tommaso Campanella had built a universe on excremental foundations (in the early Italian acceptance of this term), in a 'popular' ode, in which the many faceless, anonymous 'workers' were in their element, and men/worms were born and nestled in the womb of the God/world:

---

[30]   C. Ginzburg, *Il formaggio e i vermi*, p. 63.
[31]   J. Cardan, *De rerum varietate*, Avignon, 1558, p. 611.
[32]   This is Campanella's own gloss on the sonnet which we quote below, in *La città del Sole e Poesie*, ed. A. Seroni, Milano, 1962, p. 64.

The world is a great and perfect animal,
A statue to God, that praises God and resembles Him:
We are imperfect worms, a lowly family,
That within his belly we have life and laws . . .
We are of the earth, a great animal
Within the greatest, we are as lice
To our bodies are, and yet they do us harm . . .

If worms and lice were used to symbolize the relationship between mankind and God, their impact on the imagination and allegorical/symbolic power must have been incisive, lasting and creative.

For Campanella, mankind, 'like the worm in our stomachs', lives inside the belly of the world and stands in relation 'to the earth as lice do to our heads; and we do not know that the world has a soul and love, as worms and lice do not know by reason of their smallness of our soul and intelligence; and thus they do us harm without respecting us'. The world was seen in terms of an entomic ratio: the worm is to man's belly, as man/worm is to the belly of the world. Additionally, man is to the earth as lice are to the head of man which they inhabit.

'In strength and spirit and body the lion surpasses all other beasts, yet the minutest midge in Mesopotamia overwhelms him . . .':[33] the miniscule destroys the gigantic. Apologues and moral reflections, omens and forecasts, dreams and medicines – all signs of a different rapport with insects – were extracted from these 'little beasts'.

The cosmogonic medley of the miller from Friuli emanated from confused Augustinian memories (heard second-hand perhaps) and from analogies with everyday naturalistic rituals and feeding patterns. Without delving too far into geological depths, or penetrating increasingly packed and mysterious strata, which were demonized and obliterated by the predominant culture and by ecclesiastical power, it seems nevertheless possible to perceive in these simple tokens of faith, a profound example of the coming together of sacred and 'lay' cultures, of theological abstraction and the physical world of objects and the natural processes of fermentation. Evil lies not in its 'chains' but in premises relating to the interaction of God and Chaos, order and disorder, genesis over time and the spontaneous reproduction (and therefore diabolic) of matter which constantly self-perpetuates itself. 'Every creature of God is good' (I Tim., 4). 'Everything surely that is natural, in its proper rank is good.'[34] This is fundamentally a kind of anomalous, deviant, rough-and-ready version of intellectual Manichaeism. If in place of Chaos we

---

[33]   U. Aldrovandi, *De animalibus insectis*, c. [III], 'Ad lectorem'.
[34]   St Augustine, *Contra Faustum Manicheum*, in Migne, *Patrologia latina*, II, col. 235.

substitute demonization of matter, which St Augustine identified with the name Beelzebub, we shall understand why inquisitional orthodoxy could not take Menochio's undigested *pot-pourri*, probably finding inadmissible above all his obtuse fixation and obstinate reluctance to betray his own premises.

The image of the god/worm in the Bible (Psalm, 7) /Italian Bible, but Psalm, 6 in Authorised Version/. 'But I am a worm, and no man', is taken up by St Augustine in order to prove that in the same way as the worm is not born through copulation and therefore through animal parturition (as in the case of mankind), so too was Christ born of a virgin birth, a birth homologous with that of the worm, the fruit of self-reproduction. The mythological potential of *ex putri* birth seems to grow weightier the more aware one becomes of its capacity to evoke a mental frame of reference and inspire disturbing analogies in the realm of the religious even at its highest levels.

'"But I am a worm": This is the son of man, not a man like he who was not the son of man',[35] writes St Augustine in a letter. For this great Father of the Church, the worm's purpose is to illustrate the paradox of man who is not the son of man.

So perfect is the ambivalence of function and symbolism between his two aspects, that man is *putredo, pellis morticina* [carrion skin], *sanies fetida*, and at the same time a *magnum miraculum* [a great wonder], a fascinating and marvellous edifice ('... whence the body's shape? whence its various limbs? whence its beauteous form? And he wonders at things outside himself, the wonderer who is himself the great wonder'), and the worm, too, has a sober and linear beauty of its own. The *vermiculi laus* [praise of the worm] fits in with the principle of 'nothing is ordered that is not clean'.[36] Augustinian anthropology has room for the *laus vermis*, for man-worm (or worm-man):

> ... yet I could speak at great length without any falsehood in praise of the worm. I could point out the brightness of its colouring, the slender rounded shape of its body, the fitness of its parts from front to rear, and their effort to preserve unity as far as it is possible in so lowly a creature. There is nothing anywhere about it that does not correspond to something else that matches it.... I am speaking of any kind of living worm. Many have spoken fully and truly in praise of ashes and dung ('Cato and Cicero' in *Catone majore*). What wonder is it then if I say that a

---

35   St Augustine, *Epistolarum classis III*, in Migne, *Patrologia latina* XXXIII, col. 548.

36   . St Augustine, *De vera religione*. Translation & ed. by J. H. S. Burleigh, 'Of true religion' in *St Augustine: earlier writings*, London, 1953, p. 265.

man's soul, which, wherever it is and whatever its quality, is better than any body, . . .[37]

God is a worm because he is not born of copulation, man, too, is a worm because worms are born, again, not from copulation, but from the putrefaction and decomposition of his flesh. 'But I am a worm, and no man, namely, I am the son of man, and not a man: which is to say, I am Christ who breathes life into all; not Adam in whom all dies' (cf. 1 Corinthians XV, 22).

It is reasonable to suppose that swarms of dangerous, irksome, disgusting and repellent 'little animals', noxious to man, orchards, fields and granaries (a peril which constantly threatened not just the processes of farming, but also the preservation of foods basic to survival), must in some way have acted on people's mental outlook and imagination, suggesting (through the channels of anxiety) purifying mythologies, eliciting dreams of uncorrupted worlds not subject to the pestilential and badgering presence of parasites and small monsters of uncontrolled provenance.

The terror of the myriads of 'tiny animals' (slimy frogs, voracious mice, blood-sucking mosquitoes, villainous worms, moths, bedbugs, cockroaches, ticks, gadflies, grasshoppers or locusts, flies of all sorts, maggots, snails), the whole destructive arsenal vomited by the chaos of the night and by putrefaction, engendered by rotting corpses, by the wicked juices of menstruation and rotten seed, cannot but have carried a certain (and perhaps decisive) weight in the visionary genesis of worlds immune to corruption, abstracted from the flesh's degeneration and the rust of years, sheltered from the contaminant pollution of an infinitude of filthy and murderous 'little animals', born of organic fermentation and unpredictable products of *calor vivificus* [life's warmth]. And yet we may reasonably suppose that the idea of man as a living incubator of *animalcula*, or as a factory (in life) of bugs, worms, gadflies and (in death) of these and of snakes has been difficult to swallow. The horrible earthworm was man's inseparable companion in death as in life, splashing about in his putrefying guts and rotting flesh. It must have taken a great deal to overcome the repugnance involved to sustain the conviction that the body (threatened perpetually by physiological imbalance, ever on the verge of plunging into fever and decay) nourished with its sorry humours colonies of indomitable ruffian insects, of barbarous killers. Nor is it surprising if in this context of anxiety about 'entomata', of daily revulsion, a paradise should slowly blossom, devoid of worms, putrescence, fermentation, controlled by the Almighty, where flesh would be unchanging, preserved *in aeternum*, becoming 'impassi-

[37]   St Augustine, *De vera religione*, p. 265.

ble' and not corruptible or productive of base and abject creatures. It would be a world in which the body, its humours perfectly balanced and therefore immortal and non-perishable, was not responsible by reason of its black and melancholic juices, its overproduction of phlegm (a secretion of catarrh not dissimilar to the smear left by a snail's trail), its organic sewage, the dung-heap within, for the proliferation of animal 'evil'. The perfectly tempered humours brought with them a heavenly state of perfect sterility.

Beelzebub, the fly-god, the 'prince of flies' (St Augustine), protector of witches, of 'fly-eating old women' (St Bernardino of Siena), is the king of filth, of putrefaction, producer of slimy, foul little monsters, a demon ruling over occult, inflexible and uncontrollable forces of corruption, releasing decomposing matter: self-reproducing matter, spawned *ex putri*, without the assistance of seed or even of Divine creation. Demoniacal also were the sites where obscure processes of (fertile) putrefaction occurred, as for instance dung-heaps, delicate sanctuaries to the spirits of fertility upon whose threshhold were laid, in the agricultural world of the Slavs, propitiatory offerings. Cellars, where musk, fermenting and boiling its way to become wine and passing, after a miraculous metamorphosis, to a new life, were presided over by sprites and will-o'-the-wisps. Enzyme/sprites, yeast/sprites stimulated and governed the processes of transformation and putrefaction: the curdling of cheese (in which a host of the tiniest worms take part, 'mites, which are often seen in cheese');[38] the fermentation of milk for yoghurt, widespread among sheep-rearing societies of the East; the fermentation of barley whereby it becomes beer; the fermentation of bread, that by the addition of yeast, rises, grows, becomes big: 'we say thus that leaven causes things to rise up' (Ramón Lull).[39] The oven, which it was customary to protect from certain taboos; the stable that superstition surrounded with apotropaic amulets to repel the *incubus* that preyed upon livestock, the diabolic forces of the night that descended on men and beasts alike (like the evil eye that could afflict both).

Milk, curdling (whereby a fragment of rotting intestine of lamb sets up the process of coagulation of the liquid), yoghurt, cheese, worms . . . whole cosmologies based on teeming fermentation, angel/worms, demon/enzymes, spirits that metamorphize matter: the impenetrable and elusive forces that presided over transformations, the 'great mystery' mentioned by Paracelsus, the fermentation through which things were re-shaped, reconstituted, both in form and substance:

[38]   B. Codronchi, *De morbis qui Imolae et alibi* . . . , p. 25.
[39]   R. Lull, *Testamentum. Duobus libris universam artem chymicam complectens* . . . , Coloniae Agrippinae, 1573, c. 50r.

> Milk is the mystery of cheese [wrote the visionary creator of the *homunculus* made of the fermentations from enriched sperm, in his *Philosophia ad Athenienses*, I, 3], cheese is the mysterium of worms that develop within it, and worms are the mystery of their excreta.

The religion of the miller who lives among his granaries only too aware of the canker hiding in his grain (*Robigo* was the name the Romans gave the deity whose task it was to repel rust from cereals) is allied to that of shepherds and livestock breeders. The universal belief in the widespread presence of worms, in decay born 'of corruption in breeding and presently breeding in corruption',[40] in the occult power of fermenting agents, of leaven and enzymes, supply the culture out of which angel-worms are engendered.

Nature demonic and fermenting ('nature and gross and corrupt in its matter'), brimming over with mystery, a machine for proliferation, a sublime and perverse organism, uncontrollable and secret in its ways, had to be stopped, stalled, re-thought, re-created, turned on its head. A sudden thrust into a contrasting world of divine and not demoniacal character, was called paradise. In this way was the genetic free-for-all exorcised. It is therefore quite understandable how the decline in the idea of paradise, the melancholic fading of this imposing mythological and consolatory edifice, followed the descending curve of belief in birth *ex putri*. As, on the one hand, repugnance and distaste for putrefaction, the mother of monsters, falters, so too has the myth of the place where there is no corruption entered upon the path to extinction.

The dream of nature incorrupt, incorruptible, unperishable and impassible unfolds itself against a backcloth of anxiety about pervasive, ubiquitous and oppressive verminousness. It dissipates the nightmare of impromptu autogenesis by hosts of maggots and little monsters, out of damp, oozing, paludial, festering warmth, and 'flesh liquescent in its rottenness'.[41] It is only at the birth of the new parasitology (heralded by Francesco Redi) that the realization is reached that only life can engender life (*omne vivum ab ovo* [all life comes from the egg]), that putrescence generates nought, that the old, haunting, millenial dream of death as begetter of living creatures, of putrefaction as the seedbed of proliferating masses of *animalcula*, entered into a slow, irreversible decay. Very slow indeed, if one takes into account the trouble Lazzaro Spallanzani had in convincing one English cleric, Needham, that the 'doctrine' of spontaneous generation was untenable. Only then, and

40   Ibid. c. 8r.
41   A. Vallisnieri, *Considerazioni ed esperienze intorno alla generazione de' vermi ordinarj del corpo umano*, Padova, 1710, p. 17.

imperceptibly, did the sterile and ascetic rapport between man and death begin to change. And even the supernatural world began to be regarded in a different light. The parasitological revolution brought about a fundamental *volte-face* in the vision of life beyond the tomb. Antisepsis completed the mental revolution by drying out and sterilizing the fertile reservoirs of putrescence.

Slow, relentless decline had overtaken the long dark ages of the mind, the microbe had put the worm to flight; life, it was now understood, could only originate in life, and from death, putrefaction and decomposition, are born only phantoms, monsters and *mirabilia*. Changed scientific outlook could only lead to a gradual change of mental attitude. The ancient cosmogonic structures of the agricultural, grain-growing and 'carnivalesque' societies were now to be eroded. The death/life dialectic, the closed circuit, eternally repeating itself and interlocking with beliefs about birth in putrescence, birth in death, birth from nothingness, would slowly die its own death.

The deadly funeral pyre had been built upon which the antique emblem of the phoenix reborn of her ashes would finally, and irrevocably, end its days, never to return; like a final curtain upon the age-old drama of ambivalent fire: fire that destroys and simultaneously purifies and regenerates, a myth to which the concept of a 'third world' is not foreign, where fire purges and cleanses. The obsession with rebirth, rejuvenation, regeneration of life by fire and magical waters, by enchanted potion, by alchemic elixir begins to fade. Likewise, the old belief in the reviving power of fermentation and putrescence is doomed to extinction. The 'worm immortal' dies opening the way to 'God's death'. Prophets, ascetes, hermits; the cult of holiness, the horrors of the flesh, bodily decay, man defined as nothing better than an obscene excrement produced by rotting blood and corrupted sperm; the cult of ubiquitous worminess which had placed the maggot on a pedestal as a putrid, vengeful and destructive angel, begins to lose its most repellent but irreplaceable ally. The cult of disintegration and putrefaction, of teeming and squirming monsters, of the mortuary and of the worm (connected with manure heaps, dung-heaps, regarded as treasure chests and catalyzers of fervent processes leading to the generation of life and the seed, and therefore associated with faeces and dung), the excremental cult that was found in this flabby, ridiculous giant, this farting and 'shitting' monster, a big brother to the baby monster that was born of melting matter and multiplied itself: all these suffer a mortal blow at the hands merely of a theory that states that only from a fertilized egg can birth take place. Hence, the vision of a new order begins to emerge that will transform the relationship of the sacred to the profane, of God to life, of man to his destiny. It emerges from the banal yet explosive observation that every living creature, be it a flea or a man, must have a parent (an egg), that the register of things that move is a genetic, measurable, classifiable and plannable mechanism. This pullulating and chaotic mass, whether demonic or angelic, magic or divine, this obsessive duality of system, this implacable ambivalence, is no match for the advancing army of a ternary system that requires two participants to produce a third: father, mother and offspring.

INDEX